THE RESTATEMENT THIRD: RESTITUTION AND UNJUST ENRICHMENT

The publication of the *Restatement Third: Restitution and Unjust Enrichment* by the American Law Institute in July 2011 was an event of major importance, not only for the development of the law of unjust enrichment in the US, but also for global scholarship relating to this important area of private law. The *Restatement First* appeared in 1937 and the *Restatement Second* was abandoned. Hence the *Restatement Third* is the most significant survey of the American law on this topic for over 70 years. Private law has been a comparatively neglected area of study in US law schools for several decades, and this is particularly true of the law of unjust enrichment. However, the appearance of the *Restatement Third* has prompted a renewal of interest in the subject among US scholars and it is hoped that the present volume of essays will contribute to this revival, while reflecting on the lessons to be learned from the *Restatement* by other legal systems. Written by leading scholars from the UK, Germany, South Africa, Canada, Hong Kong and Australia, the essays undertake a critical and comparative assessment of the *Restatement*, and offer fresh insights into the rules that it articulates.

Volume 6 in the series Hart Studies in Private Law

The Restatement Third: Restitution and Unjust Enrichment

Critical and Comparative Essays

Edited by
Charles Mitchell
and
William Swadling

•HART•
PUBLISHING
OXFORD AND PORTLAND, OREGON
2013

Published in the United Kingdom by Hart Publishing Ltd
16C Worcester Place, Oxford, OX1 2JW
Telephone: +44 (0)1865 517530
Fax: +44 (0)1865 510710
E-mail: mail@hartpub.co.uk
Website: http://www.hartpub.co.uk

Published in North America (US and Canada) by
Hart Publishing
c/o International Specialized Book Services
920 NE 58th Avenue, Suite 300
Portland, OR 97213-3786
USA
Tel: +1 503 287 3093 or toll-free: (1) 800 944 6190
Fax: +1 503 280 8832
E-mail: orders@isbs.com
Website: http://www.isbs.com

British Library Cataloguing in Publication Data
Data Available

ISBN: 978-1-84946-408-6

Typeset by Hope Services, Abingdon
Printed and bound in Great Britain by
Lightning Source UK Ltd

PREFACE

This collection of essays takes a critical and comparative look at the American Law Institute's *Restatement Third: Restitution and Unjust Enrichment* ('R3RUE'), published in 2011. This was an event of major importance, both for the development of the law of unjust enrichment in the US and for global scholarship relating to this important area of law. The *Restatement First* appeared as long ago as 1937 and the *Restatement Second* was abandoned. Hence, R3RUE is the most significant survey of the law on this topic in the US for over 70 years.

For the benefit of English and other readers who are unfamiliar with the American Law Institute (ALI) and its work, it may be helpful to give a brief description of these. The ALI was founded in 1923 with the purpose of improving the law. It currently has around 3,000 members, most of whom are practising lawyers, though they include judges and legal academics. Its best-known publications are its *Restatements.* These are exercises in codification, designed to summarize and clarify selected areas of the law as they have developed in all the American states. However, the *Restatements* are not intended to lead to legislation and, besides stating the law in the form of 'black letter' summaries, they critically assess the law in the manner of an academic commentary, set out in the Reporter's Notes, explanatory comments and illustrations that are generally drawn from decided cases.

The process by which *Restatements* are brought into being has been helpfully described by Lionel Smith:

> In principle, the author of a restatement is the ALI itself, although most of the work is done by the reporter of any particular restatement. . . . The reporter generates draft text (black letter and supporting commentary), called a 'preliminary draft'; this text is circulated for comment among a self-selecting group of ALI members, namely the Members Consultative Group, which exists for each pending restatement. This group may also be invited to a meeting to discuss the draft. When it is ready, the draft, now designated a 'council draft', is submitted to the Council of the ALI, a body of thirty senior members. The council may require amendments or revision, but when it has approved the text, it becomes a 'tentative draft'. This draft is available to all members and is presented and discussed at an annual meeting of the ALI. This leads to one of the most striking features of the process, which is that the whole membership of the ALI must approve this draft; the black letter will be presented, section by section, to a room of hundreds of lawyers, any one of whom has standing to intervene and raise questions on anything from the substantive rule that is proposed to the choice of words or punctuation in the draft. Not surprisingly, the production of the whole document takes years, but the result is that when it is complete, it has the authority that comes from the successful negotiation of this complex procedure.[1]

[1] L Smith, 'Book Review' (2012) 57 *McGill Law Journal* 629, 631–32.

This account makes it clear that the task of a Reporter is a challenging one, and in the case of R3RUE, it has been doubly so, for the law of unjust enrichment has become virtually lost from sight to many American lawyers. The main reason for this lies in the way in which the law of obligations has been taught in US law schools over the past forty years. In Douglas Laycock's words:

> The restitutionary causes of action dropped out of the curriculum of American law schools in the third quarter of the twentieth century, largely by accident. . . . The result is that hardly anyone who graduated from law school in the last forty years has taken a restitution course, and at least by 1989 (probably a good bit earlier), there was no restitution casebook in print. When a lawyer or judge encounters a restitution problem today, there is a substantial risk that she will view it as an isolated problem, only dimly aware that there is a large body of law on restitution and unjust enrichment and that arguments about her particular problem can be tested and refined in light of larger principles.[2]

It is to be hoped that R3RUE's appearance, following years of work by the Reporter, Professor Andrew Kull of Boston University, will stimulate American scholars to direct more of their attention towards the topic,[3] and will enable judges and practising lawyers in the US to gain a better appreciation of what it entails. Our purpose in assembling this collection of essays has been to contribute to this process and at the same time to reflect on the lessons to be learned from R3RUE by other legal systems. With this end in mind, we arranged for all the contributors to meet and discuss a series of papers on R3RUE at a symposium held in May 2012 at Brasenose College, Oxford. The essays collected in this book are a result of that meeting. On behalf of all the contributors, we thank the symposium participants for their constructive engagement with the contributors' work. We also thank Andrew Kull, who came over from the US to be with us and to participate in our debates. It is a measure of his great achievement that his work has stimulated such a high level of interest and engagement among foreign scholars, as well as those from his home country.

Charles Mitchell
William Swadling

[2] D Laycock, 'Restoring Restitution to the Canon' (2012) 110 *Michigan Law Review* 929, 930. See too J Langbein, 'The Later History of Restitution' in WR Cornish, R Nolan, J O'Sullivan and G Virgo (eds), *Restitution: Past, Present and Future* (Oxford, Hart Publishing, 1998); C Saiman, 'Restitution in America: Why the US Refuses to Join the Global Restitution Party' (2008) 28 *OJLS* 99.

[3] A process that seems to be under way, with the appearance of R3RUE-related special issues of the *Washington and Lee Law Review* and the *Boston University Law Review*: (2011) 68 *Washington and Lee Law Review* 865–1641 and (2012) 92 *Boston University Law Review* 763–1079.

CONTENTS

CONTRIBUTORS

Andrew Burrows QC FBA is a Fellow of All Souls College, Oxford, and Professor of the Law of England at the University of Oxford.

Gerhard Dannemann is the Professor of English Law, British Economy, and Politics at Humboldt-Universität zu Berlin, and a Research Fellow at the Institute of European and Comparative Law, University of Oxford.

Jacques du Plessis is a Professor of Law and Head of the Department of Private Law at the University of Stellenbosch.

James Goudkamp is a Fellow and Tutor in Law at Balliol College, Oxford, and a University Lecturer in Law at the University of Oxford.

Birke Häcker is a Senior Research Fellow at the Max Planck Institute for Tax Law and Public Finance in Munich, and a Fellow of All Souls College, Oxford.

Lusina Ho is Harold Hsiao-Wo Lee Professor in Trusts and Equity at the Faculty of Law of the University of Hong Kong.

Nicholas McBride is Director of Studies in Law and a Fellow of Pembroke College, Cambridge.

Ben McFarlane is a Professor of Law at University College London.

The Hon Keith Mason AC QC is a Professorial Visiting Fellow at the Faculty of Law, University of New South Wales. He was formerly Chairman of the New South Wales Law Reform Commission, Solicitor General of New South Wales and President of the Court of Appeal of New South Wales.

Charles Mitchell is a Professor of Law at University College London.

Steve Smith is James McGill Professor at the Faculty of Law, McGill University.

William Swadling is a Fellow of Brasenose College, Oxford, and a Reader in the Law of Property at the University of Oxford.

Frederick Wilmot-Smith is a Prize Fellow of All Souls College, Oxford.

TABLE OF CASES

Australia

Canada

France

Germany

Israel

New Zealand

United Kingdom

United States of America

TABLE OF LEGISLATION

United Kingdom

United States of America

International Instruments

TABLE OF OTHER MATERIALS

1

Rights and Value; Means and Ends

BEN McFARLANE*

A. Overview

One of the themes of this chapter is the importance of considering means as well as ends. One of the aims of the *Restatement Third: Restitution and Unjust Enrichment*[1] is to protect and advance the 'central achievement' of its 1937 predecessor: 'the identification of unjust enrichment as an independent basis of liability in common-law legal systems'.[2] However, one of the means adopted towards this end is the adoption of a largely functional and contextual approach, based on the assumption that the law of restitution and unjust enrichment can be adequately described without attempting to answer fundamental structural questions as to how the concept of unjust enrichment should best be defined. Of course, very few things are produced purely to please purists, and Restatements do not form part of that select group. Quite rightly, the chief aim of R3RUE is to assist practitioners and judges in the US and, in collecting and examining a wide number of different legal rules absent from the casebooks and other Restatements, R3RUE provides an invaluable *tabula* in the *naufragio* that is contemporary American private law. Indeed, R3RUE's Reporter has referred to another important assumption underlying the project: that he and his colleagues were 'writing for a legal profession that knew no more about restitutionary claims and remedies than do reasonably bright first-year law students'.[3]

Two points are nonetheless worth making. First, as academics know to their cost, bright first-year students are often the source of the most searching questions about the nature and structure of a subject: they want to know, for example, why specific topics are taught in one module and not another. Second, and more importantly, the end of providing practitioners with clear and workable rules may

* I am grateful to Toby Boncey for research assistance and to the Leverhulme Trust for the support of a Philip Leverhulme Prize.

[1] American Law Institute, *Restatement Third: Restitution and Unjust Enrichment* (St Paul, MN, American Law Institute Publishers, 2011) (hereinafter 'R3RUE'). References to section numbers, unless otherwise stated, are to sections of R3RUE.

[2] § 1, Comment a.

[3] A Kull, 'Three Restatements of Restitution' (2011) 68 *Washington and Lee Law Review* 867, 876.

in fact require careful attention to the definitions of fundamental concepts such as 'unjust', 'enrichment' and 'at the expense of'. R3RUE warns (in vituperative terms) of the 'specious precision'[4] of formulas that courts may adopt when deciding if the defendant (D) has been unjustly enriched at the expense of the claimant (C); however, it is no surprise that courts, and therefore practitioners, should wish for some general guidance in interpreting unjust enrichment, a liability principle that may, after all, be applied directly, even in a context outside those covered by the specific sections of R3RUE.[5] Moreover, as this chapter will discuss, an inquiry into the general structure of the liability principle allows for the discovery of limits that, unlike those discussed in § 2, are internal to, and an inherent part of, the liability principle. The clear identification of such limits is, of course, of great practical use, not least in addressing the persistent fear that the unjust enrichment liability principle is a licence for the judicial redistribution of assets.

One possible limit to unjust enrichment depends on the structural distinction with which this chapter is concerned: that between rights and value. The potential relevance of this distinction to the law of unjust enrichment was first noted by Robert Chambers,[6] who has argued that, in applying the general model developed by Peter Birks, it is crucial to distinguish between those cases in which D's enrichment takes the form of a right and those in which it consists of a different form of value. This chapter accepts the importance of that distinction and therefore owes a great deal to Chambers' insight, but it adopts a different view. On this view, the distinction has greater significance than suggested by Chambers: rights cases and value cases are not seen as corresponding to the same general pattern of liability. Rather, the strict, unilateral liability principle with which unjust enrichment is synonymous applies only in cases where the same event involves both C's loss of a right, or gain of a duty, and D's acquisition of a right, or loss of a duty. Outside such cases, it is suggested, the strict, unilateral liability principle does not apply, and so any successful claim of C against D must have a different basis. I have argued elsewhere that such a 'rights-based' analysis provides important insights into the operation of English and Australian law and offers the best way of capturing the distinct unjust enrichment principle that R3RUE hopes to identify.[7]

Such a 'rights-based' view is, of course, controversial: as discussed in Part C below, it means that not all enrichments are equal and so, for example, mistaken payment cases are governed by different principles compared to cases of mistakenly provided services. This chapter is not the place for further discussion of the general advantages of, or problems with, such a rights-based analysis. Rather, it aims to analyse each of the four parts of R3RUE in the light of the distinction

[4] § 1, Comment d.

[5] The possibility of such direct applicability is noted in § 1, Comment a: 'cases may arise that fall outside every pattern of unjust enrichment except the rule of the present section'.

[6] R Chambers, 'Two Kinds of Enrichment' in R Chambers, C Mitchell and J Penner (eds), *Philosophical Foundations of the Law of Unjust Enrichment* (Oxford, Oxford University Press, 2009) 242.

[7] B McFarlane, 'Unjust Enrichment, Rights and Value' in D Nolan and A Robertson (eds), *Rights and Private Law* (Oxford, Hart Publishing, 2011) 581.

between a liability principle that focuses specifically on the loss and acquisition of rights and one which treats enrichment as a broader concept, encompassing not only rights but also other forms of value. In so doing, it aims not only to point out some of the situations in which R3RUE departs from English and Australian law, but also to consider how the means adopted by R3RUE have affected those end results.

B. Introduction

Whilst disavowing any attempt to define the concept of unjust enrichment, its Introduction explains that R3RUE excludes some cases that may 'correspond fully to the plain meaning' of that term.[8] For example, it is said that 'essentially historical' reasons lie behind the exclusion of examples such as an owner's right to recover stolen property or to remove a trespasser from land; a bailor's right to recover a chattel from a bailee; and a lender's right to payment of a debt. Given the general rule set out by § 1, however, the absence from R3RUE of specific rules covering those areas does not prevent a party from arguing that a particular case should be decided by reference to the general liability principle. It would therefore be useful in practice, as well as more intellectually satisfying, if the exclusion of those cases could be explained on conceptual rather than contextual grounds. Indeed, as shown by each of the three *Restatements of Trusts*, one strategy in defining a concept is to explain why certain cases fall outside its operation.[9]

A focus on rights, as opposed to value, can assist in justifying the exclusion of the examples given above. For example, if an owner asks for the return of his stolen property from D, the basic right on which his claim stands is a proprietary right that pre-dates any interference by D. Certainly, an owner in such a case is not asking for the return of any right, as the theft, whilst it may involve a loss of factual possession, does not involve any loss of that owner's right. This point, in fact, is noted elsewhere in R3RUE: § 55, Illustration 10 concerns a case in which bankrupt Debtor holds $500 in identifiable currency stolen from Victim. The following explanation is given. Victim is entitled to remove that $500 from Debtor's insolvent estate and the means to this end is not a constructive trust, but rather '[an action in] replevin'. A constructive trust cannot arise as Debtor (being a thief) does not have title to the money. In contrast, had Debtor used that same $500 to purchase a watch, 'thereby obtaining title to the watch', that watch (by

[8] § 1, Comment g.

[9] See §§ 5–16 of the American Law Institute, *Restatement First: Trusts* (St Paul, MN, American Law Institute Publishers, 1935) and *Restatement Second: Trusts* (St Paul, MN, American Law Institute Publishers, 1959), listing situations (such as bailment) that do not count as trusts. See now American Law Institute, *Restatement Third: Trusts*, vol I (St Paul, MN, American Law Institute Publishers, 2003) § 5.

which must be meant that title to the watch) is held on constructive trust for Victim.[10]

One can quibble with the analysis of this illustration: a thief of money, like a thief of any physical thing, acquires a title simply by the act of taking possession and it is therefore possible for the thief to hold that possessory title on trust.[11] As Chambers has noted, however, such a trust cannot be explained on the basis of the thief's unjust enrichment at the expense of the owner: '[s]ince the victim's rights to possession and damages are not affected by the thief's gain, it is difficult to see how that gain comes from the victim in any meaningful legal sense'.[12] Yet, the thief's use of the stolen proceeds to acquire a new right changes things: in claiming a trust of those proceeds, the owner of the initial money is clearly asserting a new right, and the need to prevent an unjust enrichment of the thief may (or may not) be the source of that right.

It is, of course, possible to take a different view.[13] Indeed, Peter Birks argued that an unjust enrichment claim may be possible even in a case where the claimant's property right has not passed to the defendant,[14] and this view is adopted in the current edition of *Goff & Jones*.[15] In one sense, this debate could be seen as precisely the sort of arid academic controversy that R3RUE can safely ignore: after all, the disagreement is not as to the result, but rather as to the possible means available to reach that result. The point, however, is that the stance taken in such a debate can have repercussions for broader structural questions (such as the meaning of enrichment or of 'at the expense of') on which many practical issues do turn. As R3RUE does not engage with such issues directly, it does not provide the general guidance that might have been of great practical use to lawyers and judges in cases that call for the interpretation of R3RUE's black letter.

Establishing R3RUE's stance on such structural issues therefore requires a good deal of inference. For example, if the decision to exclude cases in which an owner asserts a pre-existing property right is based on purely historical grounds, this suggests support for the view of Birks, and *Goff & Jones*, that such a case *does* involve D's unjust enrichment at C's expense. Similarly, practical rather than con-

[10] English and Australian law also seem to allow for the existence of such a trust of the proceeds of stolen property: see, eg, *Westdeutsche Landesbank Girozentrale v Islington LBC* [1996] AC 669 (HL) 716 (Lord Browne-Wilkinson); *Black v S Freedman & Co* (1910) 12 CLR 105. Dicta in the latter case also state that a trust also arises over the initially stolen property, but the case itself involved a trust of the proceeds of such property.

[11] For the acquisition of title through the possession of stolen property, see, eg, *Costello v Chief Constable of Derbyshire* [2001] EWCA Civ 381, [2001] 1 WLR 1437. The possibility of such a title being held on trust is noted by J Tarrant, 'Thieves as Trustees: In Defence of the Theft Principle' (2009) 3 *Journal of Equity* 170.

[12] R Chambers, 'Trust and Theft' in E Bant and M Harding (eds), *Exploring Private Law* (Cambridge, Cambridge University Press, 2010) 223, 234. See also *Shalson v Russo* [2003] EWHC 1637 (Ch), [2005] Ch 281, 317 (Rimer J).

[13] However, the view is supported by W Swadling, 'Ignorance and Unjust Enrichment: The Problem of Title' (2008) 28 *OJLS* 627.

[14] P Birks, *Unjust Enrichment*, 2nd edn (Oxford, Oxford University Press, 2005) 63–68.

[15] C Mitchell, P Mitchell and S Watterson (eds), *Goff & Jones: The Law of Unjust Enrichment*, 8th edn (London, Sweet & Maxwell, 2011) [8-34]–[8-36].

ceptual reasons are given to explain the absence from R3RUE of the law of 'fraudulent conveyance'.[16] The extensive statutory regulation of the area, it is said, has led to the exclusion of principles that would otherwise fall very naturally within § 48. The rule of this section, which is also said to lie behind the more specific rule in § 47, may reveal something of importance about R3RUE's general approach. The rule is that:

> If a third person makes a payment to the defendant to which (as between claimant and defendant) the claimant has a better legal or equitable right, the claimant is entitled to restitution from the defendant as necessary to prevent unjust enrichment.

Whilst the black letter refers only to payment, § 48, Comment a notes that 'cases of non-money benefits may be decided by analogy'. The comment also avers that the action by a defrauded creditor against the fraudulent transferee would 'make a prime example of a claim in restitution within the rule of § 48'. Such an analysis depends on a broad interpretation of what it means for D to be unjustly enriched at C's expense. As will be discussed further in Part C below, it seems that liability in unjust enrichment is viewed as a mechanism for ensuring the reversal, or avoidance, of situations in which D has acquired some value which would more appropriately be available to C. For example, § 48 would seem to be potentially applicable even in a case where X, who is contractually obliged to perform a particular service for C, instead performs that service for D. In such a case, C's claim falls outside the limits imposed by § 39, as C need not claim that D must disgorge profits made from the wrongful conduct of X or from any wrongful conduct of D; indeed, it may well be that D had no knowledge of the prior contract. If D has made payment to X prior to C's claim, D may argue (by analogy to § 25(2)(b)) that his unjust enrichment is thereby reduced or eliminated, but it may seem surprising that even a prima facie liability should exist in such a case.

Further evidence for this broad view of enrichment can be found in, for example, § 46, which states that D can be liable in unjust enrichment to C where, as a result of 'fraud, duress, undue influence or other intentional misconduct', assets that would otherwise have passed by donative transfer to C are instead diverted to D. It is notable that the black letter does not require that D himself has interfered with the planned transaction. As is the case with § 48, there is no need for any transactional link between C and D: C need not show that D's benefit has been directly acquired from C. Similarly, § 11(3) states that a claim in restitution can be made by C, an intended donee, against D, an unintended recipient, if the donor, at the time of his death or incapacity, mistakenly believes that he has completed a gift to C. In some cases, as where the donor mistakenly makes a gift to D rather than C, the effect of the rule is simply to shift D's liability in unjust enrichment to C and away from the donor or donor's estate. However, the rule also applies even if D acquires the intended gift as a successor of the donor.

[16] § 1, Comment g. See also § 48, Comment a. For the equivalent English rule, see Insolvency Act 1986, s 423.

Another example is provided by § 25, which allows for the possibility of a claim (subject to a number of conditions) where C's performance of his contract with X leads to D's acquisition of a benefit. One of these conditions, imposed by § 25(2)(b), is that C's performance would otherwise go uncompensated and D would otherwise retain the benefit of that performance without payment. The possibility of such liability, as well as the nature of that condition, again suggests that the focus is not on establishing a clear link between C and D, but is rather on the end of moving value from D to C in a case where, overall, that is thought to be the best solution.

It thus seems that R3RUE rests on a broad, but not explicitly stated, model of what it means for D to be unjustly enriched at C's expense. Certainly, R3RUE recognises liability in some cases where C would have no claim in other common law jurisdictions. For example, consider the case where X dies in the mistaken belief that he has made a gift of certain shares to C, whereas in fact no such gift has been made. The shares then pass to D, X's residuary legatee. In English law, C would face insuperable obstacles in attempting to make an unjust enrichment claim against D. First, can it be said that D has been enriched at C's expense? Second, if so, can it be said that there is any unjust factor, any reason why that enrichment should be given up? The main point is not that the English result is necessarily more appropriate than the R3RUE solution; rather, it is that the conceptual tests applied by the former differ markedly from the contextual approach of the latter.

This difference means not only that R3RUE recognises liability in some cases where C would have no claim in English or Australian law, but also that R3RUE includes within its scope some situations which, to an English or Australian lawyer at least, seem more naturally to lie outside the scope of unjust enrichment. For example, secret trusts fall within § 46, as noted by § 46, Comment g; however, whilst numerous academic and judicial attempts have been made to explain the basis of such trusts,[17] unjust enrichment has rarely featured, for the simple reason that it would seem to lead to the intended trustee's being under a duty to restore the intended trust assets to the testator's estate. Similarly, to judge from the existing authorities, English or Australian judges would be unlikely to show much enthusiasm for the principle behind § 25.[18] Of course, this does not, by itself, mean that the analysis of R3RUE, which seeks to elucidate the law as applied in jurisdictions within the US, must be rejected. The more serious consequence, however, is for the operation of R3RUE itself. As there are very few internal limits on the unjust enrichment liability principle, R3RUE, which of course does not seek to impose new swathes of liability, has to identify and emphasise external

[17] For a recent discussion, see S Gardner, 'Reliance-Based Constructive Trusts' in C Mitchell (ed), *Constructive and Resulting Trusts* (Oxford, Hart Publishing, 2010) 63. For the present author's view, see B McFarlane, 'Constructive Trusts Arising on a Receipt of Property *Sub Conditione*' (2004) 120 LQR 667.

[18] See, eg, *Pan Ocean Shipping Co Ltd v Creditcorp Ltd* [1994] 1 WLR 161 (HL); *Lumbers v W Cook Builders Pty Ltd (in liq)* [2008] HCA 27, [2008] 232 CLR 635.

countervailing concerns that can restrain the broad prima facie liability. For example, the principle that liability in restitution 'may not subject an innocent recipient to a forced exchange', set out in § 2(4), is often pressed into service to deny liability. So, in a case such as *Ulmer v Farnsworth*,[19] the principle must be used to explain why C has no claim where his draining of his own land also benefits D's land. Similarly, a somewhat complicated set of rules, laid out in §§ 49–53, governs the calculation of money judgments in restitution.

This point again raises the question of ends and means, and also the possibility that there may be good practical reasons for engaging more thoroughly with structural, conceptual questions. To give a specific example, on the rights-based analysis (which will be discussed further in Part C below), there is no prima facie liability in a case such as *Ulmer*, as D has acquired no right from C. To consider the utility of conceptual analysis more broadly and to borrow from an analysis of property law, it is worth noting the argument made by Henry Smith that there may be sound functional reasons for adopting a formal, conceptual approach. In the field of property law, for example, such an approach may emphasise the single organising idea of a core right to exclude others from a thing, in contrast to a more realist or contextual approach in which property is deconstructed into a bundle of varied rights to use resources.[20] According to Smith, the functional benefits of a formal approach depend on the higher information costs, for parties, their advisers and the courts, imposed by the contextual approach. On this view, there may be efficiency gains from a switch away from a realist approach, with its focus on end results and its scepticism towards the concepts used by courts to reach those results. It can similarly be argued that, if we are interested in the ease and efficiency with which the law of unjust enrichment can be communicated to practitioners and courts, a concentration on the definition of underlying concepts, which are relatively invariant to context, may serve us well. As will be suggested in the next three parts, the conceptual distinction between rights and other forms of value may be one such helpful means to that practical end.

C. Liability

In considering how best to organise and present the circumstances in which a liability in unjust enrichment may arise, an important question soon arises: to what extent, if at all, do different rules apply to different types of enrichment? One view is that the liability principles remain essentially the same whatever the particular nature of D's enrichment. For example, in his book *Unjust Enrichment*, Birks used the core case of the duty of an innocent recipient to return the value of a unilaterally mistaken payment as, literally, the prime example of an independent liability

[19] *Ulmer v Farnsworth*, 80 Me 500, 15 A 65 (1888): see § 30, Illustration 1.
[20] H Smith, 'Property as the Law of Things' (2012) 125 *Harvard Law Review* 1691.

principle based on D's unjust enrichment at C's expense.[21] His strategy was then to generalise from that core case in various ways: one such generalisation was from D's receipt and retention of money to D's receipt and retention of an abstract enrichment, where enrichment is an acquisition measureable in money; a second was from a transfer by D to C to an enrichment of D at C's expense. Similarly, in its treatment of mistake as a ground for restitution, the current edition of *Goff & Jones* departs from its previous editions, in which separate chapters discussed the receipt of different types of benefit.[22] Whilst noting that '[c]omparatively few cases have recognised that the value of non-money benefits can be recovered' on the grounds of mistake, the editors urge that 'former inhibitions should fall away'[23] so that, for example, the same general rules should apply to mistaken services cases as to mistaken payment cases. In contrast, the *Restatement First: Restitution*, in its discussion of mistake of fact, separately examined and distinguished in §§ 39–43 between various forms of non-money benefits. For example, §§ 40 and 41 made clear that, subject to the rules in § 43 relating to the performance of D's duty or the discharge of a lien over D's land, a claim in restitution did not arise simply because of C's unilateral mistake in rendering services which were of benefit to D and for which D was not otherwise under a duty to pay.

The difference between these two types of approach is fundamental: it concerns the validity of Birks' generalisations from the core case of a unilaterally mistaken payment and this, in turn, raises the question of why liability arises in that core case. For example, as noted above, it is possible to argue against the move from that core case, which involves the transfer of a right from C to D, to cases (such as those involving the provision of services) that involve no transfer of a right. Cases involving the transfer of a right are susceptible to particular justifications that do not apply in a services case. For example, it can be argued that the core mistaken payment case exemplifies a liability principle that may cause D to come under a duty to C even though D has no responsibility for a flaw (such as C's unilateral mistake), provided that the flaw is a cause of C's loss, and D's gain, of a right.[24] The scope of this suggested principle is limited to cases in which the same event involves *both* C's loss of a right[25] *and* D's gain of a right.[26] The transfer of a right from C to D is the principal, but not the only, example of such a case.[27] The purpose of the principle is to protect C's initial legal position. As a result, it does not

[21] Birks (n 14) ch 1.

[22] *Goff & Jones* (n 15) [9-01]–[9-05].

[23] ibid [9-02].

[24] McFarlane (n 7). It should be emphasised that this model, whilst it builds on the distinction between rights and value, is not the model advocated by Chambers (n 6).

[25] Or C's loss of a power, or gain of a duty (as where C's payment to D is made from C's overdrawn bank account) or liability. Future reference to this principle will refer, for shorthand, to C's loss of a right.

[26] Or D's gain of a power, or loss of a duty (as where C's payment to D is made into D's overdrawn bank account) or liability (as where C's payment discharges a lien on D's property). Future reference to this principle will refer, for shorthand, to D's gain of a right.

[27] For example, usurpation of office cases in which X's payment to D discharges X's duty to C, eg, *Arris v Stukely* (1677) 2 Mod 260, 86 ER 1060.

extend to cases where C simply suffers a factual loss, even if that loss correlates to a factual or legal gain of D. This does not mean, of course, that liability can never arise in, for example, a services case; it does suggest, however, that any such liability will require more than the mere fact of C's having mistakenly conferred a gain on D.

On this narrow view, the liability principle in the core mistaken payment case exists to protect an interest of C that is already recognised as a legally valid entitlement. The function of the principle is to mitigate the effects on C of other legal rules that recognise a particular event as causing both: (i) for C's part, the loss of a right; and (ii) for D's part, the acquisition of a right. This means that the liability principle must be understood as part of the logic of the underlying legal rule that has had that effect on C and D. It is therefore justified at one remove: its 'second order'[28] flavour comes from the fact that the function of the principle is to justify the operation of *other* legal rules regulating the acquisition and loss of legal rights.

Such an analysis, of course, gives the liability principle operating in the core mistaken payment case a more limited scope than that proposed by Birks. It also raises the question of whether the label of 'unjust enrichment' can be usefully applied to this principle. After all, the principle can apply even if D makes no net factual gain: this is the case, for example, when it operates to allow C to rescind a contract entered into with D as a result of D's innocent misrepresentation, even though this contract is at a price that is fair or even advantageous to C. R3RUE does, in fact, recognise that such rescission falls within the basic § 1 principle, even though D 'cannot plausibly be said to have been enriched';[29] it seems to view this observation as an argument against rather than in favour of further exploration of the concept of enrichment. Moreover, at those points when the general definition of unjust enrichment is explicitly touched on, some of the language used in R3RUE is consistent with the narrow view of the liability principle. For example, in R3RUE's Foreword,[30] the 'key words' – unjust enrichment – are said to identify 'a transfer of money or other valuable assets to an individual or company that is not entitled to them'; there is also the suggestion in § 1, Comment b that unjustified enrichment 'results from a transaction that the law treats as ineffective to work a conclusive alteration in ownership rights'. It is, for example, difficult to conceive of a services case as involving a transfer of a valuable asset, or an alteration, conclusive or otherwise, of ownership rights.

Those straws in the wind aside, R3RUE clearly does not adopt a narrow approach, based on the distinction between rights and value, to the scope of the liability principle. In contrast to its predecessor, there is no separate section dealing with services cases: as the parallel tables make clear, the nearest equivalent to § 41 of the *Restatement First: Restitution* is § 2(4), which does not involve an internal limit on the definition of unjust enrichment but sets out the external

[28] R Stevens, 'Is There a Law of Unjust Enrichment?' in S Degeling and J Edelman (eds), *Unjust Enrichment in Commercial Law* (Sydney, Lawbook Co, 2008) 11, 23.

[29] See § 1, Comment c and § 13, Comment e.

[30] Written by Lance Liebman, the Director of the American Law Institute.

constraint of not imposing a forced exchange on an innocent D. Whilst § 9 does deal specifically with benefits other than money, § 9, Comment a makes it clear that, as far as establishing (rather than quantifying) liability is concerned, the sole issue is, again, as to compliance with § 2(4). Moreover, § 10 makes it clear that even this concern may have to give way in cases involving the mistaken improvement of another's property.

A good example of R3RUE's approach is provided by § 7, which concerns C's mistaken performance of D's obligation. In such a case, the full or partial release of D's obligation means that it is simple to establish that D has acquired a benefit. Where C's performance consists of mistakenly paying a debt owed by D to X, even the narrow principle set out above is satisfied as the same event (C's payment) involves both C's loss of a right and D's loss of a duty. In contrast, that narrow principle has no application where C, acting under a unilateral mistake, performs services which D was in fact under a duty to perform. As is made clear by § 7, Comment c and Illustrations 8 and 9, R3RUE does allow for recovery in the case where, due to a unilateral mistake, C performs D's unliquidated obligation. It is not clear, however, that this rule is supported by the relevant American case law.

For example, Illustration 9 is based on *Sykeston Township v Wells County*,[31] in which the claimant township repaired a gravel road in the mistaken belief that the claimant, rather than the defendant county, was responsible for such repairs. The claimant was allowed to recover its expenses, but the Supreme Court of North Dakota expressly based its decision on an innocent misrepresentation made by the defendant to the claimant that led to, or at least confirmed, the claimant's mistaken belief. Indeed, a previous decision[32] was distinguished on the basis that no such misrepresentation had been made in that case, and the court was careful to state that:

> This is not a case where a township, without the knowledge and approval of the board of county commissioners, performed maintenance work upon a county road and thereafter billed the country for the work which was done.[33]

Illustration 8 is based on *McClary v Michigan Central Railroad Company*,[34] in which the Supreme Court of Michigan allowed the claimant to recover the value of his services in carrying mail for the defendant railroad company, mistakenly believing that he was obliged to carry that mail under a separate contract with the government, when in fact the defendant was, under the postal laws of the US, bound to carry to and from the post office all mail at terminal points of its roads. The treatment of the legal question is very brief, but it should be noted that the defendant 'permitted the services to be performed'[35] and so, again, it does not seem to be a case of unilateral mistake.

[31] *Sykeston Township v Wells County*, 356 NW 2d 136 (ND 1984).
[32] *Rolette State Bank v Rolette County*, 56 ND 571, 218 NW 637 (1928).
[33] *Sykeston* (n 31) 142.
[34] *McClary v Michigan Central Railroad Company*, 102 Mich 312, 60 NW 695 (1894).
[35] ibid 696.

Indeed, § 7, Comment c notes that there is '[t]raditional authority' against liability in a unilateral mistake case; however, referring to *Rohr v Baker*,[36] it argues that such cases fail to 'distinguish a liability in unjust enrichment from a liability in contract'. It is true that in *Rohr*, the language of the Supreme Court of Oregon may suggest that a real (as opposed to quasi-) contract is required for recovery, but the result in that case may nonetheless be defended. Both Rohr and Baker had contracts with the city of Portland to extract earth. Rohr, by mistake and without Baker's knowledge, excavated some earth on ground covered by Baker's contract. When Baker completed the work and received payment, Rohr attempted to recover the actual cost of his work. Given the purely unilateral nature of Rohr's mistake and the fact that it did not result in any transfer of a right to Baker, the denial of liability is no surprise: after all, to paraphrase Pollock CB,[37] if one digs part of another's hole, what can the other do but keep on digging?

A further concern with the accuracy of the approach taken in § 7 relates to the extent of C's recovery in *Sykeston* and *McClary*. On the R3RUE model, C's claim is based simply on D's saving of a necessary expense through C's unilateral mistake in performing an obligation of D. As D is thus, in the language of § 50(1), an 'innocent recipient', D's liability in unjust enrichment for an unrequested benefit is, under § 50(2)(a), 'measured by the standard that yields the smallest liability in restitution'. Under the possible measures set out in § 49(3), that smallest liability could well be that set out by § 49(3)(a): 'the value of the benefit in advancing the purposes of the defendant'. Given D's position as a party with an established operation for, respectively, repairing roads and delivering mail, the cost to D of performing the duty is likely to be lower than the cost to C of performing those services, or even the market value of such services. Yet, in neither case did the court consider this possibility: indeed, in *Sykeston*, C simply recovered its costs of performance. This, of course, is no surprise if the essence of the claim lies not (or, at least, not only) in the benefit received by D, but rather in C's reasonable reliance on D. Indeed, it is interesting to compare these cases with § 52, Illustration 3. In this scenario, C, mistaking the boundary line, spends $50,000 on building a barn on what turns out to be the land of D, his neighbour. D notices C's mistake (presumably at a point when building has only just started) and says nothing, hoping to benefit from the error. The presence of the barn increases the value of D's land by $35,000. Even if D has no use for the barn and no plans to sell his land, R3RUE tells us that 'D's enrichment from the mistaken improvement' will be measured at $50,000. The result that D should be liable for the full sum of C's costs, although not based on a specific authority, is plausible; however, as D's liability exceeds even any factual gain he has made from C's conduct, unjust enrichment is surely not the appropriate means by which to reach that result.[38]

[36] *Rohr v Baker*, 13 Or 350, 10 P 627 (1886).

[37] *cf Taylor v Laird* (1865) 25 LJ Ex 329, 332: 'One cleans another's shoes. What can the other do but put them on?'

[38] It could be said that D's enrichment consists of his saved expense in not having to construct the barn himself. Again, however, as in *Sykestown*, there is no reason to think that it would necessarily have

This point leads us to § 10, which deals specifically with mistaken improvements to another's property. The rule states that:

> A person who improves the real or personal property of another, acting by mistake, has a claim in restitution as necessary to prevent unjust enrichment. A remedy for mistaken improvement that subjects the owner to a forced exchange will be qualified or limited to avoid undue prejudice to the owner.

As noted above, the separate treatment given to such cases results in a 'more liberal formula' which 'is necessary to accommodate numerous decisions that grant relief to a mistaken improver even where the remedy requires an innocent property owner to submit to an involuntary exchange'.[39] R3RUE admits that the approach in § 10 differs from the common law's 'traditional reluctance to relieve the mistaken improver', but asserts that this reluctance resulted not from a view that such a party is less deserving of restitution, but rather from the fact that 'effective relief to the improver may in some circumstances impose unjustified hardship on the owner'.[40] It is certainly the case that the liability acknowledged by § 10 is wider than any yet acknowledged by English or Australian courts.[41] As the law stands in those jurisdictions, it is necessary for C, the mistaken improver, to show that D has some form of responsibility for C's error: D must have created or encouraged a belief in C that C did, or would, have a right in the land, or, at least, that C would receive some reward for his work.[42] It may be that D can come under a duty even without making an express commitment to C: this may occur, for example, if, as in § 52, Illustration 3, D, knowing of C's belief, simply stands by and fails to correct C's error.[43] In any case, however, liability can only arise if D can bear at least some responsibility for C's decision to spend his time and effort in building: the simple, unilateral model of the core mistaken payment case does not apply. Further, as noted above when considering § 52, Illustration 3, D's responsibility for the error may lead to D's being under a liability to C that extends beyond any benefit acquired by D.[44]

In many cases, of course, one could view the absence of liability in a unilateral mistaken improvement case as depending on the absence of any benefit to D, and thus as consistent with the R3RUE model. The critical case, then, is one in which D cannot deny that he has benefitted from C's improvements. For example, it

cost D $50,000 to have built the barn, or that D would have built the barn in the same way had he decided to spend $50,000 of his own money on it. Compare the comment of HHJ Kirkham in *JS Bloor Ltd v Pavillion Developments Ltd* [2008] EWHC 724 (TCC), [2008] 2 EGLR 85 [45].

[39] § 10, Comment a.

[40] ibid.

[41] For Australian authority, see, eg, *Brand v Chris Building Co Pty Ltd* [1957] VR 625 (Supreme Court of Victoria); S Degeling and B Edgeworth, 'Improvements to Land Belonging to Another' in LB Moses et al (eds), *Property and Security: Selected Essays* (Sydney, Lawbook Co, 2010) 277.

[42] See, eg, *Cobbe v Yeoman's Row Management Ltd* [2008] UKHL 55, [2008] 1 WLR 1752.

[43] See, eg, dicta of Lord Cranworth and Lord Wensleydale in *Ramsden v Dyson* (1866) LR 1 HL 129, 140–41, 168. For discussion, see K Low, 'Non-feasance in Equity' (2012) 128 LQR 63.

[44] Indeed, C can have a claim in proprietary estoppel even where C's reliance confers no benefit on D, as in *Crabb v Arun DC* [1976] Ch 179 (CA).

may be said that D is 'incontrovertibly benefited' if C can show that the work done on D's land was work which D, in any case, intended to procure at his own expense. The Privy Council considered just such a case in *Blue Haven Enterprises Ltd v Tully*.[45] C established a coffee plantation on D's land, mistakenly believing that C had the best title to that land. Lord Scott, noting that D himself had bought the land in order to develop it as a coffee plantation, stated that:

> [T]here is no doubt whatever that [D] has been enriched at [C's] expense . . . The critical question is not whether [D] has been enriched at [C]'s expense but whether the circumstances in which that enrichment came about place [D] under an equitable obligation to compensate [C] accordingly.[46]

To answer that question, Lord Scott turned to the law of proprietary estoppel, which requires some 'acquiescence or encouragement or other species of representation by [D]'.[47] This approach, followed by Judge Kirkham in *JS Bloor Ltd v Pavillion Developments Ltd*,[48] is consistent with the narrow liability principle proposed above. C's mistaken improvement of D's land is not an event that involves both the loss of a right by C and the gain of a right by D, and so the unilateral liability model of the mistaken payment case cannot apply; rather, it is necessary for C to show that D has some form of responsibility for C's error.

As in the discussion of § 25 and § 46 in Part B, it is not suggested that R3RUE has fallen into error by its departure (in this case, a conscious one) from other common law jurisdictions. Indeed, as noted elsewhere by R3RUE's Reporter, the different development of the American law may depend on two local problems not arising in England: 'the chaotic land titles of an earlier day' and 'the difficulties of surveying the wide open spaces'.[49] Moreover, academic suggestions that mistaken improvements cases should fall within the basic liability principle of the mistaken payment case have been made[50] and, indeed, have recently won the support of *Goff & Jones*.[51] Nonetheless, two points can be made.

First, a focus on the distinction between value and rights can provide conceptual support for the traditional common law view, which can then be seen, contrary to R3RUE's view,[52] as concerned not solely with valuation or liquidity problems but rather as recognising the distinction between cases in which D makes a factual gain at C's expense and those in which an event causes both C's loss of a right and D's gain of a right. Indeed, the judgment of Justice Story in *Bright v Boyd*,[53] which was influential in the liberalisation of the American

[45] *Blue Haven Enterprises Ltd v Tully* [2006] UKPC 17.

[46] ibid [20].

[47] ibid [24].

[48] *Bloor* (n 38).

[49] A Kull, 'Mistaken Improvements and Restitution Calculus' in D Johnston and R Zimmerman (eds), *Unjustified Enrichment: Key Issues in Comparative Perspective* (Cambridge, Cambridge University Press, 2002) 369, 369–70. See also § 10, Comment b.

[50] T Wu, 'An Unjust Enrichment Claim for the Mistaken Improver of Land' [2011] *Conveyancer* 8.

[51] *Goff & Jones* (n 15) [9-04].

[52] § 10, Comment a.

[53] *Bright v Boyd* (1841) 4 Fed Cas 127 (No 1,875) (Cir Decisions, Maine).

approach, drew explicitly on civil law rather than common law principles, and so it may be no surprise that the common law, properly interpreted, does not assist C in a unilateral mistaken improvement case.

Second, and more importantly, this traditional common law limit may be seen to involve a less costly way of delineating the law. The converse approach, demonstrated by § 10 and §§ 49–52, is to allow a prima facie liability but to base the actual outcome (in the words of the Supreme Court of West Virginia) 'largely upon the circumstances and the equities involved in each particular case'.[54] It is of course true that the English law of proprietary estoppel has its own complexities and requires a court to 'look at the matter in the round'.[55] Nonetheless, it is accepted that C's unilateral mistake in improving land will not suffice for liability, and C needs to show that he has reasonably relied, to his detriment, on a representation or assurance made by D.[56] In comparison, the § 10 approach is less structured and requires consideration of circumstances that, as noted in Comment b, can include an owner's expectations, and the purposes for which an owner holds his title to the land, with the result varying depending on whether it is held for investment or occupation. As noted by Chambers in a different context, the use of such factors to determine legal results carries the risk of uncertainty and may even imperil the basic principle of equality before the law.[57] More generally, such an approach, whilst undoubtedly allowing for more carefully gradated outcomes than the traditional common law rule, necessarily involves greater costs in establishing the parties' entitlements.

Of course, this is not to deny what R3RUE's Reporter has elsewhere called the intolerable injustice that resulted when an honest yeoman, by a mistake about title or boundaries for which he was in no way responsible, spent years of labour cultivating Blackacre and building a modest dwelling for his family, only to discover that the few acres he had cleared and improved were part of a larger tract of wilderness belonging to an absentee speculator.[58]

However, it may well be that, as suggested by Simone Degeling and Brendan Edgeworth in their analysis of the relevant Australian decisions,[59] such hardship is best tackled by specific statutory intervention rather than by a modification and possible distortion of common law rules. R3RUE naturally refers to the 'betterment' acts in force in many US jurisdictions, which do provide such statutory relief, but draws attention to their limits and arbitrary operation. It may seem unduly optimistic to argue that the possible hardship to the mistaken improver should be dealt with by the amendment of such legislation, but there is a real con-

[54] *Somerville v Jacobs* (1969) 153 W Va 613, 629; 170 SE 2d 805, 813–14.

[55] *Gillett v Holt* [2001] Ch 210, 225.

[56] See, eg, *Thorner v Major* [2009] UKHL 18, [2009] 1 WLR 776 [29].

[57] R Chambers, 'The Importance of Specific Performance' in S Degeling and J Edelman (eds), *Equity in Commercial Law* (Sydney, Lawbook Co, 2005) 431, discussing suggestions in the Canadian and Australian case law that the availability of specific performance in the case of a contract to transfer title to land depends on the particular use to which the purchaser intends to put the land.

[58] Kull (n 49) 377.

[59] Degeling and Edgeworth (n 41).

cern as to whether a Restatement focusing on unjust enrichment is the best vehicle to remedy those statutory defects. After all, in the example quoted by the Reporter, is the unfortunate yeoman's complaint really as to the *benefit* acquired by the speculator or is it rather as to the detriment he will suffer if forced to leave the land without compensation?

The treatment of mistaken improvements within § 10 thus marks a clear difference between the R3RUE approach to defining unjust enrichment and that taken in England and Australia. This practical difference can be seen to depend on a willingness to look beyond the narrow case where C loses, and D gains, a right to other cases where D makes a factual gain at C's expense. The same can be said for another important area in which R3RUE departs from English and Australian law: the claims available to trust beneficiaries against an innocent third party donee who acquires trust assets transferred in breach of trust. First, consider the case in which D acquires knowledge of the breach of trust only after disposing of the trust assets and their traceable proceeds. In such a case, as when D receives $500 of trust money and spends this money on his monthly groceries, D may nonetheless retain the abstract value inherent in those assets. In English and Australian law, C has no claim against D: D is not liable to account to C as a constructive trustee (to use the language of the cases) as there is no point in time at which D held the trust assets, or their traceable proceeds, with knowledge of the initial trust in C's favour.[60] In contrast, the R3RUE position is that D is liable to C, as, despite D's innocence, a prima facie liability arises under § 17 (consider Illustration 9) and D's retention of an abstract enrichment prevents D's relying on the defence set out in § 65. No authority is cited for this proposition, but it is consistent with the position adopted (again without reliance on authority) by both the *Restatement First: Trusts* and *Restatement Second: Trusts*; as will be considered further below, the recent *Restatement Third: Trusts*, rather surprisingly, is content to leave the issue to be dealt with by the provisions in R3RUE.

It has, of course, been argued that the traditional understanding of English and Australian law on this point is incorrect[61] or that the law should be changed.[62] The current position is, however, perfectly explicable if we focus not on the *value* received by D, which can perhaps be seen as acquired at the expense of C, but rather on the *right* received by D, for the right acquired by D was formerly held by T, the trustee, not by C. A trust exists because, whilst T holds the right, he is under a duty to C to use that right for C's benefit, and not for T's own benefit. Nevertheless, the existence of the trust does not alter the fact that the right itself

[60] See, eg, *Re Montagu's Settlement Trusts* [1987] Ch 264 (Ch); *Bank of Credit and Commerce International (Overseas) Ltd v Akindele* [2001] Ch 437 (CA); *Farah Constructions Pty Ltd v Say-Dee Pty Ltd* [2007] HCA 22, (2007) 230 CLR 89. Of course, if D has dishonestly assisted in the breach of trust, he may be liable as a constructive trustee under the so-called 'second limb' of *Barnes v Addy* (1874) LR 9 Ch App 244 (CA).

[61] See, eg, the decision of the Court of Appeal of New South Wales in *Farah Constructions Pty Ltd v Say-Dee Pty Ltd* [2005] NSWCA 309, in which Mason P presided.

[62] See, eg, Lord Nicholls, 'Knowing Receipt: The Need for a New Landmark' in WR Cornish et al (eds), *Restitution: Past, Present and Future: Essays in Honour of Gareth Jones* (Oxford, Hart Publishing, 1998) 231.

belongs to T – indeed, that is an essential feature of the trust in common law jurisdictions.[63] The absence of a strict liability claim for C against D in our example is thus compatible with a focus not on rights as an alternative to value but rather on rights as distinct from value. Whilst the value gained by D may have come from C, the *right* acquired by D came from T, not from C. As a result, the example falls outside the narrow liability principle.

The R3RUE position, in contrast, reflects the broader view that sees D's enrichment consisting not of a right derived from T but rather as any value derived from, or due to, C. Indeed, the trust example forms a very useful means of distinguishing between the narrow and the broader views as it, unusually, involves a distinction between T, the holder of the right, and the trust beneficiaries who are (at least as against T) entitled to (at least some of) the value of that right. In fact, this feature of the trust seems to have been important in some early American attempts to explain the very basis of liability in unjust enrichment. In the very first article of the very first volume of the *Harvard Law Review*,[64] James Barr Ames argued that the ability of a trust beneficiary to assert a right against an innocent recipient of trust assets rested on the same foundation as quasi-contracts (which were, in his view, really a means of enforcing an equitable liability): that a 'court of equity will compel the surrender of an advantage by a defendant whenever, but only whenever, upon grounds of obvious justice, it is unconscientious for him to retain it at another's expense'.[65] Indeed, Ames explicitly rejected the view (which remains all too common) that the beneficiary has a form of equitable ownership of the trust assets and that this ownership right explains the liability of the innocent transferee. He noted that: 'A *cestui que trust* is frequently spoken of as an equitable owner of the land. This, though a convenient form of expression, is clearly inaccurate.'[66] Ames instead took the at first sight somewhat mysterious view that 'What the *cestui que trust* really owns is the obligation of the trustee'. The idea that the same liability principle operates in a quasi-contract case as in such a case of a constructive trust was also adopted by Ames' colleague, William A Keener, in a later contribution to that first edition of the *Harvard Law Review*.[67] Keener argued that, in the core mistaken payment case, D can be compelled to restore money to C 'not because the Court does not regard [D] as the legal owner thereof, but because it is inequitable that he should retain it'.[68]

[63] There are some trust-like structures that do not require the party equivalent to the trustee to hold the subject matter, as it suffices that the trustee has control of that right: the South African *bewind* and Quebecois *fiducie* are examples. See T Honoré, 'Trusts: The Inessentials' in J Getzler (ed), *Rationalizing Property, Equity and Trusts: Essays in Honour of Edward Burn* (London, LexisNexis, 2003) 7. Such structures fall within the scope of the Hague Convention on the Law Applicable to Trusts and their Recognition, Art 2.

[64] JB Ames, 'Purchase for Value without Notice' (1887) 1 *Harvard Law Review* 1. For discussion of Ames' role in identifying and developing the unjust enrichment liability principle, see A Kull, 'James Barr Ames and the Early Modern History of Unjust Enrichment' (2005) 25 OJLS 297.

[65] Ames (n 64) 3.

[66] ibid 9.

[67] WA Keener, 'Recovery of Money Paid under Mistake of Fact' (1887) 1 *Harvard Law Review* 211.

[68] ibid 211.

It is easy to understand the attraction of the analogy between the core mistaken payment case and the transfer of trust assets, in breach of trust, to an innocent donee. One puzzle in the former case is to explain why the law both recognises that a right has indeed been transferred from C to D (for example, where C pays D in the mistaken belief that he has a duty to do so, this mistake does not prevent title to the money passing to D) and, at the same time, may require D to return the value of that right to C. This trap, in fact, continues to ensnare commentators who wish to adopt a 'proprietary' explanation of the liability in the former case.[69] The trust example is invoked by Ames and Keener to explain the puzzle: in such a case, it is clear that D does acquire T's right, but, due to the breach of the trust, the transaction is ineffective in allowing D to gain unencumbered access to the value of that right. This, it seems, is the point that R3RUE aims to capture in the statement, noted above, that unjustified enrichment 'results from a transaction that the law treats as ineffective to work a conclusive alteration in ownership rights'.[70] The trust analogy thus depends on a distinction between rights and value: in simple terms, D's dealing with T suffices to transfer a right to D, but, as it is a breach of trust, it does not operate to transfer the *value* of the right from C to D. As far as explaining the core mistaken payment case is concerned, the means of distinguishing between rights and value is therefore shared by both the trust analogy and the narrow principle set out above. However, the end of each analysis is radically different: the trust analogy leads to a broader definition of enrichment, in which D is enriched when acquiring value which is more properly due to C; the narrow principle excludes the trust case, as it is one in which D's right is acquired from T, not from C. R3RUE's adoption of the broader view, which may perhaps be ultimately traced back to Ames' analysis, is thus inconsistent with each of the narrow principle and the English and Australian approach to third party liability for breach of trust.

It may of course be said that the practical impact of R3RUE's approach is limited: the difference with other common law jurisdictions arises in the relatively rare case where the innocent donee retains the value of the right received in breach of trust but holds neither that right nor a right that counts as its traceable proceeds. The practical differences, however, are more pronounced as, rather surprisingly, the *Restatement Third: Trusts* seems to leave the question of the impact of a beneficiary's right on a recipient of trust assets entirely to the R3RUE. §§ 107 and 108 of the *Restatement Third: Trusts* are consistent with that Restatement's approach to entifying the trust[71] (and are thus inconsistent with the prevailing common law approach to the trust) as they are headed 'Third Party Liability to Trust' and so, oddly, do not specifically consider the third party's direct liability to

[69] See, eg, P Watts, 'Restitution – A Property Principle and a Services Principle' [1995] *Restitution Law Review* 49; P Watts, 'Property and "Unjust Enrichment": Cognate Conservators' [1998] *New Zealand Law Review* 151. See also C Webb, 'Property, Unjust Enrichment, and Defective Transfers' in Chambers, Mitchell and Penner (n 6) 335.

[70] § 1, Comment b.

[71] See, eg, *Restatement Third: Trusts* (n 9) vol I, § 2, Comment a.

a beneficiary. This is all the more surprising as the Reporter's Note to § 2 of the *Restatement Third: Trusts* states that, although the proposition has not been universally accepted, there is 'probably general agreement in the United States that a trust involves a division of legal and equitable ownership'.[72] Despite this, it seems, Ames' analysis has been adopted: the protection of a beneficiary against a third party receiving trust assets in breach of trust depends *entirely* on the law of unjust enrichment and *not* on the proprietary nature of the beneficiary's right. It should be emphasised that, as far as the Restatements are concerned, this is not a novelty: whilst the *Restatement First: Trusts* and *Restatement Second: Trusts* did set out specific rules as to third party liability,[73] those rules were premised on unjust enrichment[74] and so are entirely consistent with the model now applied solely by R3RUE.[75]

In our first example, in which an innocent D spends the trust assets on his ordinary expenses, the R3RUE analysis gives C, a trust beneficiary, additional protection beyond that available in England or Australia. In other cases, however, an unjust enrichment analysis reduces C's rights against D. For example, consider a case in which D innocently receives $500, transferred in breach of trust, and, relying on his belief that he is thereby better off, spends an unrelated $500 on a holiday. The standard position, applying in England and Australia, is that, as D retains the trust assets or their traceable proceeds, D remains vulnerable to a claim from C: to use the language of Lord Browne-Wilkinson in *Foskett v McKeown*,[76] C's claim depends on 'hard-nosed property rights', not on unjust enrichment. On this view, as C can identify a specific right in D's hands that is either the right initially held on trust for C or a traceable product of that right, D must give up that right, and no change of position defence is available. In practice, whilst the 'hard-nosed' model relied on in *Foskett* may seem to be insufficiently sensitive to particular fact situations, there may, again, be efficiency savings in delineating the beneficiaries' rights through transactional rather than causal notions. Certainly, in *Foskett*, the House of Lords were keen to avoid the refinements, and consequential complications, that would come from extending the inquiry beyond the location of the trust assets and their traceable proceeds in order to consider the defendant's abstract enrichment.

Indeed, *Foskett* itself reveals a further difference, again operating to the disadvantage of the beneficiary. In English law, if D innocently invests the $500 received in breach of trust in some shares, and those shares increase in value,

[72] It further cites AW Scott Jr, 'The Importance of the Trust' (1967) 39 *University of Colorado Law Review* 177, 179: 'it is generally agreed in England as well as in the United States that the beneficiaries of a trust have the proprietary interest in the subject matter of the trust and not merely a personal claim against the trustee. Although the trustee has the legal title, the beneficiaries are equitable owners. The chancellors created a new type of property interest'.

[73] See *Restatement Second: Trusts* (n 9) §§ 289 and 292.

[74] See, eg, ibid § 292, Comment h.

[75] For instance, the result in the first example considered above, in which D spends the trust assets on his everyday expenses and remains liable, was the same under ibid § 292, Comment j.

[76] *Foskett v McKeown* [2001] 1 AC 102 (HL) 109.

C has the choice of claiming a trust of the shares themselves.[77] In contrast, § 53(3) ensures that C has no claim to that increased value.[78] Indeed, the decision in *Foskett* seems to depend on what might be called a purely transactional approach to tracing: in that case, trust assets were used to pay some of the premiums on a life insurance policy, and a claim was allowed in relation to the insurance pay-out, even though the policy would have remained in force had the particular premiums for which trust assets were used not been paid. The decision thus demonstrates that if a particular trust asset is used in the acquisition of another asset, a beneficiary may be able to assert a claim in relation to that new asset, even if there is no causal link between that new asset and the trust asset.

It has been tentatively suggested by Lionel Smith that, when courts of equity first allowed a beneficiary to assert a right not only against a trustee but also against an innocent recipient of trust assets, a general notion of unjust enrichment may have motivated that intervention.[79] However, it will be surprising to many non-American lawyers to think that such third party liability is, today, a direct application of unjust enrichment. The triumph of Ames' reasoning is an unlikely one, even in the American context, given the general adoption there (principally at the urging of one of the Reporters of the *Restatement First: Restitution*)[80] of the proprietary model of the trust. Again, of course, it cannot be suggested that English or Australian law provides the yardstick by which R3RUE must be judged. Nonetheless, both a conceptual and a practical point can be made. Conceptually, the R3RUE model of third party liability arising on innocent receipt of trust assets may overlook the point that the establishment of a trust does not give a beneficiary an abstract right, good against all but a bona fide purchaser, to the value of a trust asset. After all, as confirmed by the *Restatement Third: Trusts*,[81] if a third party tortiously destroys or damages trust assets, the claim to payment of the value of those assets is made by the trustee: in the absence of special circumstances,[82] there is no direct claim available to the beneficiary. As against the rest of the world, then, it is the trustee, if anyone, who has an abstract right to the value of the trust asset. The beneficiary's interest depends on the fact that the trustee is under a general duty to the beneficiary not to use the trust assets for the trustee's own benefit but, instead, to use the assets for the benefit of the beneficiaries. It is therefore difficult to justify the third party effect of the beneficiary's interest by claiming that the trustee's duty to the beneficiary gives the beneficiary an abstract entitlement to value, good against all but a bona fide purchaser. Indeed, the weaknesses of the trust analogy, as used by Ames and Keener, may lie in its very use to separate the holding of a right from an entitlement to the value of such a right. If C simply holds a right (as he does at the start of the mistaken

[77] See too *Trustee of FC Jones & Sons v Jones* [1997] Ch 159 (CA).

[78] The same position applied under *Restatement Second: Trusts* (n 9): see § 292, Comment g.

[79] L Smith, 'Unravelling Proprietary Restitution' (2004) 40 *Canadian Business Law Journal* 317.

[80] See, eg, AW Scott, 'The Nature of the Rights of the "*Cestui Que Trust*"' (1917) 17 *Columbia Law Review* 269.

[81] § 107.

[82] See § 107(2).

payment case), does it make sense to think of C holding an entitlement to the value of that right separately from the right itself?

Indeed, as will be discussed further in the next part, the 'proprietary' effect of a beneficiary's interest under a trust may be seen to depend on the fact that the trustee's duty to the beneficiary relates to a specific right held by the trustee. So, just as a legal property right depends on a link between its holder and a physical thing, an equitable property right may be seen to depend on a link between its holder and another right: in the case of a trust, a link between C and the trust assets. One advantage of this 'proprietary' feature of a beneficiary's right is the possibility of following the trust assets into the hands of a third party, just as one advantage of a legal property right is the possibility of asserting a claim against anyone who comes to have possession of the physical thing to which the legal property right relates. As Henry Smith has recently argued, the concept of a thing has an important 'modular' effect in property law, lowering information costs to courts and third parties by delineating rights through the concept of exclusion from a specific thing, rather than by distributing varied liberties to use that thing.[83] Where trusts are concerned, the organising module can again be seen as the subject matter of C's right: in this case, not a physical thing, but rather the rights held by T. Just as the identification of C's right with a specific thing, or a specific right of T, gives C particular advantages, it also carries particular risks. As Lionel Smith has noted,[84] there is a necessary arbitrariness to such rights: if, for example, a lightning strike destroys my bike and none of the other bikes locked nearby, I must bear that loss. Similarly, it may be entirely a matter of chance as to whether D, who received trust assets in breach of trust and who always lacked knowledge of the trust in C's favour, has retained or disposed of those assets or their traceable proceeds. Yet this does not mean that it is arbitrary for the law to attach importance to the fact that D happened to spend the trust assets (rather than, as he might equally well have done, some of his other assets) on his everyday expenses, or on a profitable investment. After all, the possibility of C's having a claim against D at all depends on D's receipt of a particular right, and the fate of that claim may then depend on the fate of that right.

D. Remedies

The preceding two parts have suggested how the distinction between rights and value may be of use in establishing whether D has been unjustly enriched at C's expense. The particular nature of D's enrichment may also be crucial when considering the appropriate remedy. For example, if D's initial enrichment consists of

[83] Smith (n 20).

[84] Smith (n 79); L Smith, 'Philosophical Foundations of Proprietary Remedies' in Chambers, Mitchell and Penner (n 6) 281.

the acquisition of a right from C, but D no longer holds that right, there is a strong case for D's liability (subject to, for example, the change of position defence) being to pay the objective value of that right to C, even if D put a lower value on that right.[85] However, the discussion here will focus on a more fundamental distinction, between what R3RUE refers to as 'Restitution Via Money Judgment' (§§ 49–53) and 'Restitution Via Rights in Identifiable Property' (§§ 54–61). This distinction, in broad terms, may be seen to track the distinction between value and rights. Crucially, in a case where D's enrichment consists of the acquisition of a particular right, D may come under a specific duty to C in relation to that particular right rather than merely a general duty to pay C a sum of money. Indeed, as Chambers has suggested, where D's enrichment takes the form of a right acquired from C, the appropriate response, the 'most perfect form of restitution',[86] would seem to require the return of that right to C. It can further be argued that the distinction between duties relating to a right held by D, and other duties of D, precisely marks the divide between cases in which C has an equitable property right, such as a right under a trust, and cases in which C has only a personal right against D.[87] In this way, a focus on the conceptual distinction between rights and value can provide a useful means for a court to decide if, for example, D's unjust enrichment must be addressed via the recognition of a constructive trust. On this view, the selection between a constructive trust and a monetary remedy does not depend on the discretion of the court, on any wider questions of policy or indeed on the nature of D's conduct: it turns simply on whether D's duty to C relates to a particular right held by D, which may in turn depend on whether D's enrichment consists in the acquisition of a right from C.[88] The conceptual distinction between rights and value can thus provide a practically straightforward means for a court to recognise the appropriate response to D's enrichment at C's expense.

In the preceding two parts, we saw that, when considering the initial question of D's liability, R3RUE does not make use of the potentially helpful distinction between rights and value. Where remedies are concerned, however, R3RUE comes extremely close to adopting that very distinction. For example, § 55(1) states that a constructive trust may arise if D is 'unjustly enriched by the acquisition of title to identifiable property at the expense of [C]'. The reference to title is perhaps unnecessary, as it may confirm the misconception that only legal ownership of property can be held on trust; of course, the general position is that any right held

[85] See J Edelman, 'The Meaning of Loss and Enrichment' in Chambers, Mitchell and Penner (n 6) 212; McFarlane (n 7). See also *Cressman v Coys of Kensington (Sales) Ltd* [2004] EWCA Civ 47, [2004] 1 WLR 2775, in which D was ordered to pay the market value of a registration mark to C, even though D claimed that he had subjectively placed a lower value on that mark.

[86] Chambers (n 6) 267 (quoting L Smith (n 84) 294).

[87] See, eg, Chambers (n 6); Smith (n 79); B McFarlane and R Stevens, 'The Nature of Equitable Property' (2010) 4 *Journal of Equity* 1.

[88] See further B McFarlane, 'The Centrality of Constructive and Resulting Trusts' in Mitchell (n 17) 183.

by T may be the subject matter of a trust.[89] As will be seen in Part E, this misconception is reflected in the wording of § 66, with regrettable practical consequences. This aside, however, the statement confirms the difference between, for example, the core mistaken payment case and a pure services case: a constructive trust clearly cannot arise in the latter case, as D's enrichment does not consist in the acquisition of a specific right at C's expense. Similarly, as noted by § 55, Comment f and Illustrations 14 and 15, such a trust cannot arise where D's pre-existing right has increased in value as a result of C's services (although, it seems, a lien may be appropriate in such a case). § 55's limit to the acquisition of title (or, more accurately, to the acquisition of rights) also rules out a possibility which, given R3RUE's broad view of enrichment, might otherwise arise. For example, consider the case discussed in Part C above, in which D, an innocent recipient of $500 transferred to him in breach of trust, spends that money on his monthly groceries. It may be that D had previously intended to spend the $500 remaining in his bank account on those groceries. As noted by Smith,[90] a broad causal view of unjust enrichment could lead to the assertion that D's enrichment now consists specifically of the right to the bank account and that D should now hold that right on constructive trust for C. § 55, however, impliedly adopts a transactional view by limiting such a trust to cases in which D's enrichment consists in the *acquisition* of a right.

The bare wording of § 55 may thus suggest that R3RUE adopts a formal approach to the question of whether or not a constructive trust has arisen, focusing on the question of whether D's duty to C relates to a specific right held by D. On one view,[91] this is precisely the approach taken by English and (albeit subject to some recent challenges) Australian law.[92] However, this is not the case. Again, R3RUE's focus seems to be on ends rather than means. This is perhaps inevitable, given that the American view of constructive trusts depends almost entirely on a realist perspective, in which the trust is seen as essentially an empty but convenient vehicle to reach results which may be desirable on policy grounds. For example, in 2004, R3RUE's Reporter noted that:

> [I]t is nothing less than extraordinary, to a United States lawyer, to hear anyone describe a constructive trust as a species of trust. To us this seems just as old-fashioned, and just as fundamentally misleading, as to describe a quasi-contractual obligation as a species of contract.[93]

[89] See, eg, *Don King Productions Inc v Warren* [2000] Ch 291; *Barbados Trust Co v Bank of Zambia* [2007] EWCA Civ 148. For discussion of the limited exceptions, see McFarlane and Stevens (n 87) 10-15.

[90] Smith (n 84) 303–04.

[91] See, eg, McFarlane (n 88).

[92] For consideration of some relevant Australian decisions, see B McFarlane, 'Trusts and Knowledge: Lessons from Australia' in J Glister and P Ridge (eds), *Fault Lines in Equity* (Oxford, Hart Publishing, 2012) 169. The recent challenge comes from the High Court's decision in *John Alexander's Clubs Pty Ltd v White City Tennis Club Ltd* [2010] HCA 19, (2010) 241 CLR 1.

[93] Of course, such scepticism as to constructive trusts is not confined to legal realists: see, eg, W Swadling, 'The Fiction of the Constructive Trust' (2011) 64 *Current Legal Problems* 399.

Against this background, R3RUE can only be praised for its rejection of some of the worst excesses of legal realism, such as the view, adopted by the court in *Re Omegas Group Inc*,[94] that a constructive trust does not exist until a court order in C's favour.[95] Yet it seems that, had R3RUE taken the formal concept of the constructive trust more seriously, this concept might have performed some important explanatory work.

For example, consider § 13, Illustration 11: D fraudulently induces C, his mother, to transfer to him her land, goods and two cheques. It is stated that 'Mother is entitled to recover land, cattle and money by whatever remedies are most convenient, including rescission, cancellation, and constructive trust'. Whilst the constructive trust is here seen as just one available means to the desired end, it can be formally justified as depending on D's holding of rights acquired from C with knowledge of the reason meaning that C's consent to the transfer of the rights was defective.[96] In § 13, Illustration 14, C is induced by fraud to convey Blackacre to X. X then re-conveys to D, who purchases with notice of X's fraud. The illustration notes that C is entitled to recover Blackacre from D and that one way to achieve this result is via the cancellation of both deeds. A constructive trust analysis can equally explain why C has a claim against D if we accept that X held title to the land on constructive trust for C from the moment of X's fraudulent acquisition of that right and that, like any trust, a constructive trust is capable of binding a third party who acquires trust assets with notice of the facts giving rise to the trust. The problem for R3RUE, however, is the view, set out in § 55, Comment b that a constructive trust, 'used correctly to designate a remedy for unjust enrichment, is only a manner of speaking' or a 'metaphor'. On this view, in the words of this comment, the term is shorthand for a court's declaration that D's 'legal title to X' [ie, D's right] is subject to C's superior equitable claim, and that D must 'surrender X' [ie, transfer the right] to C.

So, despite R3RUE's distaste for the approach in *Re Omegas Group Inc*, it does not seem to allow for the possibility of a constructive trust being used not merely as a conclusion, but rather as a step in the court's reasoning. In other words, a constructive trust is only an end, never a means to an end. For example, consider § 41, Illustration 11:[97] daughter (X) and co-conspirators fraudulently obtain millions of dollars in mortgage loans from C, a bank. A total of $250,000 of those proceeds is paid by X to D, her mother. It is stated that D is prima facie liable to C's claim in restitution, whether or not she had notice of the source of the funds; in the absence of notice, she may be able to rely on the § 67 bona fide payee defence if, for example, some or all of that money was used to discharge loans previously made by D to her daughter. The assumption here seems to be that,

[94] *Re Omegas Group Inc*, 16 F 3d 1443 (6th Cir 1994) 1451.

[95] See § 55, Comment e.

[96] See further McFarlane (n 92).

[97] The facts of the illustration are based loosely on *Chicago Title Insurance Co v Ellis*, 409 NJ Super 444, 978 A 2d 281 (App Div 2009), although the bank's claim in that case was founded on conversion. For a similar consideration of the relationship between conversion and unjust enrichment, see *Heperu Pty Ltd v Belle* [2009] NSWCA 252, (2009) 76 NSWLR 230.

although the right acquired by D came from X, not from C, it is possible to view D as unjustly enriched at C's expense. This illustration may therefore help to supply an answer to one of those fundamental structural questions not expressly addressed in R3RUE, namely, can an indirect recipient be said to have received a benefit 'at the expense of' C? Yet the example, like so many of the English cases said to support the liability in unjust enrichment of such indirect recipients,[98] can equally be said to depend on C's assertion against D of a right under a trust, that trust arising when X fraudulently acquired rights from C. Similarly, as noted by Birke Häcker,[99] the Illustrations given, in §§ 40, 41 and 43, demonstrating the liability of D where D has received a benefit as a consequence of X's wrongdoing against C, can also all be understood as cases in which there is an equitable proprietary link between C and D, as the assets received by D (not a bona fide purchaser) were held by X on constructive trust for C.[100]

Again, it might be said that, as the same ends are reached on each analysis, the particular means employed are not of importance. First, however, there are important practical differences between a broad analysis of enrichment, which extends to indirect recipients, and a more limited view, such as the narrow principle set out above, which can then be complemented, in particular cases, by claims based on the receipt of assets subject to a pre-existing constructive trust. For example, consider a case in which C mistakenly gives two $50 notes to X. X pockets those notes and, believing himself to be $100 better off, withdraws $100 from his bank account and makes a gift of that cash to D. On a broad analysis of enrichment, which is inconsistent with that taken by Goulding J in *Re Byfield*,[101] D can be said to be enriched at C's expense; on the narrow view, there is no such enrichment: the event causing D to acquire a right (X's transfer of $100 to D) did not also cause C to lose a right. Nor can C make any claim based on an equitable property right, as the notes received by D are not the traceable product (on a transactional view of tracing) of the notes mistakenly given by C to X. A further practical difference arises in the case where there is an increase in the value of the rights acquired by D, the innocent third party. For example, § 41, Illustration 13 concerns X's wrongful misappropriation of $10,000 from C. X passes that money, as a gift, to D and D uses it to buy shares which he would not otherwise have bought and which increase in value. It is stated that if D had no notice of the misappropriation, C's claim in restitution is limited to an equitable lien on the shares, securing a claim to $10,000 plus interest. This result is not surprising within the context of R3RUE, as it is consistent with its treatment of an innocent recipient of trust assets (as discussed in Part C), yet it can also be said to overlook the standard tracing rules, which allow for a trust obligation to extend to rights acquired with the initial trust assets.

[98] See, eg, *Banque Belge pour l'Etranger v Hambrouck* [1921] 1 KB 321 (CA); *Lipkin Gorman (a firm) v Karpnale Ltd* [1991] 2 AC 548 (HL). For discussion, see B McFarlane, 'Unjust Enrichment, Property Rights and Indirect Recipients' [2009] *Restitution Law Review* 37.

[99] See Chapter 2 of the present volume, at pp 49–50.

[100] In addition to § 41, Illustration 11, see also § 41 Illustrations 9, 10 and 13.

[101] *Re Byfield* [1982] Ch 267 (Ch).

Second, an analysis which allows the constructive trust to play a formal role in explaining liability may also assist in giving a simpler explanation of particular results. For example, consider § 52, Illustration 10, in which C, a bank, mistakenly credits D's account, with a prior balance of $0,[102] with $20,000. D immediately notices the error but does not inform the bank. D later withdraws the $20,000 and uses it to purchase shares. When C later discovers the error, D sells those shares for $40,000 and offers C $20,000 plus interest. It is stated that, even if D has committed no actionable wrong, D's 'bad faith makes him liable in restitution for a consequential gain that an innocent recipient would be free to retain' and C is thus entitled to recover $40,000 from D. The result, whilst not based on specific authority, seems reasonable, but the explanation given for it in § 52, Comment e is far from straightforward. It depends on § 52(2)(c), which concerns responsibility for enrichment, and allows more extensive recovery for C in a case where D's unjust enrichment is 'attributable to D's bad faith or reprehensible conduct': in such a case, the enrichment may be measured as though D were a conscious wrongdoer and thus under the rule of § 51(4). This means of reaching the result is thus somewhat tortuous and D can of course object that his initial receipt of the money, which first constituted the enrichment, was solely due to an error by C. An alternative, and perhaps simpler, means of reaching the same result is to follow the approach advocated by Lord Browne-Wilkinson in *Westdeutsche Landesbank Girozentrale v Islington LBC*[103] and applied by White J in the New South Wales Supreme Court in *Wambo Coal Pty Ltd v Ariff*.[104] Under that approach, if D, having innocently acquired a right mistakenly transferred to him by C, becomes aware of C's mistake whilst still holding that right or its traceable product, D will hold that right on trust for C. The tracing rules mentioned above can then explain C's ability to make a claim in relation not only to the mistakenly transferred right, but also to its proceeds.

The *Westdeutsche* analysis of this point is controversial[105] and, whilst it can be defended, there is not room to do so here.[106] It is nonetheless worth noting one of its advantages: it draws together cases of fraud, misrepresentation, receipt of assets transferred in breach of trust, mistake and indeed all cases in which there is some reason for saying that D's receipt of a right has led to D's unjust enrichment at C's expense, and asks a simple question: is there any point at which D held that right, or its proceeds, with knowledge of the facts (for example, the fraud, misrepresentation, etc) constituting such a grounds of liability in unjust enrichment?[107] If the

[102] The illustration itself does not state that the prior balance was $0. However, it does state that D later withdraws '*the* extra $20,000' (emphasis added), and such specificity can only be possible if the prior balance was $0.

[103] *Westdeutsche* (n 10) 715, explaining the decision of Goulding J in *Chase Manhattan Bank v British-Israel Bank* [1981] Ch 105 (Ch).

[104] *Wambo Coal Pty Ltd v Ariff* [2007] NSWSC 589.

[105] For a differing view, see, eg, R Meagher et al (eds), *Meagher, Gummow & Lehane's Equity: Doctrine and Remedies*, 4th edn (Sydney, LexisNexis, 2002) [14-010].

[106] See rather McFarlane (n 92).

[107] Of course, the simple question has to be modified when the transfer occurs under an initially valid contract, as noted by Rimer J in *Shalson* (n 12) 318. In such a case, unless and until C exercises a power to set the contract aside, the contract provides a basis for D to retain the enrichment; compare § 62.

answer to the question is yes, then a trust can arise, as D is thus under a duty to C in relation to a specific right held by D. Such a trust, whether labelled as constructive or resulting, is no mere metaphor: in fact, it has the exact characteristic of a standard express trust as it rests on D's being under an obligation to C in relation to a specific right held by D.[108] It is therefore not just a means of stating a conclusion that D must make specific restitution to C: it is also a *reason* for a conclusion that a recipient of the right from D may also come under a duty to C (as in § 13, Illustration 14 or § 41, Illustration 11, for example, or as in *Wambo*, where a recipient from D was held to be liable under the first limb of *Barnes v Addy*),[109] or for the conclusion that D should account to C for the proceeds of the initial right held on trust for C (as in § 52, Illustration 10). Unfortunately, however, R3RUE's view of the constructive trust as no more than a conclusion prevents its use as a concept that may assist in elucidating and simplifying such claims. Indeed, it is stated in § 55, Comment i that '[u]nless [C's] remedy in restitution involves specific restitution (one form of which may be priority over competing creditors), the idea of constructive trust is at best superfluous and at worst misleading'. On this view, a constructive trust can never be used as an explanation of D's duty to account to C. This is a telling example of the fact that R3RUE sees the recognition of a constructive trust only as the end of a reasoning process rather than as a means to a conclusion. For example, on the *Westdeutsche* approach, if D gives away a right after discovering that the right was mistakenly transferred to him by C, D can be liable to account to C for the value of that right, just as an express trustee is liable to account to a beneficiary. This duty to account depends on the fact that D was under a duty to C in relation to a specific right, and it exists even when D no longer holds that right.

It therefore seems that, whilst the basic wording of § 55 impliedly acknowledges the importance of distinguishing enrichments consisting in the acquisition of a right from other forms of enrichment, R3RUE has, understandably, been unable to shake off the realist legacy that sees the constructive trust simply as the statement of a conclusion rather than as a formal concept. As we saw in Part C, when considering liability, this rejection of conceptual formality may result in undue complexity in the presentation of the law, as unifying general ideas are overlooked.

E. Defences

As the final part of R3RUE is that in which the distinction between rights and other forms of value is at its least significant, this section can be relatively brief. Two points will be made: one, which is rather technical, can be quickly made; the

108 See, eg, Smith (n 79); McFarlane (n 88).
109 *Barnes* (n 60).

other, which is more abstract, is potentially very significant and so cannot be fully examined here.

The first point concerns what seems to be an inadvertent oversight in the coverage of the bona fide purchaser defence as set out in § 66. The problem is that the black letter refers to a purchaser for value and without notice who 'acquires the legal interest that the grantor holds and purports to convey'. The misconception that a trust necessarily involves the trustee holding a legal interest was noted above in relation to § 55, and it has important consequences here. It means that the defence does not seem to be available to D if, for example, he acquires an equitable interest from X. This is uncontroversial in a case where, for example, T holds title to land on trust for C and then grants an equitable mortgage over that land to D: both C and D have a right against T's right to the land, and in the contest between these two rights, C's, which comes first in time, takes priority. Consider, however, a case in which T holds an equitable interest on trust for C and then transfers that interest to D, a bona fide purchaser. Whilst D has not acquired any legal interest, he is a bona fide purchaser of the subject matter of the trust in C's favour and should therefore be protected against any claim of C. Indeed, the necessity of protecting D in such a case was the main argument of Ames' article, referred to above, with which the *Harvard Law Review* opened.[110] Moreover, such protection was explicitly given to D in the *Restatement First: Trusts*[111] and *Restatement Second: Trusts*[112] as well as in the *Restatement First: Restitution.*[113] As was noted in Part B, the *Restatement Third: Trusts*, perhaps surprisingly, leaves the elaboration of the bona fide purchaser defence to R3RUE, which means that, on the scheme of the Restatements, a gap has now appeared in the protection available to a bona fide purchaser of an equitable interest. It should not be thought that such purchases are rare: after all, dealings in intermediated securities are almost always dealings in equitable interests, and so almost all share purchases are in fact purchases of an equitable interest.[114] Of course, as the Restatements are not statutes, this oversight is not formally significant, but given that, 125 years on from Ames' article, there seems to be doubt in English law as to whether a bona fide purchaser of an equitable interest takes free from a sub-trust of that equitable interest, it is unfortunate that the Restatements can no longer provide a clear point of reference.

The second, broader point concerns the operation of the change of position defence set out in § 65. As far as the distinction between rights and value is concerned, the significance of the defence comes from its close link to the unjust enrichment liability principle discussed in Part C. Indeed, § 65, Comment a notes that the defence 'gives effect to inherent limitations of a liability based on unjust

[110] JB Ames, 'Purchase for Value without Notice' (1887) 1 *Harvard Law Review* 1, 9.

[111] *Restatement First: Trusts* (n 9) § 285.

[112] *Restatement Second: Trusts* (n 9) § 285.

[113] See § 172, Comment d.

[114] See further B McFarlane and R Stevens, 'Intermediated Securities: Practical Problems and Conceptual Solutions' in L Gullifer and J Payne (eds), *Intermediated Securities: Legal Problems and Practical Issues* (Oxford, Hart Publishing, 2010) 33.

enrichment' and is 'an important device by which the law of restitution justifies the imposition of liability independent of fault'. This notion of an inherent limit may contrast with the external limiting principles set out in § 2, and it offers the possibility that an exploration of the defence may tell us something significant about the nature and justification of the strict liability unjust enrichment principle. The adoption of such a conceptual approach could provide useful general rules which may assist a court in applying the widely-phrased black letter of § 65. Again, however, R3RUE shies away from such a formalist approach, and instead emphasises the function of the defence as a 'loss-allocation device'.[115] Whilst there is, of course, some truth to that functional view, it may be of limited assistance to a court attempting to assess whether a claimed obligation to make restitution would be, in light of the D's change of position, 'inequitable'.

A potentially fruitful alternative approach could make use of the structure that may apply to constructive trusts. It was suggested in Part D that the existence of such a non-express trust in an unjust enrichment case should depend on D's holding of a right acquired from C (or its traceable proceeds) in circumstances where D has knowledge of the facts constituting the reason for which there is no legal basis for D, as against C, to have the benefit of that right. D's knowledge may have a similarly important role to play in cases where C does not allege that a trust has arisen, but rather argues that he has a purely personal claim against D. As noted by Stephen Smith,[116] it is difficult to argue that an innocent recipient of a mistaken payment has an immediate duty to pay its value to C. Once, however, D is aware of C's mistake, many (indeed, I would say all) of those difficulties disappear. The change of position defence can therefore be seen not simply as a loss-allocation device, but as a conceptual means to give effect to the idea that the strict liability unjust enrichment claim depends on D's holding a surviving enrichment, acquired from C and derived from a right of C, with knowledge of the facts, meaning that there is no legal basis for D, as against C, to have that benefit. A personal unjust enrichment claim, asserting that D is under a duty to pay money to C, may therefore have the same basic structure as an equitable 'proprietary' unjust enrichment claim, asserting that D is (or was) under a duty to C in relation to a specific right held by D. In each case, D's duty depends not only on some facts (such as C's unilateral mistake), meaning that there is no legal basis for D, as against C, to have the benefit of a right, but also on D's knowledge of those facts. In the former case, the duty responds to D's unconscientious retention of value derived from C's right;[117] in the later case, it responds to D's unconscientious retention of a right derived from C's right.[118] It might be possible to use this parallel to organise the more detailed principles of the law, thus retaining the

[115] See § 65, Comment a.

[116] In ch 10 of the present volume.

[117] For a formulation of C's claim depending on D's unconscientious retention of a benefit, see, eg, *Roxborough v Rothmans of Pall Mall Australia Ltd* (2001) 208 CLR 516 [104] (Gummow J). See also *Equuscorp Pty Ltd v Haxton* [2012] HCA 7, (2012) 86 ALJR 296 [34] (French CJ and Crennan and Kiefel JJ).

[118] See, eg, Nourse LJ in *Akindele* (n 60).

symmetry between cases of quasi-contract and of constructive trusts, noted by Ames and Keener, and developed by the *Restatement First: Restitution*.

F. Conclusion

R3RUE rightly identifies the 'central achievement' of its 1937 predecessor: 'the identification of unjust enrichment as an independent basis of liability in common-law legal systems'.[119] It is a bitter irony that the benefits of this insight have, in the main, been reaped outside the US. Set in the context of declining academic and practical interest in private law doctrine, the mere existence of R3RUE is a triumph. It rightly aims to protect and advance the central achievement of Scott and Seavey's Restatement. This chapter has suggested two ways in which that end might have been better served.

First, closer attention to the distinction between the acquisition of rights and the more general acquisition of value would have made R3RUE more coherent and a more powerful statement of the nature of the unjust enrichment liability principle. Indeed, this chapter has relied on the argument that the principle is a narrower one than is often thought and its characteristic strict, unilateral liability depends on the same event having caused both C's loss of a right (or acquisition of a duty) and D's acquisition of a right (or loss of a duty). Many of the differences between, on the one hand, R3RUE and, on the other, English and Australian law can be attributed to the former's implicit rejection of this narrow view of the liability principle.

Of course, this narrow view of the liability principle is a controversial one, and it would be dangerous to say that R3RUE was wrong not to have adopted it. This leads us, however, to the second, and more important, point. The criticism is not that R3RUE adopts a particular view of what counts as an enrichment, or when D's enrichment is at C's expense, or when D's enrichment is unjust; rather, it is that R3RUE simply does not engage with these fundamental conceptual questions, adopting instead a predominantly functional and contextual approach. Given the discussion in the previous four parts, each corresponding to a part of R3RUE, it must be concluded that such an approach has proved an unsuitable means to the end of entrenching and explicating unjust enrichment as an independent basis of liability.

This should not be taken as a criticism of R3RUE itself, but rather as a reflection of the American legal culture in which R3RUE must operate. The pervasive and enduring influence of legal realism makes it very difficult to present a Restatement that examines, and is organised around, well-defined formal concepts, such as the distinction between rights and value. The irony is that a focus on concepts as well as results – that is, on the means by which legal conclusions

[119] § 1, Comment a.

are reached as well as the conclusions themselves – may in fact have great functional benefits in allowing for the simpler delineation of the law, and hence of parties' rights. After all, the virtue of concepts lies in their relative invariance to context and thus in their applicability to a broad range of situations.[120] Indeed, a focus on the distinction between rights and other forms of value may thus be particularly beneficial, as rights, unlike value, are already delineated (and have their value set) by other areas of law beyond unjust enrichment. It can also be suggested that, in private law in particular, when we seek to explain to D why precisely he should transfer some money or a right to C, a conceptual justification of that duty may have valuable explanatory force: in some cases, after all, the means may justify the end.

[120] This point is developed by H Smith (n 20).

2

Direct and Indirect Enrichment at the Claimant's Expense in Three-Party Cases

BIRKE HÄCKER

A. Introduction

The topic of enrichment in three-party situations under the *Restatement Third: Restitution and Unjust Enrichment*[1] is one that I tackle with some trepidation. This is not only because I claim no particular expertise in US law, but also because multi-party restitution cases are notoriously difficult within those legal systems with which I am best acquainted: the English and the German. Some decades ago, it was indeed rumoured in German academia that the authorities in charge of running the State Examination in Law had decided never to set problem questions involving more than two parties in an unjust enrichment scenario since it would be practically impossible to mark such a paper.[2]

Over time, numerous different approaches have been developed to cope with multi-party cases. In Germany, lawyers seek to resolve many of the issues by identifying particular 'performance relationships' which predetermine the patterns of potential restitutionary liability.[3] In England, one finds proponents of a 'directness' requirement or a restitutionary 'privity principle' (both admitting for exceptions),[4] but also those favouring a simple causal test (conversely subject to

[1] American Law Institute, *Restatement Third: Restitution and Unjust Enrichment* (St Paul, MN, American Law Institute Publishers, 2011) (hereinafter 'R3RUE').

[2] See HH Jakobs, 'Die Rückkehr der Praxis zur Regelanwendung und der Beruf der Theorie im Recht der Leistungskondiktion' [1992] *Neue Juristische Wochenschrift* 2524.

[3] The German sources are too numerous to list in a representative way. For accounts in English with further references, see R Zimmermann and J du Plessis, 'Basic Features of the German Law of Unjustified Enrichment' [1994] *Restitution Law Review* 14, 31–36; G Dannemann, *The German Law of Unjustified Enrichment and Restitution* (Oxford, Oxford University Press, 2009) 29–34, 50–60.

[4] A Burrows, *The Law of Restitution*, 3rd edn (Oxford, Oxford University Press, 2011) 69–85; G Virgo, *The Principles of the Law of Restitution*, 2nd edn (Oxford, Oxford University Press, 2006) 105–12. See also B McFarlane, 'Unjust Enrichment, Property Rights and Indirect Recipients' [2009] *Restitution Law Review* 37, especially 56–59; L Smith, 'Restitution: The Heart of Corrective Justice' (2001) 79 *Texas Law Review* 2115, especially 2155–74. And *cf Investment Trust Companies (in liq) v HMRC* [2012] EWHC 458 (Ch) [51]–[67] (Henderson J).

restrictions)[5] in order to establish when a defendant has been enriched at the claimant's expense. Closely intertwined are disagreements over whether a claim in unjust enrichment only ever lies between one claimant and one defendant (or sets of these) or whether there can in fact sometimes be several potential claimants or defendants in different capacities.[6] Excellent comparative scholarship has highlighted the various similarities and differences between civilian legal systems and common law jurisdictions, making a meaningful dialogue possible.[7]

My initial instinct was therefore to see where R3RUE fitted into all of this and to produce a full comparative account and assessment of the approach adopted by its draftsmen. It became quickly obvious, however, that this would be far too big a task for several reasons. First, the barest upfront outline of the concepts and debates informing the comparative perspective would take up so much space that too little would remain for the actual analysis of the *Restatement*. Second, although R3RUE contains two chapters expressly exploring 'performance rendered to a third person' and 'benefits conferred by a third person' respectively,[8] the problems raised by multi-party situations are in fact addressed in other places as well, relevant examples being spread out over the entire 1,400-odd pages. Third, a number of these examples concern cases which civilian – and certainly German – lawyers would not recognise as having anything much to do with unjustified enrichment as that area of the law is conventionally understood. Finally, even within the common law tradition, there are inconsistencies in the usage of ostensibly straightforward terms like 'direct' and 'indirect' enrichment. Take the example of A asking his bank B to

[5] P Birks, '"At the Expense of the Claimant": Direct and Indirect Enrichment in English Law' in D Johnston and R Zimmermann (eds), *Unjustified Enrichment: Key Issues in Comparative Perspective* (Cambridge, Cambridge University Press, 2002) 493; P Birks, *Unjust Enrichment*, 2nd edn (Oxford, Oxford University Press, 2005) 75–78, 86–98, especially 89 ff, 93 ff; C Mitchell, P Mitchell and S Watterson (eds), *Goff & Jones: The Law of Unjust Enrichment*, 8th edn (London, Sweet & Maxwell, 2011) [3-58]–[3-92] and especially [6-12]–[6-62]; S Watterson, '"Direct Transfers" in the Law of Unjust Enrichment' (2011) 64 *Current Legal Problems* 435. See also C Mitchell, 'Liability Chains' in S Degeling and J Edelman (eds), *Unjust Enrichment in Commercial Law* (Sydney, Thomson Reuters, 2008) 131, especially 142–45; R Williams, 'Three Quarrelling Parties, Two Oral Contracts and a Claim in Restitution?' [2010] *Restitution Law Review* 51, especially 61–74. And *cf Relfo Ltd (in liq) v Varsani* [2012] EWHC 2168 (Ch) [85]–[90] (Sales J).

[6] On the relationship between the alleged 'directness' requirement and the postulate that an enrichment can only ever be gained by one party or at one other party's expense, see especially *Goff & Jones* (n 5) [6-13].

[7] See especially JP Dawson, 'Indirect Enrichment' in E von Caemmerer, S Mentschikoff and K Zweigert (eds), *Ius Privatum Gentium: Festschrift für Max Rheinstein zum 70. Geburtstag am 5. Juli 1969*, vol 2 (Tübingen, Mohr Siebeck, 1969) 789; S Meier, 'Mistaken Payments in Three-Party Situations: A German View of English Law' (1999) 58 *Cambridge Law Journal* 567; A Schall, 'Three-Party Situations in Unjust Enrichment Epitomised by Mistaken Bank Transfers' [2004] *Restitution Law Review* 110; P Schlechtriem, *Restitution und Bereicherungsausgleich in Europa*, vol 2 (Tübingen, Mohr Siebeck, 2001) ch 7, 285–398; D Solomon, *Der Bereicherungsausgleich in Anweisungsfällen: Rechtsvergleichende Untersuchung zum deutschen Recht und zu den Rechtsordnungen des Common Law* (Tübingen, Mohr Siebeck, 2004); D Visser, 'Searches for Silver Bullets: Enrichment in Three-Party Situations' in D Johnston and R Zimmermann (eds), *Unjustified Enrichment: Key Issues in Comparative Perspective* (Cambridge, Cambridge University Press, 2002) 526. More generally, a thorough comparative analysis of the English and German law of unjust(ified) enrichment is provided by Dannemann (n 3).

[8] R3RUE (n 1) vols 1 and 2, pt II, ch 3, topic 2 (§§ 23–25) and ch 6 (§§ 47–48).

pay C a certain amount of money. On one view, irrespective of the payment mechanism, this is an 'immediate' or direct enrichment of A by B and at the same time of C by A, so that C is at most 'remotely' or indirectly enriched at B's expense.[9] Others describe such an account as 'counter-intuitive' in light of the fact that the funds flow straight from B to C.[10] There can thus be a measure of disagreement about what properly counts as a two- or three-party case.

To avoid burdening the present chapter with such preconceived difficulties, I have decided to approach R3RUE in a rather more naïve way by simply going through the rules and examples it provides for instances in which a (potential) restitutionary liability is said to exist between two parties in circumstances where a third party was in some way involved in the conferral or receipt of the benefit that actually changed hands. The aim of this exercise will be to distil from R3RUE whatever patterns it may yield, to raise questions where this seems necessary or appropriate and to seek out any answers that there be. In doing so, I cannot – of course – discard the comparative baggage completely, not least because one's perspective is always informed by that with which one is familiar. But my comments should be seen as haphazard thoughts inspired by what I have read rather than any systematic attempt to assess R3RUE comparatively. As far as possible, I will try to leave aside issues dealt with in other chapters, such as the relevant unjust factors,[11] remedies and defences, yet these are sometimes so closely interwoven with the topic under consideration that the picture would be incomplete without reference to them. This is because R3RUE does not tell us in the abstract when a person is to be treated as enriched at another's expense; instead, it focuses on specific situations giving rise to restitutionary liability in three-party cases. If my account is therefore primarily a descriptive summary, I hope that it is at any rate one which will provide a solid foundation for further analysis.

Any useful description requires a clear structure. As already mentioned, R3RUE distinguishes between, on the one hand, the 'performance rendered to a third person' scenario and, on the other hand, that of 'benefits conferred by a third person'. This can be a helpful way of looking at three-party cases so long as one does not forget that who counts as a 'third person' depends on the viewpoint one adopts. Going back to the above example of A, B and C: as far as a potential restitutionary claim by A against C is concerned, B may be seen as the third party (unless one regards the case as a straightforward two-party situation),[12] while in the relationship between A and B, the third party is C, and in that between B and C, it is A. Bearing this in mind, however, the distinction suggested by R3RUE

[9] Birks, 'Direct and Indirect Enrichment' (n 5) 503; Birks, *Unjust Enrichment* (n 5) 87–88. German law reaches the same conclusion by its particular notion of 'performance': see n 3 and accompanying text.

[10] *Goff & Jones* (n 5) [6-19]; Watterson (n 5) 440. See also Schall (n 7) 120–21.

[11] Although R3RUE (n 1) vol I, 4–6, expresses a slight preference for the 'absence of basis' perspective over the traditional common law 'unjust factor' approach (§ 1, Comment b), for exposition purposes it still adheres to the categorisation of cases according to the latter, dealing, for example, with mistake (in §§ 5–12) and other defects of consent such as duress (in § 14) or undue influence (in § 15).

[12] See the text following n 10.

affords a good basic structure for the inquiry, mainly because it allows us to 'feed in' the various three-party scenarios we find discussed in places other than those expressly headed as such. To mark the fact that this chapter therefore takes the liberty of a little reorganisation, I shall devote one part (dealing with 'benefits rendered to a third person' broadly conceived) to the problem of identifying the defendant, and the other (dealing with 'benefits conferred by a third party' broadly conceived) to the problem of identifying the claimant. Within each of these two parts, a further subdivision is apposite and inherent in R3RUE, namely the distinction between 'primary' claims which are established immediately and without more, and 'secondary' claims typically contingent on a party to the primary claim dropping out of the picture at a later stage. I shall call the parties to such claims the 'primary/secondary claimant' and the 'primary/secondary defendant' only so as to avoid the connotations which would otherwise be imported by the language of 'directness', 'immediacy' or 'remoteness'. This is not to say that it would be illegitimate to describe, for example, the primary defendant as the 'immediate enrichee' or the secondary claimant as a 'remote enricher'.[13]

B. Who Has Been Enriched? Identifying the Defendant

Normally, where C effects a conveyance to X or personally renders some service to X, we can observe for a fact that the resulting shift of assets, wealth or value emanates from C and moves to X. In a very basic sense, X is enriched at C's expense. The question with which this part is concerned is whether and when another party, D, must (also) be treated as being enriched at C's expense, either in addition to, or instead of, X. R3RUE contains several examples of cases where D may be liable to C in unjust enrichment from which we can infer that it regards C as having enriched D, X being the third party. However, since § 1 imposes restitutionary liability only on 'a person who is *unjustly* enriched at the expense of another' (and only to the extent that the enrichee has no valid defence), we must take care to separate out – as far as R3RUE will allow us – the enrichment issue from the unjust factor or lack of basis[14] pertaining between C and D and any defences applying in the relationship between C and X. As such, the first section within this part deals with cases where the circumstances of C's 'performance' to X are such that R3RUE treats D as unjustly enriched at C's expense from the outset. The second section concerns situations where X is the (sole) primary defendant and D becomes liable to C only as a consequence of X somehow dropping out.

[13] In fact, on the defendant side, the present distinction is similar to that made by Birks, 'Direct and Indirect Enrichment' (n 5) between 'immediate enrichees' and 'remote recipients'.

[14] *cf* n 11. Emphasis added in the quote from §1.

(1) Primary Claims Where Performance is Rendered to a Third Person

(a) Performance to the Defendant's Agent

R3RUE does not directly raise the question of who has been enriched where the claimant (C) renders performance to the defendant's (D's) agent (X), presumably because it regards the answer as obvious. Performance to an agent is a form of performance straight to the principal. We may infer this from a passage in § 65, concerning the change of position defence. Under the heading 'payment over by a representative', the commentary explains 'payment over' as a specific application of the change of position defence, also noting that the mere status of being a representative does not afford the agent a defence.[15] Instead, the position in a mistaken payment case, for example, is as follows:

> Until Agent has paid the funds to Principal, the claimant may seek restitution from either Agent (who has possession of the funds) or Principal (who can direct Agent to return them). By contrast, as soon as Agent has paid the funds over to Principal or to Principal's creditors, or has expended them for Principal's benefit, it is evident that Principal has been enriched and that Agent has not.[16]

It therefore seems to be D's control over the agent X which allows C to treat D as enriched even before X has actually surrendered the money to D. Until payment over in good faith occurs, D is liable to C alongside X,[17] and thereafter exclusively.

(b) Mistaken Performance of the Defendant's Obligation

§ 7 addresses the 'mistaken performance of another's obligation' and provides that this 'gives the performing party a claim in restitution against the obligor to the extent of the benefit mistakenly conferred on the obligor'.[18] So, if C mistakenly pays D's debt to X, D is unjustly enriched at C's expense to the extent that X's enforceable claim against D is validly discharged. The commentary makes it clear that, in theory, there are two potential defendants: X, to whom the performance was rendered, and D, who benefits to the extent that his debt is discharged. However, 'on the hypothesis that [C's] payment has discharged a valid debt . . . [C's] claim against [X] will be barred by [X's] affirmative defence as a bona fide payee in any case where [X] takes payment without notice of [C's] mistake'.[19]

[15] R3RUE (n 1) vol II, 516 (§ 65, Comment e). But *cf* n 17.

[16] ibid 517.

[17] Some authors would, in fact, argue that the agent X is never enriched in the first place because X is at all times accountable to his principal D for what he has received: *cf* the discussion in *Goff & Jones* (n 5) [6-36]–[6-37] and especially [28-02], drawing on JP Moore, 'Restitution from Banks' (unpublished DPhil thesis, University of Oxford, 2000).

[18] R3RUE (n 1) vol I, 79.

[19] ibid 80. The bona fide payee defence is dealt with in § 67. For discussion by Andrew Burrows, see ch 7 in the present volume.

Several points should be noted here. While it is possible to say that both X and D are enriched by C's performance, R3RUE assumes that in practice there will only be one primary claim. This is because X will either have recognised C's mistake, in which case he does not qualify as a bona fide payee and there is typically no valid discharge,[20] or the existence of the bona fide payee defence confines C to suing D whose liability to X has been reduced. R3RUE envisages a similar alternative liability for the special case of negotiable instruments where the rules tie in with those under the Uniform Commercial Code:[21]

> Frequently, (as when a bank pays a check in disregard of its customer's order to stop payment) it will be the case that one of two parties – either the drawer or the payee – has been unjustly enriched by the bank's mistake, depending on the underlying transactions between the drawer, payee, and any holder in due course. If payment discharged a valid obligation of the customer/drawer, the bank's restitution claim is against the drawer under the rule of this section; while if the payee has received a payment of money not due, the bank's restitution claim is against the payee under the rule in § 6 [dealing with the mistaken payment of money not due in a two-party scenario].[22]

The reason why *Barclays Bank Ltd v WJ Simms, Son & Cooke (Southern) Ltd*[23] would be decided differently in the US than in England is that the bank's payment on the cheque countermanded by its customer, the drawer, would be regarded as effective to discharge the drawer's obligation on the cheque, so that the payee would have a complete defence to any restitutionary liability.[24]

The crucial first question is therefore always whether C's performance has actually discharged a debt of D's. Without a valid discharge, D is not enriched. Unfortunately, R3RUE contains little indication – still less conclusive answers – as to when this is the case. Does the appropriation of the payment to any particular debt depend on the payer or the payee perspective? How exactly does the payer's mistake or the payee's awareness of it affect the validity of the discharge?[25] Where there is, for whatever reason, no valid discharge, does the payer C nevertheless have the choice of 'abandoning' his claim against the payee X and elect to pursue the debtor D instead?[26] These are issues to tackle and resolve largely outside R3RUE, though it will be seen that the resulting problems do not pass it by completely.

An essential element of liability under § 7 is that C should have been mistaken in discharging D's debt. Other parts of R3RUE deal with situations where C knowingly

[20] But see nn 39–40 and accompanying text.

[21] *cf* Uniform Commercial Code, § 3–418 and § 4–407.

[22] R3RUE (n 1) vol I, 83 f.

[23] *Barclays Bank Ltd v WJ Simms, Son & Cooke (Southern) Ltd* [1980] 1 QB 677 (QBD Comm). Contrast the case of *Lloyds Bank plc v Independent Insurance Co Ltd* [2000] QB 110 (CA).

[24] For a critical discussion of *Simms* from the US perspective, see A Kull, 'Rationalizing Restitution' (1995) 83 *California Law Review* 1191, 1228 ff. Contrast Birks, 'Direct and Indirect Enrichment' (n 5) 506, who questions the American 'discharge for value' defence. And compare Andrew Burrows' contribution in ch 7 of the present volume.

[25] The effect of the payee being aware of the payer's mistake for the availability of the bona fide payee defence is addressed in n 39 and accompanying text.

[26] *cf* the comparative discussion of such questions by Dawson (n 7) 809–15.

or deliberately relieves D of the obligation to X. Such a conscious discharge may or may not lead to a restitutionary claim by C against D, depending on all the circumstances of the case.[27] What one can perhaps infer from § 7 is that D is always to be regarded as enriched at C's expense where C's performance to X validly discharges a debt owed by D to X, the ensuing potential liability between C and D turning (where appropriate)[28] on the correct valuation of this enrichment and on the existence of a relevant unjust factor or on the absence of a justificatory basis.[29] D will, in any event, not be prejudiced by a substitution of creditors, since any defences he might have been able to raise against X will also hold good against C.[30]

A final comment concerns the notion of a 'mistaken performance' and the examples given in § 7 to illustrate the rule. Broadly speaking, they fall into two categories. In one set of cases, C erroneously believes himself to be X's debtor, so that he is subjectively trying to discharge his own liability when rendering performance to X.[31] In another set, C is fully aware of discharging D's debt, his mistake consisting in believing himself under an obligation to do so when in fact he is not.[32] It is a pity that these two types of mistaken performance cases are not distinguished more clearly in R3RUE,[33] since they present wholly different challenges.

Take the following examples which reflect typical situations mentioned by R3RUE. In the first example, C pays a tax that should have been borne by D either (i) because C's property has been incorrectly assessed by the tax authority for improvements actually located on D's land or (ii) because C has sold the relevant property to D and has simply forgotten to stop paying taxes for it.[34] According to R3RUE, C is here mistaking D's liability for his own. However, one may wonder whether there really is a valid discharge, particularly in scenario (i).[35] Apart from the fact that – according to cases discussed elsewhere in R3RUE – US law is slow to afford the bona fide payee defence to a taxing authority, at least where the authority is itself primarily responsible for the payer's misapprehension,[36] the obvious objection to scenario (i) is that it is not clear how or why C's compliance with his over-assessment should relieve D of any liability.[37]

[27] See the text to nn 50–74 (on §§ 22–24).

[28] See especially Comment c to § 7 on 'unliquidated' obligations: R3RUE (n 1) vol I, 81 f.

[29] *cf* n 11.

[30] R3RUE treats this as a general rule concerning the valuation of D's enrichment: R3RUE (n 1) vol I, 79 ff.

[31] For example, Illustrations 1, 2, 3 and 8: R3RUE (n 1) vol I, 80 ff.

[32] For example, Illustrations 4, 6, 11 and 12: ibid 81 ff.

[33] The Reporter's Note (ibid 86) merely explains why, as far as the second type of case goes, an insurer's payment resulting from a mistake about the extent of policy coverage (*cf* text to n 38) should not be treated as 'voluntary' vis-à-vis the insured.

[34] See § 7, Illustrations 1 and 3: R3RUE (n 1) vol I, 80.

[35] The problem also arises in 'unliquidated obligation' scenarios, such as where C erroneously believes himself to be bound to perform a service to X when in fact D is the person contractually obliged (*cf* § 7, Illustration 8: ibid 82). If performance of the service in question by C to X makes it impossible for D to do the same, then D's obligation to X is discharged by frustration; it is not a matter of C having truly 'performed' D's obligation.

[36] *cf* § 19 on the recovery of overpaid tax, especially the discussion in the Reporter's Note of *Mayer v Mayor of the City of New York*, 63 NY 455 (1875): R3RUE (n 1) vol I, 275.

[37] Illustrations 8 and 9 in § 19 (R3RUE (n 1) vol I, 264) do not shed much light on the matter either.

In the second example, differing from the first category of case, negligent tortfeasor D, who has liability insurance with company C, is found to be liable to pay victim X the sum of $10,000. Overlooking the fact that the policy limits C's liability to $5,000 per occurrence, C pays X the entire amount due under the judgment.[38] Here there is much less doubt about the validity of the (full) discharge, since C has deliberately freed D from his liability to X, albeit for a mistaken motive. Yet here the question arises as to whether we are really dealing with an either-or scenario under all circumstances. What if X is aware of C's mistake when accepting the money? Will X then not qualify as a bona fide payee (as an illustration in § 67 would seem to suggest)[39] and will C therefore – on the assumption that the validity of the discharge nevertheless remains unaffected – have concurrent claims to the overpaid $5,000 against X or D?[40] Or is C always confined to suing X first? If the answers to such concerns are contained in R3RUE, they are certainly not easy to find.

(c) Mistaken Discharge of a Lien Benefiting the Defendant

In connection with § 7, brief mention must also be made of § 8(2), which provides:

> If the use of the claimant's funds to discharge a lien confers an unintended benefit on another person as the result of the claimant's mistake about title to the encumbered property, the existence of intervening liens, or other relevant circumstances, the claimant is entitled to restitution via subrogation to the discharged lien (§57(1)(a)) as necessary to prevent unjust enrichment.[41]

This is not the place to discuss the remedy of subrogation in any detail.[42] Suffice it to note that – like § 7 – § 8(2) is concerned with one party's (the payer C's) performance to a third party (the security holder X) which inadvertently benefits D rather than C himself.[43] No question is raised about the validity of the discharge; § 8(2) simply presupposes that the lien has been validly discharged.[44] In contra-

[38] See § 7, Illustration 4: ibid 81.

[39] According to § 67, Illustration 12, in the case where an insurer pays a patient's full hospital bill of $200,000 not realising that coverage under the policy is in fact limited to $125,000, the bona fide payee defence means that 'Hospital is not liable to Insurer *if Hospital obtains payment before learning of Insurer's mistake*' (emphasis added): R3RUE (n 1) vol II, 564.

[40] The formulation quoted above (in the text to n 19) suggests that a debt which D owes to X can be validly discharged by C without X necessarily being able to invoke the bona fide payee defence vis-à-vis C.

[41] § 8(2): R3RUE (n 1) vol I, 87.

[42] The remedy of subrogation is dealt with extensively by § 57: R3RUE (n 1) vol II, 352–79.

[43] The commentary notes that although § 8(2) is limited to cases in which D's unjust enrichment at C's expense originates in C's mistake, 'there are other reasons why application of [C's] funds to discharge a lien on [D's] property might likewise result in the unjust enrichment of [D] at [C's] expense'. The relevant examples given in Comment a are of fraud, duress or undue influence (§§ 13–15) or of C performing a legal duty or otherwise acting reasonably to protect an interest of his own (§§ 23–24, 26): R3RUE (n 1) vol I, 87 f.

[44] As in § 7, we are left in the dark about the exact conditions under which a discharge is to be treated as valid. The examples provided to illustrate § 8(2) apparently assume that C informs the

distinction to § 7, D need not have been under any personal liability to X, which explains why § 8(2) confines C to the remedy of subrogation.[45] If C's payment also happens to discharge a concurrent monetary debt of D's, then § 7 ensures that C acquires an appropriate personal restitutionary claim against him.

(d) Protecting the Defendant from Liability

In § 21 (concerning the 'protection of another's property' as an aspect of 'emergency intervention'), we find a discussion of the case where C bestows a benefit on X with the result that a liability owed by D to X is smaller than it would otherwise have been:

> If one party intervenes in an emergency to reduce (or prevent altogether) a liability to which another would have been subject in the absence of the intervention, the first party has at least a theoretical claim under this section.[46]

Thus, if C salvages X's ship after it has been damaged in a collision for which D is responsible, C may claim restitution from D to the extent that D's liability to X is diminished or avoided as a result of C's intervention, though not exceeding the amount of C's actual outlay or the salvage award that C could otherwise have demanded from X.[47]

Here D's enrichment at C's expense consists not in the discharge of an existing obligation, but in the protection from a liability D would otherwise inevitably have incurred towards X. C may or may not know that his intervention ultimately benefits D rather than X. Any limits placed on C's ability to recover from D indicate not a lack of enrichment (which exists in the form of saved expenditure), but possibly a lack of an unjust factor. They stem from the need to bring the unjust enrichment regime into line with the principles governing necessitous intervention. Liability can only be imposed – in the words of § 21 – 'if the circumstances justify the decision to intervene without request'.[48] Where C's intervention is not justified, for example where he knows that X and D do not want him involved, he is an officious intermeddler whose enriching performance (to either X or D) will be deemed 'voluntary'.[49]

security holder X about his intention to discharge the lien, but R3RUE itself does not tell us what – if any – effect it has if X realises that C is acting under a misapprehension about title to the encumbered property or similar relevant circumstances.

[45] See R3RUE (n 1) vol I, 91 (§ 8, Comment c): 'subrogation (as opposed to a monetary claim to the value of the benefit conferred) protects the defendant against the imposition of any new or enlarged obligation in consequence of the claimant's mistake. If the lien discharged secured an obligation on which the defendant was not personally liable, for instance, a judgment for money might impose a liability in restitution in excess of the benefit conferred'.

[46] R3RUE (n 1) vol I, 301 (§ 21, Comment f).

[47] See § 21, Illustration 12: ibid 302.

[48] R3RUE (n 1) vol I, 295.

[49] On 'voluntariness' as a limiting principle *cf* § 2(3): ibid 15.

(e) Performance of the Defendant's Duty

§ 22 is headed 'performance of another's duty' and touches on a closely related issue of emergency intervention. It reads:

> A person who performs another's duty to a third person or to the public is entitled to restitution from the other as necessary to prevent unjust enrichment, if the circumstances justify the decision to intervene without request.[50]

Various circumstances are outlined which may justify an unrequested intervention. As regards the three-party scenario, they are named as the payment of another's money debt 'if there is no prejudice to the obligor in substituting a liability in restitution for the original obligation' and the performance of 'another's duty to furnish necessaries to a third person, to avoid imminent harm to the interests of the third person'.[51]

In the first case, C discharges D's monetary debt to X. The situation differs from that addressed by § 7 because C is not mistaken in any way. In line with the general principles governing necessitous intervention, R3RUE requires C to have a special justification for interfering with D's affairs before it will allow C to recoup the enrichment bestowed upon D. The commentary to § 22 explains that R3RUE expands on the old rule which restricted recovery to the payment of debts for 'necessaries'.[52] However, the new rule is not as wide as the wording of § 22 might suggest. It is by no means the case that payment by C is always justified when D suffers no prejudice through a substitution of creditors. Instead, justification additionally requires 'some degree of urgency', 'some obstacle to prior agreement' between C and D, and that C is 'a proper party to intervene'.[53] On the latter requirement, the commentary observes:

> One who paid another's debt without being requested to do so, having no interest in the matter other than a desire to become the other's creditor, would probably be denied restitution under the rule of this section; but such cases are mostly hypothetical.[54]

In the second case, the supply by C of necessaries to a third party X in circumstances where this is imperative to avoid imminent harm to X and where it would have been D's duty to look after X, we may assume that the abovementioned conditions are automatically met. However, one would expect the amount of D's enrichment at C's expense to be less easily quantifiable than in the monetary debt case, yet we are told that since D will ordinarily be responsible for bringing about the situation which invited the claimant's intervention, his

> unjust enrichment may properly be measured by the costs reasonably incurred by [C] in performance of [D's] obligation, even if [D] might under other circumstances have been able to employ less expensive means.[55]

[50] § 22(1): ibid 308.
[51] § 22(2)(a) and (b), respectively: ibid.
[52] R3RUE (n 1) vol I, 311 (§ 22, Comment f).
[53] ibid 312, referring to the tests set out in Comment b.
[54] ibid 310.
[55] ibid 311 (§ 22, Comment e), referring to § 49(3)(b) and § 52(2).

(f) Performance of a Joint Obligation

§ 23 is the first in a set of three consecutive sections expressly entitled 'performance rendered to a third person' which forms part of the wider context of 'unrequested intervention'. Headed 'performance of a joint obligation', §23 provides as a basic principle:

> If the claimant renders to a third person a performance for which the claimant and defendant are jointly and severally liable, the claimant is entitled to restitution from the defendant as necessary to prevent unjust enrichment.[56]

It then goes on to specify:

> There is unjust enrichment in such a case to the extent that (a) the effect of the claimant's intervention is to reduce an enforceable obligation of the defendant to the third person, and (b) as between the claimant and the defendant, the obligation discharged (or the part thereof for which the claimant seeks restitution) was primarily the responsibility of the defendant.[57]

We are here dealing with the problem of indemnity and contribution as between joint debtors. Where C and D are jointly and severally liable to X (as business partners or as joint tortfeasors, for example) and C pays up, his payment also extinguishes D's debt. C and D are then left to sort out their internal relationship. Often, the distribution of the economic burden between them will be governed by express contract. If it is not, then a claim in unjust enrichment may lie.[58] This depends on the extent to which – as between C and D – the 'primary' responsibility for discharging the joint obligation lay with D. Thus, a surety who has satisfied the creditor will typically be able to demand a complete indemnity from the principal debtor, while a joint tortfeasor will often be confined to seeking a contribution that reflects the other's proportionate share of responsibility.[59] R3RUE does not purport to outline the proper internal allocation of liability, but presupposes that such a division exists, being determined by other areas of the law.[60]

It is not entirely clear what § 23 can tell us about the enrichment question. Assume that C and D are jointly and severally liable to X for an amount of $10,000 in circumstances where their internal responsibility is divided half and half. If C discharges the debt in full, one can certainly regard X as enriched to the tune of $10,000, albeit that there is no unjust factor or absence of basis and X has a

[56] § 23(1): R3RUE (n 1) vol I, 328.

[57] § 23(2): ibid.

[58] R3RUE (n 1) vol I, 329 ff, regards express contractual arrangements as ousting the law of restitution, but sees a cause of action in unjust enrichment potentially overlapping with implied contract or breach of duty as grounds for liability: *cf* n 59 immediately below.

[59] In these cases, the claim to an indemnity/contribution may rest purely on unjust enrichment or may alternatively be based on implied contract (in the surety example) or possibly breach of duty (though query the extent to which joint tortfeasors owe each other a duty of care): ibid 330 ff.

[60] R3RUE (n 1) vol I, 331 ff, referring in particular to two other modern *Restatements*: American Law Institute, *Restatement Third: Suretyship and Guaranty* (St Paul, MN, American Law Institute Publishers, 1996) especially §§ 22–31 and §§ 55–57; and *Restatement Third, Torts: Apportionment of Liability* (St Paul, MN, American Law Institute Publishers, 2000) especially §§ 22–23.

complete defence as far as any repayment goes. At the same time, under § 23, D is to be treated as unjustly enriched at C's expense, but only by $5,000. Are we to see this as the extent of D's actual enrichment? Or is D in fact enriched by $10,000, with no more than $5,000 being 'unjust' vis-à-vis C? The latter view appears preferable if one understands the performance of a joint obligation as merely a special instance of one person discharging another's debt, as R3RUE seems to do,[61] a sufficient justification for the unrequested nature of the payment (from the other debtor's perspective) being provided by the payer's own liability towards the creditor.

What about the case where an immunity or particular limitation of liability applies in the relationship between D and X? C and D may, for example, both be car drivers whose negligent collision injures X, D's wife. They are in a jurisdiction which imposes joint and several liability between tortfeasors but at the same time recognises interspousal immunity for negligence.[62] The question arises whether C, having compensated X for her injuries, may seek a proportionate contribution from D.[63] Under R3RUE, the answer is 'no'. This is because D is not enriched insofar as he would have been immune from suit by X.[64] If that solution is correct, it suggests that D's enrichment at C's expense must indeed be determined exclusively by reference to D's relationship with X and without reference to the relationship between C and D.

(g) Performance of an Independent Obligation

The scenario addressed by § 24, the 'performance of an independent obligation', is in many respects similar to that dealt with in § 23, the only difference being that C and D are not joint debtors but are typically both independently liable to X for the same performance.[65] The section reads:

> (1) If the claimant renders to a third person a performance for which the defendant would have been independently liable to the third person, the claimant is entitled to restitution from the defendant as is necessary to prevent unjust enrichment.
> (2) There is unjust enrichment in such a case to the extent that (a) the claimant acts in the performance of the claimant's independent obligation to the third person, or otherwise in the reasonable protection of the claimant's own interests; and (b) as between the claimant and the defendant, the performance in question (or the part thereof for which the claimant seeks restitution) is primarily the obligation of the defendant.[66]

[61] *cf* Reporter's Note on § 23: R3RUE (n 1) vol I, 341.

[62] Example based on § 23, Illustration 10: ibid 336.

[63] In German law, this problem is discussed under the heading '*gestörter Gesamtschuldnerausgleich*'.

[64] R3RUE (n 1) vol I, 335, pointing out that the tort law applicable within a given jurisdiction may well hold D liable to contribute irrespective of his immunity vis-à-vis X.

[65] Note that R3RUE does not strictly require X to have an enforceable claim against C (as older decisions did), but lets it suffice that C's intervention rested on a reasonable need to protect his own interests: R3RUE (n 1) vol I, 348 ff (§ 24, Comment d). According to § 23, Illustration 6, this may be the case when C owes an independent duty to the public to perform the act for which D would have been liable to X: ibid 334.

[66] R3RUE (n 1) vol I, 344.

An example is provided by title insurer C compensating the purchaser of land X for an undisclosed encumbrance affecting the title and diminishing its value in circumstances where the vendor D has provided a warranty against encumbrances.[67] In line with common practice, R3RUE describes C's claim against D as 'equitable subrogation', but is careful to point out that § 24 is merely concerned with establishing a personal liability in unjust enrichment and that it says nothing about whether and when the remedy of 'subrogation' is available to C.[68]

As in the context of § 23, it is submitted that – on the view underlying R3RUE – D is enriched at C's expense to the extent that an enforceable debt owed by D to X is discharged as a result of C's performance,[69] with this enrichment being 'unjust' only insofar as D's obligation to X ranks as 'primary' vis-à-vis C.[70] An interesting case discussed in the commentary to § 24 concerns the relationship between a casualty insurer and a tortfeasor. Where an insurer C pays money to its client, policyholder X, to compensate X for a tort committed by D and this payment discharges D's liability to X, there is no problem about holding D liable to C in unjust enrichment. However, some US jurisdictions still follow the so-called 'collateral source' rule, according to which evidence of the insurer's performance is inadmissible in proceedings determining the tortfeasor's damages liability to the victim. In such jurisdictions, C's payment to X does not reduce D's liability. In keeping with the principles outlined above, D should not therefore be subject to any restitutionary liability as such. R3RUE nevertheless seeks to accommodate the solution within an unjust enrichment framework:

> The collateral-source rule itself prevents the unjust enrichment of the tortfeasor (since the tortfeasor remains liable), but it creates a new problem of unjust enrichment in the potential double recovery of the policyholder. Subrogation of the insurer (the 'collateral source') to the policyholder's rights corrects this problem. The result is indemnity to the policyholder and reimbursement to the insurer at the ultimate expense of the tortfeasor, with no double recovery and no double liability.[71]

In short, § 24 is invoked to explain why C has a 'restitutionary' claim against D despite the fact that D's liability to X is unchanged: by allowing C rather than X to enforce X's persisting right (the tort claim) against D, we are told, X's unjust enrichment at C's expense is prevented and restitution is accomplished.[72] While the practical outcome is wholly plausible and may indeed relate to preventing X's unjust enrichment,[73] it is hard to see how – *inter partes* – D's liability to C can be placed directly onto an unjust enrichment footing.[74]

[67] § 24, Illustration 1: ibid 344 f.

[68] ibid 345 ff (§ 24, Comment b). Subrogation as a remedy is dealt with by § 57.

[69] This view is also supported by the commentary to § 25, Illustrations 14 and 15: ibid 376 ff.

[70] On determining 'primary' and 'secondary' liability between C and D *inter se*, sometimes described as identifying which party has the 'superior equity', see R3RUE (n 1) vol I, 355 ff (§ 24, Comment g).

[71] ibid 347.

[72] ibid 348 (discussion of Illustration 5).

[73] *cf* the discussion in *Goff & Jones* (n 5) [21-01]–[21-23], especially [21-13].

[74] It would just about be possible to interpret the phrase 'as necessary to prevent unjust enrichment' at the end of § 24(1) as referring to the prevention of X's unjust enrichment at C's expense, but since

(h) Contractual Performance

The final section of the trio entitled 'performance rendered to a third person' is § 25. It is – in a sense – only indirectly relevant under the present heading and will be dealt with in greater detail when we come to consider the position of 'secondary' defendants whose liability depends on the 'primary' enrichee dropping out. The basic provision reads as follows:

> If the claimant renders to a third person a contractual performance for which the claimant does not receive the promised compensation, and the effect of the claimant's uncompensated performance is to confer a benefit on the defendant, the claimant is entitled to restitution from the defendant as necessary to prevent unjust enrichment.[75]

The interesting feature about this section is that it assumes, without further explanation, that the person primarily liable to the performing party is his contract partner and not the party who was – in physical terms – the immediate recipient of the performance. A typical example is where subcontractor C is asked by general contractor X to do some work on the land of property owner D.[76] Although D is the person whose land becomes more valuable as a result of C's work, R3RUE regards C as performing to X, presumably on account of the triangular contractual setup. This assumption reflects the performance notion adopted by German law[77] and it also chimes with the abovementioned 'counter-intuitive' view of an 'immediate' enrichment,[78] but it is nonetheless remarkable. Re-adjusting the parties' roles and designations so as to comply with the style here employed, we may conclude for present purposes that where subcontractor C has a contract with main contractor D (formerly X) under which he is obliged to make a transfer or render some service to property owner X (formerly D), it is primarily the contract partner D who has been enriched at C's expense, albeit that X may under certain circumstances also become liable to C as 'secondary defendant' under § 25.

Of course, C's claim against his contract partner D will in most cases not be rooted in unjust enrichment. D's enrichment at C's expense is justified by their contractual relationship, and C's claim against D will be the contractual right to the agreed remuneration. A question this scenario does throw up, however, is what happens where C's contract with D is for some reason defective or yields no claim. For example, how does the inference from § 25 sit with the bank or insurance cases discussed above? Under § 7, where C mistakenly performs D's obligation to X thinking that a valid contract between C and D requires him to do so, C will have a restitutionary claim against D if and only if D's debt to X is discharged

the wording is predicated on the claimant being 'entitled to *restitution from the defendant*' (emphasis added), this does not ultimately help. The only conceivable argument, namely that tortfeasor D would be factually – albeit not legally – enriched at the insurer C's expense if X as the victim refrained from suing D upon being compensated by C, makes too much of the notion of factual enrichment.

[75] R3RUE (n 1) vol I, 368.

[76] See only § 25, Illustrations 1 and 2: ibid 370.

[77] See n 3 and accompanying text.

[78] See nn 9 and 10 and accompanying text.

and/or X qualifies as a bona fide payee.[79] So, a bank overlooking its customer's stop order on a cheque and paying out to the drawee is properly regarded as having enriched the customer-drawer whenever the payment was effective to discharge the drawer's obligation to the drawee.[80] The obvious difference between the rule in § 7 and that implied by § 25 is that the latter does not care whether C's performance discharges any debt of D's. D is always enriched at C's expense. This must be on account of the contractual relationship between them and D's request. It also explains why C's contract partner D (or the 'third person' in the terminology of § 25) is invariably regarded as the recipient of C's 'performance',[81] while the wording of § 7 leaves the matter of direction open.

(2) Secondary Defendants

(a) Uncompensated Performance under a Contract with a Third Person

The most relevant section to look at when it comes to identifying 'secondary' defendants is again § 25 – this time from a different angle. As already mentioned, the section concerns 'uncompensated performance under [a] contract with [a] third person' and is exemplified by the scenario of the subcontractor C who is employed by general contractor X to do work on a site owned by D. Under certain conditions, § 25 allows C to seek restitution for unjust enrichment from D. R3RUE here recognises a form of *actio de in rem verso*, something that French lawyers have done since the famous *Boudier* case[82] and that both current English law[83] and the German Civil Code[84] firmly reject. To prevent a claim by C against D from undermining the contractual setup, especially the doctrine of privity, liability under § 25 is hedged around with various restrictions.[85] They are conveniently summarised by the accompanying commentary as follows:

> [§ 25] authorizes restitution only as the claimant's secondary recourse: only if the defendant will otherwise retain the benefit without paying for it; only if restitution is not displaced by the parties' contractual arrangements; and only if restitution will not subject the defendant to a forced exchange.[86]

Perhaps most importantly for present purposes, C must pursue a viable contractual claim against X before suing D.[87]

[79] *cf* the text to nn 18–40.
[80] See the discussion of *Barclays Bank v Simms* in the text to nn 23 and 24.
[81] Dawson (n 7) 802 speaks of a 'two-sided performance with an inevitable by-product for a third party'.
[82] *Patureau-Miran v Boudier*, Cass req, 15 June 1892, DP 1892.1.596, S 1893.1.281. The *Boudier* case also provides the basis for § 25, Illustration 8: R3RUE (n 1) vol I, 374.
[83] The leading case is now *MacDonald Dickens & Macklin (a firm) v Costello* [2011] EWCA Civ 930, [2012] QB 244. *cf* also the discussion in *Goff & Jones* (n 5) [3-67]–[3-76].
[84] But see n 99 and accompanying text.
[85] See R3RUE (n 1) vol I, 369 ff (Comment b).
[86] ibid 373. *cf* the conditions set out in § 25(2). On 'forced exchange', see also § 2(4).
[87] *cf* ibid 370.

How are we to understand these restrictions and what do they tell us – conceptually – about the enrichment enquiry? If C's contractual performance means that it is X who is primarily enriched at C's expense (albeit perhaps not unjustly),[88] then we can fairly assume that D's enrichment must derive primarily from X. However, there could not be any restitutionary liability by D to C under § 25 if D were not – at least on a secondary level – also enriched at C's expense. Yet R3RUE contains a rather puzzling remark in its commentary on the limiting conditions:

> Section 25 takes as a starting point the proposition, inherited from [the *Restatement First: Restitution*] . . . that when [C] confers a benefit on [D] as the performance of [C's] contract with [X], [X's] failure to render the performance promised to [C] does not necessarily mean that [D] has been enriched at [C's] expense; nor does it mean that any enrichment of [D] is necessarily unjust.[89]

While it is easy to see how the limiting conditions might prevent an enrichment being 'unjust', it is much harder to comprehend why D should sometimes be regarded as enriched at C's expense and sometimes not. Are we to say that there can only ever be one enricher and that X ceases to be that person when he finally fails to pay C, for example when he becomes bankrupt? One could perhaps adopt this view, albeit not without some difficulty, if one regarded subtraction as a 'zero-sum game'.[90] The problem is that R3RUE does not expressly commit to this view in other places; instead, it appears quite happy accepting that a single enrichment may have several sources and several destinations. In one place, the rule in § 25 is indeed expressly linked up with that in § 24:

> If work performed by the claimant [C] under contract with a third party [X] discharges an independent obligation of the defendant [eg, an obligation owed by D to a fourth party Y], the benefit to the defendant [D] is to that extent established.[91]

A second comment relates to the substantive merits of allowing C to sue D under the conditions specified in § 25. In his seminal paper on 'Indirect Enrichment', Dawson argued in respect of the subcontractor case:

> If [property owner D] has not yet paid [builder X], the sub [C] might be given a direct claim to any balance due, *but this balance is an asset that should be subject to the claims of the builder's creditors*, one of whom is this particular sub; the net result would be a preference to the sub.[92]

The Reporter's Note responds to this criticism by stating that

> the problem does not appear to arise in practice. The assumption is that [C's] performance has left [D] obligated to [X], so that [C's] restitution claim against [D] is a means of reaching an asset ([D's] debt to [X]) that properly belongs to [X's] creditors gener-

[88] See the text following n 75.
[89] R3RUE (n 1) vol I, 369.
[90] *cf* LD Smith, 'Three-Party Restitution: A Critique of Birks' Theory of Interceptive Subtraction' (1991) 11 *OJLS* 481, especially 482 ff.
[91] R3RUE (n 1) vol I, 376.
[92] Dawson (n 7) 803 (emphasis added).

ally. Under the rule of this section, however, if [X] (or [X's] trustee in bankruptcy) has an enforceable claim against [D], [C's] claim is already foreclosed by § 25(2)(b).[93] While the decided cases commonly refer to [X's] bankruptcy . . . there is never any suggestion that [X] (or [X's] trustee in bankruptcy) has a pending claim against [D]. More often than not, the circumstances of [X's] default and exit from the [C–D–X] transaction make it highly unlikely that [X] has left behind any viable claims against [D]'.[94]

This may, of course, be the case where bankruptcy proceedings are not instituted at all (owing to a lack of assets, for example), but if X's claim against D is not 'viable' because of various counterclaims, set-offs and similar defences, the logic of R3RUE demands that such defences also be available against C.[95] In that case, at any rate, nothing is won through § 25.

(b) Reaching Secondary Enrichees Outside the Contractual Setting

What about the situation where C confers a benefit on X in circumstances entitling C to restitution for unjust enrichment, but where X has meanwhile passed the benefit received from C on to D? Can C's claim to restitution (which is primarily directed against X) ever reach D, and under what circumstances? The scenario differs from that envisaged by § 25 in two respects: first, C's primary claim against X is based on unjust enrichment, not contract; and second, C will not – or at any rate not normally – have had any previous dealings with D, whereas under § 25 he will have performed to X typically by rendering some service straight to D, as in the subcontractor case. Assume for present purposes that, having transferred money or conveyed an asset directly to X, C discovers that he has been labouring under a liability mistake. Before he can claim restitution, however, X has in good faith changed his position either (i) by gratuitously passing the asset in question on to D or (ii) by making a gift of an equivalent amount of money to D in reliance on his receipt. Alternatively, (iii) X may have acted in bad faith when making the relevant transfer to D and then become bankrupt. Can C now sue D as a secondary defendant?

R3RUE does not address this question directly. That is a pity, for the example goes right to the heart of the so-called 'leapfrogging' issue.[96] In England, the problems raised by the example are usually discussed in connection with *Lipkin Gorman (a firm) v Karpnale Ltd*,[97] and their solution hinges on the proper interpretation of this decision.[98] German law, much as it objects to the *actio de in rem*

[93] § 25(2)(b) provides that there is unjust enrichment for the purposes of § 25(1) only if, inter alia, 'the defendant will retain the benefit of the claimant's performance free of any liability to pay for it': R3RUE (n 1) vol I, 368.

[94] ibid 382 f.

[95] See n 30 and accompanying text.

[96] The term 'leapfrogging' is here used in the broad sense of reaching someone other than the immediate recipient of an enrichment, not (merely) in the sense of trying to skip over the counterparty within a contract.

[97] *Lipkin Gorman (a firm) v Karpnale Ltd* [1991] 2 AC 548 (HL).

[98] See especially Birks, 'Direct and Indirect Enrichment' (n 5) 514–19; Birks, *Unjust Enrichment* (n 5) 93–98; McFarlane (n 4) 45–47.

verso in general, actually allows C to seek restitution from D, at least in the first disenrichment scenario (i).[99] As far as R3RUE is concerned, we have to rely on tentative inferences from individual illustrations. Although the section dealing with change of position (§ 65) treats gifts which would not have been made but for an enriching receipt as prime instances of the defence,[100] it fails to tell us anything about the position of the donee vis-à-vis the claimant enricher. Slightly more helpful is an illustration hidden away in § 17, where 'lack of authority' is discussed: a mother who acts as the trustee of a testamentary trust in favour of her children gratuitously transfers some trust property to her innocent niece and then dies, leaving no estate. We are told that, in principle, the children have a claim in unjust enrichment against the niece, who – despite being innocent – took the trust property as donee.[101] However, the illustration continues, if the niece has passed the trust property on to a cousin before anyone is aware of the mother's breach of trust, the children's claim against the niece is foreclosed by her change of position, but they are instead entitled to recover the trust property and any interim proceeds from the cousin.[102]

We can conclude from this illustration that C would have a restitutionary claim against D in our example (i) where the primary enrichee X has changed his position by passing on the asset originally received. Here, at any rate, R3RUE regards D as enriched at C's expense. Yet this does not mean that the same is necessarily true of examples (ii) and (iii). A special feature of the aunt-and-niece case is that it could be explained by some sort of 'proprietary link' reasoning.[103] If a legal system recognises proprietary restitution after impaired consent transfers in the simple two-party scenario (eg, by imposing a resulting or constructive trust),[104] it can allow for restitution of the original asset or its traceable proceeds[105] from third party donees without categorising this as a form of 'genuine' leapfrogging. The bona fide purchase defence then does the work of protecting innocent recipients for value against claims by the original transferor. Whether C has a claim against D where X is disenriched as a result of making a gift of (other) money to D is therefore left open by R3RUE. If C did have a right to seek restitution from the donee D as a secondary defendant, a connected question would arise whether such a right might also be exigible where X is bankrupt rather than disenriched.

[99] § 822 BGB reads: 'If the recipient [here the primary enrichee X] gratuitously bestows what he has obtained upon a third party [here D], then, to the extent that the recipient's liability to make restitution [to C] is in consequence excluded, the third party is obliged to surrender what he has received as if he had, without legal cause, received it from the creditor [here C].' There is a debate as to whether § 822 BGB also applies where X has changed his position by passing on an asset different from that received (the money scenario (ii)) or where X cannot rely on the disenrichment defence but recovery is factually impossible (the bankruptcy scenario (iii)).

[100] R3RUE (n 1) vol II, 522 ff.

[101] § 17, Illustration 4: R3RUE (n 1) vol I, 234.

[102] § 17, Illustration 5: ibid.

[103] Or possibly even by 'transactional links', as, for example, where X has passed on to D the traceable proceeds of the asset originally received from C. For an explanation and analysis of 'proprietary' and 'transactional' links, see *Goff & Jones* (n 5) [6-35]–[6-45].

[104] For the position under R3RUE, *cf* §§ 54 ff, especially § 55 on the US-style 'constructive trust'.

[105] *cf* n 103.

Despite the dearth of examples, an argument could nevertheless be made for saying that genuine leapfrogging is supported by R3RUE, provided only that there is a sufficiently clear causal nexus between C's performance to X and D's enrichment. It runs along the following lines: considering that § 25 allows C in appropriate circumstances to skip over his contract partner X in order to bring a claim against D, R3RUE already acknowledges certain cases where C can reach right to the end of the enrichment chain C–X–D.[106] Yet if the possibility of such a claim is not ruled out in the contractual scenario, then it must *a fortiori* exist outside valid contractual relationships. The concerns displayed by § 25 for D's protection (no forced exchange, integrity of bargains, etc) are either irrelevant in the present context or can be adequately catered for. D is simply being asked to give up a gratuitous benefit to the extent that he is still enriched by it. In terms of the security of his receipt, it makes no difference whether or not the asset gratuitously bestowed upon him by X was the same that C had previously conveyed to X (and thus whether or not a 'proprietary link' might be established) or even whether it was a traceable product of the original asset.

(c) Restitution for Wrongs: Claims against Third Parties

By contrast with the 'leapfrogging' problem just discussed, R3RUE does address the liability of secondary defendants in connection with 'restitution for wrongs'. § 40 provides:

> A person who obtains a benefit by the act of trespass or conversion, by comparable interference with other protected interests in tangible property, *or in consequence of such an act by another*, is liable in restitution to the victim of the wrong.[107]

Similarly, § 41 states:

> A person who obtains a benefit by misappropriating financial assets, *or in consequence of their misappropriation by another*, is liable in restitution to the victim of the wrong.[108]

Again, § 43, dealing with fiduciary duties and confidential relations, holds liable 'a person who obtains a benefit . . . (c) *in consequence of another's breach of [a fiduciary or equivalent] duty*'.[109] This links in with the abovementioned aunt-and-niece case where the innocent niece's primary restitutionary liability towards the children was explained by reference to the aunt's breach of trust.[110] Finally, the subsidiary catch-all provision of § 44 states in sub-section (1):

> A person who obtains a benefit by conscious interference with a claimant's legally protected interests (*or in consequence of such interference by another*) is liable in restitution

[106] Recall that § 25 treats C's contract partner X as the immediate enrichee and D as being only remotely enriched, irrespective of how the physical conferral of the benefit took place: see the text following n 75.

[107] R3RUE (n 1) vol II, 4 (emphasis added).

[108] ibid 18 (emphasis added).

[109] ibid 52 (emphasis added).

[110] See n 101 and accompanying text.

as necessary to prevent unjust enrichment, unless competing legal objectives make such liability inappropriate.[111]

Two questions arise in this context. First, are we dealing here with restitution for unjust enrichment or restitution for wrongs? In the light of the relevant section headings, those who strictly distinguish between these causes of action[112] might well say: the latter. However, there are good reasons for thinking that 'unjust enrichment' is what these sections actually have in mind as far as the innocent recipient is concerned. If X commits a wrong vis-à-vis C and thereby or subsequently bestows a relevant benefit upon D,[113] X's liability to C will be wrongs-based, but D's will not (unless D was in some way involved in the wrongdoing). This is because D has not breached any duty towards C. Assume now that D is a subsequent transferee from the wrongdoer X. The commentary to §§ 41 and 43 clearly envisages the scenario of X wrongfully obtaining an asset from C and passing it or some traceable substitute on to innocent D.[114] If R3RUE holds D liable to C in unjust enrichment, it must regard D as having been enriched at C's expense.

The second question is whether §§ 40–44[115] tell us anything about 'genuine' leapfrogging. The wording merely requires D to have obtained a benefit 'in consequence of' the wrong committed by X. It could easily accommodate a purely causal analysis. Yet the relevant illustrations are all amenable to analysis in terms of 'proprietary' or 'transactional' links.[116] On closer consideration, this should perhaps not surprise us. It is extremely hard in practice to establish a relevant causal connection between X's wrongdoing and D's gain without at least some transactional link, given that a wrongdoer will not be able to rely on the security of any receipt. In the case of an enrichment chain C–X–D, we are therefore unlikely ever to encounter a case where D's restitutionary liability to C does not turn on the issue of bona fide purchase.[117]

[111] R3RUE (n 1) vol II, 76 (emphasis added).

[112] R3RUE draws no such clear distinction, holding that besides its derivative connotation, 'the consecrated formula "at the expense of another" can also mean "in violation of another's protected rights"': R3RUE (n 1) vol I, 3 (§ 1, Comment a).

[113] If D obtains the benefit as an immediate consequence of X's wrong without X at any time appropriating the benefit to himself, such that the benefit passes directly from C's into D's patrimony, then D should probably be classed as a 'primary' rather than as a 'secondary' defendant because his liability to C arises immediately and without more. However, since not much turns on the distinction, it is convenient for exposition purposes to deal with §§ 40–44 in the present context of secondary defendants.

[114] R3RUE (n 1) vol II, 23 ff (§ 41, Comment e), 65 (§ 43, Comment g). Both passages specifically deal with 'claims against third parties'.

[115] Although § 42 (concerning the 'interference with intellectual property and similar rights') does not contain the phrase 'or in consequence of . . .', which appears in the other sections, the use of the words 'misappropriation' or 'infringement' (rather than 'misappropriating' or 'infringing') suggests that liability is intended to extend to third parties reaping the benefits of someone else's wrong: see the discussion by Nicholas McBride in ch 11 of the present volume (at pp 259–60).

[116] See especially § 41, Illustrations 9, 10 and 13: R3RUE (n 1) vol II, 24 f. Comment g to § 43 makes D's liability to C depend on whether D qualifies as a bona fide purchaser: ibid 65. *cf* McBride, ch 11 in this volume, pp 259–60.

[117] Note, however, that pure causal link cases are conceivable in other scenarios. Some problematic hypotheticals are floated by McBride, ch 11 in this volume, pp 259–60.

C. At Whose Expense is the Enrichment? Identifying the Claimant

This part concerns the opposite question to the question addressed in the previous part. There, we considered what R3RUE tells us about 'who has been enriched' in circumstances where the enricher is known. Here, our concern is with cases where the enrichee is easily identifiable, but the enricher is not. Our inquiry therefore focuses on the person 'at whose expense' a particular enrichment is received when a third party is involved in the conferral of the benefit. Again, it is convenient to distinguish situations in which a claimant C may seek restitution from the defendant D right from the moment of receipt ('primary claims') and those in which the claimant's right to restitution is subject to a prior claim by some other party, typically that of the primary enricher X, not being pursued ('secondary claims'). Cases already dealt with will be left to one side.

(1) Primary Claims Where Benefits are Conferred by a Third Person

(a) Performance by an Agent on the Claimant's Behalf

Let us again start by considering the agency context. Where an agent X renders some performance to D on behalf of the principal C, R3RUE normally treats it as an enrichment of D at C's expense. This is evident from § 17, although R3RUE does not say so expressly. The section deals with cases where the agent (X) lacks the principal's (C's) authority to make a transfer, providing that such transfers are 'subject to rescission and restitution' and holding the transferee (D) liable in restitution to the principal (C) 'as necessary to avoid unjust enrichment'.[118] Yet if D is enriched at C's expense where X is acting without C's authority, then *a fortiori* this must also be true where X is properly authorised to make the transfer. A claim to restitution by C against D will then, of course, only lie if D's enrichment at C's expense is unjust, for example, as a result of some invalidating mistake.

It should be noted, however, that § 17 is only concerned with the case of the agent transferring (or purporting to transfer) an asset belonging to the principal.[119] This leaves open the question of the proper claimant where agent X, acting on C's behalf, passes one of his own assets to D in pursuance of some relationship or transaction pertaining between C and D. Yet the answer can be no different. Irrespective of whether D's enrichment should properly be described as stemming from X,[120] there can be little doubt that we must (also) treat it as being at C's expense, for C will have come under a liability to reimburse his agent.

[118] R3RUE (n 1) vol I, 231.
[119] *cf* especially Comment a: ibid 231–32.
[120] See n 17 for the parallel issue in the converse case.

(b) Payment to the Defendant in Respect of the Claimant's Property

§ 47 is the first of two sections explicitly concerned with 'benefits conferred by a third person'. Headed 'payment to defendant in respect of claimant's property', it provides:

> If a third person makes a payment to the defendant in respect of an asset belonging to the claimant, the claimant is entitled to restitution from the defendant as necessary to prevent unjust enrichment.[121]

A prime example is where tenant X pays rent to D whom he believes to be the owner of the rented property, when in fact the owner is C.[122] Under § 47, D is liable to make restitution to C of the amount received from X.[123]

R3RUE must therefore regard D as enriched at C's expense, although there can be little doubt that D is at the same time also enriched at X's expense. This is a point to which we shall have to return. For the time being, it is worth noting that the reason for treating C as D's enricher is that C's entitlement to the asset in respect of which X made the payment is superior to D's.[124]

(c) Payment to the Defendant to which the Claimant Has a Better Right

Before pondering further over these issues, we need to look at § 48, the second section concerned with 'benefits conferred by a third person'. R3RUE itself sees both sections as closely related, with § 47 being merely a specific instance of 'the more general, residual rule' in § 48.[125] The latter provides:

> If a third person makes a payment to the defendant to which (as between claimant and defendant) the claimant has a better legal or equitable right, the claimant is entitled to restitution from the defendant as necessary to prevent unjust enrichment.[126]

§§ 47 and 48 are described as the 'logical converse' of §§ 23 and 24.[127] There, C discharged a debt to X which – in the relationship between C and D – should have been discharged by D; here, we are dealing with cases where X makes a payment to D which – as between C and D – should have gone to C. The comparison between §§ 47 and 48 and §§ 23 and 24 is helpful, but should be taken with a pinch of salt. An obvious inroad into the symmetry is that §§ 23 and 24 deal with all kinds of 'performances' (including, for example, the rendering of a service), while §§ 47 and 48 are nominally confined to 'payments'.[128] Within the general

[121] R3RUE (n 1) vol II, 130.

[122] *cf* § 47, Illustration 1: ibid.

[123] Because X was mistaken when paying D, there is a parallel mistake-based claim (under § 6) in the relationship between X and D. D is relieved of both liabilities when he makes restitution either to X or to C: ibid. See the discussion in the text following n 131.

[124] See R3RUE (n 1) vol II, 131–32 (§ 47, Comment a).

[125] ibid 130, where the introductory note to ch 6 emphasises that 'the two sections should be considered together'.

[126] R3RUE (n 1) vol II, 144.

[127] ibid 129. See also ibid 132 and 145.

[128] Note, however, that the commentary envisages §§ 47 and 48 being applied 'by analogy' for non-money cases: ibid 131 (§ 47, Comment a) and 145 (§ 48, Comment a).

rule of § 48, we find covered various situations. Thus, the parallel to § 23 (performance of a joint obligation) is discussed in the commentary to § 48 under the heading 'joint obligees',[129] and the parallel to § 24 (performance of an independent obligation) prompts a lengthy discussion of the rules governing 'equitable priorities between independent obligees'.[130]

Where C and D are joint creditors and X's payment to D automatically discharges the debt to C as well, it is easy to understand how the payment leads to D being enriched at C's expense. C loses his claim against X. In the absence of statute or a contract fixing C's and D's respective entitlements, § 48 therefore affords C a restitutionary claim against D to the extent that D's enrichment at C's expense is 'unjust' vis-à-vis C because, as between C and D, C had a better right to the money. What about the more common case, however, where X's payment to D leaves C's claim against D wholly unaffected? Suppose, for example, that X owes $500 to C, but – as a result of an identity mistake – erroneously sends the relevant payment to D, to whom X owes nothing.[131] Here, it is clear that X's payment has not discharged the debt to C and that X would be able to bring a mistake-based restitutionary claim against D for the repayment of $500 (under § 6). We are nevertheless told that the recipient D is 'alternatively' liable to C as the intended payee and that D's payment of $500 to either X or C discharges both liabilities.[132] Yet it will be recalled that under §§ 23 and 24 – and also under § 7 – D could only be regarded as having been enriched at C's expense where C's performance to X actually discharged an obligation of D's.[133] So how can this be?

It is submitted that the answer turns on C's position. Where C is the performing party, it is not up to him to determine whether D's debt to X is ultimately discharged. By contrast, where C is the creditor and X's payment to D happens not to discharge the debt automatically, there is no reason why the law should not allow C to ratify the transaction and seek restitution from D, thereby relieving X of his liability. It would then be C's choice that establishes whether or not D is enriched at his expense. Until C has made a binding choice of this kind, D can be left free to make restitution either to X or C.[134] If he repays X, then X and C are both in the position they were in before X made the mistaken payment. If D instead passes the money on to C, then X has achieved what he intended and C is in the same position as if he had received payment straight from X.

The only quibble one might have with R3RUE's formulation of D's 'alternative' restitutionary liability is thus that D's enrichment cannot be finally regarded as 'coming from' C in any meaningful sense unless and until X's liability to C is discharged or payment over has actually occurred. Yet if we take seriously the fact that §§ 47 and 48 give C a primary claim against D in all cases, this must be on

[129] Comment c on § 48: ibid 147 ff.

[130] Comments c–h on § 48: ibid 148 ff.

[131] See § 48, Illustration 2: ibid 146.

[132] ibid 145 ff. It would therefore appear that C and X are now joint creditors.

[133] See especially the text to nn 18–26, 56–57 and 69–70.

[134] *cf* also § 6, Comment b, especially Illustration 1: R3RUE (n 1) vol I, 60.

account of 'interceptive subtraction'-type reasoning[135] along the following lines: the mere fact that X intended the payment received by D to go to C and that D has 'intercepted' it (albeit perhaps inadvertently) means that D's enrichment is at C's expense all along. The idea of interceptive subtraction would at least explain the straightforward case of a misdirected payment, though the rent case discussed in connection with § 47 (where X is not mistaken about the identity of the recipient payee as such, but rather about the issue of ownership)[136] poses a somewhat greater challenge.[137]

(2) Secondary Claimants

(a) Misdirected Gifts: Claims by the Intended Donee

In two places, R3RUE deals with a situation which is in some respects related to the misdirected payment case just considered in the context of § 48: misdirected gifts. The first place is § 11(3), one of the provisions pertaining to 'mistake in inter vivos gifts', which reads:

> If a donor attempts to make a gift and dies or becomes incapacitated in the belief that the gift has been perfected, and as a result of mistake the attempted gift (a) is wholly or partly ineffective; . . . or (c) transfers property to someone other than the intended donee; the intended donee has a claim in restitution as necessary to prevent the unjust enrichment of the unintended recipient or of the donor's successors, as the case may be.[138]

The second place is § 46, entitled 'wrongful interference with donative transfer', which provides in sub-section (1):

> If assets that would otherwise have passed by donative transfer to the claimant are diverted to another recipient by fraud, duress, undue influence, or other intentional misconduct, the recipient is liable to the claimant for unjust enrichment. The misconduct that invalidates the transfer to the recipient may be the act of the recipient or of a third person.[139]

Like the abovementioned rules in §§ 40–44, § 46 contains a mix of restitution for wrongs and restitution for unjust enrichment. Where the misconduct that

[135] On the notion of 'interceptive subtraction' and the debate surrounding it, see Birks, *Unjust Enrichment* (n 5) 75–78; Burrows (n 4) 79–84; *Goff & Jones* (n 5) [6-52]–[6-62]; Smith (n 90); M McInnes, 'Interceptive Subtraction, Unjust Enrichment and Wrongs – A Reply to Professor Birks' (2003) 62 *Cambridge Law Journal* 697.

[136] See the text to nn 122–23.

[137] This is because X's payment to the supposed owner D may then actually have discharged a debt owed by X to D (if there was a valid tenancy agreement between them), though not necessarily a debt owed by X to C (with whom there may not be a contract).

[138] R3RUE (n 1) vol I, 136.

[139] R3RUE (n 1) vol II, 114. § 46(2) provides that § 46(1) applies to donative transfers in any form, including testamentary and inter vivos gifts.

invalidates the transfer to the intended recipient is the act of a third person, the (innocent) actual recipient's liability to make restitution to the intended recipient can only be based on his unjust enrichment.

For present purposes, § 11(3) and § 46 may be illustrated by the following generalised example: donor X intends to make a gift to C, but – as a result of some mistake or the wrongful intervention by an outsider Y – the gift ends up in D's hands. Under certain circumstances, § 11(3) and § 46 allow C to seek restitution from D.[140] The provisions are here mentioned in connection with claims by 'secondary' enrichers because (unlike under § 48) C's claim against D does not arise automatically at the moment of D's receipt. Rather, D's unjust enrichment is primarily at the donor X's expense, and X must in the first instance be free to decide what to do about it. § 11(3) therefore makes D's right to restitution expressly contingent on X dying or becoming incapacitated in the (still mistaken) belief that the gift has been perfected as intended. Although no similar restriction is contained in the wording of § 46, the commentary makes clear that 'it is only in unusual circumstances that a claim under § 46 will be brought during the lifetime of a competent donor' because '[u]sually a donor having legal capacity will either take steps to rectify the unintended disposition or, failing to do so, be deemed to ratify it', but that '[t]hese considerations no longer obtain when the wrongful diversion of assets comes to light following the donor's death or incapacity'.[141]

The pattern is, in a sense, the converse of that described by the term 'leapfrogging'. In a leapfrogging case, there is an immediate (or, better, primary) enrichee, and the question arises whether and under what circumstances a remote (or, better, secondary) enrichee can be reached where the claim against the primary enrichee fails. Here, we have the donor as the immediate (or primary) enricher, and §§ 11(3) and 46 tell us that when the donor is not in a position to assert or pursue his restitutionary claim against the enrichee, the intended donee steps in as a remote (or secondary) enricher. The question again arises whether the intended donee C is only enriched at the expense of the actual recipient D where the donor X is dead or incapacitated, or whether D is to be regarded as always enriched at C's expense, albeit that the enrichment is 'unjust' vis-à-vis C only where X drops out of the picture. In light of the view taken by R3RUE in the misdirected payment case discussed in connection with § 48,[142] the latter seems more likely. D's enriching receipt of the gift is at C's as well as X's expense simply because X subjectively intended it to go to C. The idea of 'interceptive subtraction' may again be made serviceable.

[140] Somewhat worrying from a policy point of view is the prospect that § 11(3) and § 46 can potentially undermine (eg, testamentary) formality requirements by making failed gifts work.

[141] R3RUE (n 1) vol II, 115. A primary claim by C against D is (only) conceivable in the case of testamentary gifts where the testator X will necessarily have died by the time the misdirected transfer to D becomes effective.

[142] See the text accompanying nn 131–35.

(b) Where the Primary Enricher Has 'Passed On' the Loss

Finally, we must consider an inference from § 64 arising in connection with the so-called 'passing on' defence outlined there. In contrast to the English common law[143] or the German basic position, US law allows an innocent recipient of a payment not due (typically a tax erroneously levied) to defend himself against the payer's restitutionary claim by proving that

> (a) the economic burden of the payment has been passed on by the claimant to third persons (typically customers of the taxpayer), yet (b) restitution to the claimant would not facilitate recovery by the persons ultimately entitled to relief.[144]

The claimant can be regarded as having passed on the economic burden of the payment to a third person 'if and to the extent that such third person would be entitled to restitution of the payment from the claimant, if restitution were made by the recipient to the claimant'.[145] Transposed into the terminology used by this chapter, this means that where, for example, a service provider or retailer X has collected from his customer C a tax for services or goods and passed this tax on to the defendant taxing authority D, and it later emerges that the tax should never have been levied, then although D is unjustly enriched at X's expense, a restitutionary claim by X against D may be denied on the basis that the economic burden of the tax was not borne by X himself but ultimately by C.[146]

Although § 64 does not say so in express terms, the section clearly envisages that – where the passing on defence operates so as to preclude a claim by X – C has a right to demand restitution for D's unjust enrichment.[147] As the commentary notes, '§ 64 emphasizes that the third persons [here customers in C's position] to whom the economic burdens have been passed on are the parties ultimately entitled to restitution'.[148] The part of the commentary specifically devoted to discussing 'restitution to the third person' explains that this is because '[D] (the recipient) has been unjustly enriched at the expense of [X's customer C]' and that 'the object of the law is to facilitate restitution – directly or indirectly – from [D] to [C]'.[149] The indirect route is chosen where restitution from D to X would actually facilitate recovery by C,[150] but otherwise X's claim against D is displaced (via

[143] Note, however, the statutory provision in s 80(3) of the VAT Act 1994.

[144] § 64(1): R3RUE (n 1) vol II, 503.

[145] § 64(2): ibid. § 64(3) specifies that such restitutionary claims by 'third persons' against the 'claimant' would lie under § 48 (see the text to n 126) 'If a claimant obtains restitution from a recipient of payments to which third persons have a better legal or equitable right': ibid.

[146] Under § 64(1)(b), the passing on defence does not operate where the transactions are sensibly unwound in the relationship D–X and then X–C, so that restitution by D to X actually facilitates recovery by C. See text to n 150.

[147] This right to restitution is structurally similar to the claim recognised by Henderson J in the *Investment Trust Companies* case (n 4), although the reason why the primary enrichers could not recover in that case was different.

[148] R3RUE (n 1) vol II, 505.

[149] ibid 508.

[150] *cf* § 64(1)(b), quoted in n 146.

the passing on defence) in favour of a direct claim by C against D.[151] We must therefore conclude that once X has passed on the economic burden to C, D's enrichment is no longer (merely?) at X's expense, but at C's.

D. Summary and Conclusion

A short survey like the present one can hardly do justice to the complex and multi-facetted mechanisms underlying R3RUE. What I have sought to do in this chapter is to collect information – sometimes expressly provided, but more often implicitly assumed – on R3RUE's stance towards the problem of 'indirect' enrichment in three-party situations. For this purpose, I have compiled a list of all the situations in which R3RUE gives C a 'primary' or 'secondary' claim to restitution for unjust enrichment against D, although the benefit in question has prima facie been bestowed by C on X or by X on D.

If one were to draw some tentative conclusions from the foregoing discussion, they might be the following: R3RUE does not subscribe to a 'directness' or 'privity' requirement as a basic starting point, as is sometimes postulated in England. Nor, however, does it unequivocally commit to a more liberal 'causal' approach. Although it accepts a form of the *actio de in rem verso*, thus allowing claimants under certain limited circumstances to 'leapfrog' out of a valid contract, it does not openly encourage 'leapfrogging' in general. Judging by the examples provided, where a primary defendant in unjust enrichment X has passed on the value received to D and is disenriched as a result, the only means of C claiming directly from D appears to be via some sort of 'proprietary' or perhaps 'transactional' link. Nevertheless, there is an argument to be made for a more relaxed stance, since the spirit of R3RUE is certainly not incompatible with the notion of leapfrogging. Interestingly, R3RUE seems to see enrichment as a 'zero-sum game' in some places, but more often envisages that D's enrichment may come from X and C at the same time. It is by and large open to accepting the idea of there being several potential enrichers and several potential enrichees. A follow-on question worth discussing might be whether the 'bona fide payee' and 'bona fide purchase' defences resemble 'change of position' in presupposing the defendant to have been initially enriched at the claimant's expense, or whether they actually prevent the relevant enrichment from occurring in the first place.[152] All in all, it may be concluded that R3RUE provides many answers to three-party cases, but it does so in a rather haphazard way and consequently leaves a number of important issues unresolved.

[151] R3RUE (n 1) vol II, 508 ff.

[152] In connection with this question, compare the distinction between 'denials' and 'defences' drawn by James Goudkamp and Charles Mitchell in ch 6 of the present volume.

3

§ 38 and the Lost Doctrine of Failure of Consideration

FREDERICK WILMOT-SMITH

A. Introduction

The *Restatement Third: Restitution and Unjust Enrichment* was published in 2011, 74 years after its grandfather, the *Restatement First*.[1] Hopefully it will revitalise discussion of unjust enrichment in American law schools,[2] overcoming the view of the topics as 'too doctrinal, almost too legal for modern American scholars'.[3] What can a lawyer schooled in English law add? Only so much. However, there is a 'peculiar interplay' between England and America in this field, the story of which is well known.[4] This makes comparative analysis of the doctrine particularly fruitful. Furthermore, conceptual truths are not established by authority: it is always open to us to say that the authority's classification is impoverished.

This chapter is about § 38 of R3RUE, which deals with 'Performance-Based Damages'. § 38 classifies these as remedies for breach of contract as opposed to unjust enrichment. On that account, § 38 is an imposter: it does not belong in R3RUE. I argue that beneath the banner of performance-based damages, there are two separate remedies. While one of these is correctly seen as a remedy for breach of contract, the other is part of the law of unjust enrichment. The reason for the mistake is twofold: American writers have lost the concept we know in other common law countries as 'failure of consideration', and may have missed the value of this concept by adopting an impoverished theory of contract. A number of errors that the misclassification has engendered, or risks engendering, are also examined.

[1] American Law Institute, *Restatement of Restitution* (St Paul, MN, American Law Institute, 1937); *Restatement Third: Restitution and Unjust Enrichment* (St Paul, MN, American Law Institute Publishers, 2011) (hereinafter 'R3RUE'). The second attempt at restating the law of this area was aborted; so disastrous was the experience that the American Law Institute (ALI) moved onto the third volume without attempting to finish the job.

[2] In this chapter, I will use 'America' as used as shorthand for the United States of America.

[3] D Partlett and R Weaver, 'Restitution: Ancient Wisdom' (2003) 36 *Loyola of Los Angeles Law Review* 975, 977.

[4] JH Langbein, 'The Later History of Restitution' in W Cornish et al (eds), *Restitution, Past, Present and Future: Essays in Honour of Gareth Jones* (Oxford, Hart Publishing, 1998) 57, 60.

B. Restitution and Contract in R3RUE

(1) A Very Brief Overview

Andrew Kull, the Reporter of R3RUE, has said that: 'The relation between restitution and contract is notoriously confused.'[5] Chapter 4 of R3RUE tries to clarify things. It divides up the law in this manner:

Chapter 4. Restitution and Contract

Topic 1. Restitution to a Performing Party with No Claim on the Contract

§ 31. Unenforceability
§ 32. Illegality
§ 33. Incapacity of Recipient
§ 34. Mistake or Supervening Change of Circumstance
§ 35. Performance of Disputed Obligation
§ 36. Restitution to a Party in Default

Topic 2. Alternative Remedies for Breach of an Enforceable Contract

§ 37. Rescission for Material Breach
§ 38. Performance-Based Damages
§ 39. Profit from Opportunistic Breach

The next section will look in greater detail at § 38, explaining the important claims made therein. It shows that § 38 contains two separable remedies.[6] Although this is not controversial,[7] it is a necessary distinction for the main claims of the chapter to be made.

(2) § 38 in Detail

(a) Introduction

§ 38 states, in full:

(1) As an alternative to damages based on the expectation interest (Restatement Second, Contracts § 347), a plaintiff who is entitled to a remedy for material breach or repudiation may recover damages measured by the cost or value of the plaintiff's performance.
(2) Performance-based damages are measured by
  (a) uncompensated expenditures made in reasonable reliance on the contract, including expenditures made in preparation for performance or in perform-

[5] A Kull, 'Rescission and Restitution' (2005) 61 *Business Lawyer* 569, 569.
[6] This does not beg the question of the chapter: the remedies could be separable but best considered together. That is the position of R3RUE.
[7] Until late in the day, R3RUE classified the remedies separately: see, eg, Tentative Draft No 3 (2004), § 38.

ance, less any loss the defendant can prove with reasonable certainty the plaintiff would have suffered had the contract been performed (Restatement Second, Contracts § 349); or

(b) the market value of the plaintiff's uncompensated contractual performance, not exceeding the price of such performance as determined by reference to the parties' agreement.

(3) A plaintiff whose damages are measured by the rules of subsection (2) may also recover for any other loss, including incidental or consequential loss, caused by the breach.

Sub-section (1) sets the scene. The meat of § 38 is in sub-sections (2)(a) and (2)(b). They set out separate methods of calculating a damages award. The provisions are complicated. They each contain a prima facie award with a qualification to that sum. While sub-section (1) suggests an underlying similarity between the awards, and sub-section (3) does apply to both awards, this apparent equivalence must be treated with care. Not only are the prima facie awards calculated differently, the qualification to the prima facie award is different in both (a) and (b).

To illustrate how these various sections function, consider the following example:

> Roosevelt employs Hoover to build a dam for $50. The two fall out, and Roosevelt fires Hoover, in breach of contract. The evidence shows that: (i) 50 per cent of the work has been completed; (ii) at a cost of $50 to Hoover. Further, (iii) the market value of Hoover's work is $40; and (iv) the cost for Hoover to complete would be $30.[8]

Hoover's normal remedy in such circumstances would be to sue Roosevelt for breach of contract, seeking an expectation award. That award would here be calculated by 'the loss in value to [Hoover] of [Roosevelt's] performance', deducting for 'any cost . . . that [Hoover] has avoided by not having to perform'.[9] In other words, Hoover's award would be $50 (the value of Roosevelt's performance) minus $30 (the cost for Hoover to complete): $20. Notice that had the deal been performed, it would have had a net value of *minus* $30 on Hoover's balance sheet.

§ 38(2) gives Hoover two alternative methods to formulate his claim for damages. His first claim, under § 38(2)(a), is for his reliance costs. His prima facie entitlement is the value of 'uncompensated expenditures made in reasonable reliance on the contract', ie, $50. Assuming Hoover's expectation interest was unknown, Hoover could claim $50 under this section. However, the prima facie sum is qualified. We must deduct 'any loss [Roosevelt] can prove [Hoover] would have suffered had the contract been performed'. As the previous paragraph demonstrated, Hoover would have lost $30 had the contract been fully performed.[10] So, under this section, Hoover would be awarded $50 – $30 = $20. Notice, further, that this award does not give Hoover more than the expectation award: qualification to the section functions to cap reliance awards at the expectation interest.[11]

[8] Based closely on R3RUE (n 1) vol I, 637, Illustration 17.

[9] American Law Institute, *Restatement Second: Contracts* (St Paul, MN, American Law Institute Publishers, 1981) § 347(a) and (c).

[10] Roosevelt bears the burden of proving this.

[11] This language is consonant with R3RUE (n 1) vol I, 626.

Hoover's second claim is under § 38(2)(b). The prima facie value of the claim is 'the market value of [Hoover's] uncompensated contractual performance', which is $40. Again, there is a qualification to this prima facie sum – but a different one from that under (a). § 38(2)(b) caps the award at the price of performance 'as determined by reference to the parties' agreement'. Half the contract work is completed and the contract price is $50, so the value of the work done, measured according to the contract, is $25. The value of Hoover's claim is reduced, accordingly, to $25.

Finally, to illustrate the operation of sub-section (3), suppose instead that $10 of Hoover's total costs were caused by Roosevelt's failure to make interim payments of the contract price.[12] This changes the calculation of the prima facie sum under (a) to $40. Combined with the projected expense of completion of $30, Hoover would have spent $70 on the dam. He would therefore have lost $20 overall. This means that the qualifier to (a) reduces the prima facie sum to $30 (to bring Hoover's balance sheet from negative $50 to negative $20). This claim can be combined with the claim for damages under § 38(3), which amounts to $10.[13]

(b) The Key Claims of § 38

There are two important claims made in this section. The first claim emerges from the title of Topic 2 when compared with earlier drafts. The topic used to refer to *restitutionary* remedies.[14] No longer. The shift is to accommodate § 38(2)(a), which awards the claimant a remedy for 'uncompensated expenditures made in reasonable reliance on the contract' (ie, the cost of performance). While the cost of the claimant's performance will 'frequently' quadrate with the value of the claimant's performance to the defendant, it will not always do so.[15] The cost to the claimant may exceed the value accrued to the defendant. In other words, awards made under § 38 are not *necessarily* restitutionary.

The second claim is also made explicit in the title of Topic 2. The remedies of this topic have always been said to be 'for breach'. Andrew Kull has voiced his objection to restitution as 'merely a description of the end result, not a reference to the basis of liability.'[16] By this he means that we should classify according to the cause of action (the 'basis of liability') rather than the response (the 'end result'). In keeping with this position, the ALI claims that the remedies of this topic are contractual, in that the cause of action is breach of contract.[17] They are both 'a second-best, "fall-back" alternative to damages measured by expectancy.'[18] The

[12] Based on R3RUE (n 1) vol I, 637, Illustration 18.

[13] There is no change to the § 38(2)(b) claim, but Hoover could still combine that claim with the $10 under § 38(3).

[14] eg, Tentative Draft No 3 (n 7) § 38.

[15] R3RUE (n 1) vol I, 627.

[16] A Kull, 'Rationalizing Restitution' (1995) 83 *California Law Review* 1191, 1219.

[17] R3RUE (n 1) vol I, 638 (Reporter's Note, Comment a).

[18] ibid vol I, 626.

unjust enrichment explanation, preferred by the *Restatement Second: Contracts*,[19] is said to be 'fictional'.[20]

R3RUE anticipates that a claimant will use the remedies under this section when proof of the expectation award is difficult. This shifts the cost of raising the evidence to the defendant. The idea is that each section should establish a presumption that the expectation measure would have been *at least* the measure available under either (a) or (b). So, (a) is premised on the presumption that 'the plaintiff's earnings from performance would have been at least sufficient to defray the plaintiff's reliance expenditures' and (b) is premised on the view 'the plaintiff's unknown expectancy would have been at least equal to the market value of the plaintiff's performance.'[21] However, as the example of Hoover's dam proves, there is a category of cases where (b) will yield more than an expectation award.

(c) Two Separate Remedies

R3RUE aligned the two remedies of § 38 under one paragraph as it views the two remedies as different presumptions to vindicate the expectation interest in circumstances of evidential uncertainty. The claim that both (a) and (b) are a 'single alternative damage remedy'[22] is the claim that this chapter seeks to assess. It is important to bear in mind, though, that this proposition can only be made at the end of the analysis. The two remedies are strikingly distinct in important ways: both the quantum of the prima facie award and the qualification to that award differ. The awards can therefore give different awards in the same fact scenarios, as the Hoover dam example illustrated. It may be that they are ultimately justified in the same manner, as R3RUE claims, but it is by no means obvious. This is all to make a simple point: the two sections were separate, are separable and can be investigated separately.

C. Are the Remedies of § 38 Correctly Classified?

(1) Introduction

The basic structure of Chapter 4 of R3RUE and of § 38 in particular should now be clear. The question for this part is whether § 38 is correct that the remedies under both (a) and (b) are for breach of contract. We first examine the proper way to determine the cause of action giving rise to a remedy. A three-step process is suggested, examining the facts giving rise to the cause of action, the structure of

[19] For the analogous remedy of § 38(2)(b) and the unjust enrichment analysis, see *Restatement Second: Contracts* (n 9) §§ 344–45; § 373, Comment a; and Chapter 16, Topic 4, Introductory Note (1981).

[20] R3RUE (n 1) vol I, 646.

[21] ibid vol I, 626.

[22] ibid vol I, 626.

the remedy, and the rational coherence between the proposed cause of action and the remedy. This three-step process is then applied to both (a) and (b) in turn. It is suggested that (a) is correctly classified, but that R3RUE goes wrong in its treatment of (b).

(2) How to Classify According to Cause of Action

(a) Introduction

Dorothy Parker, on being informed of the death of Calvin Coolidge ('Silent Cal'), quipped: 'How could they tell?'[23] Just so here. It is often claimed that a particular response is sourced in unjust enrichment or breach of contract. But how can we tell? While a great deal has been written on the proper way to categorise the law, little has been written about how to distinguish actual cases.[24] It is important to do so, as we presuppose the ability to make such distinctions all the time. Indeed, the emergence of unjust enrichment as a separate source of obligations presupposes this ability. This sub-section suggests a structure to make these distinctions.

(b) Different Kinds of Classification

There are numerous ways to divide up the law. One common approach is to classify contextually, as textbooks on 'commercial law' do.[25] Whether a particular rule belongs in a book on a contextual category is not a matter of analytic precision; it is a matter of pragmatic convenience. If lawyers dealing with commercial issues might have reason to know a particular rule, the rule can sensibly be put in a book on commercial law. Another way is to categorise according to the cause of action.[26] For instance, the ALI classifies the remedies of § 38 as remedies for breach of contract.[27]

It is tempting,[28] but misguided, to suppose that this kind of claim can be verified empirically by simply looking to what judges say about the source of the remedy.[29] However, there are two reasons why such an approach cannot be conclusive.

[23] A Sloane, *Humor in the White House: The Wit of Five American Presidents* (Jefferson, NC, McFarland, 2001) 49.

[24] See, for example, P Birks, *An Introduction to the Law of Restitution* (Oxford, Oxford University Press, 1985) 28–74 and the essays in P Birks (ed), *The Classification of Obligations* (Oxford, Clarendon Press, 1997); more recently, see C Rickett and R Grantham (eds), *Structure and Justification in Private Law: Essays for Peter Birks* (Oxford, Hart Publishing, 2008).

[25] P Birks, 'Restitution and Freedom of Contract' (1983) 14 *CLP* 141, 146; Birks, *Introduction* (n 24) 73–74; P Birks, 'Definition and Division: A Meditation on *Institutes* 3.13' in Birks (ed), *Classification* (n 24) 1, 34.

[26] In addition to the two approaches to classification suggested in the text, a recent trend in private law scholarship has been to classify according to the underlying rights of parties: eg, R Stevens, *Torts and Rights* (Oxford, Oxford University Press, 2007). Whether this is an appropriate form of classification probably depends on the question we want to answer.

[27] R3RUE (n 1) vol I, 625.

[28] *cf* K Low, 'The Use and Abuse of Taxonomy' (2009) 29 *Legal Studies* 355, 358–59.

[29] In this particular case, for instance, *Schwasnick v Blandin*, 65 F 2d 354, 357 (2d Circ 1933) (Learned Hand J).

First, the judicial statements are unlikely to be entirely consistent. Otherwise, identifying the cause of action would be unlikely to emerge as a controversial issue. Second, the fact that a judge claims to be deciding a case on the basis of a particular principle does not necessarily mean that the decision is best justified in that manner. Judges can misunderstand individual doctrines, accepting (or rejecting) their application too swiftly. Their reasons can also simply be inadequate. Judges used to claim that the right to restitution arose from a quasi-contract. Since 1937, American lawyers have understood that to be obfuscating and untrue.[30]

(c) The Three Steps to Classification

So, what should we look for when we seek to classify a remedy under a particular cause of action? The key is to keep in mind the kind of claim being made with this form of categorisation. While contextual categories do not lay claim to a normative unity (the law being grouped together by dint of its relation to categories in the world), classification according to the cause of action is different; it is subject to a greater rational burden.[31] When one claims that a particular remedy is sourced in a particular cause of action, one claims that (1) (relevantly) similar facts trigger (2) a remedy governed by a (relevantly) similar remedial structure because (3) the justifications of the remedies are coherent. All three features should be analysed for any particular remedy.

The three connections between remedies originating from the same cause of action provide us with three features to examine when the cause of action of a particular remedy is in question. We compare the remedy in question with other remedies uncontroversially within the cause of action being tested. In the comparison, we aim to discover whether (1) similar facts trigger (2) a similar remedy for (3) similar reasons. Let us examine each step in detail.

(i) Similar Facts

'A cause of action is simply a factual situation the existence of which entitles one person to obtain from the court a remedy against another person.'[32] So, the first way to test the source of a remedy is by examining the facts that a claimant must prove to establish an entitlement to the remedy in question, and comparing those facts with the ingredients of the cause of action in question.[33] If the remedy in question requires similar facts to be proven as an established cause of action, that gives us reason to classify the remedy as emanating from that cause of action; equally, if certain facts are required by a particular cause of action but are unnecessary for the

[30] The *Restatement of Restitution* (1937) was key to this move, although earlier examples can be found, eg, H Maine, *Ancient Law*, 4th edn (London, John Murray, 1870) 344.

[31] C Webb, 'What is Unjust Enrichment?' (2009) 29 *OJLS* 215, 237.

[32] *Letang v Cooper* [1965] 1 QB 232 (CA), 242 (Diplock LJ).

[33] Compare the contextual approach to classification: the facts of the cases need share no legally significant features.

remedy in question, this gives us reason to be suspicious. For instance, a claimant who seeks damages for a breach of contract must prove, inter alia, the existence of a contract with the defendant and the defendant's breach of the contract. In some cases where a claimant seeks restitution from a defendant, both of these facts must be proven too. This gives us reason to say that the two remedies (compensation and restitution) arise from the same cause of action: breach of contract.[34]

However, for two reasons, the first step is not conclusive. First, the same factual situation might give rise to more than one cause of action. In the case of a negligent misstatement, for instance, it is possible that the same facts can give rise to liability in both tort and breach of contract. The presence of the breach of contract, and the liability to pay damages, should not blind us to the presence of a concurrent action in tort – a separate action that would (or could) remain even if the contract were for some reason unenforceable.[35]

Second, we should be cautious when stating the facts necessary to establish the cause of action, as there is a danger of an invalid universal inference. That a particular fact circumstance establishes a particular cause of action does not mean that the cause of action requires that precise set of facts. For instance, a mistake is often present in a claim for unjust enrichment, but even if the only recognised instances of unjust enrichment were mistake cases, we should be careful about the further claim that a mistake is *necessary* for the cause of action to be established.

(ii) Similar Remedial Structure

The second step to classification based on the cause of action examines the structure of the remedy awarded. Different causes of action often have different rules on issues such as limitation periods, remoteness and choice of law. Equally, these rules (herein categorised under the label 'remedial structure') are broadly similar in remedies emanating from the same cause of action.[36] So, we can work forwards – from cause of action to remedial structure – in individual cases. If we know that the cause of action in a particular case is *p*, we have good reason to align the remedial structure of the case with that of other cases of *p*. However, we can also work backwards, from remedial structure to cause of action. If a particular remedy shares features characteristic of remedies for *p*, this fact gives us reason to categorise the remedy as sourced in *p*.

This process can be inverted to give us reason to doubt that a remedy is sourced in a particular cause of action. If a remedy shares few characteristic features of *p*, this gives us reason to doubt that *p* is the source of the remedy. For instance, the

[34] This does not entail that R3RUE is wrong in its classification of the remedy of § 39, which is classified as a remedy for unjust enrichment: one could argue that, despite the factual similarity between remedies for breach of contract and the remedy of § 39, there are other reasons to classify the remedy as sourced in unjust enrichment.

[35] The leading case in England, demonstrating this point, is *Henderson v Merrett Syndicates Ltd* [1995] 2 AC 145 (HL).

[36] For example, the *Restatement Second: Contracts* (n 9) § 350(1) states a general principle that damages factually caused by a breach of contract are not recoverable where the claimant 'could easily have avoided them without undue risk [or] burden'.

normal response to an unjust enrichment is restitution. Indeed, the 'near universally held view'[37] is that restitution is not simply the most common response but the *only* response to an unjust enrichment.[38] Therefore, anyone who claims a non-restitutionary remedy is sourced in unjust enrichment has his work cut out.[39]

There are three problems with this approach, though, which mean that the strength of the reasons that these arguments give is comparatively weak. First, many features of the remedial structure are shared across a range of causes of action. Second, insofar as the remedial structure is conditioned by the classification itself, one must beware allowing the classification to be determined by fiat alone. For example, suppose that a remedy is classified as contractual for the purposes of a limitation statue. In a subsequent case, that decision will stand as a reason in favour of the very question of the first case – whether the remedy is contractual. But it cannot be determinative. The reasons given by such matters must, accordingly, be quite weak. Finally, a related concern is that the remedial structure can only go so far in establishing the cause of action for the remedy. Without a reason to suppose that the remedy serves the values of the cause of action, the theorist will always be open to argue that the link between the two is not conceptual, but a mere matter of probability.[40] This leads us to the final step.

(iii) The Rational Continuity of Cause of Action and Remedy

The final step in the classification process is the most theoretically demanding. It requires that we examine whether the justification of a remedy for a cause of action is instantiated and well served by the remedy in question. The remedy for a particular cause of action will be justified, in large part, by the reasons for the institution underlying the cause of action. That makes the inquiry peculiarly difficult, as we require a theory about the institution in question.[41] For instance, a good case can be made that the institution of contract aims to secure both instrumental and normative goals.[42] The instrumental benefits of the institution are the facilitation of 'a form of reliance, co-operation, or co-ordination between

[37] R Williams, 'Preventing Unjust Enrichment' [2000] *Restitution Law Review* 492, 513.

[38] P Birks, 'Annual Miegunyah Lecture: Equity, Conscience, and Unjust Enrichment' (1999) 23 *Melbourne University Law Review* 1, 8; A Burrows, *The Law of Restitution*, 3rd edn (Oxford, Oxford University Press, 2011) 9; R3RUE (n 1) vol 1 § 1.

[39] That the remedial structure is an important but not conclusive factor in the process of classification is shown by the fact some writers do make such claims: see, for instance, C Mitchell, *The Law of Contribution and Reimbursement* (Oxford, Oxford University Press, 2003) [3.10]–[3.12]; K Barker and L Smith, 'Unjust Enrichment' in D Hayton (ed), *Law's Future(s)* (Oxford, Hart Publishing, 2000) 411, 414–15; Williams (n 37) 512–14.

[40] As, for instance, demonstrated by the claims of the writers listed in the previous footnote.

[41] So difficult, in the case of unjust enrichment, that R3RUE had to be 'written on the assumption that the law of restitution and unjust enrichment can be usefully described without insisting on' such an inquiry: R3RUE (n 1) vol I, 4. See, further, D Dobbs, *Law of Remedies*, 2nd edn (St Paul, MN, West Publishing Co, 1993) § 4.1(2). To make claims about the cause of action, however, we cannot avoid this thorny issue.

[42] The account suggested here is taken from D Kimel, *From Promise to Contract: Towards a Liberal Theory of Contract* (Oxford, Hart Publishing, 2005).

people',[43] a reliance not dependent on trust between individuals; the normative value is 'the value of personal detachment'.[44] Remedies which vindicate those goals (by protecting the institution and its participants from harm) are sensibly categorised as contractual remedies.[45] The expectation remedy, for instance, aims to erase the harm that the claimant would suffer from the defendant's failure to perform (reflecting the claimant's entitlement to the defendant's performance).[46] In other words, the expectation measure aims to secure the claimant's entitlement in the contract.[47] That it does so gives us good reason to categorise it as a contractual remedy.[48] This process of inquiry is herein described as one into the rational continuity between a particular cause of action and a particular remedy.

Before turning back to the main task, a confusion that arises at the third step must be cleared away. Some theorists would deny our quiver this arrow. For instance, Birks says:

> [T]he measure of the law's response [to a civil wrong] ... is in principle a mere matter of policy. The law has a free choice of what it shall be, subject only to extrinsic considerations such as the values of proportionality, determinacy, humanity, and so on.[49]

If this were true, it would be troubling for two reasons. First, it would make classification very difficult. It threatens both the second and third stages of our classification process, for if the law can in principle respond to a wrong in any way, then we can never eliminate wrongdoing from the possible causes of action by reference to the response. The facts giving rise to the claim become the only way we might distinguish between a wrong and (say) a claim in unjust enrichment. Second, it suggests a necessary irrationality at the core of our law in the remedies it supplies for civil wrongs. The suggestion seems to be that reason cannot itself determine or fix a response, hence why the law has a 'free choice'.

Birks wanted to counter those who asserted that remedies for civil wrongs can only be compensatory. To be sure, one should not simply assert that compensation is the only justifiable response. However, to make this point, we should not be forced to make the move he did, as his claim must be wrong. The institution of contract is more rational if it gives expectation damages for a breach of contract than if the response is for a defendant to perform an interpretive dance for the

[43] ibid 65.

[44] ibid 78.

[45] This approach suggests that some caution is required when dealing with the monolithic Birksian category of 'wrongs': see P Birks, 'The Concept of a Civil Wrong' in D Owen (ed), *Philosophical Foundations of Tort Law* (Oxford, Oxford University Press, 1997) 31, 47–48. Sensible distinctions can be drawn between breach of contract and breach of, say, a duty not to commit trespass to the person. For one thing, the harm done to the institution by breach may well differ: see Low (n 28) 357. This may explain why gain-based awards are more readily available for some wrongs than others.

[46] J Raz, *The Morality of Freedom* (Oxford, Oxford University Press, 1986) 414: 'one harms another when one's action makes the other person worse off than he ... is entitled to be'.

[47] Kimel (n 42) 94.

[48] *Restatement Second: Contracts* (n 9) § 347.

[49] Birks (n 45) 47. See, perhaps most startlingly, Birks, 'Definition and Division' (n 25) 1, 31. For this kind of argument in the context of remedies for breach of contract, see R Craswell, 'Contract Law, Default Rules, and the Philosophy of Promising' (1989) 88 *Michigan Law Review* 489.

claimant.[50] Why? Because the institution of contract aims to secure various goods and the remedies should protect and promote those goods if they are to be rational.[51] And, if that is so, we are able to establish the cause of action giving rise to a remedy by an examination of the rational coherence between a particular cause of action and a particular remedy.

(3) § 38(2)(a): Reliance Damages

Having laid extensive groundwork, it is time to turn to the claims of R3RUE itself. The first remedy to consider is that of § 38(2)(a), which, recall, allows a claimant to recover:

> [U]ncompensated expenditures made in reasonable reliance on the contract . . . less any loss the defendant can prove with reasonable certainty the plaintiff would have suffered had the contract been performed.

As explained, this remedy provides for a part-performing claimant to recover for her expenses incurred, capped by the expectation interest. The ALI claims that the cause of action is breach of contract.[52] To test this, we need to apply the three steps described above to the remedy in question.

(a) The Facts

First, the facts. Some of the same facts are required to raise a claim under this section as for recovery of expectation damages: a claimant must prove (1) a breach of (2) a contract. One clear difference is that a claimant need not prove the value of her expectation interest, but must prove her reliance costs. However, when we move to the second step, on the structure of the remedy, this difference in the ingredients of the cause of action is explained.

(b) The Remedial Structure

Under this section, the expectation interest caps the prima facie award for reliance losses. This explains the difference in the facts required to establish the cause of action: the vindication of the expectation interest is the purpose of the award, but this object is, for practical reasons, pursued obliquely. As Chief Judge Learned Hand explained:

[50] It is startling that such a claim seems to be conceptually impossible on Birks' account. It is not even clear from Birks' account whether the *defendant* need be the one responsible for the law's response.

[51] My account is influenced by the 'continuity thesis' of J Gardner, 'What is Tort Law For? Part 1. The Place of Corrective Justice' (2011) 30 *Law and Philosophy* 1, 28–37. See also J Raz, 'Personal Practical Conflicts' in M Betzler and P Baumann (eds), *Practical Conflicts: New Philosophical Essays* (Cambridge, Cambridge University Press, 2004) 189.

[52] Beyond the many references in R3RUE, see, further, *Restatement Second: Contracts* (n 9) § 349.

> It is often very hard to learn what the value of the performance would have been; and it is a common expedient, and a just one, in such situations to put the peril of the answer upon that party who by his wrong has made the issue relevant to the rights of the other.[53]

In other words, it would be unfair if the claimant went without a remedy because her contractual expectancy is hard to prove.[54] The law puts the burden of proof on the defendant, allowing the claimant to vindicate her expectancy as far as the evidence will allow. The law presumes that the claimant would not have made an unprofitable bargain. By implication, it can presume that the claimant would not have spent more than she would eventually have made under the deal. So, the claimant is prima facie entitled to the amount she has spent on the deal. However, if the defendant can prove the expectation level and that it is less than the amount the claimant spent, the justification for the prima facie award falls away. The law then effectively awards the expectation award. This explains why different facts must be proved for the orthodox expectation award and the reliance award. There is a fundamental affinity between the two remedies. In the words of an English judge, 'reliance losses are a species of expectation losses'.[55]

(c) The Rational Continuity of Cause of Action and Remedy

It was suggested above that the expectation remedy is a sensible way of vindicating the goals of contracting. In other words, the expectation remedy is sensibly (and, clearly, uncontroversially) understood as a remedy for breach of contract. The third step of the analysis is therefore easy. As explained, § 38(2)(a) is no more than a proxy for the expectation interest. The expectation award aims to remedy a breach of contract. As such, § 38(2)(a) is sensibly categorised as a remedy for breach of contract, as it vindicates the goals of contracting as best we can in circumstances of evidential uncertainty.[56] Conversely, if there was a genuine reliance remedy (ie, compensating a promisee only for losses incurred in reliance on a promise to the full extent of those losses), the remedy would 'make non-optional a completely different course of conduct' to an expectation measure.[57] It would be harder to justify such a remedy as a response to a breach of contract.[58]

[53] *L Albert & Son v Armstrong Rubber Co* (1948) 178 Fed Rep 182, 189.

[54] A similar principle is at work in *Summers v Tice*, 199 P 2d 1 (1948); *Cook v Lewis* [1951] SCR 830; and *Fairchild v Glenhaven Funeral Services Ltd* [2002] UKHL 22, (2003) 1 AC 32: the wrongdoer is put to the evidential burden she has helped create.

[55] *Omak Maritime Ltd v Mamola Challenger Shipping Co* [2010] EWHC 2026 (Comm) [42] (Teare J). For this reason, we should perhaps jettison the language of 'reliance interest' in a contract: D McLauchlan, 'Reliance Damages for Breach of Contract' [2007] *New Zealand Law Review* 417.

[56] *cf* A Kull, 'Restitution as a Remedy for Breach of Contract' (1993) 67 *South California Law Review* 1465, 1466, who says that the remedy 'consists in something other than enforcement of the bargain'. This proposition is true, but trivially so: the justification of the remedy is the same as the justification of enforcement.

[57] Kimel (n 42) 94; see, further, D Friedmann, 'The Performance Interest in Contract Damages' (1995) 111 *LQR* 628, 635–38.

[58] Compare, however, J Raz, 'Promises in Morality and Law' (1982) 95 *Harvard Law Review* 916, 934.

Therefore, the analysis of R3RUE is correct. Although R3RUE reaches its conclusion via a different route to this Chapter, its analysis is broadly consonant with that here.[59] The explanation also has a good pedigree in American law.[60] Finally, the analysis is also shared in a number of different jurisdictions.[61]

(4) § 38(2)(b): Performance Damages

However, on § 38(2)(b), there is rather less harmony. This section, recall, provides the claimant with:

> [T]he market value of [her] uncompensated contractual performance, not exceeding the price of such performance as determined by reference to the parties' agreement.

This chapter does not contest that breach of contract can be the basis of recovery where the contract provides for such a claim expressly or impliedly. [62] The question arises, however, when the contract is silent on the matter. As will be explained in greater detail below, R3RUE's classification of this remedy as one for breach of contract sets itself against both the English law[63] and the position of the *Restatement Second: Contracts.*[64] This section applies the three-step test to the remedy.[65] It argues that R3RUE is wrong: the cause of action is best understood as part of the law of unjust enrichment.

(a) *The Facts*

R3RUE's claim that the remedy of (b) is for breach of contract might be thought to find some support at this stage of the inquiry. It initially seems that to qualify for the remedy, a claimant must establish the existence of a contract and a qualifying breach of contract by the defendant. In this respect, the remedy seems analogous to the expectation award for breach of contract.[66] However, there are three reasons why this is not conclusive. First, as the expectation level does not need to

[59] See the explanation of R3RUE (n 1) vol I, 626.

[60] See, for instance, *Holt v United Security Life Insurance & Trust Co*, 76 NJ 585, 597; 72 A 301, 306 (1909).

[61] England and Wales: *Omak Maritime* (n 55); Canada: *Bowlay Logging v Domtar Ltd* (1978) 87 DLR (3d) 32; Australia: *Commonwealth of Australia v Amman Aviation Pty Ltd* (1991) 174 CLR 64. Compare Israel: CA 3666/90, 4012/90, *Tzukim Hotel Ltd v Municipality of Netanya* 46(4) Piskei Din (PD) 45 (1992).

[62] JW Carter and GT Tolhurst, 'Conditional Payments and Failure of Consideration: Contract or Restitution' (2001) 9 *Asia Pacific Law Review* 1, 1; T Baloch, *Unjust Enrichment and Contract* (Oxford, Hart Publishing, 2009) 178.

[63] See below, p 81.

[64] See above, n 19.

[65] The history of the remedy has been examined in detail by Tariq Baloch, who concluded that unjust enrichment was the superior analysis: Baloch (n 62) especially chs 1 and 5; compare R3RUE (n 1) vol I, 609–12.

[66] This seems to be enough for Joseph Perillo: JM Perillo, 'Restitution in a Contractual Context and the *Restatement (Third) of Restitution and Unjust Enrichment*' (2011) 68 *Washington and Lee Law Review* 1007, 1023.

be proved and is not recovered, we would need a further argument, similar to the one just mentioned (for reliance damages), to justify the classification as for breach. (This point is examined in greater detail below.)

Second, it is not clear that either of the two facts supposedly necessary to the claim is, in truth, essential to the remedy. One can conceive of a similar remedy to that under § 38(2)(b) where there is no breach of contract. For example:

> Obama agrees to buy 100 cartons of cigarettes from Emanuel, paying $1/carton, plus an allocated sum of $50 which Emanuel is to pay to the federal government by way of tax under a federal health law. The tax is found unconstitutional. The law could allow Obama to recover $50 of his performance.[67]

One can even conceive of a similar remedy to that under § 38(2)(b) where there is no contract in the first place. For example:

> Rajoy agrees to an interest rate swap with Merkel under a contract void for lack of formality. Rajoy pays Merkel $10,000 before the contract is found to be void. The law might well say Rajoy could claim back the $10,000.[68]

These examples give us reason to think that the two facts are inessential to the remedy, properly understood. In both examples, performance is rendered on the basis of an assumption that turns out to be false. The factual basis of the claim in both cases is, in this respect, strikingly similar to that of § 38(2)(b). That a similar remedy is available in materially similar circumstances suggests that the existence of the contract in one case is not fundamental to the principle at hand. It suggests, instead, at a broader underlying principle, of which the fact scenario of § 38(2)(b) is but one manifestation.

Finally, and related to the second reason, § 31 demonstrates that the presence of the two facts does not conclusively establish breach of contract as the appropriate classification. Under this section, a claimant who 'renders performance under an agreement that cannot be enforced against the recipient'[69] has a claim under that section for the 'benefits directly conferred as the performance required'.[70] Both the facts and the remedial structure of this claim are the same as § 38(2)(b): a contract is formed and is breached; that it is unenforceable does not change those facts. R3RUE, in accordance with the law of other jurisdictions, accepts that this remedy is sourced in unjust enrichment.[71] Therefore, the similar facts and remedial structure are clearly not determinative of the classification.

What of the suggestion of the *Restatement Second: Contracts* that the remedy is sourced in unjust enrichment? Quite what a claimant must prove in America for

[67] Example based on the Australian case of *Roxborough v Rothmans of Pall Mall Australia Ltd* (2001) 208 CLR 516 (HCA).

[68] Example based on the English cases of *Westdeutsche Landesbank Girozentrale v Islington London Borough Council* [1996] AC 669 (HL) and *Haugesund Kommune v Depfa ACS Bank* [2010] EWCA Civ 579, [2012] Bus LR 1.

[69] R3RUE (n 1) § 31(1).

[70] ibid § 31, Comment a.

[71] § 31 refers to 'a claim in restitution . . . as necessary to prevent unjust enrichment'; see, further, *Pavey & Matthews Pty Ltd v Paul* (1987) 162 CLR 221 (HCA).

a prima facie case is not clear. R3RUE rejects a 'checklist of factors' approach to the subject as 'they can lend a specious precision to an analysis that may be simple or complicated but which at any rate is not susceptible of this form of statement'.[72] Instead, R3RUE says that liability arises upon 'the receipt of a benefit whose retention without payment would result in the unjust enrichment of the defendant at the expense of the claimant.'[73] R3RUE says that an enrichment is unjustified where it is 'without adequate legal basis'.[74] Therefore, it seems that (at least) two elements are required: (1) an enrichment (2) without an adequate legal basis.[75] Therefore, we should examine whether these elements can be made out in the fact scenario of § 38(2)(b) claims.

Andrew Kull has consistently argued that unjust enrichment cannot explain this remedy. His argument has primarily been that the remedy should not (regardless of its source) be used to allow a claimant to escape a bad bargain.[76] However, I suggest that he has two arguments as regards the cause of action:[77] (1) the *enrichment argument* (of which there are two formulations); and (2) the *injustice argument.* These arguments deny that two facts essential to the unjust enrichment analysis can be established in this context.[78] By examining the arguments in turn, it is suggested that the two facts *can* be made out. Unjust enrichment is thus a plausible candidate as a cause of action.

Kull's enrichment argument claims that:

> [W]e have no standard by which to judge enrichment or its absence other than the terms of the parties' agreement. Because we view the parties' agreement as the proper measure of value between them, a rationalized (enrichment-based) law of restitution has no independent role as a remedy for disputes arising out of the breach . . . of a valid contract.[79]

It is odd to suggest that we have *no* standard by which to value an enrichment without a contract. Money is, by definition, capable of valuation regardless of any contractual structure. The value of services, too, *can* be quantified without regard to the contract in question: for instance, by reference to the market value of the services transferred. The second sentence contains a more reasonable claim: that the parties' agreement is the 'proper measure of value'.[80] This chapter does not,

[72] R3RUE (n 1) vol I, 8.

[73] ibid vol I, 3.

[74] ibid vol I, 6.

[75] Compare the three-stage analysis of *Banque Financière de la Cité v Parc (Battersea) Ltd* [1999] 1 AC 221 (HL) 227 (Lord Steyn) and 234 (Lord Hoffmann). The fourth stage of the analysis, defences, is a separate question.

[76] Kull (n 56) 1481. R3RUE suggests that this problem is rare, arising only in a 'handful of untypical cases': R3RUE (n 1) vol 1, 644. However, the problem is said to be 'constantly recurring' in England: WE Peel (ed), *Treitel on the Law of Contract*, 13th edn (London, Sweet & Maxwell, 2011) 851, n 13. It is hard to know who is right: neither cites evidence for his claim.

[77] Compare Kull (n 16) 1209: note 54 suggests that Kull may see the point as a single argument.

[78] Of course, even if valid, the arguments do not show that the cause of action is breach of contract.

[79] Kull (n 16) 1209.

[80] See, further, R3RUE (n 1) vol I, 608 (Introductory Note, No Necessary Relation with Unjust Enrichment); I think, but am not sure, that this is the argument of JM Perillo, 'Restitution in a Contractual Context' (1973) 73 *Columbia Law Review* 1208, 1216.

and need not, deal with that claim.[81] It is simply a non sequitur to move from this position, a claim about the quantification of an enrichment, to the claim that unjust enrichment 'has no independent role' in this context.[82]

Kull elsewhere offers another enrichment argument. This argument, if valid, eliminates unjust enrichment as a possible analysis. He argues that performance is not enriching because 'a party *who is liable in damages* is . . . not enriched at all'.[83] Under any fact situation to which § 38(2)(b) applies, the defendant will be liable to pay the claimant expectation damages. Kull argues that it is incoherent, in such circumstances, to claim that the receipt of performance enriches the defendant. The defendant has received something of factual value in the contractual performance. On receipt, she also comes under a duty to counter-perform or a liability to pay damages on non-performance. Kull's argument requires: (1) that the cost to the defendant of counter-performance equals the value of the performance received; *and* (2) that the law must net the value of the performance received against the liability the defendant thereby incurs.

The argument is an intriguing one, particularly as, to my knowledge, it has never been made in England. However, neither of these points can be made out. The first point is, in effect, no more than a reformulation of Kull's first enrichment argument that the contract is the proper measure of the enrichment. As to the second point, the law of unjust enrichment could decide to net claims against enrichments transferred in that manner. However, it need not do so. The law can allow the separate claims to proceed side by side, allowing the claimant to choose between the two. The law might deny the claimant this choice to prevent her escaping a bad bargain, but that is a quite separate question to the enrichment inquiry. Here, Kull has to demonstrate that it is incoherent to claim that a defendant is enriched by the receipt of performance for which she incurs a liability to pay. He does not give us such an argument and I cannot think of one.

The first fact necessary for an unjust enrichment claim, an enrichment, can be established. The next question is whether it is possible to say that the circumstances of § 38(2)(b) denote an instance where the enrichment is legally unjust(ified). An enrichment is unjustified where it is 'without adequate legal basis'.[84] The concept of legal basis is never explicated, nor is that of adequacy explained. It is said that unjustified enrichment results from 'a transaction that the law treats as ineffective to work a conclusive alteration in ownership rights'.[85] This pushes the inquiry to the kinds of factors that the law treats as undermining transfers. 'Broadly speaking', the law will treat as ineffective 'nonconsensual'

[81] But see p 85.

[82] ie, this may simply seek to ensure that the claimant gets 'no more than the value of the benefit which he has conferred upon the other party': American Law Institute, *Restatement First: Contracts* (St Paul, MN, American Law Institute, 1932), § 107.

[83] Kull (n 56) 1482, 1467 (emphasis in original). See, further, 1479–80; and Kull (n 16) 1221, n 92. This argument is the only claim Kull makes which can separate § 31 from § 38(2)(b).

[84] R3RUE (n 1) vol I, 6.

[85] ibid vol I, 6.

transactions.[86] By that metric, can the transaction under § 38(2)(b) be said to be unjustified? It could not be so if the fact of the initial agreement for the transfer sufficed to satisfy the desiderata of 'consent'. However, it is clear that R3RUE takes a broader view of things than that, as it includes unenforceable contracts as instances of unjust enrichment. In those cases, there is consent sufficient to form a contract – but it is not adequate to effect a conclusive transfer, because the contract itself is unenforceable. Since the circumstances are not as the parties anticipated, the transaction is non-consensual. The same analysis can be applied here: the parties anticipated that the contract would be performed, and the failure of performance undermines that initial assumption.

Kull has, in his own work, sought to contradict this simple position. His injustice argument claims that:

> [W]here a benefit is conferred pursuant to a valid contract, the presence or absence of *unjust enrichment* – the starting point of analysis in restitution – can only be determined by reference to the parties' bargain.[87]

The point is developed:

> [W]e have no standard by which to measure either justice or injustice in a contractual exchange apart from the parties' agreement, actual or imputed.[88]

The enrichment argument is about establishing the *existence* or *extent* of the enrichment; this argument is about establishing the *injustice* of the enrichment.[89] Kull argues that this inquiry cannot be divorced from 'contract interpretation'[90] and so (he implicitly claims) any remedy must be for breach of contract. It is clear that the contract is important to establish the claim under § 38(2)(b), as the claim only arises where contractual relations break down. However, the fact that we must have 'reference' to the parties' bargain does not mean that the parties' bargain is all that we may have reference to. An extra step is needed from the fact that the claim arises out of the breakdown of contractual relations to the proposition that the solution to this problem is contractual.

Elsewhere, Kull denies that the injustice of the transfer can be established thus:

> The enrichment that results from a voluntary exchange is what the law of contracts exists to promote, and it is a form of enrichment that the law of restitution will never classify as unjust.[91]

[86] ibid vol I, 5 and 164. *Quaere* the case of void contracts: vol I, 543. The caveat is to accommodate cases where the claimant overpays tax: vol I, 261.

[87] Kull (n 16) 1200 (emphasis in original); R3RUE (n 1) vol 1, 609 (Introductory Note, No Necessary Relation with Unjust Enrichment).

[88] Kull (n 16) 1209, n 54. I think that this is also Jaffey's objection: P Jaffey, *The Nature and Scope of Restitution* (Oxford, Hart Publishing, 2000) 43.

[89] The two are not so easily separated. See, further to the above, Kull (n 16) 1200.

[90] Kull (n 16) 1209, n 54. This may also be what Hedley means: S Hedley, 'Implied Contract and Restitution' (2004) 63 *CLJ* 435, 452, n 45.

[91] Kull (n 56) 1481.

This seems to beg the question. The argument has force only in the claim that the exchange is 'voluntary' (ie, consensual), but the question is whether the transaction is sufficiently voluntary to be justified. We are here given no reason to doubt the earlier suggestion that the initial voluntariness is negated by the defendant's failure to perform.

Therefore, the facts of the claim in unjust enrichment can be made out. Unjust enrichment remains a plausible candidate as a cause of action.

(b) The Remedial Structure

The second step in our analysis of the remedy is to examine how the remedial structure fits with the central remedies of a particular cause of action. The closer the remedy in question fits those central cases, the stronger the claim to be classified with them; the weaker the fit, the weaker the classificatory analogy. R3RUE accepts that this step is required in the analysis, as it justifies its classification in part with the claim that 'a concern with unjust enrichment cannot explain some notable features of the remedy'.[92] There are two distinctive features of the remedy: (1) the claimant recovers the value of performance transferred to the defendant (2) as measured under the contract.

As regards the first of these features, normal contractual remedies are not a good fit. Remedies for breach of contract are normally unconcerned with the benefits accruing to the defendant in the course of performance (though the law does sometimes concern itself with the benefits which come to the defendant from *breach*).[93] Instead, 'Contract damages are ordinarily based on [the claimant's] expectation interest.'[94] This fact supported the classification of § 38(2)(a) as contractual: the existence of the expectation cap showed that the remedy merely sought to vindicate the expectation interest as the evidence best allows. However, the first feature of the remedy fits well with the normal remedies in unjust enrichment, which measure 'liability by the extent of the benefit' received by the defendant.[95]

The second distinctive feature of the remedy is that the claimant is limited by the price of the performance transferred as specified by the parties' deal. It is tempting to link the remedy to a contractual source from this fact.[96] However, this would be to miss a crucial distinction between § 38(2)(a) and § 38(2)(b). The cap in § 38(2)(a) is at the claimant's expectation interest. As explained, this is a suitable cap to place on an award that seeks to remedy a breach of contract. However, § 38(2)(b) does not have an expectation cap. Instead, it refers to the contract simply to value the performance transferred. Perillo has called this a

[92] R3RUE (n 1) vol I, 608.

[93] Though this would not support R3RUE's case, as it regards disgorgement as a remedy for unjust enrichment: R3RUE (n 1) vol 1 § 39. English law regards § 39 cases as restitution for the wrong of breach of contract.

[94] *Restatement Second: Contracts* (n 9) § 347; further, Kull (n 56) 1474.

[95] R3RUE (n 1) vol I, 7.

[96] As R3RUE (n 1) vol I, 608 (Introductory Note, No Necessary Relation with Unjust Enrichment).

'peculiar distinction' to draw between (a) and (b).[97] If both awards aimed to do the same thing, it would be peculiar.[98] However, if (b) aims to reverse an unjust enrichment, R3RUE's approach is much more defensible. The law of unjust enrichment can make reference to the parties' contractual valuations in its quantification of the enrichments transferred. This appears to be the approach of (b). Therefore, this feature of the remedy suggests that the cause of action is unjust enrichment, not breach of contract.

Kull has a further argument, drawing on the law and economics tradition, in favour of the contractual understanding of the remedy. It is appropriately considered at this step as it concerns the structure of the response. The argument has this form:

(1) The remedies of contract law should be 'defensible as contractual default rules: as provisions . . . to which the parties would agree in *ex ante* negotiations'.[99]
(2) Parties would agree to the most efficient remedies.[100]
(3) The performance award meets this standard.[101]

This argumentative structure could clearly *exclude* a possible contract remedy or deny that a remedy is plausibly sourced in breach of contract. If (3) claimed 'remedy *p* does *not* meet this standard', Kull would say that we have reason to doubt that *p* is (or should be) a remedy for breach of contract.[102] However, it is unclear whether the argument is capable of establishing a positive case for a cause of action. While one could disagree with any of (1)–(3) on their own terms, one could accept all three points and yet still deny that the cause of action of § 38(2)(b) is breach of contract. By way of analogy, consider § 31. Suppose, not implausibly, that it is optimific. Regardless, the cause of action of the rule is unjust enrichment, not breach of contract. Therefore, the efficiency argument could eliminate breach of contract as a plausible analysis; it cannot demonstrate that it is the only analysis.

Whatever positive case the argument can make must come from the intuition that the remedy is in some sense agreed to (or that the concept of agreement does some work in the justification of the remedy). There are two problems with this: first, the concept of agreement which the argument must have in mind is so abstracted as to have little normative force; second, the remedy does not seem to satisfy the interests of the agreement we know exists. If the defendant agrees to perform some service for the claimant, and does not, then the normative force of the agreement seems to justify giving the claimant the best approximation of that

[97] Perillo calls this an 'innovation': Perillo (n 66) 1023. That is untrue, but it does show that the approach of § 38(2)(b) is unusual when viewed from a contractual standpoint.

[98] See, however, R3RUE's explanation of its approach at vol I, 636 (Comment d) and 643.

[99] Kull (n 56) 1476, referencing R Epstein, 'Beyond Foreseeability: Consequential Damages in the Law of Contract' (1989) 18 *Journal of Legal Studies* 105.

[100] ibid 1502.

[101] ibid 1483. See, further, A Kull, 'Disgorgement for Breach, the Restitution Interest, and the Restatement of Contracts' (2000) 79 *Texas Law Review* 2021, 2041, n 49.

[102] Recall that Birks' understanding of remedies for wrongdoing would not permit us this claim: see the text to nn 49 ff.

service as possible. It is counter-intuitive to suggest that by unwinding the contract – giving the claimant back what she transferred – we are satisfying the parties' agreement. This seems an appropriate link to the next section, where we consider the values served by the remedy.

(c) The Rational Continuity of Cause of Action and Remedy

So far, the unjust enrichment analysis has seemed more plausible both as an explanation of the facts and as an explanation of the remedial structure. This section examines whether the remedy serves the values that the cause of action seeks to protect and promote. It is suggested that this step gives us no reason to prefer breach of contract as an analysis.

The normal remedy for a breach of contract is the expectation remedy, as this best satisfies the protection and promotion of the goods of the institution of contract. The value of contracts in this respect is, essentially, that it allows parties to attain their contractual expectancy – ideally *in specie*; alternatively, in the law's next-best approximation to the expectancy (in the event of breach). This point is well expressed by Friedmann's well-known phrase '[t]he essence of contract is performance.'[103] For that reason, 'performance is the only genuine contractual interest'.[104] However, the remedy under § 38(2)(b) does not appear to vindicate that interest and so does not obviously vindicate the value of contracting: rather than going *forwards*, to fulfil the expectation, it goes *backwards*, to undo the value transferred. Therefore, in order to justify the remedy as sourced in breach of contract, more steps are required. R3RUE claims that the remedy embodies a similar presumption to the reliance award, that 'the plaintiff's unknown expectancy would have been at least equal to the market value of the plaintiff's performance.'[105] The argument would then be as above: the remedy aims to repair a breach of contract in a state of evidential uncertainty.

This interpretation of the remedy under § 38(2)(b) is, I believe, novel – and ingenious. It is a plausible explanation of the remedy with no easy refutation. However, with some trepidation, it must be rejected, for two reasons. First, the fact that the presumption *could* explain the remedy does not mean that it *does*. The same presumption could be used for § 31, but breach of contract clearly does not explain that remedy. Second, if the remedy were ultimately sourced in breach of contract, one would expect a different remedial structure. The cap to the award is in the value of performance transferred, as agreed by the parties. However, as explained, this is inconsistent with § 38(2)(a) – and this suggests that the expectation under the contract is not the ultimate justification of the remedy.[106]

[103] Friedmann (n 57) 632.

[104] ibid 632.

[105] R3RUE (n 1) vol I, 626. This is premised on the 'rebuttable presumption that the plaintiff was [not] performing . . . at less than market value': ibid 626.

[106] Compare the explanation of R3RUE for preferring performance to expectation: R3RUE (n 1) vol I, 636 (Comment d) and 643. See, further, EA Farnsworth, 'Legal Remedies for Breach of Contract' (1970) 70 *Columbia Law Review* 1145, 1178–80.

The alternative claim, that the remedy is sourced in unjust enrichment, faces two difficulties. First, we do not have a similarly pithy explanation of the values served by unjust enrichment as we do of the values served by contract. This problem is particularly clear if we seek to assess R3RUE on its own terms: it explicitly disavows any such claim.[107] However, R3RUE suggests that the basic unity to the law comes from the idea that there is some inadequacy (broadly conceived) to the transfer of wealth between the parties.[108] Peculiar to the law of unjust enrichment is the fact that the remedy given by the law does not aim to make good the inadequacy,[109] but rather aims to reverse the *transfer itself*. Second, it is not clear what values the performance award serves.[110] Why might we allow a claimant to recover the value transferred under a contract where the defendant does not perform the contract? R3RUE suggests that the value is an indirect vindication of the expectation interest. However, as we have just seen, that is implausible: the remedy has no rational connection with the expectation interest. Another explanation is needed.

The performance award is justified by the value in allowing a claimant to retrieve herself from a course of conduct when things do not turn out as anticipated.[111] Implicit to this story is the sense that remedies for breach of contract do not always secure a perfect alternative to performance for a claimant.[112] After a remedy for breach of contract, there is often a 'rational remainder . . . [ie] unsatisfied or imperfectly satisfied reasons' to perform the original course of conduct.[113] The reasons remain because the claimant's expectation was performance, and remedial options are rarely, if ever, actual performance. The claimant's project was, in some sense, frustrated.[114] That is why breach of contract is a wrong.[115] It should also give us some pause before we accept that the remedies for breach of contract are exclusive.

The law, as a concession to the fact that its remedy for breach may be unsatisfactory, can (and, here, does) allow the claimant another course. The claimant may recover the value transferred in order that she may use it in pursuit of another project. This does not seek to address the rational remainder head-on; instead, it allows the claimant to re-open her options. Put another way, the law does not seek to give the claimant what she sought to achieve; instead, it allows her to try again. This forces the question of what kind of harm the law seeks to address, or

[107] R3RUE (n 1) vol I, 4. See above, n 41.

[108] ibid vol I, 5.

[109] Compare breach of contract: the claimant is given what she sought to achieve.

[110] Or, in the words of Perillo, what the 'rationale for restitution' is: Perillo (n 66) 38.

[111] The law here distinguishes a claimant's 'hopes' from genuine conditions: F Wilmot-Smith, 'Replacing Risk-Taking Reasoning' (2011) 127 *LQR* 610, 612. The distinction is important: not every breach of contract justifies this kind of remedy.

[112] S Williston, 'Repudiation of Contracts' (1901) 14 *Harvard Law Review* 317, 330.

[113] Gardner (n 51) 34.

[114] Note that this account also explains why the law of unjust enrichment has no part to play where the parties have agreed on their remedies or sought to exclude those remedies in unjust enrichment.

[115] It is interesting to note R3RUE's ambivalence towards this proposition: at 636, it is willing to '[assume] for the sake of argument' that breach of contract is a wrong. As argued below, this may explain why R3RUE has gone wrong on § 38(2)(b).

what value it seeks to promote, by such an approach. This has not received a satisfactory answer in the unjust enrichment literature. However, one thing is clear. The harm is not the harm of dashed expectations: the law does not try to secure the expectation of the claimant. This undermines the contractual explanation.

Instead, perhaps the harm the remedy addresses is more like that of regret, the emotion which fills the gap when we cannot make our mistakes right. While the law cannot put the situation entirely right, it can give the claimant the option of beginning again.[116] In this way, the award allows for greater autonomy of disposition: the claimant is permitted to re-open the options she forwent in pursuing the relevant course of conduct, a course of conduct which did not turn out as she wished. Therefore, the defect in the transfer arises from a breach of contract, but it is not the breach of contract that the law seeks to remedy. The breach of contract is merely the fact precipitating the defectiveness of the transfer.[117] The distinction is a fine one, but it is fundamental. Moreover, it suggests that the remedy is sensibly categorised as a remedy for unjust enrichment: the breach of contract leads to an inadequate legal basis that, in turn, makes the enrichment unjustified. Therefore, § 38(2)(b) allows for restitution to undo the unjust enrichment.

(5) Conclusion

This part has examined the two remedies under § 38. R3RUE is correct to classify § 38(2)(a), the reliance award, as a remedy for breach of contract; however, it is wrong to classify § 38(2)(b), the performance award, in the same way. The necessary facts of the claim, the remedial structure, and the rational continuity of cause of action and remedy all suggest that unjust enrichment is a better explanation of the remedy than breach of contract.

D. Why Did the *Restatement* Go Wrong?

The previous part suggested that R3RUE was wrong in its classification of § 38(2)(b). This section suggests why the ALI mis-stepped. I think that there are two contributing causes. First, the American commentators never developed a coherent picture of the concept underlying § 38(2)(b). The section began to look anomalous and an alternative, contractual explanation was sought. The second reason is more speculative. I suggest that the way in which the law of contract is considered by some American writers is inadequate, blinding them to the possible harm that a remedy for breach of contract does not address.

[116] It is important to say that this award will not necessarily guarantee this result: the point is simply that it *aims* to do so.

[117] However, the characterisation of the defendant's actions as a breach is, in principle, irrelevant to this. This may explain why the cases have referred to a 'consideration that *happens to* fail': *Moses v Macferlan* (1760) 2 Burr 1005, 1012; 97 ER 676, 682 (Lord Mansfield) (emphasis added).

The first, major reason why R3RUE went wrong has to do with a concept now lost within American texts, generally known – when it is known – as failure of consideration. To explain the concept, a glance at the English law may be helpful. The key English case is *Fibrosa Spolka Akcyjna v Fairbairn Lawson Combe Barbour Ltd.*[118] There, the claimants made an advance payment of £1,000 towards the purchase of £4,800 worth of machinery from the defendants. When war broke out between England and Germany, the contract was frustrated and the claimants sought restitution of the money paid. Their Lordships said that restitution should be ordered because there had been a 'total failure of consideration'.[119] This phrase is apt to confuse.[120] However, Lord Wright explained the reason for restitution perspicaciously:

> The payment was originally conditional. The condition of retaining it is eventual performance. Accordingly, when that condition fails, the right to retain the money must simultaneously fail.[121]

Failure of consideration therefore represents a kind of injustice to a transfer of wealth, arising where there is a condition attaching to a transfer, and the condition fails. For this reason, it has been suggested that 'failure of condition' is a sensible name for the concept.[122] One great benefit of this term is that it does not risk equating failure of consideration with failure of counter-performance, allowing for the conceptual structure of the claim to be made clear. The possible conditions do not arise from the contract and are not limited to counter-performance.[123] As Lord Wright said, the claim is 'not like a claim for damages for breach . . . nor is it a claim under the contract.'[124] Instead, the House of Lords clarified that the case fell 'within a third category of the common law'[125] (beyond tort and contract) which we now refer to as the law of unjust enrichment.[126]

[118] *Fibrosa Spolka Akcyjna v Fairbairn Lawson Combe Barbour Ltd* [1943] AC 32 (HL).

[119] ibid 49 (Viscount Simon LC), 51 and 53 (Lord Atkin), 56 (Lord Russell), 61 (Lord MacMillan), 69 (Lord Wright) and 74 (Lord Roche).

[120] See, eg, C Mitchell, P Mitchell and S Watterson (eds) *Goff & Jones: The Law of Unjust Enrichment*, 8th edn (London, Sweet & Maxwell, 2011) [12-10]–[12-15].

[121] *Fibrosa* (n 117) 65 (Lord Wright). See, further, P Birks, 'Restitution and Freedom of Contract' (1983) 14 *CLP* 141, 151.

[122] eg, *Anderson v McPherson (No 2)* [2012] WASC 19 [235] (Edelman J). Others prefer the term 'failure of basis', but such accounts often speak in terms of conditionality when explaining that term: eg, *Goff & Jones* (n 119) [12-01].

[123] *Fibrosa* (n 117) 48 (Viscount Simon LC). For earlier recognition, see *Cantiare San Rocco v Clyde Shipbuilding & Engineering Co Ltd* [1924] AC 226 (HL), 238 (Earl of Birkenhead).

[124] *Fibrosa* (n 117) 65 (Lord Wright).

[125] ibid 61 (Lord Wright).

[126] *Lipkin Gorman v Karpnale Ltd* [1991] 2 AC 548 (HL) 558h (Lord Bridge), 568c (Lord Ackner) and 578c (Lord Goff of Chieveley). English scholars tend to differ from the ALI in their preference for the category of 'unjust enrichment' alone, labelling it by the event, not the response: see P Birks, 'A Letter to America: The New Restatement of Restitution' (2003) 3 *Global Jurist* 2. While it is orthodox to see failure of consideration as part of the law of unjust enrichment, this is not uncontested amongst commentators: see, for instance, P Atiyah, *The Rise and Fall of Freedom of Contract* (Oxford, Oxford University Press, 1985) 489.

The concept of failure of consideration (or condition) gives a conceptual clarity to § 38(2)(b) that would otherwise be lacking. So long as § 38(2)(b) is considered alone, as a particular remedy arising only on a breach of contract, it looks odd – and the explanation proffered by R3RUE is understandably alluring. However, once § 38(2)(b) is seen as an example of a wider category of cases, where the law recognises a category of conditional transfers, it is more readily appreciable as an instance of unjust enrichment. Therefore, it is a reasonable hypothesis that when the concept of failure of consideration is lost, the proper characterisation of § 38(2)(b) is threatened.

The history of the treatment of the remedy of § 38(2)(b) shows an early appreciation that it was explained by failure of consideration. However, the concept of failure of consideration was never developed sufficiently to give it coherence or stability. At the beginning of the nineteenth century, failure of consideration received scant treatment in the texts, and then only really as a defence to an action on a contract.[127] There was, however, a clearly recognisable line of authority developing in the cases, allowing recovery of money paid on a consideration which failed.[128] Textbooks then began to distinguish total and partial failures of consideration in considering when rescission for breach of contract was possible.[129] In this context, references to total failure of consideration often seem to equate the concept with a lack of binding contractual consideration.[130] However, while the cases did not always reason in terms of failure of consideration,[131] writers generally accepted that money paid on a total failure of consideration could be recovered back.[132] There are two important points to notice about this: first, the doctrine was not clearly separated from the contractual domain (for which the misleading word 'consideration' should probably shoulder the blame); and second, cases where money was recovered on non-performance of a contract were not considered with other analogous cases (such as recovery of money paid on an unenforceable contract).

[127] T Peake, *A Compendium of the Law of Evidence* (Philadelphia, PA, Josiah Randall, 1812) 324; W Selwyn, *An Abridgement of the Law of Nisi Prius*, 2nd American from the 5th London edn (Albany, NY, Henry Wheaton, 1823) vol I, 246.

[128] *Sanford v Dodd*, 2 Day 437 (1807); *Boyd v Anderson*, 1 Tenn 438 (1809).

[129] Eg, WW Story, *A Treatise on the Law of Contracts Not Under Seal* (Boston, MA, Little Brown, 1844) § 153; (2nd edn, 1847) § 480–81; (3rd edn, 1874) § 480.

[130] eg, ibid; CG Addison, *A Treatise on the Law of Contracts and Rights and Liabilities Ex Contractu*, 1st American edn (Philadelphia, PA, Lea and Blanchard, 1847) 24; T Parsons, *The Elements of Mercantile Law* (Boston, MA, Little, Brown & Co, 1856) 36. Parsons' *The Law of Contracts*, the 8th edition of which was edited by Samuel Williston, contained similar claims.

[131] See, eg, F Wharton, *A Commentary on the Law of Contracts* (Philadelphia, PA, Kay and Brother, 1882) § 742: of the 14 cases cited for the proposition, only three contain reference to failure of consideration.

[132] eg, J Chitty, *A Practical Treatise on the Law of Contracts*, 5th American edn, from the 3rd London edn (Springfield, MA, G and C Merriam, 1842) 622; CG Addison, *A Treatise on the Law of Contracts and Rights and Liabilities Ex Contractu*, 2nd American edn (Philadelphia, PA, Lea and Blanchard, 1857) 150; Parsons (n 129) 36.

Keener's casebook classified the cases differently.[133] The second chapter is entitled 'Failure of Consideration'. It has three sections: (1) Mistake; (2) Failure of the Defendant to Perform the Contract; and (3) Failure of the Claimant to Perform a Condition of the Contract. The second section included, inter alia, unenforceability for breach of the statute of frauds. This promised an interpretation of failure of consideration avoiding the two points we have just noted, and giving the concept the kind of unity and breadth it required to be intelligible. The casebook is remarkable in its approach. The suggestion that failure of consideration is the basis of recovery for mistake cases, for instance, is radical, even today.[134] However, this clarity of classification was abandoned in Keener's eventual *Treatise*.[135] This book separated out what had been considered together into three separate chapters (2, 4 and 5). While Keener did not entirely abandon the claim that failure of consideration was a uniting concept,[136] the importance of that claim was obscured by the shift in the presentation. The cause of the shift is unclear, but it is interesting to note that the book is dedicated to James Barr Ames, whose work had such an important influence on the structure of the first *Restatement*.[137]

As that brief window of opportunity passed, failure of consideration was treated with increasing scepticism. Harriman's textbook said that: 'Strictly speaking, there can be no such thing as a "failure of consideration".'[138] His objection, one which will chime with those familiar with the English law, was essentially to using a single phrase to denote two different ideas – consideration as a precondition to contractual validity, and consideration in the sense of performance.[139] Brantley said that '[t]he expression, "failure of consideration", sometimes used to designate a breach of contract, is a vague term which has no definite technical import'.[140] Woodward's *The Law of Quasi Contracts* does not even refer to the term.[141]

It is therefore not entirely surprising that the *Restatement of Restitution* did not present the law using the concept of failure of consideration. While Williston, a member of the ALI's committee on restitution, continued to defend the term in his own work, prevailing scholarly opinion held that the term did more harm than good. The concept is referred to in the *Restatement First: Contracts* to refer to the discharge in the contractual duty of one party if the other party fails to

[133] WA Keener, *A Selection of Cases on the Law of Quasi-Contracts* (Cambridge, MA, CW Sever, 1888–89).

[134] *cf* P Matthews, 'Money Paid under Mistake of Fact' (1980) 130 *NLJ* 587, 588–89.

[135] WA Keener, *A Treatise on the Law of Quasi-Contracts* (New York, Baker, Voorhis and Company 1893).

[136] ibid 119, 292.

[137] ibid, dedication page; see A Kull, 'James Barr Ames and the Early Modern History of Unjust Enrichment' (2005) 25 *OJLS* 297.

[138] EA Harriman, *The Law of Contracts*, 2nd edn (Boston, MA, Little, Brown, 1901) § 524.

[139] See, further, E Patterson, 'Constructive Conditions in Contracts' (1942) 42 *Columbia Law Review* 903, 921–22. Patterson formed part of the ALI's committee on restitution for the first *Restatement*.

[140] WT Brantly, *Law of Contract*, 2nd edn (Baltimore, MD, HB Scrimger, 1912) § 203.

[141] FC Woodward, *The Law of Quasi Contracts* (Boston, MA, Little, Brown & Co, 1913). The term does appear in quotes in the text, but never in the main body of the work.

perform.[142] Failure of consideration is described only in terms of non-performance (thus omitting important aspects of the concept, such as cases where a purpose fails[143] or a contract is void)[144] and the language has a contractual flavour.[145] The *Restatement Second: Contracts* took the logical step (from that perspective) of renaming the term 'failure of performance'.[146] This term has two major problems: first, it obscures the conceptual foundations of failure of consideration and makes the link between § 38(2)(b) cases and (for instance) § 31 cases much harder to perceive; and second, the label with the historical pedigree to show scholars the underlying conceptual unity was lost.

So, when the drafters of R3RUE came to their task, they were faced with a body of rules allowing recovery of money on the breakdown of a contract. There was no obvious analogy in the law of unjust enrichment. The case must have appeared to be an outlier. Small wonder, therefore, that they explained the remedy as part of the law of contract. However, perhaps with a revitalisation of the concept of failure of consideration, or condition, the remedy would look less peculiar from the unjust enrichment perspective – and § 38(2)(b) would become an accepted part of R3RUE.

The second reason why I suggest the American law took a wrong turn is more speculative. However, I believe that the Holmesian turn in contractual analysis amongst American scholars may have led them to ignore the rational remainder, the residual harm left after a remedy for breach of contract is awarded. Holmes famously called the duty to keep a contract 'a prediction that you must pay damages if you do not keep it'.[147] Whether this is quite what Holmes meant is unclear,[148] but this point is unimportant to the claim made here. Holmes has been understood as it sounds as though he intended to have claimed that a contract is nothing more than an agreement to pay damages in the event of non-performance.[149] R3RUE says that there is a 'substantial truth' in this proposition.[150] This fallacy has

[142] American Law Institute, *Restatement First: Contracts* (St Paul, MN, American Law Institute, 1932) § 274. Patterson lamented the usage of the term as 'inconsistent with the basic definition of "consideration"': E Patterson, 'The Restatement of the Law of Contracts' (1933) 33 *Columbia Law Review* 397, 406.

[143] eg, *Wales v Wetmore*, 3 Day 252 (1808).

[144] eg, *Dill v Inhabitants of Wareham*, 7 Metcalf 438, 48 Mass 438 (1844).

[145] Equally, Williston's textbook continued to defend the use of the term, but only as failure of *performance* of a *contractual* obligation: WHE Jaeger (ed), *Williston on Contracts*, 3rd edn (Mount Kisco, NY, Voorhis & Co, 1959) § 814; RA Lord (ed) S Williston, *The Law of Contract*, 4th edn (St Paul, MN, West Publishing, 1992) § 7:11.

[146] See *Restatement Second: Contracts* (n 9) § 237, Comment a and the Reporter's Note.

[147] OW Holmes, 'The Path of the Law' (1897) 10 *Harvard Law Review* 457, 462.

[148] Compare M Howe (ed), *Holmes-Pollock Letters: The Correspondence of Mr Justice Holmes and Sir Frederick Pollock, 1874–1932* (Cambridge, MA, Harvard University Press, 1941) 233 (letter of Dec 11, 1928); *PP Emory Mfg v Columbia Smelting & Refining Works*, 60 NE 377 (1901) (Holmes J). See, generally, J Perillo, 'Misreading Oliver Wendell Holmes on Efficient Breach and Tortious Interference' (2000) 68 *Fordham Law Review* 1085.

[149] See, for instance, D Friedmann, 'The Efficient Breach Fallacy' (1989) 18 *Journal of Legal Studies* 1, 1; JP Nehf, 'Contract Damages as Substitute for Full Performance' (1999) 32 *Indiana Law Review* 765, 765–66.

[150] R3RUE (n 1) vol I, 648.

been abetted by the economic turn in American scholarship, as some lawyer-economists have lent credence to the claim in their analysis of 'efficient breach'.[151] This means that breach of contract is not regarded as a wrong but as an option at the defendant's election.[152] From this position, it becomes difficult to see why the claimant should be given an additional power to pull back her performance in the event of the defendant's exercise of the election. The claimant's normative position has not, on this analysis, been materially affected. However, once the breach of contract is perceived as a wrong, the harm described above becomes more readily discernible.

E. Why It Matters

So far, I have suggested that R3RUE gets its classification of § 38(2)(b) wrong and I have given two reasons why it might have gone wrong. But why does it matter, either way? This section suggests seven points of consequence, both for the law represented in § 38(2)(b) and for the law represented in the rest of Chapter 4. The first point is that the reclassification pushes us to reconsider – if not necessarily reject – the cap on the claim under § 38(2)(b). As described, the claimant's recovery is valued at the contractual rate; in other words, she is prevented from escaping a bad bargain by claiming in unjust enrichment. There is much to be said for this rule. However, it should be re-examined in the light of the proper classification of the cause of action. In particular, it should be scrutinised in the light of the justification of the remedy. The remedy is justified in part by the inadequacy of the contractual award. It may be that the value in the claimant being able to re-open her options can only be properly satisfied if she can recover the market value of her services: the contractual valuation of her performance was, after all, premised on counter-performance. Furthermore, whatever is concluded on this matter, there should be greater internal coherence across the remedies of Chapter 4. If the measure of § 38(2)(b) is a good one, then it is surely a good one in all cases where the parties have valued performance under a contract. However, R3RUE does not use the measure for the remedies of Chapter 4, Topic 1. So long as § 38(2)(b) is classified as a remedy for breach of contract, this does not appear to be inconsistent; when it is understood as a remedy for unjust enrichment, the anomaly is clear.

Second, the applicable rules on alternative and cumulative remedies following the breach of contract must be reconsidered. If the claimant satisfies the particular rules on special damages, she may combine a claim under § 38(2)(b) with a claim

[151] eg, *Patton v Mid-Continent Systems*, 841 F 2d 742, 750 (1988) (Posner J). Compare Friedmann (n 148).

[152] By comparison: 'Legal concepts like failure of consideration . . . reek of the need for actual performance': K Llewellyn, 'Our Case-Law of Contract: Offer and Acceptance, II' (1939) 48 *Yale Law Journal* 779, 790.

to 'recover for any other loss, including incidental or consequential loss, caused by the breach'.[153] If § 38(2)(b) is understood to be a remedy for breach, this is uncontentious. However, once the remedy is seen as one for unjust enrichment, the point is less clear. In *Neel v Deens*, the claimant, an 'elderly widow lady', paid the defendants, 'dealers and traders in negroes', for a 'negro girl'.[154] A third party, one Captain Smily, testified that the slave was 'so diseased . . . that he would not have had her as a gift'.[155] The widow brought an action for money had and received 'to recover money for a consideration which failed'. She was successful, but the jury also awarded $100 'smart-money' (punitive damages). The defendant appealed and Gantt J found that 'from the nature of the present action, damages by way of "smart-money," ought not to have been given'.[156] This colourful – and, for all but the slave girl, entirely disreputable – episode illustrates two very important points. As a matter of principle, it is undeniable that a claim for restitution of unjust enrichment should not be used to award sums which are to repair a breach of contract (or to punish the wrongdoer). R3RUE makes this point perilously unclear. There is a great danger of judges awarding consequential damages when the claimant's claim is, properly understood, to reverse an unjust enrichment. It is also contested whether damages for breach of contract can be combined with a claim for restitution for unjust enrichment in this manner.[157] The point should be dealt with on its merits and not ignored by reason of a classificatory error.[158]

Third, the applicable limitation period for the claim may differ depending on the cause of action. I do not want to labour this point as it turns on the limitation rules of individual states, but a limitation statute could clearly distinguish the two bases of claim for the purposes of limitation.[159]

Fourth, claims for contribution and reimbursement may be affected depending on the characterisation of the remedy. For instance, in *Boeing Co v Aetna Casualty and Surety Co*,[160] a question arose as to whether the response costs for which the insured was liable counted as 'damages' or a liability in 'restitution'. Such a question could just as easily arise where recovery is sought for liability under § 38(2)(b).

Fifth, whether the remedy is protected by the contracts clause of the United States Constitution (and other similar provisions of state constitutions) will depend on whether the cause of action is sourced in breach of contract or unjust

[153] R3RUE (n 1) § 38(3) and vol I, 636–38.

[154] *Neel v Deens*, 1 Nott & McC 210 (1818).

[155] ibid.

[156] ibid.

[157] See, generally, Dobbs (n 41) §§ 4.5(5), 9.4 and 12.7(6); G Palmer, *Law of Restitution* (Boston, MA, Little Brown, 1978) §§ 4.8 and 4.13; S Watterson, 'Alternative and Cumulative Remedies: What is the Difference?' [2003] *Restitution Law Review* 7.

[158] See, for example, K Barker, 'Restitution of Passenger Fare: The Mikhail Lermontov' [1993] *Lloyd's Maritime & Commercial Law Quarterly* 291; *Giedo van der Garde BV v Force India Formula One Team Ltd* [2010] EWHC 2373 (QB) [291], noted (2011) 128 *LQR* 23.

[159] Dobbs (n 41) § 4.1(1).

[160] *Boeing Co v Aetna Casualty and Surety Co*, 113 Wash 2d 869, 784 P 2d 507 (1990); Dobbs (n 41) § 4.1(1).

enrichment. For instance, in *Coombes v Getz*,[161] the question arose as to whether a liability initially arising under the Constitution of California[162] was protected from repeal by the contracts clause.[163] The majority of the court, finding that the liability arose 'upon the contractual liability created in pursuance of [the Constitutional provision]', held that the cause of action was so protected.[164] The dissent was premised on his view that the liability was contractual 'only in a qualified sense, as the expression of a legal fiction'.[165] A similar debate could arise over a liability under § 38(2)(b).

Sixth, the relevant rules on the conflict of laws can vary according to the proper classification of the remedy. For instance, as regards choice of law, the second *Restatement on the Conflicts of Laws* clearly distinguishes contract cases from restitution cases.[166] The applicable rules, while similar,[167] can clearly come apart in some cases.[168]

The final point does not concern § 38(2)(b) itself, but the coherence of R3RUE as a consequence of the error in § 38(2)(b). The precise reason for restitution in §§ 31–35 is not made clear. Instead, the factual circumstances which lead to recovery are described. The unfortunate consequence – particularly when combined with the unwillingness to explain the basis of unjust enrichment as a category – is that the chapter has overlapping categories (§ 31 and § 33 are, for instance, both about restitution for unenforceability of the contract) of questionable coherence. The chapter is so structured not only because of the methodological stance of R3RUE, but also because the concept of conditional transfers, embodied by the failure of consideration doctrine, was not available to the drafters. However, §§ 31, 33 and 34 are all hornbook examples within other jurisdictions of restitution for failure of consideration.[169] They should have been considered – and categorised – together with § 38(2)(b).[170] Keener would have agreed, and there is support for the classification in the history, before the concept was lost.[171] This would have made the reason for restitution in those cases must easier to understand and would probably have made Chapter 4 much shorter and easier to follow.

[161] *Coombes v Getz*, 285 US 434, 52 S Ct 435 (1932).
[162] California Constitution of 1879, s 3, Art 12.
[163] United States Constitution, Art 1, s 10, cl 1.
[164] *Coombes* (n 160) 442 and 436 (Sutherland J).
[165] ibid 449 and 439 (Cardozo J, with Brandeis and Stone JJ).
[166] Compare American Law Institute, *Restatement Second: Conflicts of Laws* (St Paul, MN, American Law Institute Publishers, 1969) §§ 186–88 with § 221.
[167] The distinction between § 188(2) and § 221(2) is marginal.
[168] Most obviously where there is a choice of law agreement under § 187.
[169] Other sections could also plausibly be so categorised: §§ 28 and 36.
[170] It is worth pointing out that, consistent with his analysis of the section as a claim for breach of contract, Professor Kull disagrees with this categorisation of 38(2)(b).
[171] eg, *Thompson v Gould*, 20 Pick 134; 37 Mass 134 (1838) 137 (Wilde J).

F. Conclusion

The claim of this chapter is, in one sense, very modest. It has looked in detail at one small part of a very large *Restatement* and suggested that half of the section is incorrectly classified. However, a great deal turns on that small point. The rediscovery of the concept of non-contractual conditions would allow much of Chapter 4 to be presented in a simpler and more intelligible form. The rationalised presentation would both aid the busy practitioner and illuminate the connections within the law of Chapter 4, forcing a reconsideration of a number of aspects of the law as presented there.

This point hints at a broader problem of R3RUE, at least to English eyes. The *Restatement* covers an enormous distance. In part because of this, it is difficult to get a handle upon the whole. However, its methods do not always help. The contextual approach complicates the endeavour as it entails needless overlapping of topics. The contextual approach is also more forgiving of conceptual impurity. The English obsession with such matters is often thought too dry for the dynamic pragmatism of the American lawyer. This chapter suggests that the former approach may serve the latter aim.

4

Duress and Related Forms of Pressure: A Comparative Perspective

JACQUES DU PLESSIS

A. Introduction

In deciding whether to order restitution of a transfer, legal systems generally regard it as relevant that the claimant acted under duress or related forms of pressure. However, they do so in quite different ways,[1] especially in terms of the relative prominence they accord to the fact that the claimant acted under pressure, compared to other circumstances, such as that the transfer exceeded what was owed under a valid contract or statutory obligation. These differences may have important implications for practical issues such as the distribution of the burden of proof and for theoretical debates on the choice of appropriate schemes for structuring or representing enrichment law.[2] The purpose of this chapter is to investigate the approach of the *Restatement Third: Restitution and Unjust Enrichment*[3] to these matters and to evaluate it from a comparative perspective. Before investigating these issues further, it is first necessary to achieve clarity in relation to some key concepts.

[1] For comparative overviews, see P Schlechtriem, *Restitution und Bereicherungsausgleich in Europa*, vol 1 (Tübingen, Mohr Siebeck, 2000) 73–112 and 158–88; I Englard, 'Restitution of Benefits Conferred without Obligation' in *International Encyclopedia of Comparative Law*, vol X, ch 5 (Tübingen, Mohr Siebeck/Martinus Nijhoff, 1991) 22–32; M Chen-Wishart, 'In Defence of Unjust Factors: A Study of Rescission for Duress, Fraud and Exploitation' in D Johnston and R Zimmermann (eds), *Unjustified Enrichment: Key Issues in Comparative Perspective* (Cambridge, Cambridge University Press, 2002) 159; J du Plessis, 'Fraud, Duress and Unjustified Enrichment: A Civil Law Perspective' in Johnston and Zimmermann (eds), *Unjustified Enrichment* (above) 194.

[2] The focus here is therefore only on determining whether a claim of restitution should be allowed, and not on the relevance of pressure in quantifying such a claim.

[3] American Law Institute, *Restatement Third: Restitution and Unjust Enrichment* (St Paul, MN, American Law Institute Publishers, 2011) (hereinafter 'R3RUE').

B. The Meaning of Duress and Related Concepts in R3RUE

(1) A Framework of Relevant R3RUE Provisions

Part II of R3RUE contains the main divisions of liability, or 'circumstances that give rise to a claim in restitution and unjust enrichment'.[4] The following table identifies the main divisions relating to duress and related forms of pressure.

Part II. Liability in Restitution

Chapter 2. Transfers Subject to Avoidance

Topic 2. Defective Consent or Authority

§ 14. Duress

Topic 3. Transfers under Legal Compulsion

§ 18. Judgments Subsequently Reversed or Avoided
§ 19. Recovery of Tax Payments

Chapter 3. Unrequested Intervention

Topic 1. Emergency Intervention

§ 22. Performance of Another's Duty

Topic 2. Performance Rendered to a Third Person

§ 23. Performance of a Joint Obligation (Indemnity and Contribution)
§ 24. Performance of an Independent Obligation (Equitable Subrogation)
§ 25. Uncompensated Performance under Contract with Third Person

Chapter 4. Restitution and Contract

Topic 1. Restitution to a Performing Party with no Claim on the Contract

§ 31. Unenforceability
§ 35. Performance of Disputed Obligation

(2) Duress (§ 14)

Chapter 2, Topic 2 deals with various grounds for rescission and avoidance of a transfer that is 'imperfectly voluntary' or has been made due to 'defective consent'.[5] One of these grounds is duress. It is defined in § 14(1) as 'coercion that is wrongful as a matter of law'. This essentially means that the victim must have

[4] ibid vol I, 43.
[5] ibid vol I, 45.

been subjected to a wrongful threat or refusal.[6] A lawful threat, for example, a threat of litigation to enforce a demand, does not constitute duress unless the demand was made in bad faith, in pursuit of a claim known to be unjustified.[7] Although some definitions of duress further require that the threat must 'overcome' the victim's will, the drafters of R3RUE rightly regarded this element as superfluous. Their view is in line with the civil law notion that it is not the lack of volition on the side of the victim which deprives consent of its force, but the use of improper means to obtain consent, namely an unlawful threat.[8] Similar approaches have for some time been supported in English law: it is not the overborne will but the unacceptable nature of the means used to influence a person's will that lies at the heart of duress.[9]

The general definition of duress is subject to an important qualification. In cases of unjust enrichment, when it is easy to prove that the defendant is enriched by receiving an overpayment, the claimant may rely on § 14 without having to prove wrongful coercion.[10] These cases may, for want of a better expression, be termed 'duress light'. It suffices if the defendant was subjected to a lawful threat of civil litigation made in good faith, as long as he would suffer substantial prejudice, beyond merely having to defend a lawsuit.[11] Thus, if a lender mistakenly but in good faith threatens to foreclose a mortgage unless the borrower makes a payment which is not due, and the borrower pays to prevent foreclosure from interfering with the anticipated sale of the property, the payor may claim restitution of the excess payment.[12] Other cases deal with undue payments by an insured to prevent an insurer from terminating an insurance policy and forfeiting payments,[13] or by a customer to prevent a municipality from cutting off its water supply.[14] One may add in passing that the position in English law is stricter, inasmuch as

[6] ibid vol I, 186 and 195. See also American Law Institute, *Restatement Second: Contracts* (St Paul, MN: American Law Institute Publishers, 1981) § 176, which refers to an 'improper threat'. Duress is distinguished in R3RUE from undue influence (§ 15) on the ground that undue influence 'is the result of persuasion that the law regards as excessive, but such persuasion need not reach the level of wrongful coercion' (vol I, 203–4). However, it is accepted that the elements overlap and that 'it is not always possible (or necessary) to isolate the precise ground of relief' (vol I, 204; also see vol I, 182).

[7] ibid vol I, 188, 192–95 and 200–02. See Illustration 23 for an example: a seller demands immediate payment of an outstanding account, on threat of litigation, even though the seller knows that the buyer's account is current (ibid vol I, 193).

[8] See, for example, BGB (the German Civil Code), § 123 I. This notion can be traced to Paulus D.4.2.21.5 (*voluntas coacta tamen voluntas est*); for comparative perspectives, see J du Plessis, 'Threats and Excessive Benefits or Unfair Advantage' in HL MacQueen and R Zimmermann (eds), *European Contract Law: Scots and South African Perspectives* (Edinburgh, Edinburgh University Press, 2006) 151, 152–57.

[9] See *Lynch v DPP of Northern Ireland* [1975] AC 653, 695; E McKendrick 'The Further Travails of Duress' in A Burrows and Lord Rodger of Earlsferry (eds), *Mapping the Law: Essays in Memory of Peter Birks* (Oxford, Oxford University Press, 2006) 181; for a historical and comparative overview, see T Schindler, *Rechtsgeschäftliche Entscheidungsfreiheit und Drohung – Die englische Duress-Lehre in rechtsvergleichender Perspektive* (Tübingen, Mohr Siebeck, 2005).

[10] R3RUE (n 3) vol I, 182 and 188–90.

[11] ibid vol I, 189.

[12] See R3RUE (n 3) § 14, Illustration 14; vol I, 189 and cases referred to at 199.

[13] See R3RUE (n 3) § 14, Illustration 15: vol I, 189–90, and the reference at 199 to *Still v Equitable Life Assurance Society of United States*, 165 Ten 224, 54 SW 2d 947 (1932).

[14] See R3RUE (n 3) § 14, Illustration 16: vol I, 190 and cases referred to at 199.

restitution would be denied if the demand for payment creating the pressure was made in good faith.[15]

Thus far, the focus has been on situations involving pressure arising from threats which amount to duress in the context of § 14. However, R3RUE also provides for claims where undue transfers have been made under pressure that did not arise from a threat at all. These situations concern cases of 'legal compulsion' (§§ 18–19) and cases where performance was demanded of a disputed contractual obligation and it would be prejudicial not to accede to the demand (§ 35). These will be considered in turn.

(3) Legal Compulsion: Transfers Made to Satisfy Judgments that Are Later Reversed (§ 18) and Undue Tax Payments (§ 19)

As the table indicates, Chapter 2 of R3RUE not only deals with transfers subject to avoidance due to defective consent or authority (Topic 2, which includes duress in § 14), it also deals with transfers subject to avoidance due to legal compulsion (Topic 3). Although it is argued that transfers under legal compulsion are usually made involuntarily or due to defective consent, they are located in a separate category because 'the quality of the transferor's consent is not what distinguishes a valid transfer under legal compulsion from one that is subject to avoidance'.[16] The basis for the distinction lies elsewhere. Because the explanation is quite sophisticated, it is quoted in full:

> The most direct explanation of the restitution claims within this Topic lies in the recognition that the use of legal compulsion to effect a transfer presupposes a conclusion about the existing obligations between the transferor and transferee – namely, that justice (whether embodied in the civil law of obligations or the tax code) requires a transfer from one to the other. If that conclusion about the parties' entitlements is subsequently believed to be erroneous, the effect of legal compulsion will have been to create an improper distribution, rather than to correct one.[17]

The main examples of transfers made under legal compulsion are transfers made to satisfy a judgment that is subsequently reversed (§ 18) and payments of taxes in excess of the taxpayer's actual legal liability (§ 19). There is no need to prove duress in terms of § 14 and, more specifically, no need to prove a threat.[18]

[15] See, eg, *CTN Cash & Carry Ltd v Gallagher Ltd* [1994] 4 All ER 714 (CA); G Dannemann, 'Unjust Enrichment as Absence of Basis: Can English Law Cope?' in Burrows and Rodger (n 9) 363, 373–77. On English law, see C Mitchell, P Mitchell and S Watterson (eds), *Goff & Jones: The Law of Unjust Enrichment*, 8th edn (London, Sweet & Maxwell, 2011) [10-81]–[10-86]; A Burrows, *The Law of Restitution*, 3rd edn (Oxford, Oxford University Press, 2010) 257. It is not convincing to attempt to circumvent the difficulty of not being able to rely on duress by finding that the compelled transferor was somehow mistaken (see *Nurdin & Peacock v DB Ramsden & Co Ltd* [1999] 1 All ER 941).

[16] R3RUE (n 3) vol I, 244. See 260 on overlapping between § 14 and § 19; see further the general comments on overlapping provisions at 43.

[17] ibid vol I, 244.

[18] On the absence of duress in these cases, see also MP Gergen, 'Self-Interested Intervention in the Law of Unjust Enrichment' in R Zimmermann (ed), *Grundstrukturen eines Europäischen Bereicherungsrecht* (Tübingen, Mohr Siebeck, 2005) 243 and 262–63.

It will immediately be apparent to English lawyers that there is a significant difference between the way in which R3RUE and English lawyers define 'legal compulsion'. For example, according to Burrows, 'legal compulsion' is the 'legitimate application of the legal process', which covers the compulsory discharge of another's liability.[19] It therefore clearly does not deal with the transfer made to satisfy a judgment that is subsequently reversed or with a payment of taxes in excess of the taxpayer's actual legal liability,[20] which is of course the domain of *Woolwich Equitable Building Society v IRC*.[21] R3RUE, in turn, does not regard cases of compulsory discharge of another's liability as instances of 'legal compulsion', but as instances of 'unrequested intervention', covered by Chapter 3 of R3RUE.[22]

An outsider who is not familiar with these contrasting definitions of 'legal compulsion' may be forgiven for finding them rather perplexing. However, the outsider may take some consolation from the fact that insiders have their difficulties too, especially in terms of what precisely constitutes the pressure or compulsion to which the transferor is subjected in cases of unlawfully demanded tax, and whether it really is important enough to make 'legal compulsion' the topic heading in presenting these cases in R3RUE.[23] We will return to these matters later on.[24]

(4) Disputed Obligations (§ 35): Payments Not Owed under a Contract and Made under Protest or Reservation of Rights

Legal compulsion is not the only category of situations where R3RUE provides claims for restitution of undue transfers which may have been made under pressure. According to § 35, if one party demands a payment in excess of what he is entitled to under a contract and the other party pays under protest or reservation, the payor may reclaim the payment. However, it must have been reasonable for

[19] Burrows (n 15) 436. See also G Virgo, *The Principles of the Law of Restitution*, 2nd edn (Oxford, Oxford University Press, 2006) 220.

[20] Burrows (n 15) 498–520. See further Virgo (n 19) 242–43 and 400–24.

[21] *Woolwich Equitable Building Society v IRC* [1993] AC 70.

[22] More specifically, there are situations when the claimant performed an obligation of his own, but thereby discharged an obligation of the defendant as well. The provisions dealing with these cases of 'performance rendered to a third person' are § 23 on performance of a joint obligation (indemnity and contribution), § 24 on performance of an independent obligation (equitable subrogation) and § 25 on uncompensated performance under contract with a third person. The *Restatement First* brought cases of 'discharge by one person of duty also owed by another', including indemnity and contribution, under its Chapter 3 on 'coercion': American Law Institute, *Restatement of the Law of Restitution: Quasi Contracts and Constructive Trusts* (St Paul, MN, American Law Institute Publishers, 1937) 327–431.

[23] See Gergen (n 18) 260–63 for a rather dismissive view on the decision to include § 19 under this broader heading ('compulsion is only a . . . throw-away argument to explain a new rule in terms that would be familiar to the audience': 263). For criticism of the use of the term 'legal compulsion' in English law, see S Meier, 'No Basis: A Comparative View' in Burrows and Rodger (n 9) 360–61; C Mitchell *The Law of Contribution and Reimbursement* (Oxford, Oxford University Press, 2003) paras 3.24–3.29.

[24] See Part C, section (3) and Part E, section (4) below.

the payor to have acceded to the demand rather than to insist that liability should immediately be determined.[25]

Some important differences exist between the circumstances under which restitution would be awarded in terms of § 35, compared to the cases of duress which belong under § 14.[26] An obvious difference is that § 35 is limited to a demand for a performance that is not due under a contract, whereas § 14 is more general in scope. In addition, the claimant who relies on § 35 does not have to describe the pressure as wrongful;[27] he only has to prove the specific circumstances of a demand to which it was reasonable to accede, and that he made the performance under protest or reservation of rights. He therefore does not have to prove actual duress under § 14, but only a 'species of coercion akin to duress'.[28]

However, R3RUE recognises that the distinction between these categories is at times fine: it is admitted that the § 35 cases are closely related to the § 14 cases which find that there is duress in the event of a good faith threat that carries disproportionate consequences of harm (ie, the cases of 'duress light').[29] It is said that the benefit of relying on § 35 is that it 'provides an alternative explanation of the same results, without the need to condemn the defendant's threats as wrongful coercion'. The application of this major innovation, which was inspired by Gergen,[30] can be illustrated by some examples. A borrower may claim restitution under § 35 if the lender demands payment of more than he is entitled to for releasing the borrower from a mortgage, and the borrower then under protest pays the amount demanded to ensure that he is released in time to prevent a delay in the anticipated sale of the property. The borrower does not have to prove that the lender made a threat, as in the example of the threat to foreclose the mortgage discussed in the context of § 14. However, the situations are indeed close to each other: in both instances, the payor may fear that the other party could take steps that would harm him. The same may be said when an insurer makes an unfounded demand for payment of a premium or when a utility demands payment of a disputed surcharge. They need not make an express threat, but the insured or customer knows that a failure to pay may result in the cancellation of the policy or termination of the service.[31]

[25] § 35 reads as follows: 'If one party to a contract demands from the other a performance that is not in fact due by the terms of their agreement, under circumstances making it reasonable to accede to the demand rather than to insist on an immediate test of the disputed obligation, the party on whom the demand is made may render such performance under protest or with reservation of rights, preserving a claim in restitution to recover the value of the benefit conferred in excess of the recipient's contractual entitlement.'

[26] The claimant may choose whether to rely on § 14 or § 35: R3RUE (n 3) vol I, 189.

[27] ibid vol I, 572.

[28] ibid vol I, 582.

[29] ibid vol I, 182.

[30] M Gergen, 'Bridge over Troubled Contractual Waters' (2002) 71 *Fordham Law Review* 709 – see R3RUE (n 3) vol I, 582. For positive comments, see JM Perillo, 'Restitution in a Contractual Context and the Restatement (Third) of Restitution and Unjust Enrichment' (2011) 68 *Washington and Lee Law Review* 1007, 1020.

[31] See R3RUE (n 3) § 35, Illustrations 1–3: vol I, 574–75 and cases referred to at 582.

C. The Consequences of Duress and Related Forms of Pressure According to R3RUE

(1) Introduction

Having explored key provisions dealing with duress and related forms of pressure, we may now proceed to examine their consequences. All these provisions refer to a claim for restitution. But, to return to the question posed at the outset, what is the exact relevance of the pressure in awarding such a claim? We will first consider the answers provided by R3RUE, paying particular attention to how it views the relationship between the relevance of proof of the various forms of pressure and proof that a transfer was not due. Thereafter, we will investigate civil law approaches to related fact patterns and doctrinal issues with a view to drawing comparative conclusions.

(2) Duress: § 14

According to § 14(2), 'a transfer induced by duress is subject to rescission and restitution. The transferee is liable in restitution as to avoid unjust enrichment'. A comment on this provision adds that a finding of duress 'invalidates a transfer only to the extent that the transfer finds no basis in the transferor's underlying obligation to the transferee'.[32] In the light of these statements and the earlier distinctions drawn between various forms of duress,[33] it appears that duress could have the following consequences.

When a transferor seeks restitution of a transfer induced by duress, it is crucial to determine whether the transfer is supported by some underlying obligation, for example, a contract, will or other instrument. If there is such an obligation, the claim will fail. It is presumably either up to the transferor to prove from the outset that the obligation is absent, for example, by seeking rescission of a contract,[34] or for the recipient to rely on the presence of such an obligation as a type of defence. One way in which the recipient may try to establish from the outset that the transfer was supported by such an obligation is to indicate that it was made pursuant to a contract (for example, an agreement of compromise or settlement), which is invalid and may be rescinded because it was concluded under duress. But the transferor need not necessarily rescind underlying obligations to succeed. He

[32] R3RUE (n 3) vol I, 183–84. According to § 14(3), if the effect of duress is tantamount to physical compulsion, a transfer induced by duress is void. If not, a transfer induced by duress conveys voidable title. Note that § 14 is not limited to contractual obligations, but could also be 'the basis for asserting the invalidity of a will, deed or other instrument': R3RUE (n 3) vol I, 181.

[33] See Part B, section (2).

[34] See § 54 on the specialised rules that govern claims for rescission and restitution of mutual performances under failed contracts.

could also establish that he has made an overpayment of a liquidated, previously subsisting obligation (for example, an obligation to pay an insurance premium). As we have seen earlier, he then only has to prove that the transfer was induced by 'duress light'.[35] However, once it is established that there was indeed a valid underlying obligation and that the transfer fulfilled it, the transfer cannot be reclaimed, irrespective of the type of duress which induced it. The duty to make restitution is only imposed if there is unjust enrichment, and there can be no unjust enrichment if the transfer fulfilled a valid obligation.[36] As the comment on § 14 states, 'the use of bad means to coerce payment of a just debt may be illegal, but it does not present a problem in unjust enrichment'.[37]

These principles must be read in conjunction with a doctrine of American law which traditionally views matters from the perspective of the defendant and enables him to defeat a claim for restitution of an undue payment. According to the doctrine of voluntary payment, such a claim is barred if the transferor elected to 'satisfy a doubtful claim in the face of a recognized uncertainty as to the underlying liability'.[38] The transferor is regarded as having assumed the risk of overpayment. The defendant would not be able to bar the claim for restitution if the claimant proves that he was subjected to duress and that the payment was therefore involuntary.[39]

(3) Legal Compulsion: §§ 18 and 19

It will be recalled that the category of legal compulsion comprises transfers made to satisfy judgments that were reversed (§ 18) and certain undue tax payments (§ 19).

Under § 18, the disadvantaged party who made the transfer in consequence of the subsequently reversed or avoided judgment is entitled to restitution. This claim is only recognised inasmuch as it is necessary to avoid unjust enrichment. Restitution would be denied if a party was compelled to pay under an invalid or erroneous judgment, and it transpires on appeal that he was in any event liable to pay, but only on different grounds. According to the comment on § 19:

[35] See Part B, section (2).

[36] See R3RUE (n 3) vol I, 197. For discussion of the question whether the presence of a contract justifying the defendant's enrichment should be seen as a defence or as a denial that the defendant's enrichment is unjust, see ch 6 in the present volume by James Goudkamp and Charles Mitchell at pp 151–52; and contrast Andrew Burrows' views in ch 7 in the present volume at pp 174–78.

[37] ibid vol I, 184.

[38] ibid vol I, 189. See also the definition in *Carey v Fitzpatrick*, 301 Mass 525, 527, 17 NE 2d 882, 883 (1938) quoted at 199: 'Money voluntarily paid under a claim of right, with full knowledge of the facts on the part of the one making the payment, cannot be recovered back unless there is fraud or concealment or compulsion by the party enforcing the claim.' It is disputed whether it is desirable for English law to recognise a comparable construct in the form of a defence of 'submission to an honest claim': Burrows (n 15) 255–56; *Goff & Jones* (n 15) 323–24 (deviating from earlier editions); Virgo (n 19) 668–71; Dannemann (n 15) 375.

[39] ibid vol I, 189. Proof of duress can also show that the payor did not intend to settle or compromise a dispute: ibid vol I, 184–85 and 189.

> [A]n invalid or erroneous judgment that gives effect to a valid liability does not create unjust enrichment: the ensuing transfer has a sufficient legal basis in the underlying liability, notwithstanding the deficiencies in the judgment.[40]

This suggests that the primary motivation behind awarding restitution in these cases is not a problem with volition arising from legal compulsion, but the lack of a legal basis for retaining the enrichment. This suggestion regarding the relevance of the problems with volition is strengthened by the fact that the voluntary payment rule does not apply if a debtor chooses to pay a judgment that he regards as invalid, without waiting for steps to be taken to enforce it.[41]

According to § 19:

> [T]he payment of a tax by mistake, or the payment of a tax that is erroneously or illegally assessed or collected, gives the taxpayer a claim in restitution against the taxing authority as necessary to prevent unjust enrichment.

The comment on this provision recognises that a variety of rationales or justifications exist for allowing such a claim.[42] These include mistake or duress, if it is of the quality demanded by § 14. However, the claim is usually regarded as *sui generis*, with its own special rules. The drafters therefore decided not to distribute the relevant authorities under headings like mistake and duress (which would in any event not be appropriate in cases where the mistake of law rule applied or the pressure was negligible),[43] but to allocate them to their own special provision, albeit within the broader category of 'legal compulsion'.[44] It is apparent, though, that within this *sui generis* category, it is of central importance that the transfer was not due.[45] According to the comment on § 19:

> It is not the taxpayer's willingness to pay that is the relevant consideration, but whether the payment corresponds to a proper legal liability. To the extent that it does not, the result is a transfer that lacks an adequate legal basis.[46]

[40] ibid vol I, 248–49.

[41] ibid vol I, 246–47 and 255.

[42] ibid vol I, 259–60.

[43] See, in the context of English law, the remarks of Lord Goff in *Woolwich* (n 21) 173.

[44] See Part B, section (3). As indicated earlier, English commentators do not regard claims for restitution of unlawfully demanded tax to be claims for the recovery of money paid under legal compulsion. They recognise that the duty of restitution is triggered by its own 'unjust factor', described as, for example, 'public authority exaction and payment': Burrows (n 15) 498–517.

[45] In the context of English law, it is worth pointing out that after his conversion to the absence of basis approach, Peter Birks strongly argued that undue payments of taxes to public authorities should simply be reclaimed because they were made to discharge obligations when there were none. As such, he came to consider that the 'diversion' through duress or principles of public law was unnecessary: P Birks, *Unjust Enrichment*, 2nd edn (Oxford, Oxford University Press, 2005) 133–35, discussing *Woolwich* (n 21) and *Mason v New South Wales* (1959) 102 CLR 108.

[46] R3RUE (n 3) vol I, 261. R3RUE recognises that these transfers differ from undue transfers made between private parties. Public authorities are regarded as bound by a special duty not to raise revenue in violation of statutory or constitutional limits. Thus, the taxpayer's transfer is not only one that lacks a legal basis ('the usual and sufficient condition of a claim in restitution'), but also one that the law 'implicitly forbids': ibid 261.

The voluntary payment rule also applies to claims for restitution of undue taxes.[47] Thus, if the defendant can prove that the transferor paid the tax despite knowing that it was erroneously or illegally assessed, it would indicate that the payment was made voluntarily and restitution would be denied. However, the payment would not be regarded as voluntary, despite such knowledge, if the transferor can show (i) that the payment resulted from duress or (ii) in certain jurisdictions, that the payment was made under protest; restitution would then be awarded.[48] Nevertheless, it is difficult to avoid the impression that it would often be artificial to regard an undue payment to public authorities as 'voluntary'. This impression is strengthened by a Reporter's Note which recognises that a finding that the payment was voluntary might hide a policy decision to protect a public authority's finances.[49] In this regard, § 19(2) allows courts to limit the taxpayer's right to restitution if it would disrupt orderly fiscal administration or result in severe public hardship.[50]

(4) Undue Contractual Performances: § 35

As indicated earlier, § 35 essentially allows a claim in restitution of a payment made under protest or reservation when a party demanded a payment in excess of what he was entitled to under a contract, and it was reasonable for the payor to accede to the demand. According to the Comment on § 35, the basis of the claim is not the statement that the performance is made 'under protest' or 'without prejudice' and the like.[51] The reason for restitution is 'that the claimant has performed under compulsion, conferring a benefit to which the defendant was not entitled under the contract'.[52] It therefore appears that a combination of circumstances trigger the duty of restitution: a contractual context that determines that the claimant is not obliged to make the performance (ie, that it is not owed) *and* the fact that the performance was made under 'compulsion'. The concept of 'compulsion' is not defined, but it presumably covers some form of pressure-inducing conduct falling short of an actual threat.

Claims for restitution under § 35 are subject to the voluntary payment rule.[53] The examples given in Part B, section (4) above, of the payments to the lender, insurer and public utility, suggest that a payment would be regarded as involuntary if the payor had no practical alternative but to submit to the demand. This is essentially the case if resistance by the party facing the demand would have created the risk of consequential harm going beyond the ordinary expense of legal

[47] ibid vol I, 269 and 278–79.
[48] ibid vol I, 269 and 278–83.
[49] ibid vol I, 278–99.
[50] For additional discussion of this point, see ch 6 of the present volume by James Goudkamp and Charles Mitchell at pp 159–61.
[51] R3RUE (n 3) vol I, 580.
[52] ibid vol I, 580.
[53] ibid vol I, 574–77 and 582–84.

proceedings.[54] It should therefore be apparent that even though § 35 does not expressly require proof that the claimant acted under pressure, such proof could be vital in showing that the voluntary payment rule should not bar the claim for restitution.

D. Civil Law Contrasts

(1) Introduction

A cornerstone of the civil law of unjustified enrichment is the requirement that the defendant must be enriched without legal ground. To determine whether this requirement has been met, the point of departure is to establish in what way the enrichment has been obtained. Traditionally, the most prominent manner of enrichment is where the claimant deliberately conferred a benefit on the defendant, ie, if he has made a transfer to him. This is the domain of the *condictiones*. It is then said that transfers are made for specific purposes, and if these purposes are not achieved, it indicates that the defendant is enriched without legal ground.[55] Each typical situation involving the failure of the purpose of a transfer could then be linked to its own specific enrichment claim or *condictio*.[56] It is therefore necessary to determine the purpose of a transfer in order to determine whether a duty of restitution should be imposed.

Historically, there has been some uncertainty about how to make this determination in cases where the claimant made a transfer due to unlawful threats of harm and related forms of pressure emanating from the recipient. It is generally accepted that the claimant's claim belongs to the category dealing with transfers made without legal ground, ie, that it is a *condictio* or some of its modern manifestations. However, there are different views on the possible purpose of a transfer

[54] Examples of the types of harm that arise from these cases of compulsion include losses that may result from the cancellation of the sale of property, the cancellation of the policy or the termination of services provided by a public authority, for example, the supply of water or electricity: R3RUE (n 3) vol I, 574 and 582–84.

[55] This argument has been used to explain why a *condictio* was awarded in Roman law: F Schwarz, *Die Grundlage der Condictio im klassischen römischen Recht* (Münster, Böhlau, 1952) 212; M Kaser, *Das römische Privatrecht*, 2nd edn (Munich, Beck, 1971) vol I, 595. It is also a popular explanation for awarding the *Leistungskondiktion*, which is the successor to the *condictio* in German law: HJ Wieling, *Bereicherungsrecht*, 3rd edn (Berlin, Springer, 2004) 15; R Zimmermann and J du Plessis, 'Basic Features of the German Law of Unjustified Enrichment' [1994] *Restitution Law Review* 14, 26. The argument also enjoys qualified support in South African law: D Visser, *Unjustified Enrichment* (Cape Town, Juta, 2008) 229–53; J du Plessis, *The South African Law of Unjustified Enrichment* (Cape Town, Juta, 2012) 66–67.

[56] Various provisions in the German Civil Code echo the *condictiones* of earlier uncodified law. See, eg, S Lorenz, *J von Staudingers Kommentar zum Bürgerlichen Gesetzbuch mit Einführungsgesetz und Nebengesetzen, Band 2: Recht der Schuldverhältnissen §§ 812–822 (Ungerechtfertigte Bereicherung)* (Berlin, Sellier de Gruyter, 2007) 176–99; Wieling (n 55) 23–42; Zimmermann and Du Plessis (n 55) 20–24 and 27.

obtained under pressure and hence on which *condictio* applies. The main possibilities will be considered in turn.

(2) The Enrichment Claim Based on the Failure of a Transfer to Achieve the Purpose of Fulfilling an Obligation (the *Condictio Indebiti*)

If a transfer is made with the purpose of fulfilling an obligation, but fails to do so, civil law systems traditionally awarded an enrichment claim called the *condictio indebiti*. In deciding whether this claim should be awarded, the pressure can be relevant in at least two ways.

First, proof of pressure may show that the obligation which a transfer was supposed to fulfil was invalid. This would generally be the case if the pressure took the form of unlawful threats that induced the claimant to conclude a contract, and the transfer was made in fulfilment of such a contract; the unlawful threat could then invalidate the contractual obligation, thereby rendering the transfer undue.[57]

However, civil law systems do not automatically award restitution of a transfer merely because it is not due or not owed. They take further circumstances into account in deciding whether the claimant should succeed. In this context, the pressure could again be relevant. Here different approaches have been adopted within the civilian tradition. Let us first consider the modern civilian approach, represented by German law.

(a) The Modern Civilian Approach: The Claimant Must Prove that the Transfer Was Not Owed; the Defendant May Respond with the Defence that the Transferor Knew that the Transfer Was Not Owed; the Claimant May then Defeat this Defence by Proving that He Acted under Certain Forms of Pressure

According to German law, a claimant seeking restitution of an undue transfer must prove that he made a transfer and that it was not due.[58] However, this is no guarantee of success. The transfer is only prima facie recoverable. According to

[57] See Englard (n 1) 51–55. It is accepted in the modern civilian approach that the claim for restitution arising from invalidity of a contract is the modern version of the *condictio* – the enrichment claim based on a transfer, more specifically the claim for restitution of a transfer which was aimed at fulfilling a (contractual) obligation, but which failed to do so: Lorenz (n 56) 177–78 and 180. Lorenz points out that even though the contract is valid until rescinded, the effect of rescission is to render the transfer made in fulfilment of it retrospectively not owed or undue. Such a transfer is consequently recoverable with an enrichment claim, namely the *Leistungskondiktion*. This claim is awarded by German law to ensure restitution of undue transfers, and it is the successor to the *condictio indebiti* of Roman law. Historically, it was said that if something is done as a consequence of duress (*metus*), the victim is entitled to *restitutio in integrum*, which was a remedy distinct from the *condictiones*.

[58] Lorenz (n 56) 183 and 215.

§ 814 BGB, something given with a purpose of fulfilling an obligation cannot be reclaimed if the transferor knew that he was not obliged to give it. Doubt does not count as knowledge.[59] Once the defendant proves such knowledge,[60] the ball is back in the claimant's court. The claimant may respond that he did indeed know that he was not obliged to make the transfer, but that he made the transfer under reservation of a right to reclaim,[61] or in a position of constraint (*Zwangslage*), for example, when he was threatened with enforcement of a judgment.[62] In these situations, which have been described as cases where the transferor did not act voluntarily,[63] the defence under § 814 BGB would fail and the claimant would be entitled to restitution of the undue transfer.

It has been said that the motivation behind § 814 BGB is the general notion that one should not engage in contradictory behaviour (*venire contra factum proprium*).[64] This suggests that an underlying purpose of § 814 BGB is to protect the recipient, who is first made to believe that the transferor intends him to have the transfer, but subsequently is confronted with a claim for restitution. This may explain why it was held in some cases that the defence in § 814 BGB does not apply if the recipient could not rely on being able to retain the transfer.[65] However, it has been doubted whether such a reliance-based approach could be inferred from § 814 BGB, given the provision's express focus on the state of mind of the transferor and, more specifically, on whether he knew that no debt was due, rather than on the reliance of the recipient.[66]

These difficulties are illustrated by a case where the defence of knowledge was held not to apply where a pension fund kept on depositing pension payments into the account of a deceased, even though the relatives had notified the fund of the recipient's death.[67] As Dannemann points out, it is unusual that the court found that the fund somehow did not act voluntarily and that § 814 BGB therefore did not apply.[68] The actual reason for excluding § 814 BGB, and awarding restitution, may have been that the relatives never relied on being entitled to keep the undue

[59] ibid 210.

[60] ibid 215–16; M Schwab, 'Titel 26. Ungerechtfertigte Bereicherung' in M Habersack (ed), *Münchener Kommentar zum Bürgerlichen Gesetzbuch*, 5th edn (Munich, CH Beck, 2009) 1484–85.

[61] The reservation of the right to reclaim must relate to the specific payment. It will therefore not be effective if the transferor routinely includes it in standard form notifications of payment. See G Dannemann, *The German Law of Unjustified Enrichment and Restitution: A Comparative Introduction* (Oxford, Oxford University Press, 2009) 77, and the discussion there of BGH 17.2.1982, BGHZ 83, 278, 282; OLG Koblenz 20.9.1983, NJW 1984, 135.

[62] Lorenz (n 56) 213. On the threat of execution of a judgment, see RGZ 147, 17, 21 (1939). It is less clear whether the defence would apply if the transferor knew that he was not obliged to comply with the defendant's demand for payment, yet was uncertain whether he would be able to prove that he is not liable.

[63] Dannemann (n 61) 77.

[64] Schwab (n 60) 1480; Lorenz (n 56) 209.

[65] See the examples cited in Schwab (n 60) 1482.

[66] ibid; Lorenz (n 56) 209.

[67] OLG Karlsruhe 30.12.1987, NJW 1988, 1920. Compare the similar facts of BGHZ 73, 202, 206 = NJW 1979, 763, discussed in Schwab (n 60) 1482; Lorenz (n 56) 209.

[68] Dannemann (n 61) 78.

transfer.[69] It may therefore have been preferable for the drafters of the BGB to formulate a defence which clearly indicates that restitution should be denied if the recipient does not have a protectable reliance on being able to keep the transfer. Proof that the recipient pressurised the claimant into making the undue transfer could assist in indicating that the recipient did not have such a reliance. However, this is not the route which the BGB has taken.

(b) The Traditional Civilian Approach: The Claimant Seeking Restitution Must Prove an Undue Transfer and Mistake or Certain Forms of Pressure

It was indicated in the previous section that German law regards an undue transfer as prima facie recoverable. However, not all civil law systems do so. Some require the claimant to prove at the outset that the transfer was not due (an *indebitum*) *and* that there were additional circumstances which warrant awarding restitution. Historically, the most prominent of these circumstances is that the claimant was in error or mistaken about liability. Requiring proof of an *indebitum* and an error as to liability is the essential construction of the *condictio indebiti* under what could be called the 'traditional', as opposed to 'modern' civilian approach; it was also the position in German law until codification in 1900.[70] These systems do, however, recognise that when a person makes an undue transfer under certain forms of pressure, he generally knows that the transfer is due and therefore cannot prove mistake. Their solution is to recognise that the pressure can essentially take the place of mistake[71] or that it could be an alternative circumstance that indicates that the transfer must be returned.[72]

(3) Enrichment Claims Based on Pressure and a Possible Taint of Illegality (the *Condictio Ob Turpem Vel Iniustam Causam* or the *Condictio Ex Iniusta Causa*)

In the previous section, it was shown that in the civilian tradition, the claim for restitution of an undue transfer (the *condictio indebiti*) may be used to obtain restitution of a transfer obtained by certain forms of pressure. However, this is not the only remedy favoured for obtaining restitution of such a transfer. It has been argued that when a person is compelled to make a transfer, it may be

[69] ibid: 'Importance was attached to the fact that the heirs were fully aware that they could not rely on retaining the pension, and this is presumably the policy issue which lay behind the dubious argument of voluntariness in the case.'

[70] See generally R Zimmermann, *The Law of Obligations* (Cape Town, Juta, 1990) 834–35, 841–42, 848–51 and 866–71. On the background to the shift in German law, see also D König, *Ungerechtfertigte Bereicherung: Tatbestände und Ordnungsprobleme in rechtsvergleichender Sicht* (Heidelberg, Winter, 1985) 41–42.

[71] On Austrian, French and Italian law, see Schlechtriem (n 1) 168, 170 and 171 n 607.

[72] On South African law, see J du Plessis, *Compulsion and Restitution* (Edinburgh, Stair Society, 2004) 110–11; J Beatson and E Schrage (eds), *Cases, Materials and Texts on Unjustified Enrichment* (Oxford, Hart Publishing, 2003) 392–94.

inappropriate to regard it as a transfer aimed at fulfilling an obligation.[73] On this analysis, the *condictio indebiti* would not apply, since it is by definition limited to reclaiming transfers aimed at fulfilling obligations. The transferor will have to rely on another category of enrichment claim to obtain restitution.

Different labels have been attached to this other category of claim. The most prominent are the *condictio ob turpem vel iniustam causam*, which features in Roman, Roman-Dutch and Scots law,[74] and the *condictio ex iniusta causa*, which is especially prominent in pre-codification German law.[75] The German Civil Code does not expressly require that transfers obtained by pressurising another belong to a distinct category of claim,[76] but such a development has been proposed by Detlef König in his draft codification of the German law on unjustified enrichment. Apart from a claim for restitution in § 1 I 1 for various transfers that fail to fulfil obligations (ie, a *condictio indebiti*), his draft expressly provides in § 1 III that: 'A person who transfers something to another, not in order to fulfill an obligation, but on account of compulsion or threat, may reclaim the benefit, unless the recipient proves that he had a right to the benefit.'[77] A number of examples are cited of cases which would fall under § 1 III. A threat of criminal prosecution in an unrelated matter is used to enforce a doubtful demand for payment of a purchase price. A tenant who is vacating the premises pays for repairs, even though he is not obliged to do so, because the landlord threatened that he would exercise a right to attach the tenant's property if the payment is not made. Alternatively, a representative who was dismissed by a business for being unfaithful could threaten to disclose its weak financial position to its bankers to induce the business to pay his claim for damages.[78]

Some problems arise from this practice of the civil law not to bring claims for restitution of transfers obtained by pressure under the *condictio indebiti*. If the reason for restitution is not the failure of the transfer to fulfil an obligation, what are the alternatives? One possibility, which is rather apparent from the names of

[73] See König (n 70) 47; also compare Dannemann (n 61) 34. For further analyses of what constitutes the purpose of a transfer obtained by compulsion, see Du Plessis (n 55) 66–67.

[74] On Roman law, see D.12.5.7, which suggests that this *condictio* should be awarded if money was obtained under a stipulation extorted by force. On Roman-Dutch law, see J Voet, *Commentarius ad Pandectas* (Paris, A Maurice, 1829) 12.5.1. On Scots law, see The Rt Hon Lord Coulsfield and HL MacQueen (gen eds), *The Law of Scotland by W M Gloag & R Candlish Henderson*, 12th edn (Edinburgh, W Green/Sweet & Maxwell, 2007) para 25.14. Pressure could influence the availability of the *par delictum* rule, which restricts the availability of this *condictio*: Du Plessis (n 55) 80–82 and 106–07.

[75] See König (n 70) 47; D König 'Ungerechtfertigte Bereicherung' in Bundesministerium der Justiz, *Gutachten und Vorschläge zur Überarbeitung des Schuldrechts* (Cologne, Bundesanzeiger Verlag, 1981) 1515, 1543 especially n 73; Schlechtriem (n 1) 166–67. The precise scope of this *condictio* is disputed; it covers a variety of transfers or dispositions obtained in an unlawful manner, which includes transfers obtained by compulsion.

[76] On the possible application of § 817 I BGB (the modern manifestation of the *condictio ob turpem vel iniustam causam*) in cases of compulsion, see Wieling (n 55) 34; Schwab (n 60) 1526; König (1985) (n 70) 48.

[77] König (1981) (n 75) 1522–25; the translation is from R Zimmermann, 'Unjustified Enrichment: The Modern Civilian Approach' (1995) 15(3) *OJLS* 403, 426.

[78] König (n 75) 1543.

the *condictiones* referred to above, is that the lack of legal ground for retaining the compelled transfer arises from a taint of illegality: the transfer or the transaction giving rise to the transfer could be regarded as being aimed at an unlawful purpose. According to this analysis, it does not matter that the transferor achieved the purpose of averting the harm; the purpose is in any event unlawful. In principle, there can be no objection to such an analysis as long as the taint of illegality is indeed present. This may be easy to establish in cases of extortion, such as in the case of the unfaithful representative. However, it is less convincing to find illegality in some of the lighter forms of compulsion, such as bona fide threats of resorting to lawful judicial processes to obtain payment of a contractual debt which the recipient believes to be owed to him. In these cases, there may still be pressure, and the transferor may still not intend to pay, yet it appears artificial to regard the transfer as tainted by illegality.[79]

The second problem is the recoverability of due transfers obtained by pressure. This is a complex matter, which I have dealt with in some detail elsewhere.[80] Suffice it to say that there is no uniform civilian approach to this issue. The König draft clearly favours the view that the compelled due transfer cannot be reclaimed. The victim would have to seek redress outside the law of unjustified enrichment, for example, by resorting to claims in delict. This view is also supported by civil law maxims which regard it as objectionable to reclaim something which had to be given in any event (*dolo petit qui petit quod statim redditurus est*).[81] However, an enrichment claim could potentially be allowed if it cannot be found that the compelled transfer fulfilled the obligation owed by the transferor. It remains unclear, though, under which *condictio* such a claim belongs.[82]

(4) Public Law Claims for Reimbursement

The overview of claims for restitution in the civil law can be completed by mentioning that in addition to the private law enrichment claims referred to above, certain systems recognise public law claims aimed at providing reimbursement of public law or administrative transfers that lack a legal ground for their retention.[83] Although there are clear parallels with the private law enrichment claim for a transfer made without legal ground, most notably the *condictio indebiti*,[84] the preconditions for and measure of relief may differ.[85] Most importantly, certain controls are in place to prevent the 'floodgates' problem that public finances could be

[79] See Du Plessis (n 72) 175–76; Du Plessis (n 55) 139 n 315.

[80] See Du Plessis (n 1) 213–18.

[81] See D.44.4.8pr; D.50.17.173.3.

[82] See Du Plessis (n 1) 213–18; Chen-Wishart (n 1) 193; du Plessis (n 55) 203, 249–50.

[83] See generally Lorenz (n 56) 79–90; S Meier, *Irrtum und Zweckverfehlung* (Tübingen, Mohr Siebeck, 1990) 220; B Häcker, '"Public Law Restitutionary Claims": The German Perspective' in S Elliott, B Häcker and C Mitchell (eds), *Restitution of Overpaid Tax* (Oxford, Hart Publishing, 2013).

[84] See Lorenz (n 56) 83–84.

[85] ibid 83.

severely disrupted through awarding claims for restitution of a multitude of payments which had been made under the incorrect impression that they were owed to a public authority.[86]

E. Comparative Evaluation

(1) Three Potential Roles of Duress and Related Forms of Pressure

From the overviews above, it is apparent that there are at least three ways in which duress and related forms of pressure could influence the decision to award restitution. These ways essentially relate to the prominence accorded to the pressure. First, a claimant who made a transfer could rely on the pressure to establish a prima facie right to restitution. The right is lost if it is shown that the defendant is nonetheless entitled to retain the transfer because it is owed to him. Second, the pressure could play a more modest role. The pressure could merely be something which the claimant seeking restitution must prove in conjunction with the fact that the transfer is not owed to the defendant. Finally, it may not be necessary for the claimant to allege that he was subjected to pressure to found a claim of restitution; all he may have to allege is that he made a transfer which was not owed to the recipient. It would then be up to the defendant to raise a defence which would allow him to keep the transfer. However, the pressure is not irrelevant. The claimant may in turn rely on the fact that he was subjected to pressure to defeat this defence. These three roles will be investigated in turn.

(2) Role 1: Duress and Related Forms of Pressure as Grounds for a Prima Facie Right to Restitution

As we have seen earlier, the point of departure in § 14 of R3RUE is that a transfer induced by duress is 'subject to rescission and restitution'.[87] Although the drafters have avoided engaging in doctrinal debates, it could be said that R3RUE treats duress as a type of unjust factor, which triggers a prima facie right to restitution.[88] It is only if it is established that the transfer was supported by a valid obligation that the claim would fail. This could be done, for example, by showing that the

[86] See Meier (n 83) 219–20 on time limitations that apply to challenges to administrative acts and resultant claims for restitution.

[87] See Part C, section (2).

[88] See, eg, *Goff & Jones* (n 15) 8: 'a claimant will have a prima facie right to restitution where he has transferred a benefit to the defendant by mistake, under duress, or on a basis that fails. Nevertheless, the defendant can escape liability if another rule entitles him to keep the benefit, and this rule overrides the general rule generated by the law of unjust enrichment which entitles the claimant to restitution'.

transfer was made pursuant to an underlying settlement agreement or that it compensated the defendant for losses caused by the transferor.

As indicated earlier, this type of thinking has rather curious parallels in the civilian tradition. It will be recalled that according to one strand of civilian learning, if the pressure is so strong that the transfer cannot be regarded as being aimed at fulfilling an obligation, then a claim for restitution (called a *condictio ex iniusta causa* in pre-codified German law) could be brought by the transferor. The duress then taints the transfer and renders it recoverable.[89] It will also be recalled that on this approach, restitution would be denied if the transfer was nonetheless owed to the recipient.[90] Note, however, that this approach does not draw a distinction between 'duress' and 'mistake', as in R3RUE and in lists of unjust factors in the common law. The distinction is between transfers that cannot be regarded as being aimed at fulfilling an obligation, due to the compulsion (the *condictio ex iniusta causa*), and transfers which can be regarded as being aimed at fulfilling an obligation, but then fail to achieve this aim because no debt is due (the *condictio indebiti*).

(3) Role 2: Duress and Related Forms of Pressure as Circumstances that Give Rise to a Right to Restitution When Taken in Conjunction with the Fact that a Transfer Was Not Owed

In this second category, the combination of the fact that a transfer was not due *and* that the transferor acted under pressure gives rise to a right to restitution. It appears that § 14 of R3RUE follows such an approach in cases of 'duress light', ie, good faith threats of lawful action.[91] The claimant must prove both this form of duress and the fact that there was an overpayment of a liquidated, previously subsisting obligation. This approach also characterises some civil law systems, which follow the traditional civilian approach of requiring that the transferor who seeks to reclaim a transfer that failed to fulfil an obligation must prove that it was not due *and* that he was mistaken as to liability, or that he acted under some form of pressure.[92]

At this juncture, it may be appropriate to pause briefly and consider a problem which characterises contemporary debates on approaches to enrichment liability. It concerns the old problem in comparative law of using terminology which bears a specific technical meaning in one system to describe the law of another system. Can it be said that in fulfilling this second role, mistake or pressure act as 'unjust factors' in American and civil law? Technically, the answer is quite simple: no.

[89] See Part D, section (3).

[90] See Part D, section (3).

[91] See Part B, section (2) and Part C, section (2).

[92] See Part D, section (2)(b). The civil law systems may regard the fact that the transfer was not due as more significant or important than the pressure, but this does not alter the fact that the claimant must prove that both are present.

The mistake or pressure is not an unjust factor in the sense in which this term is normally used in the common law, namely to denote a *primary* ground or reason for awarding restitution, which could be defeated by a defence that the transfer is due.[93] To refer to it as an unjust factor is misleading and confusing. The mistake or pressure plays a weaker role. It is only when it is taken in conjunction with proof that the transfer was not due that it gives rise to a claim. At best, mistake or pressure plays the role of a 'weak' unjust factor.[94] It is not clear, though, what it adds to describe civil law in these terms.[95]

Thus far, the focus has been on claims for restitution of undue transfers brought under § 14 in cases of 'duress light'. The position under §§ 35 and 19 remains to be considered. It will be recalled that these provisions cover payments made under protest or reservation, while reasonably acceding to a demand for payment in excess of what a party was entitled to under a contract (§ 35), and payments of tax that is 'erroneously or illegally assessed or collected' (§ 19). Both these provisions could cover situations involving pressure which need not emanate from a threat. But are these cases where pressure is a circumstance that, in conjunction with the fact that a transfer was not owed, gives rise to a claim of restitution? From the comment to § 35, it appears that it is indeed susceptible to such an analysis: the duty of restitution arises from the contractual context which determines that the claimant is not obliged to make the performance (ie, that it is not owed) *and* the fact that the performance was made under 'compulsion'.[96]

In the case of § 19, the position is less clear. That pressure may arise from being subjected to a process of assessment and collection of taxes cannot be doubted. However, as we have seen, there are many justifications for awarding claims for restitution against public authorities. It is therefore difficult to ascribe pressure the prominent role of being the consideration which, in conjunction with the fact that the tax is not owed, triggers a claim of restitution.[97] This analysis is also in line with the practice of some civilian systems not to award the normal private law claims for restitution of undue transfers in these cases, and rather to make use of *sui generis* administrative remedies.[98]

[93] For this definition, see *Goff & Jones* (n 15) 8.

[94] See H Scott and D Visser, 'The Impact of Legal Culture on the Law of Unjustified Enrichment: The Role of Reasons' in E Bant and M Harding (eds), *Exploring Private Law* (Cambridge, Cambridge University Press, 2010) 155.

[95] See J du Plessis, 'Comparison and Evaluation: Lessons from Enrichment Law' (2012) 76 *Rabels Zeitschrift für ausländisches und internationales Privatrecht* 947 963.

[96] See Part C, section (4); R3RUE (n 3) vol I, 580 and 572.

[97] See Part B, section (3).

[98] See Part D, section (4).

(4) Role 3: Duress and Related Forms of Pressure as Circumstances that Affect the Availability of a Defence to a Claim for Restitution of an Undue Transfer

In the third category, it is unnecessary for the claimant to prove duress or related forms of pressure as an element of his claim. It is only if the defendant raises certain defences that the claimant may seek to defeat them by proving that the recipient subjected him to pressure.

As we have seen, this approach is followed in modern German law. If the claimant proves that a transfer was made to fulfil an obligation, but failed to do so, the transfer is prima facie recoverable (§ 812 I BGB). The defendant may then raise the defence that the transferor knew that the transfer was not due (§ 814 BGB). This defence will in turn fail if the transferor proves that he reserved the right to reclaim, or that he was in a position of constraint or pressure.[99] In American law, there is of course no such general mechanism. However, aspects of the voluntary payment rule resemble § 814 BGB. Both rules effectively say that the transferor's state of mind was such that he should not have made an undue transfer, and in making this determination, both take into account whether he acted under certain forms of pressure.[100]

In the light of possible parallels between the voluntary payment rule and the defence contained in § 814 BGB that the transferor knew that no debt was due, it is appropriate to return, if only briefly, to a problem which was discussed in the context of the latter provision.[101] It was said that a possible motivation behind the defence in § 814 BGB is to protect the recipient's reliance on being entitled to retain the transfer. If it appeared that the transfer was made in the knowledge that it was not owed, the defendant would be entitled to accept that the payor may have intended to settle a dispute or to make a donation, or that he may simply not have cared that the transfer was not due. He should not subsequently act contrary to this impression. It was added that it is doubtful why such a defence should be awarded if the recipient could not rely on being entitled to retain the transfer.

A similar question could be asked about the operation of the voluntary payment rule: even if the transfer was voluntary, why should the recipient be able to bar restitution if he in any event never believed that the transfer was his to retain? This line of analysis moves the focus further away from the state of mind of the payor towards that of the recipient. Ultimately, it can be argued that if the payor proves that the transfer was not owed to the defendant, it should be up to the defendant to raise a defence that he had a protectable reliance on nonetheless being entitled to keep the transfer. Such a broad approach could potentially unify

[99] See Part D, section (2)(a).
[100] For an example of the defendant relying on the voluntary payment rule as a defence, which requires determining that the claimant acted under pressure, see *Still v Equitable Life Assurance Society*, 165 Tenn 224, 54 SW 2d 947 (1932) 949; § 14 further see Part C, sections (3) and (4).
[101] See Part D, section (2)(a).

claims for restitution of undue transfers that are now spread over provisions like §§ 14 and 35.

However, such a development would require American law to be more favourably disposed towards the payor. At present, the focus is more on his state of mind than on that of the recipient, and the expectation is that if the payor believes that he does not have to pay, or even merely doubts it, he must refuse to pay, unless he can meet the specific requirements of those provisions. Such a broad approach might also be contrary to a general preference in R3RUE not to formulate rules at such a high level of abstraction.[102]

F. Concluding Remarks

This chapter has attempted to show that when dealing with the restitution of transfers made under pressure, R3RUE adopts a nuanced approach, which, unlike its predecessor, requires quite subtle differentiations between various types of pressure. It is only in a limited set of circumstances that pressure, more specifically duress, acts as an unjust factor, ie, a primary or main 'positive' reason for awarding restitution. In some important cases, such as 'duress light', it is the combination of the fact that a transfer was not due and the pressure that trigger a duty of restitution. The pressure then cannot be regarded as the primary reason for restitution. It is at best a 'weak' unjust factor. The fact that the transfer was not owed may be just as strong a 'positive' reason for restitution.[103] This calls into question whether American law really maintains a 'confident allegiance to unjust factors', as has been suggested.[104] It is also interesting, from a comparative perspective at least, that American law at times regards pressure as relevant in determining whether a defence raised against a claim for restitution of an undue transfer should succeed. This displays curious parallels with the modern civilian approach.

[102] See more generally Gergen (n 18) 263, who contrasts the approach of R3RUE to that of Peter Birks with regard to 'trying to identify the smallest set of underlying principles or basic concepts from which . . . rules can be derived'.

[103] See Du Plessis (n 95) II.3.

[104] M McInnes, 'The Reason to Reverse: Unjust Factors and Juristic Reasons' (2012) 92 *Boston University Law Review* 1049, 1054 and 1065. A clear illustration of how the position differs from the unjust factors approach, as applied in English law, is provided by *CTN Cash & Carry* (n 15); American law would not deny restitution in such a case for want of proof of an 'unjust factor': see Part B, section (2).

5

Undue Influence: Lessons from America?

WILLIAM SWADLING

A. Introduction

The law of undue influence in England is in a mess. The purpose of this chapter is to see whether the treatment of the topic in the *Restatement Third: Restitution and Unjust Enrichments*,[1] to be found in § 15,[2] helps resolve any of the uncertainties which bedevil English law in this area. It focuses on the following eight areas: (1) the relationship between 'actual' and 'presumed' undue influence; (2) the nature of undue influence; (3) the facts necessary to raise a presumption of undue influence; (4) the facts which need to be proved to rebut this presumption; (5) the content of the presumption; (6) whether any presumption at all is involved; (7) the test of causation; and (8) the undue influence of a third hand. Unfortunately, R3RUE does not take us very much further forward as regards these issues. Indeed, in one respect at least, it fails to learn a simple lesson from English law.

B. The Relationship between Actual and Presumed Undue Influence

A pernicious division is drawn in England between two types of undue influence: 'actual' and 'presumed'. The question for English lawyers is whether they are the same thing, with the latter merely being proved with the help of a presumption, or different things altogether.

[1] American Law Institute, *Restatement Third: Restitution and Unjust Enrichment* (St Paul, MN, American Law Institute Publishers, 2011) (hereinafter 'R3RUE').

[2] The black letter provides as follows: '§ 15. Undue Influence (1) Undue influence is excessive and unfair persuasion, sufficient to overcome the free will of the transferor, between parties who occupy a confidential relation or a relation of dominance on the one side and subservience on the other. (2) A transfer induced by undue influence is subject to rescission and restitution. The transferee is liable in restitution as necessary to avoid unjust enrichment.'

The distinction derives from the seminal case of *Allcard v Skinner*.[3] A detailed account of this case is important, for it sheds light on many of the problems currently encountered in our law. The claimant was introduced by her 'spiritual director and confessor', the Rev D Nihill, to the Lady Superior of the sisterhood of St Mary at the Cross,[4] the defendant in this action. Soon afterwards, the claimant became an associate of the sisterhood, promising to devote her property to the service of the poor. She subsequently became a postulant, then a novice, before eventually joining the sisterhood itself. On becoming a sister, she took a number of vows and became subject to the rules of the order, which demanded her implicit obedience to the Lady Superior, whose voice was said to be the 'voice of God'. Moreover, she was not to seek the advice of any external person without the Superior's leave. She also took a vow of poverty, which required her to give away all her rights. Although there was no requirement that she give it to the sisterhood, there was an expectation to that effect. In fact, she gave them rights worth over £8,500, a huge sum in today's terms, all that she was able to give away. She left the sisterhood a few years later and, later still, sought to recover the rights on the ground of undue influence. Her claim failed, though only on the ground of delay.

Cotton LJ held that the claimant must be considered as being 'not in the largest and amplest sense of the term – not in mind as well as person – an entirely free agent'.[5] Lindley LJ said that though there was no evidence of any pressure, deception or unfair advantage being taken of her, the claimant was:

> [A]bsolutely in the power of the lady superior and Mr Nihill. A gift made by her under these circumstances to the lady superior cannot . . . be retained by the donee. The equitable title of the donee is imperfect by reason of the influence inevitably resulting from her position.[6]

The gift, he said, was 'so large as not to be reasonably accounted for on the ground of friendship, relationship, charity, or other motives on which ordinary men act', and therefore the 'burden was on the donee to support the gift'.[7]

Bowen LJ said that simply because the claimant was enthusiastic about religion, she was not dead in law. But while there was no duress, incompetency or want of mental power on her part:

> [Equity] will not allow a person who exercises or enjoys a dominant religious influence over another to benefit directly or indirectly by the gifts which the donor makes under or in consequence of such influence, unless it is shewn that the donor at the time of making the gift was allowed full and free opportunity for counsel and advice outside.[8]

[3] *Allcard v Skinner* (1887) 36 Ch D 145.

[4] The factual background to the case is examined in detail by Charlotte Smith in C Mitchell and P Mitchell (eds), *Landmark Cases in Restitution* (Oxford, Hart Publishing, 2006) 183–211.

[5] *Allcard v Skinner* (n 3) 172, citing Knight-Bruce LJ in *Wright v Vanderplank* (1856) 8 DM & G 133, 137.

[6] *Allcard v Skinner* (n 3) 184.

[7] ibid 185.

[8] ibid 190.

How are we to describe a case such as *Allcard v Skinner*? Unfortunately, to simply call it 'undue influence' is not enough, for that phrase is inherently uncertain. As will be seen below, the words can encompass a whole host of things, including misrepresentation and duress, neither of which was present on the facts.[9] The problem in *Allcard* was essentially a lack of emancipation on the part of the claimant from the defendant, and that is the term which will be adopted in this chapter.[10]

That undue influence might encompass more than one type of unjust factor is indeed acknowledged in the judgments of the Court of Appeal. Thus, Lindley LJ said that the fact that there was no unfair or improper conduct, no coercion, meant that there was no 'actual' exercise of influence.[11] But this was not fatal to the success of the action, he said, which was based on the operation of a presumption which operated to force the defendant to 'support the gift'.[12]

An example of what Lindley LJ called 'actual' undue influence is *Williams v Bayley*.[13] There, a son forged his father's signature on some promissory notes in order to obtain a loan of £7,000. When the forgery was discovered, the lending bank insisted on the father covenanting to pay the amount of the loan, which was to be secured by an equitable mortgage by deposit of title deeds to land held by him. Should the father refuse to sign the deed, the implicit threat was that the bank would prosecute his son for forgery, the punishment being transportation to Australia for life. With the benefit of legal advice throughout, the father signed the requisite documents; the notes with the forged endorsements were then delivered up to him. The son later absconded and, on the bank's proceedings against the father on the debt, he successfully sought a declaration that the agreement was void and for delivery up of the title deeds in exchange for the fraudulently endorsed notes. Lord Chelmsford said:

> The fears of the father were stimulated and operated on to an extent to deprive him of free agency, and to extort an agreement from him for the benefit of the bankers. It appears to me, therefore, that the case comes within the principles on which a Court of equity proceeds in setting aside an agreement where there is inequality between the parties, and one of them takes unfair advantage of the situation of the other, and uses undue influence to force an agreement from him.[14]

Despite the label used by Lord Chelmsford, this case is a clear example of what common lawyers would nowadays call 'duress' and a long way from a case like *Allcard v Skinner*. Why then was the language of undue influence used? The answer is that at the time that *Williams v Bayley* was decided, duress at common

[9] We see this, eg, in Lord Hobhouse's speech in *Royal Bank of Scotland v Etridge (No 2)* [2002] 2 AC 773 [103], where he describes undue influence as including duress and misrepresentation. The passage is reproduced below, text to nn 22.

[10] I am grateful to Elise Bant for this suggestion.

[11] *Allcard v Skinner* (n 3) 183–84.

[12] *Allcard v Skinner* (n 3) 185.

[13] *Williams v Bayley* (1866) LR 1 HL 200.

[14] ibid 216.

law was limited to duress of the person[15] and duress of goods.[16] As Lord Nicholls explained in *Royal Bank of Scotland v Etridge (No 2)*, duress at common law was originally 'narrow in scope, restricted to the more blatant forms of physical coercion'.[17] Therefore, unless equity was to be seen as flatly contradicting the common law, there was a need for some other label for duress cases falling short of threats to the person or goods. That need no longer exists, for since the decision of Kerr J in *The Siboen & The Sibotre* in 1976,[18] the common law of duress is no longer so confined. Case such as *Williams v Bayley* and all other cases of threats can now be dealt with at common law under the heading of duress. As Birks and Chin note, it is 'difficult to conceive of any pressure which will not be relieved satisfactorily, if it should be relieved at all, within the category of duress'.[19]

Therefore, when in *Allcard v Skinner* Lindley LJ spoke of 'actual' undue influence, he was referring to the sort of undue influence typified by *Williams v Bayley*, that is, duress in equity, with 'presumed' undue influence describing the fact scenario in *Allcard* itself. They were, in other words, different things. Unfortunately, the second view posited above, that actual and presumed undue influence are one and the same thing, the difference between them arising only in relation to matters of proof, seems to have taken hold of late, at least in some quarters. Thus, the authors of *Goff & Jones*, referring to the decision of the House of Lords in *Royal Bank of Scotland v Etridge (No 2)*, say that it is wrong to think there are two different things going on behind the labels. They say:

> In *Etridge*, the House of Lords held that this was a misunderstanding. They held that there is only one type of undue influence. There are two different ways of proving that undue influence has occurred, but what is being proved in either case is the same. 'Actual undue influence' should therefore be seen as undue influence that is directly proved without the need to rely on presumptions, and 'presumed undue influence' should be seen as undue influence that is proved with the help of presumptions. Actual and presumed undue influence are not mutually exclusive types of undue influence, nor are they alternatives.[20]

However, this is not quite what *Etridge* decided. Although Jonathan Sumption QC, as he then was, argued for one type of undue influence,[21] Lord Nicholls continued to distinguish between actual and presumed undue influence, as did Lord Hobhouse, who described 'actual' undue influence as:

[15] *Scott v Sebright* (1886) 12 PD 21; *Hussein v Hussein* [1938] P 159.

[16] *Astley v Reynolds* (1731) 2 Str 915.

[17] *Etridge* (n 9) [6].

[18] *Occidental Worldwide Investment Corp v Skibs A/S Avanti, The Siboen & The Sibotre* [1976] 1 Lloyd's Rep 293.

[19] P Birks and NY Chin, 'On the Nature of Undue Influence' in J Beatson and D Friedmann (eds), *Good Faith and Fault in Contract* (Oxford, Oxford University Press, 1995) 51, 64.

[20] C Mitchell, P Mitchell and S Watterson, *Goff & Jones: The Law of Unjust Enrichment*, 8th edn (London, Sweet & Maxwell, 2011) [11-06]. Curiously, at [11-32], *Williams v Bayley* (n 13) is described as a case of undue influence, though it is acknowledged that it could also be pleaded as duress. What is not noticed, however, is that *Allcard v Skinner* cannot be seen in such terms, the very point Lindley LJ was attempting to make.

[21] *Etridge* (n 9) 784.

> An equitable wrong committed by the dominant party against the other which makes it unconscionable for the dominant party to enforce his legal rights against the other. It is typically some express conduct overbearing the other party's will. It is capable of including conduct which might give a defence at law, for example, duress and misrepresentation.[22]

This is hardly what happened in *Allcard v Skinner*. Only Lord Scott might be seen as saying anything approaching what the authors of *Goff & Jones* claim for the case, but even his comments are equivocal.[23]

What is the cause of this confusion? The difficulty stems from a poor system of classification, in that the terms 'actual' and 'presumed' are not logically opposed. This seems not to be appreciated by the authors of *Goff & Jones*, who, as we have seen, view them as both concerned with proof. As will be demonstrated, only the latter is part of the law of proof. The word 'actual', by contrast, is an element of the substantive law. Let me explain.

In common parlance, the word 'actual' is normally only used for emphasis, as, for example, in the phrase 'this is the actual room in which Cromwell plotted against the King'. However, this is not its meaning in law. When we speak of 'actual' possession, 'actual' notice and so on, the word 'actual' is being used not for emphasis, but in opposition to 'constructive', so that 'actual' possession is not 'constructive' possession, and 'actual' notice is not 'constructive' notice. When, in turn, we speak of constructive possession or constructive notice, we mean to indicate that the possession or notice is 'deemed' or 'fictional'. So, for example, constructive notice is notice which a person does not have but would have had if he had made reasonable enquiries and inspections. It is attributed to him by operation of law. Similarly, constructive possession is possession a person does not have but which is attributed to him by operation of law. So, for example, the receipt of a sum of money on my behalf by my solicitor puts me in constructive, though not actual, possession of the money.[24]

'Actual', by contrast, means 'genuine' or 'real'.[25] 'Actual' notice is what I know, not what I am deemed to know; 'actual' possession is what I have in my hand, not what I am deemed to have in my hand. Moreover, the terms 'actual' and 'constructive' are concerned with rules of substantive law, not with proof of facts. Thus, in cases of constructive knowledge, it is not being said that the person involved knew the facts in question. We realise that he did not, but say it does not matter. What is being said, in other words, is that for the purposes of the rule in question, for example, the bona fide purchase defence to claims against the recipient of rights dissipated in breach of trust, the rule of substantive law is that those who have knowledge or should have had knowledge of the breach are barred from

[22] ibid [103].

[23] ibid [151]. Lord Bingham agreed with both Lord Nicholls and Lord Scott, but added the rider that should they be seen at variance on any point, he preferred the speech of Lord Nicholls: [3].

[24] *Re Fewster* [1901] 1 Ch 447.

[25] It is sometimes said that actual possession is possession in fact and constructive possession is possession in law. This is confused, for both are types of possession recognised by the law.

the defence. In other words, knowledge is not a prerequisite of the defence being barred, and the extension of the bar to those with 'constructive' knowledge is just a clumsy way of expressing this fact.[26] In such a case, it will avail the defendant nothing to bring evidence which satisfies the court that he had no knowledge himself. It is beside the point, for no rule of proof is here engaged. It is for this reason that the presence of constructive knowledge is not open to rebuttal.

The word 'presumption', by contrast, relates to questions of fact, not substantive law, and, more particularly, how facts are proved. It is a method of proof. As is well known, the general rule in litigation is that a claimant bears the burden of proof of all facts which are not admitted or of which the judge does not take judicial notice. However, in certain limited circumstances, on proof by evidence or admission[27] of one or more 'primary facts', a secondary fact will be proved by presumption, that is, without evidence or admission. The effect of such 'proof by presumption' is to place the burden of proof on the other party to the litigation, obliging him to adduce evidence demonstrating the untruth of the secondary fact. Should he fail to do so, the court is bound to find the secondary fact proved against him.[28] Such presumptions are generally known as 'presumptions of law'.[29]

An example of a presumption of law is the presumption of legitimacy, whereby on proof by evidence or admission that the husband of a child's mother had 'access' to the mother at the date of conception, a presumption arises that he is the child's father.[30] It is vital to understand that, though known as a presumption of law, no issues of substantive law are here engaged. Some person really is the child's father. It is not a case where there is no father at all, only a deemed or constructive father: we are not concerned with an immaculate conception. Instead, what is happening is that the court finds, in the absence of evidence to the contrary and as a matter of fact, that the husband is the father of the child. Crucially, however, the husband is able to adduce evidence in rebuttal. As we have seen, this would not be possible were he instead a 'constructive' father.

Thus, there is no logical contrast between 'actual' and 'presumed' undue influence: the former is a division of substantive law, the latter one of procedural law. Although it is possible to contrast 'actual' and 'constructive' undue influence, or 'proved by evidence, admission, or judicial notice' undue influence and 'proved by presumption' undue influence, any attempt to oppose actual and presumed undue influence is bound to fail, for they are categories in different series. Unfortunately, this is precisely how the subject is divided up.

The falsity of the opposition between the two types of undue influence was recently noted by Lord Clyde in *Royal Bank of Scotland v Etridge (No 2)*, who rightly said that it confused 'definition and proof'.[31] Unfortunately, not all of their

[26] *cf* L Fuller, *Legal Fictions* (Stanford, CA, Stanford University Press, 1967) 56–70.
[27] It is an empirical truth that judicial notice has no application as a trigger for any presumption.
[28] See WJ Swadling, 'Explaining Resulting Trusts' (2008) 124 *LQR* 72, 74–80.
[29] Or sometimes 'legal presumptions'.
[30] *The Banbury Peerage Case* (1811) 1 Sim & S 153; *The Poulett Peerage Case* [1903] AC 395.
[31] *Etridge* (n 9) [92].

Lordships seemed to realise this.[32] How does the confusion arise? It may well come from the fact that the word 'constructive' is sometimes seen as synonymous with 'implied', and 'presumed' likewise is often used interchangeably with 'implied'.[33] But they are different animals altogether, with the first an implication of law and the second an implication of fact.[34]

Interestingly, there is no reference to actual undue influence in R3RUE, which, despite mentioning neither category in the black letter,[35] speaks throughout the commentary to § 15 only of 'presumed' undue influence. This may be because of the view set out above that actual undue influence is nothing more than duress in equity. Indeed, US lawyers have for many years spoken of the coercion cases in equity as duress. Thus, in *Silsbee v Webber*,[36] a mother assigned security for money stolen by her son from his employer. There was a worry that her husband would be driven insane were he to discover his son's misdeeds. The case is almost identical to *Williams v Bayley*, yet Holmes J framed his judgment in terms of duress, not 'actual' undue influence; indeed, it is dealt with in R3RUE in the chapter on duress.[37] However, despite this, a clear line between duress and undue influence is not maintained by R3RUE, which in the commentary to § 15 says:

> More often than not, a suit for rescission on the basis of undue influence will be joined with claims based on fraud, duress or incapacity. Because of the important overlap between the elements of the doctrines, it is not always possible (or necessary) to isolate the precise grounds of relief.[38]

This blurring of duress and want of emancipation is unfortunate, as differences between the two unjust factors exist, not least in issues concerning the burden of proof.[39]

However, if we see actual undue influence as duress and presumed undue influence as want of emancipation, this leaves a gap, for it implies there can be no such thing as a want of emancipation claim proved without the benefit of a presumption. The reason this might be a problem is that there may be cases in which a claimant may be unable to prove by evidence the facts necessary to trigger the presumption spoken of in *Allcard v Skinner*. In such a case, it would seem perverse

[32] See, eg, Lord Scott at ibid [151].

[33] We see this, eg, in Lord Haldane's speech in *Sinclair v Brougham* [1914] AC 398, where at p 417 he said: 'to impute a fictitious promise is simply to presume the existence of a state of facts . . .'.

[34] Old editions of *Snell's Equity* formerly had chapters called 'Implied Trusts', which contained treatments of both resulting and constructive trust. This is problematic, for constructive trusts arise by operation of law, while some resulting trusts, *scil.* the presumed resulting trust, arise because of a presumption of law that a declaration of trust was made. In other words, it is a species of express trust. The point was made plain by Lord Nottingham in *Cook v Fountain* (1676) 3 Swan 585, 591, in a passage set out in n 40 below.

[35] The black letter is set out in n 2 above.

[36] *Silsbee v Webber*, 50 NE 555 (1898).

[37] § 14, Comment d.

[38] § 15, Comment a.

[39] In cases of duress, the burden of proof is squarely on the claimant, the only exception being allegations of duress to the person, where on questions of causation, the burden shifts to the defendant: *Barton v Armstrong* [1976] AC 104.

to say that they are nevertheless unable to make good all the necessary elements of their claim with evidence. To take an analogy from the law of trusts, it is sometimes possible to prove a declaration of trust with the benefit of a presumption, the so-called 'presumed resulting trust'.[40] But simply because claimants alleging declarations of trust cannot bring themselves within the fact scenarios triggering the presumption (*scil*, an *inter vivos* transfer outside certain familial relationships or provision of purchase price outside the same), there is nothing to stop them bringing evidence to prove the declaration, as, for example, where I allege that you declared yourself a trustee for me, a scenario outwith the scope of the presumption.[41]

We will see below that, in English law at least, a claimant needs to show two things to obtain the benefit of the presumption in play in cases of want of emancipation:[42] first, there must be proof by evidence of a relationship of influence; and second, there must be proof by evidence of a transaction calling for enquiry. Suppose the second requirement cannot be proved by evidence, because, for example, the case involves the guarantee by a wife of her husband's debts or the sale of property at market value.[43] Were that the case in English law, it would be impossible to bring a case of undue influence if the only route through was via the presumption. It may be that this problem does not arise in the US, for, as we will see, the second fact necessary to trigger the presumption in England does not seem to be required.[44] Nevertheless, it is a logical flaw in the scheme.

C. The Nature of Undue Influence

We have so far assumed that undue influence, at least in those cases where a presumption operates, means a want of emancipation. This was certainly the case in *Allcard v Skinner*. However, we have also noted the uncertainty surrounding the term 'undue influence', with Vaisey J in *Bullock v Lloyd's Bank* rightly describing it is an expression of 'ambiguous purport'.[45] In this respect, we could easily describe a case such as *Barton v Armstrong*,[46] where the claimant was induced to sell his shares in a company because of threats to his life, as one involving an exercise of

[40] 'All trusts are either, first, express trusts, which are raised and created by act of the parties, or implied trusts, which are raised or created by act or construction of law; again express trusts are declared either by word or writing; and these declarations appear either by direct and manifest proof, or violent and necessary presumption. These last are commonly called presumptive trusts; and that is, when the court, upon consideration of all circumstances *presumes there was a declaration*, either by word or writing, though the plain and direct proof thereof be not extant: per Lord Nottingham LC in *Cook v Fountain* (n 34) 591 (emphasis added).

[41] As, eg, in *Paul v Constance* [1977] 1 WLR 527.

[42] Text to nn 63–75.

[43] In *Etridge* (n 9), Lord Nicholls said at [30] that a guarantee by a wife was not such a transaction.

[44] Text to nn 74–75.

[45] *Bullock v Lloyd's Bank* [1955] Ch 317, 324.

[46] *Barton v Armstrong* [1976] AC 104.

undue influence. In such a case, the phrase 'undue influence' would describe a wrongful or 'illegitimate' exercise of influence. It could even describe cases of misrepresentation, that is, induced mistake, and we saw Lord Hobhouse so use it in *Etridge*.[47] Indeed, in *Allcard v Skinner* itself, Lindley LJ said that the purpose of the doctrine was 'to protect people from being forced, tricked or misled in any way by others into parting with their property'.[48] Likewise, in one of the cases given as an example of undue influence in R3RUE, it was held that a 22-year-old hotel clerk who befriended an ageing heiress, cohabited with her and received substantial gifts from her, had to prove affirmatively that the gifts were 'unaffected by any taint of undue influence, imposition or deception'.[49]

The problem with this running together of three different things (want of emancipation, imposition and deceit) is that the burden of proof does not normally shift in cases of 'imposition' and 'deceit'. The problem is only compounded by R3RUE's statement above that there is no need in undue influence cases to isolate the precise ground of claim,[50] for defendants must be able to know the case they have to meet. Fortunately, in this jurisdiction at least, undue influence has been said to be different from at least one of the triumvirate, misrepresentation. Thus, in *Royal Bank of Scotland v Chandra*, Patten LJ said:

> The two are not the same, although in certain cases they may overlap. Undue influence is concerned with the abuse of a relationship of trust and confidence by the husband exercising control over the will of the wife in order to procure her consent to the guarantee. In a case of misrepresentation that consent has been procured not by the exercise of some form of pressure or domination but by the making of a false statement which the wife . . . has relied upon.[51]

Of course, his Lordship runs together duress in equity and want of emancipation, but it is at least an improvement on the case of the bank clerk described in R3RUE.

With regard to attempts to define undue influence, Lindley LJ in *Allcard v Skinner* said that this had never been done and that this was a good thing too.[52] In English law, the tendency is merely to describe the facts which trigger the presumption and detail how that presumption might be rebutted, without getting into the question of what undue influence comprises. Does R3RUE help in this regard? Unfortunately not. The definition given is vague, with undue influence merely being said in the black letter to be 'excessive and unfair persuasion, sufficient to overcome the free will of the transferor, between parties who occupy

[47] See also *Bank of Cyprus (London) Ltd v Markou* (1999) 78 P & CR 208; *Broadway v Clydesdale Bank plc (No 2)* 2003 SLT 707 [20] (Lord Macfadyen); *UCB Corporate Services Ltd v Williams* [2002] EWCA Civ 555 [87] ('undue influence may include misrepresentation' (Jonathan Parker LJ)); *Hewett v First Plus Financial Group plc* [2010] EWCA Civ 312 [27]–[37] (Briggs J) (husband's concealment of affair amounted to misrepresentation of the nature of transaction and thus to undue influence).

[48] *Allcard v Skinner* (n 3) 183.

[49] Illustration based on *McCown v Fraser*, 327 Pa 561, 192 A 64 (1937).

[50] Text to n 38.

[51] *Royal Bank of Scotland v Chandra* [2011] EWCA Civ 192 [32].

[52] 'As no Court has ever attempted to define fraud so no Court has ever attempted to define undue influence': *Allcard v Skinner* (n 3) 183.

either a confidential relation or a relation of dominance on one side and subservience on the other'.[53]

However, the use of the word 'excessive' would at least seem to indicate that R3RUE takes the view that what is being dealt with is influence which is simply too much.[54] Indeed, in the commentary, we are told that undue influence does not necessarily involve any 'abuse' of the relationship,[55] which would seem to support this interpretation. All this is consistent with the view that we are concerned with cases of want of emancipation. However, later in the same comment, R3RUE speaks of undue influence being 'exerted', such 'exertion' being a 'threshold test of the claim'.[56] It is difficult to know what this means. Was there any 'exertion' of undue influence in *Allcard v Skinner* by the Lady Superior on the novice? Clearly not, though there is no doubt that it was a case of undue influence.[57]

The uncertainty in R3RUE is not helped by the addition of the qualifier 'unfair'. The influence, it is said, must be both excessive and unfair. But what does this mean? There is no help in the commentary, and of course the problem with the word 'unfair' is that it is nothing more than a conclusion, no different from 'unjust' or 'unconscionable', words which are completely unsuitable as tests of liability.[58] Indeed, to describe the enforcement of a transaction as 'unconscionable' has been said by the High Court of Australia to 'characterise the result rather than to identify the reasoning that leads to the application of that description'.[59] And writing extra-judicially, one judge of the same court said:

> Identifying some conduct as unconscionable or unconscientious is a statement of a conclusion which would sit as well in the discourse of an ethicist as it does in reasons for judgment. But in the law, they are not terms that invite, or even permit, recourse to a judge's idiosyncratic sense of justice. What sets apart the two fields of discourse of the ethicist and the judge is the need for the judge to articulate what it is that leads him or her to the conclusion that the conduct in question should wear this label.[60]

'Unfair' is no better than 'unconscionable' and in this particular context adds nothing.

R3RUE in the black letter also says that the influence must be between parties who occupy either a confidential relation or a relation of dominance on one side and subservience on the other.[61] This latter notion is not developed, and it is

[53] Cited at n 2 above.

[54] As in 'Fred is unduly talkative'.

[55] § 15, Comment b.

[56] ibid.

[57] 'The result of the evidence convinces me that no pressure, except the inevitable pressure of the vows and rules, was brought to bear on the Plaintiff; that no deception was practiced on her; that no unfair advantage was taken of her': *Allcard v Skinner* (n 3) 179 (Lindley LJ).

[58] So, eg, a requirement that assistance in a breach of trust be 'unconscionable' was rejected by the Privy Council in *Royal Brunei Airlines v Tan* [1995] 2 AC 378, 392 as unworkable.

[59] *Garcia v National Australia Bank* (1998) 194 CLR 394, 409 (Gaudron, McHugh, Gummow and Hayne JJ).

[60] Hayne J, 'Letting Justice Be Done Without the Heavens Falling' (2002) 27 *Monash University Law Review* 12, 16.

[61] Note 2, above.

notable that the idea that domination was part of the definition of undue influence was expressly rejected by the Court of Appeal in *Goldsworthy v Brickell*.[62] However, to be fair to R3RUE, 'dominance and subservience' is given as an alternative to excessive and unfair persuasion. It would be interesting to see where such a claim would be put in English law, though it is probably best seen as a subcategory of a want of emancipation.

D. Facts Necessary to Raise the Presumption of Undue Influence

As we have seen, there is no mention of 'actual' undue influence in R3RUE, most probably because it is seen as duress in the US; the focus is purely on presumed undue influence. We have already adverted to the fact that in English law, proof by evidence of two separate primary facts is necessary to trigger the presumption: a relationship of influence and a transaction which calls for explanation. In R3RUE, only the former seems necessary.

As to the relationship requirement, R3RUE speaks, as we have seen, of proof by evidence of one of two types of relationship: that which is 'confidential' and that which is of 'dominance and subservience'. However, little attention is paid to the latter, the reason being that judges in the US 'describe as "confidential" any relation marked by the pattern of dominance on one side and subservience on the other'.[63]

So far as confidential relations are concerned, R3RUE, like English law, divides between two types of confidential relation: those that involve certain nominate relationships and those where the relationship of influence must be 'proven as a fact'.[64] As to the former, no exhaustive list is given, but it is said to include principal/agent, trustee/beneficiary, guardian/ward and attorney/client.[65]

In this country, such nominate relationships have, somewhat unfortunately, been said to give rise to an irrebutable presumption of influence.[66] An irrebutable presumption is of course a non sequitur, because, as we have seen, presumptions shift the burden of proof in litigation. To talk of an irrebutable presumption is in truth to lay down a rule of substantive law. Thus, when we say that there is an

[62] *Goldsworthy v Brickell* [1987] Ch 378, 385 (Nourse LJ). It was argued in this case that the decision of the House of Lords in *National Westminster Bank plc v Morgan* [1985] AC 686 had made 'domination' an essential element of cause of action. This was rejected by the Court of Appeal. It was not necessary in order to raise the presumption of undue influence to show that the person in whom the trust and confidence had been reposed had assumed a role of dominating influence over the person who had effected the gift or transaction.

[63] § 15, Comment b.

[64] ibid.

[65] ibid.

[66] *Etridge* (n 9) [18] (Lord Nicholls), [103]–[107] (Lord Scott).

irrebutable presumption that a child under the age of 10 cannot commit a crime,[67] what is really being said is that there is a rule of substantive law that children of a certain age have no criminal capacity. Sir Kim Lewison has recently suggested that it would be better to say that there is a rebuttable presumption that, for instance, a solicitor has influence over his client.[68] This would seem to be the better course to take.

With regard the second type of relationship, as in England, the fact of influence must be proved by evidence. Various relationships are said by R3RUE to fall within this category, ones in which there is no rule that they are per se relationships of influence. The parent/child relationship is in this category, as is husband/wife, siblings, relatives, religious adherent/spiritual adviser, physician/patient, close friends and neighbours.[69] English law is similar in that the relationship of husband and wife is not 'presumed' to be a relationship of influence,[70] nor is the relation between siblings. However, parent/child,[71] physician/patient[72] and religious adherent/spiritual adviser[73] would seem to be within the 'presumption' in England.

However, as adverted to above, by far the biggest difference between English law and R3RUE is that there is no need according to the latter to bring evidence of any further fact beyond the relationship to trigger the presumption. Proof by evidence of a transfer within such a relationship is enough. By contrast, English law also requires proof by evidence of what used to be called 'manifest disadvantage'.[74] This was defended by Lord Nicholls in *Etridge* as follows:

> It would be absurd for the law to presume that every gift by a child to a parent, or every transaction between a client and his solicitor or between a patient and his doctor, was brought about by undue influence unless the contrary is affirmatively proved. Such a presumption would be too far-reaching. The law would be out of touch with everyday life if the presumption were to apply to every Christmas or birthday gift by a child to a parent, or to an agreement whereby a client or patient agrees to be responsible for the reasonable fees of his legal or medical adviser. The law would be rightly open to ridicule, for transactions such as these are unexceptionable. They do not suggest that something may be amiss. So something more is needed before the law reverses the burden of proof, something which calls for an explanation. When that something more is present, the greater the disadvantage to the vulnerable person, the more cogent must be the explanation before the presumption will be regarded as rebutted.[75]

That must be right. If we are to justify giving a claimant the benefit of a shift in the burden of proof, the transfer must be one which is inexplicable by ordinary

[67] Children and Young Persons Act 1933, s 50.
[68] Sir Kim Lewison, 'Under the Influence' [2011] *Restitution Law Review* 1, 9.
[69] § 15, Comment b.
[70] *Barclays Bank plc v O'Brien* [1994] 1 AC 180; *Etridge* (n 9).
[71] *Lancashire Loans Ltd v Black* [1934] 1 KB 380.
[72] *Mitchell v Homfray* (1881) 8 QBD 587.
[73] *Allcard v Skinner* (n 3).
[74] *National Westminster Bank plc v Morgan* (n 62).
[75] *Etridge* (n 9) [24].

motives. It is not clear why the approach of R3RUE is more generous in this regard.

E. Proof by Evidence of what Facts will Rebut the Presumption?

What facts proved by evidence will rebut the presumption? Ideally, we need to know the content of the presumption in order to answer this question, for rebuttal is the leading of evidence proving the untruth of the fact proved by presumption;[76] unfortunately, there is no clear account of the content of the presumption in either English law or R3RUE. As to rebuttal, in English law we are told that the defendant rebuts the presumption by proving by evidence that the claimant was able to think for himself and that the transfer was 'the result of the free exercise of independent will'.[77] Typically, this means showing that the claimant was freed from his dependence by independent information and advice. However, independent information and advice will not always be enough, for, as *Allcard v Skinner* demonstrates, claimants might be so under the spell of another that an explanation of the folly of their proposed action will make no difference. What we do know, however, is that a defendant cannot rebut the presumption by showing that he had no intention to take advantage of the other's weakness, much less by showing that he made no illegitimate threats, as *Allcard v Skinner* again demonstrates. Unfortunately, R3RUE provides little detail on rebuttal, merely stating that the transferee must prove that the transfer was 'voluntary', whatever that might mean.[78]

F. The Fact Proved by Presumption

Assume the primary facts necessary to trigger the presumption have been proved by evidence. What is the secondary fact which then arises without the need for evidence?

Surprisingly, this question is rarely asked in English law and, when it is, there is little agreement. In *Allcard* itself, Lindley LJ said that the presumption 'throws upon the donee the burden of proving that he has not abused his position, and of proving that the gift made to him has not been brought about by any undue influence on his

[76] The exact amount of evidence needed in rebuttal depends on the type of legal presumption in play. The point is discussed below, text to n 86.

[77] *Inche Noriah v Shaik Allie Bin Amar* [1929] AC 127, 135 (Lord Hailsham LC).

[78] § 15, Comment c. R3RUE notes that some states go further and require the transferee to show that it was also 'fair and reasonable'.

party'.[79] Given that there seems to have been no abuse by the Lady Superior on the facts of *Allcard*, at least in the sense of any active exercise of influence, the crucial words would here appear to be 'brought about'. In other words, what Lindley LJ is speaking about is a presumption of causation. However, as will be seen below, the position is complicated by the fact that judges sometimes speak of issues of causation as if they were separate from the presumption, though this is probably symptomatic of the general failure to discuss the content of the presumption.[80]

To the contrary, however, is the decision of the Court of Appeal in *Bank of Credit and Commerce International (Overseas) Ltd v Aboody*, where it was said that proof by evidence of a relationship of influence between the parties led the court to presume that undue influence had been *exerted*.[81] Similar comments were made by Lord Nicholls in *Etridge*, who said that on proof by evidence of the primary facts:

> [T]he stage is set for the court to infer that, in the absence of a satisfactory explanation, the transaction can only have been procured by undue influence. In other words, proof of these two facts is prima facie evidence that the defendant abused the influence he acquired in the parties' relationship. He preferred his own interests. He did not behave fairly to the other. So the evidential burden shifts to him. It is for him to produce evidence to counter the inference which should otherwise be drawn.[82]

So, 'abuse' of influence and 'unfair behaviour' are, for Lord Nicholls at least, the facts proved by presumption. Likewise, Lord Hoffmann said in *R v A-G for England and Wales* that the presumption was concerned with 'exploitation':

> Like duress at common law, undue influence is based upon the principle that a transaction to which consent has been obtained by unacceptable means should not be allowed to stand. Undue influence has concentrated in particular upon the unfair exploitation by one party of a relationship which gives him ascendancy or influence over the other.[83]

However, talk of 'the exertion of undue influence' or the 'exploitation' of the relationship cannot be right, for it was accepted in *Allcard v Skinner* that none of these things were present, yet still the presumption arising in the case remained unrebutted. Indeed, the language of wrongdoing and fault was more recently still rejected by the Court of Appeal in *Pesticcio v Huet*, where Mummery LJ said:

> A transaction might be set aside by the court, even though the actions and conduct of the person who benefited from it could not be criticised as wrongful. Although undue influence was sometimes described as an 'equitable wrong' or even as a species of equitable fraud, the basis of the court's intervention was not the commission of a dishonest or wrongful act by the defendant, but that, as a matter of public policy, the presumed influence arising from the relationship of trust and confidence should not operate to

[79] *Allcard v Skinner* (n 3) 181.
[80] Below, text to nn 100–09.
[81] *Bank of Credit and Commerce International (Overseas) Ltd v Aboody* [1990] 1 QB 923, 953 (Slade LJ).
[82] *Etridge* (n 9) [14].
[83] *R v A-G for England and Wales* [2003] UKPC 22 [21].

> the disadvantage of the victim, if the transaction was not satisfactorily explained by ordinary motives.[84]

That must be right. What seems to be persuading those who take the view that some sort of wrongdoing, some sort of oppression, is involved in cases of presumed undue influence is the malign influence of the false opposition between actual and presumed undue influence: if actual undue influence involves wrongful pressure, then so too must presumed undue influence. We see this clearly in Lord Hoffmann's analogy to duress in the passage from *R v A-G for England and Wales* cited above. Once again, the sooner this false opposition is noticed, the better will be the state of our law.

Is R3RUE of any help to English lawyers in clearing up this confusion? What does it say as to the content of the presumption? It provides as follows:

> A judicial finding that a challenged transfer took place between parties in a confidential relation, or in a relationship of dominance and subservience, does not establish that the transfer was the result of undue influence. It will in many cases give rise to a presumption that the transfer was the result of undue influence, shifting the burden of proof on the issue to the party asserting the transfer's validity.[85]

This is a difficult passage, for if a true presumption is at work here, then it does 'establish' the necessary elements of the cause of action. However, all that seems to be meant is that the presumption is rebuttable, meaning that the outcome of the case is not decided merely because the facts necessary to generate the presumption are proved. More helpfully, however, in using the language of 'result', it does seem to endorse the causation thesis advanced above.

G. Is There a Presumption at All?

We have so far assumed that the presumption in play is a presumption of law, by which is meant that it operates to shift the burden of proof to the defendant. However, that is not an entirely secure proposition, for there are some who seem to say that it is no presumption at all.

As we have seen, presumptions of law form part of the law of proof, more specifically an exception to the rule that the claimant bears the burden of proof on all aspects of his claim. Where a presumption of law is in play, the other party to the litigation bears the burden of adducing evidence to disprove the claimant's allegation with regard to the secondary fact proved by presumption. It is important to note that presumptions of law are divided into two classes: 'persuasive' and

[84] *Pesticcio v Huet* [2004] EWCA Civ 372 [20]. See also *Hammond v Osborn* [2002] 32 LS Gaz R 29, where the Court of Appeal likewise held that no fault or wrongdoing was required.

[85] § 15, Comment b.

'evidential'.[86] These terms refer to the amount of evidence required to rebut the presumption. The more difficult to rebut are persuasive legal presumptions, where the evidence adduced in rebuttal must show on a balance of probabilities the untruth of the fact proved by presumption. By contrast, an evidential legal presumption will be rebutted if sufficient evidence is adduced to make the existence of the fact proved by presumption a live issue.

Unfortunately, many other things which are not presumptions are often lumped together under this label. We have already seen that there is said to be a 'presumption' that a child under the age of 10 cannot commit a crime,[87] though it is not a presumption at all, merely a rule of substantive law; no amount of evidence that the child knew his conduct was criminal is able to rebut such a 'presumption'. It is the same with the so-called 'presumption of innocence' in criminal trials, which does no more than restate the general rule regarding the burden of proof and does not describe an exception.[88] Most confusing of all, and of relevance for our purposes, is the so-called 'presumption of fact'. Such nomenclature is especially prone to mislead, since presumptions of law also concern facts.

The phrase 'presumption of fact' describes a rule providing that upon proof by evidence of one fact, a tribunal of fact *may* find a second fact proved in the absence of sufficient evidence to the contrary. Examples of such 'presumptions' include the 'presumption of intention' (that a person intends the natural consequences of his acts)[89] and the 'presumption of guilty knowledge' (that an accused proved by evidence to have been found in possession of goods recently stolen the acquisition of which he cannot explain is 'presumed' to be guilty of handling stolen goods).[90] Though close to legal presumptions, they are different in that they are not concerned with the allocation of the burden of proof, the tribunal of fact not being compelled, as it is with legal presumptions, to find the fact in question to be proved.[91] They have therefore been described as 'no more than rational inferences to be drawn in the light of experience and common sense . . . The law does no more than recognize factual probability'.[92]

Might the 'presumption' of undue influence be nothing more than a presumption of fact – in other words, not a true presumption at all? This would seem to be the view of Sir Kim Lewison, who, writing extra-judicially, described the presumption of undue influence as 'evidential' rather than 'legal'. He said:

> [T]he nature of an evidential presumption . . . was never better explained than by Denning J in an article he wrote in the Law Quarterly Review in 1945. An evidential

[86] C Tapper, *Cross and Tapper on Evidence*, 12th edn (Oxford, Oxford University Press, 2010) 121–24.

[87] Above, text to nn 67–68.

[88] For further discussion, see WJ Swadling, 'Explaining Resulting Trusts' (2008) 124 *LQR* 72, 75–77.

[89] *R v Steane* [1947] KB 997; Criminal Justice Act 1967 s 8.

[90] *R v Schama and Abramovitch* (1914) 11 Cr App R 45; *R v Garth* [1949] 1 All ER 733.

[91] For this reason, the 'presumptions of fact' is described by *Phipson* as a misnomer: Hodge Malek QC (ed), *Phipson on Evidence*, 17th edn (London, Sweet & Maxwell, 2009) [6–17].

[92] P Carter, *Cases & Statutes on Evidence*, 2nd edn (London, Sweet & Maxwell, 1990) 77.

> presumption, he said, is a presumption in the sense that from the presumption the fact in issue may be inferred, but not in the sense that it must be inferred. As the case proceeds the evidence may first weigh in favour of the inference and then against it; thus producing a burden sometimes apparent, sometimes real, which may shift from one party to the other as the case proceeds or may remain suspended between them. At the end of the day the court has to decide as a matter of fact whether the inference should be drawn or not. These presumptions are provisional only. It is a mistake to raise these provisional presumptions into propositions having the force of law. They are recognised by the law but their force depends on good sense rather than on law. They are only guides to the court in deciding whether to infer the fact in issue or not.[93]

Of course, there is no logical divide between presumptions which are 'evidential' and those which are 'legal', for an evidential presumption is merely a type of legal presumption. What his Lordship would instead seem to be saying is that the presumption in play in cases of undue influence is one of fact, not law.

The passage from the judgment of Lindley LJ in *Allcard v Skinner* already quoted above, where he said that the burden was 'on the donee to support the gift', would, however, seem to indicate that this is a legal presumption.[94] Similar comments can be found in the judgments of both Cotton LJ[95] and Bowen LJ.[96] The issue was discussed in *Royal Bank of Scotland v Etridge (No 2)*, although the point is somewhat confused. Lord Nicholls spoke of a 'rebuttable evidential presumption' and a 'shift in the evidential burden of proof';[97] Lord Scott used the same language.[98] Both therefore seemed to see the presumption as one of law. However, Lord Hobhouse said that no presumption operated at all, though he immediately added that in the case of a transfer to a solicitor: 'The solicitor has to justify what he has done. He has a burden of proof to discharge and if he fails to discharge it he will not have succeeded in justifying his conduct.'[99] This is a difficult passage to interpret, for the difference between this type of 'defence' and the operation of a legal presumption is not obvious.

As this brief discussion shows, English law is confused on this issue. Does R3RUE help us to see whether a true presumption is in operation? In Comment c, there is talk of a shift of an 'evidentiary' burden. This would seem to mean that the presumption is one of law, though evidential, rather than persuasive; however, as the quotation from Sir Kim Lewison shows, even this proposition is not secure.

[93] Lewison (n 68) 5.

[94] *Allcard v Skinner* (n 3) 185. The passage is cited above, at text to n 7.

[95] His Lordship said that the court would set aside the transfer 'unless it is proved that in fact the gift was the spontaneous act of the donor acting under circumstances which enabled him to exercise an independent will': ibid 171.

[96] ibid 190.

[97] *Etridge* (n 9) [16].

[98] ibid [153].

[99] ibid [104].

H. The Test of Causation

The usual test of causation in cases of unjust enrichment is 'but for':[100] 'but for' the unjust factor, the enrichment would not have been conferred by the claimant on the defendant. There is, however, a different test for fraudulently induced mistakes, where it is only necessary to show that the mistake was 'a cause' of the transfer.[101] In other words, it is not fatal to the claimant's action that he would have made the transfer even if there had been no mistake. The only requirement is that the mistake be present in the claimant's mind.[102] There is similarly a more relaxed test for duress or, at least, duress to the person. Thus, in *Barton v Armstrong*, the Privy Council held that it was enough that the conferral of the enrichment was 'a cause' of the duress.[103] Indeed, in the same case, the majority shifted the burden of proof to the defendant to show that the duress was not a cause. There is thus a legal presumption of causation in cases of duress to the person. However, when we move to other cases of duress, the test seems to be the stricter 'but for' test. Thus, in cases of economic duress, there is authority to the effect that the transfer must be a 'substantial cause' of the transfer. In *Huyton SA v Peter Cremer GmbH*, Mance J (as he then was) said that the relaxed approach taken in cases of duress to the person was inappropriate and that even the 'but for' test was too generous to claimants.[104] He said instead that the pressure must be the 'decisive' or 'predominant' cause of the transfer.[105]

Of course, if the presumption in cases of presumed undue influence is one of causation, the question of the test of causation will only arise in the context of the facts needed to be proved by evidence in rebuttal. However, some courts seem to think of causation as something the claimant has to prove by evidence – in other words, something separate from the presumption itself. Thus, in *Bank of Credit and Commerce International SA v Aboody*, the Court of Appeal said that it would only order rescission of a contract alleged to have been brought about by undue influence where 'the evidence establishes that on balance of probabilities the complainant would have entered into the transaction in any event'.[106]

More recently, however, in *UCB Corporate Services Ltd v Williams*,[107] the Court of Appeal moved the subject closer towards duress of the person, holding that the influence need only be 'a cause' of the transfer. The judgment, however, is confused, with Jonathan Parker LJ saying:

[100] *Holt v Markham* [1923] 1 KB 504, 515 (Scrutton LJ).
[101] *Edgington v Fitzmaurice* (1885) 29 Ch D 459, 483 (Bowen LJ).
[102] ibid.
[103] *Barton v Armstrong* (n 46).
[104] *Huyton SA v Peter Cremer GmbH* [1999] 1 Lloyd's Rep 620, 636.
[105] ibid 638.
[106] *Aboody* (n 81).
[107] *UCB Corporate Services Ltd v Williams* [2002] EWCA Civ 555, [2003] 1 P & CR 12.

> I cannot see any reason in principle why (for example) a husband who has fraudulently procured the consent of his wife to participate in a transaction should be able, in effect, to escape the consequences of his wrongdoing by establishing that had he not acted fraudulently, and had his wife had the opportunity to make a free and informed choice, she would have acted in the same way.[108]

This is yet another example of the mistakes which are bound to occur if too broad a definition of undue influence is adopted. The analogy his Lordship draws here is with the case of a fraudulently induced mistake, which, as we have seen, operates with a very relaxed test of causation. Although this may well be justified in cases of want of emancipation, it should not become law through the operation of a confused classificatory system.

Looking at the facts proved by evidence in *Allcard v Skinner*, it would seem that the only extra fact the presumption could possibly be seen as having supplied was the element of causation: that the claimant's lack of emancipation from the influence of the Lady Superior caused her to make the transfer. No other element of the claim would seem to have been missing.

Does R3RUE cast any light on this area? As we have seen, there is talk of the presumption being 'that the transfer was the result of undue influence, shifting the burden of proof on the issue to the party asserting the transfer's validity'.[109] Beyond that, however, issues of causation are absent from the discussion.

I. Undue Influence of a Third Hand

The final question concerns want of emancipation and third parties. What is the position of defendants who themselves influence no-one, but receive enrichments as a result of the claimant's want of emancipation from a third hand?

The position taken by R3RUE is that the fact that the influence is not that of the defendant but of a third party is not normally a bar to the claim. It is said that: 'Restitution is commonly available in such circumstances, because the immediate donee in the three-party scenario – even if innocent – is likely to be a donee.'[110] This, of course, is no reason at all, for it merely states a fact, not a justification for the rule.

However, we see similar thinking in English law, where it is also the case that transferees who take gratuitously are liable to make restitution despite the fact that they are not the cause of the transfer. As Wilmot LC delightfully said in *Bridgeman v Green*:

> [W]hoever receives it, must take it tainted and infected with the undue influence and imposition of the person procuring the gift . . . Let the hand receiving it be ever so

[108] ibid [86].
[109] § 15, Comment b.
[110] § 15, Comment d.

> chaste, yet if it comes through a corrupt polluted channel, the obligation of restitution will follow it.[111]

Whatever the merits of this reasoning, the result is right. If we see undue influence, at least in its want of emancipation form, as involving a vitiation of consent to the transfer, then the defect is present, regardless of whether or not the transferee had any involvement in the transfer.

In both jurisdictions, however, a transferee who gives value in exchange in good faith and without notice of the undue influence takes free. Why is this so? R3RUE simply says that the rule operates 'by analogy to the defence of bona fide purchase'.[112] In this sense, R3RUE missed an easy lesson from English law, because the analogy with good faith purchase, which was used by Lord Browne-Wilkinson in *Barclays Bank plc v O'Brien*,[113] was exposed as false by the House of Lords in *Barclays Bank v Boulter*.[114] The reason it is false is that, in the sort of case we are dealing with, the title received by transferee is not burdened with the adverse rights of another, as is the case, for example, where a trustee transfers rights in breach of trust or a thief transfers his title to money stolen from another. Thus, in *Boulter*, Lord Hoffmann said:

> The defence of bona fide purchase for value without notice enables the purchaser to defeat a prior interest, which burdened the title . . . In the present case, however, the bank took a charge directly from Mrs Boulter. She had the necessary title to grant it. There was no prior interest, which the bank needed to defeat.[115]

What then is the explanation as to why a good faith purchaser for value without notice takes free? Although *Etridge* endorsed the reasoning in *Boulter*, Lord Nicholls was content to say that the exception was introduced into the law by *O'Brien*, and simply acknowledging that its jurisprudential basis was unsatisfactory.[116] Unfortunately, this less than rigorous approach has led to difficulties.

Instead of focusing on the rationale of the defence, Lord Nicholls focused his attention on what amounted to notice. To this question, an odd response was given. His Lordship said that a transferee would have notice where:

(i) he was aware that the claimant was in a relationship of confidence;
(ii) the transaction was not to the financial advantage of the claimant; and
(iii) the transferee had not taken steps to minimise the risk that the claimant was not unduly influenced (eg, by insisting that he take independent legal advice).[117]

This last requirement is the odd one out. This is because it has nothing to do with knowledge, actual or constructive. Whether or not a transferee has taken steps to

[111] *Bridgeman v Green* (1757) Wilm 58, 64–65.
[112] § 15, Comment d.
[113] *Barclays Bank plc v O'Brien* (n 70) 195 (described as 'the doctrine of notice').
[114] *Barclays Bank v Boulter* [1999] 1 WLR 1919.
[115] ibid 1924.
[116] *Etridge* (n 9) [38]–[43].
[117] ibid [44]–[49].

see that the claimant sought legal advice has nothing to do with whether he knows or should have known that the claimant was under the influence of another. By the same token, ensuring that the claimant has seen a solicitor cannot remove actual or constructive notice. Of course, showing that the transferee had independent legal advice is, as we have seen, something which in certain circumstances may rebut the presumption,[118] but that is a different question altogether, for constructive notice cannot be rebutted. Lord Nicholls seemed to acknowledge that this does not work as a matter of theory, but defended it in terms of practicality.[119] It may be, however, that Lord Nicholls was here making the mistake of confusing an implication of law with an implication of fact, an error we noticed above in relation to the false dichotomy between actual and presumed undue influence.[120]

J. Conclusion

There is a gap in the law of undue influence as presented in R3RUE, as is also the case in English law, in that it does not seem possible to prove the facts necessary to ground a claim in undue influence, where that phrase means 'want of emancipation', without the aid of a presumption. However, since the facts necessary to trigger the presumption are more generous in the US than in England, there being no need for proof by evidence of a transfer calling for explanation, this is probably not a problem in practice. Little help is given, however, on the key question of the content of the presumption, though, like English law, it is probably one of causation. Finally, although R3RUE is to be commended for not using the language of presumption to describe the nominate relationships, it provides no help in relation to explaining the liability of transferees who are not themselves the influencing party, for it relies on a demonstrably false analogy with bona fide purchase.

What needs to happen in both jurisdictions is a jettisoning of the language of undue influence. It is a hopelessly unstable term, capable of covering duress, deceit and want of emancipation. Moreover, a clear division must be drawn between issues of substantive law and proof. Until these things happen, the subject will be in a state of confusion on both sides of the Atlantic.

[118] Though not all. Independent advice would probably have made no difference in *Allcard v Skinner* (n 3) (Lindley LJ).

[119] *Etridge* (n 9) [42].

[120] Text to nn 23–34.

6

Denials and Defences in the Law of Unjust Enrichment

JAMES GOUDKAMP AND CHARLES MITCHELL

A. Introduction

In this chapter we argue that the rules governing the imposition of liability for unjust enrichment can be reduced to two categories. There are rules that define the elements of an action in unjust enrichment and there are rules that specify situations in which liability will not arise, or will not arise in full, even though all of the elements of an action can be established. If this is correct, then it follows that there are two and only two types of response that a defendant can make with a view to avoiding or limiting his liability in unjust enrichment: he can argue that the claimant has failed to establish an element of his action; or he can admit that the claimant has established all of the elements of his action and invoke a rule that wholly or partly exempts him from liability nonetheless. We term these responses 'denials' and 'defences' respectively.

The difference between denials and defences is recognised in the *Restatement Third: Restitution and Unjust Enrichment*.[1] The Reporter notes, for example, that the category into which a defendant's response falls may have a bearing on 'the rules of pleading and the burden of proof',[2] but, beyond this, little is made of the distinction. Chapter 8 of R3RUE, entitled 'Defenses to Restitution', concerns responses that are said to be 'presented as affirmative defenses . . . for the sake of simplicity',[3] but it is added that 'some might be understood equally well as arguments that refute an element of the plaintiff's cause of action'.[4] This treats the difference between denials and defences as if it were merely presentational or stylistic. In our view, however, the distinction between them is deeper than this, and so is the corresponding distinction between actions and defences.

[1] American Law Institute, *Restatement Third: Restitution and Unjust Enrichment* (St Paul, MN, American Law Institute Publishers, 2011) (hereinafter 'R3RUE').

[2] ibid vol II, 481.

[3] It is not explained why presenting them as defences is thought to be simpler than casting them as denials. We doubt that it is simpler, given that defences raise second-order questions while denials relate to first order questions.

[4] R3RUE (n 1) vol II, 481.

In Part B we explain the terminology that we use in this chapter. In Part C we ask whether the rules defining actions and defences comprise the whole of the law governing liability in unjust enrichment. In Part D we discuss some possible rationales for dividing the liability rules in unjust enrichment between actions and defences. Finally, in Part E we examine whether certain of the defendant's responses identified in Chapter 8 and elsewhere in R3RUE are denials or defences. The analysis in Part E is descriptive rather than normative. Our aim is to determine how the responses under review should be classified in light of their presentation in R3RUE. We do not take a position on the normative issue of how particular responses ought to operate. That issue is best addressed once the descriptive analysis that we undertake here has been completed.

B. Terminology

The main focus of our chapter is on the types of argument that a defendant can make with a view to avoiding or reducing his liability in unjust enrichment. However our analysis is premised on certain assumptions about the meaning of the terms 'action in unjust enrichment' and 'defence'. These assumptions must be made explicit.

(1) Action in Unjust Enrichment

Several points must be made to clarify what we mean by 'action in unjust enrichment'. First, R3RUE defines 'actions in unjust enrichment' to include actions for gain-based awards on the ground of wrongdoing.[5] However we do not believe this to be conceptually coherent. Our reason for holding this view is essentially the same as that given by Peter Birks for dissenting from the Reporter's position on this issue.[6] One can legitimately say that the law of restitution is the law concerning gain-based remedies, including both restitution for unjust enrichment and restitution for wrongdoing. But restitution and unjust enrichment are not the same thing. Restitution is a remedy and unjust enrichment is a source of rights and obligations. Unjust enrichment and wrongdoing are not the same thing either; they are distinct sources of rights and obligations. We shall say no more about this here. We will simply state that our chapter does not concern actions for

[5] ibid vol I, 5-6: unjust enrichment results from 'ineffective transactions' that may occur 'when the defendant acquires benefits by wrongful interference with the claimant's rights'. See too vol I, 3: 'the consecrated formula "at the expense of another" can also mean "in violation of the other's legally protected rights"'. Restitution for wrongs is dealt with in Chapter 5 of R3RUE and is discussed by Nicholas McBride in ch 11 of this volume.

[6] P Birks, 'Unjust Enrichment and Wrongful Enrichment' (2000–01) 79 *Texas Law Review* 1767; P Birks, 'A Letter to America: The New *Restatement of Restitution*' (2003) 3 *Global Jurist Frontiers* 1.

gain-based awards founded on the defendant's wrongdoing. Nor does it concern the responses that defendants can make in reply to such actions.

Second, we observe that courts in common law and civil law jurisdictions typically approach the question whether a defendant has been unjustly enriched (in common law terminology) or unjustifiably enriched (in civil law terminology) from different starting points. Courts in common law jurisdictions look for positive reasons why the transfer of a benefit should be reversed, such as the fact that the claimant made a mistake or was the victim of duress. To an English lawyer, therefore, the term 'unjust enrichment' describes a body of law that is concerned with the identification of positive reasons for restitution, or 'unjust factors'.[7] In contrast, courts in civil law jurisdictions ask whether there was a 'legal ground' for the transfer of a benefit, such as a contract or statute, and they order restitution if there was not.[8] Thus, to civilian lawyers, the term 'unjustified enrichment' describes a body of law that is concerned with the reversal of transfers for which there is no legal justification.

Most American states take the common law approach. Chapter 1 of R3RUE, concerning 'General Principles', expresses no opinion as to which approach is preferable, although the material in Chapter 2, concerning 'Transfers Subject to Avoidance', is organised by reference to unjust factors such as mistake, duress and undue influence. Chaim Saiman asserts that the neutral stance adopted in R3RUE is 'due neither to intellectual timidity, nor to its inability to decide between the competing theories', but 'proceeds from the assumption that nothing turns on' the question of which approach is taken.[9] If R3RUE makes that assumption, then we consider that it is incorrect to do so.[10] Furthermore, the Reporter's wish to avoid committing R3RUE to one approach or the other has led him to describe the circumstances in which unjust enrichment occurs in language that blurs the distinction between the two approaches.[11] Yet there are fundamental differences between them, and in this chapter we use the term 'action in unjust enrichment'

[7] For 'unjust factor' terminology, see, eg, *Banque Financière de la Cité v Parc (Battersea) Ltd* [1999] 1 AC 221, 227; *Kleinwort Benson Ltd v Lincoln CC* [1999] 2 AC 349, 363, 386, 395 and 409; *Test Claimants in the FII Group Litigation v HMRC* [2012] UKSC 19, [2012] 2 AC 337.

[8] eg, BGB (the German Civil Code), § 812 I: 'A person who obtains something as a result of the performance of another person or otherwise at his expense without legal grounds for doing so is under a duty to make restitution to him.'

[9] C Saiman, 'Restitution in America: Why the US Refuses to Join the Global Restitution Party' (2008) 28 *OJLS* 99, 120–21.

[10] Examples of cases that English and German law decide differently are identified and discussed in G Dannemann, 'Unjust Enrichment as Absence of Basis: Can English Law Cope?' in A Burrows and Lord Rodger of Earlsferry (eds), *Mapping the Law: Essays in Memory of Peter Birks* (Oxford, Oxford University Press, 2006) 363.

[11] In § 1, Comment b, the terms 'unjustified enrichment' and 'unjust enrichment' are treated as synonymous. It is also said there that 'unjustified enrichment is enrichment that lacks an adequate legal basis', but this does not mean that R3RUE necessarily espouses a civilian 'absence of legal grounds' approach. The sentence means only that restitution is ordered where an enrichment 'results from a transaction that the law treats as ineffective to work a conclusive alteration in ownership rights' – ie, 'restitution is ordered in circumstances where the courts hold that it should be', whether their idea of unjust enrichment turns on the presence of unjust factors or the absence of legal grounds.

in the common law sense, which we take to be different from the term 'action in unjustified enrichment' in the civil law sense.

Third, we note that the term 'unjust enrichment' is sometimes used to describe a moral concept which informs various areas of private law in an abstract fashion but which lacks substantive doctrinal content.[12] We do not use the term in this way. Our discussion proceeds on the different basis that the term 'unjust enrichment' describes a body of law that is constituted by rules and principles that can be discovered by the study of legal authority. Consistently with this approach, we also proceed on the footing that an action in unjust enrichment has identifiable and isolable elements. These include the requirements that the defendant must have been enriched, that this enrichment must have been gained at the claimant's expense and that this enrichment must have been unjust, in the sense that the circumstances in which it occurred must have coincided with, or been analogous to, those of a previous case in which restitution was awarded.[13] It is requirements of this sort to which we refer when we speak in this chapter of a defendant denying that a claimant has established all of the elements of an action in unjust enrichment.

In these respects, our understanding of actions in unjust enrichment corresponds to that of the English courts.[14] Likewise, R3RUE states that the justification for imposing restitutionary liability for unjust enrichment 'is not moral but legal' and that such liability is 'predictable and objectively determined' by reference to case law.[15] It states that the project undertaken in Chapters 2–6 of R3RUE is to 'classify the circumstances in which a liability in restitution will predictably be imposed – employing categories that are large enough to be significant, small enough to

[12] A recurring theme of decisions of the High Court of Australia over the past decade, asserting that judicial reliance on the concept of 'unjust enrichment' is an example of 'top-down reasoning' and is impermissible for that reason: *Roxborough v Rothmans of Pall Mall Australia Ltd* [2001] HCA 68, (2001) 208 CLR 516 [70]–[74]; *Farah Constructions Pty Ltd v Say-Dee Pty Ltd* [2007] HCA 22, (2007) 230 CLR 89 [151]; *Lumbers v W Cook Builders Pty Ltd (in liq)* [2008] HCA 27, (2008) 232 CLR 635 [83]–[85]; *Bofinger v Kingsway Group Ltd* [2009] HCA 44, (2009) 239 CLR 269 [86]–[91]. But contrast *Pavey and Matthews Pty Ltd v Paul* (1987) 162 CLR 221, 256–57; *David Securities Pty Ltd v Commonwealth Bank of Australia* (1992) 275 CLR 353, 379; *Equuscorp Pty Ltd v Haxton* [2012] HCA 7, (2012) 86 ALJR 296 [30]; *Hills Industries Ltd v Australian Financial Services and Leasing Pty Ltd* [2012] NSWCA 380 [68]–[70].

[13] It is a controversial question whether it is also an element of actions in unjust enrichment that the defendant's enrichment must not have been mandated by a contract between the parties or other source of entitlement: see Part E, section (1).

[14] eg, *Woolwich Equitable Building Society v IRC* [1993] AC 70, 196–97; *Kleinwort Benson Ltd v Birmingham CC* [1996] 4 All ER 733, 737; *Gibb v Maidstone and Tunbridge Wells NHS Trust* [2010] EWCA Civ 678, [2010] IRLR 786 [26]–[27].

[15] R3RUE (n 1) § 1, Comment a. For a critical assessment of the 'conceptualist' belief in the 'immanent rationality of the law' by which R3RUE is animated, see C Saiman, 'Restating Restitution: A Case of Contemporary Common Law Conceptualism' (2007) 52 *Villanova Law Review* 487, especially 505–16. And *cf* LE Wolcher, 'Intent to Charge for Unsolicited Benefits Conferred in an Emergency: A Case Study in the Meaning of "Unjust" in the *Restatement (Third) of Restitution & Unjust Enrichment*' (2011) 68 *Washington and Lee Law Review* 911, 919, detecting in R3RUE's approach 'a particularly acute form of legal nominalism' and denying that the only alternative is to describe the law by reference to 'loosey-goosey legal standards'.

describe cases that are perceptibly alike'.[16] It is also stresses that 'in numerous cases natural justice and equity do not . . . provide an adequate guide to decision, and would not do so even if their essential requirements could be treated as self-evident'.[17] These comments were written with an eye to many recent American decisions that are couched in the vague language of equitable discretionary remedialism.[18] R3RUE has consciously departed from such authorities and has sought to identify clear legal principles by dividing actions in unjust enrichment into certain discrete elements.[19] We observe that if it were impossible to do this because the award of restitutionary remedies was entirely at the courts' discretion, then the distinction between 'denials' and 'defences' promoted in this chapter would be meaningless. The Reporter made essentially the same point over 10 years ago when he wrote that:

> So long as liability in restitution is described in purely equitable terms – liability to restore unjust enrichment, liability to restore that which in equity and good conscience cannot be retained, and so forth – it is logically impossible to distinguish an affirmative defense from an argument that merely denies the plaintiff's prima facie case. Given the traditional, equitable conception of restitution, in other words, it is doubtful whether such a thing as an affirmative defense need ever be identified.[20]

(2) Defence

The word 'defence' is one of the most ambiguous in the lawyer's vocabulary. So we must state precisely how the word is used here. It suffices for present purposes to distinguish between four meanings that it bears in the context of unjust enrichment.

First, the word 'defence' is often used in a loose sense to capture any argument that the defendant might make in an attempt to resist the imposition of liability, in part or in full. This usage encompasses both denials that all the elements of an action in unjust enrichment have been established and pleas by the defendant that he should be wholly or partly relieved of liability on account of a rule that is independent of the definition of an action.[21] For example, a plea by the defendant that he was not enriched counts as a defence when the word is used in this way.

[16] The Reporter disparages the 'specious precision' of certain 'checklists of factors' used by some American courts 'to identify cases in which the receipt of a benefit gives rise to a liability': R3RUE (n 1) § 1, Comment d. However, his target is not formulae for liability of the kind described in the text, but formulae which include among their elements vague requirements such as that 'the circumstances [must have made] it inequitable for the defendant to retain the benefit'.

[17] R3RUE (n 1) § 1, Comment b.

[18] A phenomenon deplored in A Kull, 'Rationalising Restitution' (1995) 83 *California Law Review* 1191, 1195–96.

[19] See, eg, R3RUE (n 1) vol I, 16: 'Receipt of a benefit at the expense of another is a necessary but not a sufficient condition of liability in restitution.'

[20] A Kull, 'Defenses to Restitution: The Bona Fide Creditor' (2001) 81 *Boston University Law Review* 919, 926 n 17.

[21] eg, K Barker and R Grantham, *Unjust Enrichment* (Sydney, LexisNexis, 2008) 405: 'Analytically, the notion of a defence also includes situations where the defendant is required to show that the plaintiff has not made out all the elements of a claim. These could equally be seen as concerned with "defects" in the plaintiff's substantiation of the cause of action.'

In a second and narrower sense, the word 'defence' captures only those rules that enable the defendant to escape from liability, or reduce its extent, even if all of the elements of an action in unjust enrichment are present.[22] Denials that all of the elements of the claimant's action can be established do not count as defences when the word 'defence' is used in this way. The only rules that qualify are those which extinguish or limit liability despite the fact that the claimant's action is complete. In other words, a rule is a defence in this sense of the word only if pleading it is consistent with accepting the truth of the allegations in the claimant's statement of case. So, a plea that the claimant has not been enriched does not count as a defence in this second sense. An example of a defence within this meaning of the word is a limitation bar.[23] Limitation bars stand outside of the definition of actions in unjust enrichment. The timely bringing of such an action is not an element of the action.

Third, a rule is sometimes counted as a defence if the defendant bears the onus of pleading it and proving that it applies.[24] This meaning of 'defence' is easily conflated with the second sense in which the word is used. This is because rules that qualify as defences in the second sense must generally be pleaded and proved by the defendant.[25] Nevertheless, the third meaning of the word is distinct from the second. An example helps to illuminate the difference.[26] Under English law, the descent of a limitation bar is a defence in the second sense of the word, and yet once the defendant has put the limitation period in issue, the burden of proof is (rightly or wrongly) placed on the claimant to show that his claim was brought in time. In the words of the English Law Commission, 'the claimant has the burden of disproving a limitation defence where the defendant has pleaded one'.[27] Therefore, English law does not regard a limitation bar as a defence in the third sense of the word.[28]

[22] eg, LD Smith, R Chambers, M McInnes, JW Neyers and SGA Pitel, *The Law of Restitution in Canada* (Toronto, Emond Montgomery, 2004) 365: 'Once the plaintiff has established the elements of a claim to reverse unjust enrichment, it is then open to the defendant to invoke any applicable defences.'

[23] See below Part E, section (8).

[24] eg, R Grantham and C Rickett, 'A Normative Account of Defences to Restitutionary Liability' (2008) 67 *CLJ* 92, 95: '[F]or the purposes of the paper, defences will refer to those matters or reasons for denying or reducing liability that it is for the defendant to raise and establish.'

[25] See n 52 and accompanying text.

[26] The example given here is of a 'defence' in the second sense, the burden of disproving which is placed on the claimant. In principle, the law could also place the burden of disproving particular elements of an action on the defendant: WF Young, 'Translocations and Inertia' (2011) 68 *Washington and Lee Law Review* 1335, 1336.

[27] Law Commission, *Limitation of Actions* (Law Com No 270, 2001) para 5.29. See too Law Commission, *Limitation of Actions* (LCCP No 151, 1998) paras 9.23–9.25; *Hurst v Parker* (1817) 1 B & Ald 92, 106 ER 34; *Cartledge v E Jopling & Sons Ltd* [1963] AC 758; *London Congregational Union Inc v Harriss* [1988] 1 All ER 15; *Lloyds Bank plc v Crosse & Crosse (a firm)* [2001] EWCA Civ 366, [2001] PNLR 34 [41]; *Fiona Trust & Holding Corp v Privalov* [2010] EWHC 3199 (Comm) [135]. We are grateful to Andrew Burrows for drawing these authorities to our attention.

[28] Another example is provided by the Australian Sales Tax Assessment Act 1992 (Cth), s 51. This section states that the tax authorities need not refund money paid as sales tax that was not due if the cost of paying the tax was passed on to the taxpayer's customers. This rule was described as a 'defence' in *Avon Products Pty Ltd v Federal Commissioner of Taxation* [2005] FCAFC 63, (2005) 59 ATR 592 [56] (not considered on appeal to the High Court). Yet it has also been held that the burden of disproving

In this chapter we use the word 'denial' to describe arguments that liability should not be imposed because one or more of the elements of an action in unjust enrichment is missing. We use the word 'defence' in the second identified sense, that is, to refer to arguments that liability should not arise, or arise in full, even though all of the elements of an action in unjust enrichment are present. This is the only one of the foregoing three meanings of the word 'defence' that brings into focus the difference between the two types of response available to defendants that we discuss in this chapter. The first meaning obscures the distinction between refuting the claimant's allegations and appealing to a rule that circumvents those allegations, while the third meaning reveals a different distinction, namely that between rules that the claimant must show are applicable and rules in respect of which the defendant carries the onus of proof.

We should finally say something about a fourth use of the term 'defence' in the context of unjust enrichment. It is regularly stated by the English courts that four questions must be asked when determining whether a remedy should be awarded on the ground of unjust enrichment: was the defendant enriched; was the enrichment at the claimant's expense; was the enrichment unjust; and are there any defences?[29] However, some judges have slid from this proposition to the different proposition that the four elements of an action in unjust enrichment are: enrichment of the defendant; which was at the claimant's expense; which was unjust; *and* which was received in circumstances that do not form the basis of any defence.[30] In other words, they have included the defences question within their definition of the action. This slide from 'questions arising' to 'elements of the action' also occurs in some academic writing.[31]

Such statements attach a different meaning to the word 'defence' from the first three meanings. Unlike the third meaning, this meaning would place the burden of proving an absence of reasons to refuse restitution on the claimant. Unlike the second meaning, it would not say that defences are rules that stand outside of the definition of an action in unjust enrichment. Unlike the first meaning, it would produce the result that the only denials of elements of actions that count as defences are those that target the supposed 'no defences element'.

passing on rests on the claimant taxpayer: *Avon Products Pty Ltd v Commissioner of Taxation* [2006] HCA 29, (2006) 230 CLR 356.

[29] eg, *Banque Financière* (n 7) 227; *Cressman v Coys of Kensington (Sales) Ltd* [2004] EWCA Civ 47, [2004] 1 WLR 2775 [22].

[30] eg, *Rowe v Vale of White Horse DC* [2003] 1 Lloyd's Rep 418 [11]; *Gibb* (n 14) [26].

[31] eg A Burrows, *The Law of Restitution*, 3rd edn (Oxford, Oxford University Press, 2010) 27: 'four elements – "benefit", "at the claimant's expense", "unjust factors", and "defences" – constitute the fundamental conceptual structure of an unjust enrichment claim'.

C. Do Any Other Types of Rules Govern Liability in Unjust Enrichment?

If liability in unjust enrichment depends only on the rules that describe actions and defences, then it follows that a defendant can make two and only two types of argument to resist liability: he can deny that the claimant has made out his action or he can raise a defence. It also follows that the only arguments that a claimant can make, if he succeeds in establishing that all of the elements of his action are present, are those that are aimed at showing that the defendant has failed to make out a defence. In other words, a claimant whose allegations are met by a defence can only deny that the defence is available. He cannot answer the defendant's invocation of the defence by appealing to another rule since, if liability in unjust enrichment turns only on actions and defences, no such rules exist. However, it can be questioned whether this bipartite structure encompasses the whole of this area of law. In this part we consider two grounds on which it might be impugned as inadequate.

(1) Standing Rules

One possibility is that the law of unjust enrichment also recognises standing rules. Standing rules are rules that determine whether a given claimant is the type of person who can bring judicial proceedings. They are distinct from rules that specify the elements of actions and defences. Conventional wisdom holds that there are no standing rules in private law;[32] standing rules, according to this view, are found only in public law. This traditional learning may or may not be accurate.[33] Standing rules might exist in the law of unjust enrichment. If they do, it would be inadequate to divide the law of unjust enrichment merely into actions and defences.

[32] P Cane, *Administrative Law*, 5th edn (Oxford, Clarendon Press, 2011) 281-2: 'Standing is not normally a requirement for bringing a "private law claim" . . . There are certain private-law concepts that resemble rules of standing: for example, duty of care in the tort of negligence, the principle that breach of a statutory duty will be actionable in tort only if the duty is owed to the claimant as an individual (as opposed to the public generally), and the doctrine of privity in contract. However, these are not seen as separate from the rules that define the relevant wrong, but as part of the definition of the wrong'. *Cf* K Schiemann, 'Locus Standi' [1990] *PL* 342, 342–43.

[33] English courts often ask whether claimants have standing to bring private law actions, eg, *Burns v Shuttlehurst Ltd* [1999] 1 WLR 1449 [34], *Peer International Corp v Termidor Music Publishers Ltd* [2006] EWHC 2883 (Ch) [31] and *Pope v Energem Mining (IOM) Ltd* [2011] EWCA Civ 1043 [8] (contract); *Re Denley's Trust Deed* [1969] 1 Ch 373, 382, *Walker v Stones* [2000] All ER (D) 1003 and *Hollis v Rolfe* [2008] EWHC 1747 (Ch) [134] (trusts); *Stein v Blake* [1998] 1 All ER 724, 726 and LS Sealy, 'Problems of Standing, Pleading and Proof in Corporate Litigation' in BG Pettet (ed), *Company Law in Change* (London, Stevens & Sons, 1987) 1 (directors' duties); *City of Bradford MC v Brown* (1987) 19 HLR 16, 22–24 (trespass and 'statutory' nuisance); *Hunter v Canary Wharf Ltd* [1997] AC 655, 714 (private nuisance); *Chocosuisse Union des Fabricants Suisses de Chocolat v Cadbury Ltd* [1999] RPC 826 (passing off).

A possible example of a standing rule in the law of unjust enrichment is the rule that estops a claimant from maintaining litigation if he has made a legally binding promise not to sue the defendant. Arguably, a promise not to sue renders the claimant a type of person whom the court will not hear, to the extent that hearing him would permit him to escape from the obligation created by his promise. However, this is not the only way to understand the operation of a promise not to sue. It might be that the absence of such a promise is one of the elements of an action in unjust enrichment (in which case, pleading that the claimant made a promise not to sue would be a denial). Alternatively, the existence of such a promise might furnish the defendant with a defence. The cases simply do not tell us in which of these ways a legally binding promise not to sue functions.

A plea of illegality might also be characterised as an appeal to a standing rule, at least in some of the cases in which that plea was in issue. Lord Mansfield's famous description of the doctrine of illegality in *Holman v Johnson* is framed in language that is consistent with such an interpretation. Lord Mansfield wrote:

> No Court will lend its aid to a man who founds his cause of action upon an immoral and illegal act. If from the plaintiff's own stating or otherwise, the cause of action appears to arise *ex turpi causa*, or the transgression of a positive law of this country, there the Court says that he has no right to be assisted. It is upon this ground the Court goes; not for the sake of the defendant, but because they will not lend their aid to such a plaintiff.[34]

Lord Mansfield's references to the court's refusal to 'lend its aid' to a claimant whose action arises from an illegal transaction, and his assertion that such a claimant 'has no right to be assisted', are telling. Lord Mansfield can be read as saying that the court will shut its doors to the wrongdoing claimant even if he has a valid cause of action. However, it is far from clear that this is how the doctrine of illegality operates in the modern world, despite the courts' regular incantation of Lord Mansfield's dictum. Since Lord Mansfield's time, the courts have stressed that offenders are not persons from whom the law automatically withholds all relief.[35] The judicial Zeitgeist is opposed to construing the doctrine of illegality as a standing rule.

(2) Affirmative Answers to Defences

Just as a defendant can circumvent the claimant's allegations by invoking a defence, perhaps a claimant can avoid the impact of a defence not merely by denying that it

[34] *Holman v Johnson* (1775) 1 Cowp 341, 343; 98 ER 1120, 1121.

[35] 'The door of a court is not barred because the plaintiff has committed a crime. The confirmed criminal is as much entitled to redress as his most virtuous fellow citizen; no record of crime, however long, makes one an outlaw': *Olmstead v United States*, 277 US 438 (1928) 484 (Brandeis J); 'The medieval concept of outlawry is unacceptable in modern society. An outlaw forfeited the protection of the law. He could not invoke the assistance of the court to enforce non-existent rights. In the United Kingdom today there are no outlaws. However abhorrent the crime, whatever the subsequent conviction, the protection of the law extends to the criminal who enjoys rights not only in theory but enforceable in practice': *Cross v Kirkby* The Times, 5 April 2000 (Judge LJ).

is applicable but also by making an affirmative answer to it.[36] An affirmative answer to a defence is a plea that is consistent with accepting that the defence applies, but which asserts that the claimant's action should succeed nonetheless. If affirmative answers to defences exist in the law of unjust enrichment, then it would be incorrect to split the liability rules of this branch of the law merely into rules that define actions and rules that define defences. It would also be wrong to say that the types of response that a defendant can offer in the hope of avoiding or limiting liability are restricted to denials and defences. This is because defendants would, at the minimum, also be given the chance to show that any rule to which a claimant appeals in an attempt to circumvent a defence is inapplicable in the circumstances of the case. One party cannot be allowed to make an allegation without the other being given the opportunity to refute it.

Do affirmative answers to defences to liability in unjust enrichment exist? The law on this point is unclear. Consider the change of position defence, treated in § 65 of R3RUE, and assume, for the moment, that change of position is a defence rather than a denial.[37] A change of position will not shield a defendant from liability in unjust enrichment if the defendant changes position in bad faith. But is changing one's position in good faith an element of the defence of change of position, or is the fact that a defendant has changed position in bad faith an affirmative answer that can be given by the claimant to the defence? R3RUE gives no real guidance on this point. It provides that the defence of change of position 'is not available', or 'may not be asserted' by one who acts with notice of the facts underlying the action, or who is a conscious wrongdoer.[38] This is ambiguous as to whether the bad faith rule is part and parcel of the defence of change of position or external to it.[39] The decision to locate discussion of notice in a separate section, viz § 69, creates the impression, perhaps inadvertently, that the bad faith rule is independent of the change of position defence.

Similar observations can be made about the bona fide purchase rule treated in § 66. If we assume, for the moment, that bona fide purchase is a defence rather than a denial,[40] the question arises whether the absence of notice of prior interests is an element of this defence. Perhaps the fact that the defendant purchased the relevant property with notice of prior interests is an affirmative answer to it. Equally, is the requirement that the purchase must be for value an ingredient of

[36] The discussion here has been influenced by RA Epstein, 'Pleadings and Presumptions' (1973) 40 *University of Chicago Law Review* 556, especially 568–71.

[37] The classification of the change of position rule is discussed in Part E, section (6).

[38] R3RUE (n 1) § 65, Comments f and g.

[39] English legal scholars also tend to describe the bad faith rule, uninformatively, as one of 'disqualification': eg, Burrows (n 31) 537; C Mitchell, P Mitchell and S Watterson (eds), *Goff & Jones: The Law of Unjust Enrichment*, 8th edn (London, Sweet & Maxwell, 2011) [27-31]. Conversely, two Australian writers refer to this ambiguity and argue that the better view is that the rule is part of the defence of change of position: E Bant and P Creighton, 'The Australian Change of Position Defence' (2002) 30 *University of Western Australia Law Review* 208, 221 n 63. Unfortunately, however, they later lose sight of the distinction between defences and affirmative answers to defences, and nourish the very confusion that they sought to eliminate: ibid 224–28.

[40] The classification of the bona fide purchase rule is discussed in Part E, section (7).

the defence or is a failure to buy the property for value a freestanding rule that results in the defence being withheld? R3RUE does not does not give clear answers to these questions. It is implied in § 66, Comment d that the absence of notice is an element of the defence,[41] but the decision to house exposition of the effect of notice in § 69 creates the impression that the fact of notice is an affirmative answer to this defence.

(3) Summary

It is arguable that the law of unjust enrichment cannot be divided merely into actions and defences, and that denials and defences are therefore not the only types of arguments that a defendant to an action in unjust enrichment might make with a view to avoiding or limiting liability. However, it is far from clear whether additional responses are available, and so this chapter proceeds on the assumption that there are no additional responses open to defendants.

D. Rationalising the Distinction between Actions and Defences

The distinction between actions and defences is one of the oldest and most basic in the law of unjust enrichment. The aim of this part of the chapter is to consider whether it ought to exist. This is a neglected but important issue. It is easy to take the existence of defences for granted. However, the presence of defences is something that must be justified, since it would be possible to do away with defences by assimilating all of the liability rules in unjust enrichment into the elements of an action. Moreover, the justification needs to be powerful, as a system of liability for unjust enrichment that consisted only in actions would have the significant advantage of simplicity.

(1) Inadequate Rationales

Graham Virgo argues that the law of unjust enrichment provides for defences for two reasons:[42] first, they recognise situations in which justice favours the defendant's retaining a benefit; and second, they uphold the principle that the defendant's receipt of a benefit should be secure. However, neither argument explains

[41] The material passage reads: 'the expression "bona fide purchaser" . . . is a long-established term of art meaning "a purchaser for value without notice".' By incorporating the notice rule within the definition of the defence, R3RUE insinuates that the absence of notice is an element of the defence.

[42] G Virgo, *The Principles of the Law of Restitution*, 2nd edn (Oxford, Oxford University Press, 2006) 665–67. It is unclear whether the second argument is different from the first.

why the law of unjust enrichment recognises defences because neither is an argument for the existence of defences specifically. Rather, they are both merely arguments for limiting the circumstances in which liability in unjust enrichment arises generally. They do nothing to show, for example, that the interest in receipts being secure should be advanced by recognising defences instead of by bringing the rules that constitute defences within the net of actions in unjust enrichment. Indeed, collapsing defences into the elements of an action would advance the goals that Virgo identifies more effectively. This is because the claimant bears the burden of proving the elements of his action.[43]

Peter Birks gestured towards a different rationale for recognising defences. He claimed that defences are concerned with the 'fine tuning of the law of unjust enrichment'.[44] He also argued that the liberalisation of actions in unjust enrichment and the allocation to defences of a greater proportion of responsibility for determining when liability arises allowed the law of unjust enrichment to deliver 'more sensitive justice'[45] than was previously possible.[46] It is not clear what should be made of these passages. Do they make one argument or two? Furthermore, it is uncertain whether Birks should even be read as supporting the existence of defences. He wrote:

> Defences work because they bear on one or other of the elements of the principle against unjust enrichment. They relate to enrichment, to the phrase 'at the expense of', or to the word 'unjust'.[47]

Such language suggests that all defences are really denials because they function by 'attacking'[48] the elements of actions in unjust enrichment. Nevertheless, we do not read Birks as saying that the law of unjust enrichment does not provide for defences. He also wrote that:

> All the defences work by trumping the injustice of the defendant's enrichment. The defendant simply adds further facts which overwhelm the claimant's prima facie entitlement to restitution.[49]

[43] See the text accompanying n 52.

[44] P Birks, *Unjust Enrichment*, 2nd edn (Oxford, Oxford University Press, 2005) 40. See also at 207 and 263.

[45] ibid 40.

[46] Compare Lord Goff's claim in *Lipkin Gorman (a firm) v Karpnale Ltd* [1991] 2 AC 548, 581: 'the recognition of change of position as a defence should be . . . beneficial [because it] . . . will enable a more generous approach to be taken to the recognition of the right to restitution, in the knowledge that the defence is, in more appropriate cases, available.' Similar views are expressed in *Lincoln* (n 7) 372; *Deutsche Morgan Grenfell plc v IRC* [2006] UKHL 49, [2007] 1 AC 558 [38]; *Sempra Metals Ltd v IRC* [2007] UKHL 34, [2008] 1 AC 561 [24]. However this is not a convincing rationale for recognising defences since it does not explain why a more generous approach should be taken to recognising rights to restitution.

[47] P Birks, 'Change of Position: The Nature of the Defence and its Relationship to Other Restitutionary Defences' in M McInnes (ed), *Restitution: Developments in Unjust Enrichment* (Sydney, Lawbook Co, 1996) 49, 62.

[48] Birks (n 44) 207.

[49] ibid 207. *Cf* P Birks, *Restitution: The Future* (Sydney, Federation Press, 1992) 125–26: 'If [a defence] bears on [the qualification of the defendant's enrichment as unjust] it may impinge specifically on the reason why the plaintiff claims that the enrichment is irreversible – that is, specifically

These words, and especially the word 'trumping', strongly suggest that Birks acknowledged the existence of defences. What therefore should be made of the reason (or reasons) that he advanced in support of defences? The fatal difficulty with Birks' analysis is that it consists merely in assertions. He does not explain *why* recognising defences facilitates 'fine tuning' of the law of unjust enrichment or yields 'more sensitive justice'.

Another reason for recognising defences is offered by Andrew Burrows. He contends:

> Rather than the courts placing arbitrary restrictions on liability, the scope of restitution is now more satisfactorily and openly controlled by defences, especially the change of position defence.[50]

Again, it is unclear how many rationales for defences are being offered, as it is uncertain whether Burrows thinks that there is a difference between the scope of restitution being more 'satisfactorily' controlled and it being defined more 'openly'. However, we read him as suggesting that defences exist because they permit disputes to be resolved in a more principled manner than would be the case if the law of unjust enrichment consisted solely in actions. This analysis suffers from the same problem as Birks' discussion. As it stands, Burrows' argument does not rise above the level of assertion. He does not tell us *why* admitting defences into the law of unjust enrichment enables the law to resolve disputes less arbitrarily than it would if defences did not exist and relevant rules were packed into the elements of an action.

We also note that Burrows' claims in this regard are difficult to reconcile with some other propositions that he advances regarding defences, especially his statement that 'what counts as a defence rather than as going to the defendant's prima facie liability rests on common practice or understanding rather than clear-cut principle'.[51] By this he presumably means that the fact that a given rule is treated as part of an action in unjust enrichment or as a defence is a matter of historical accident. However, if this is the case, the distinction between actions and defences can hardly be defended on the ground that it helps the courts to solve disputes in a principled fashion. Random arrangement is the antithesis of principled organisation.

on the plaintiff's unjust factor – or it may introduce some wider but still definable concept of justice which militates against the plaintiff's claim. For example, a claim which is brought too late will meet the defence of limitation. It would be unjust for it to succeed, but the reasons why it would be so are unrelated to the quality of the defendant's receipt.' Here Birks appears to identify two types of 'unjust-related' argument open to a defendant, the first of which we would describe as a denial and the second of which we would describe as a defence.

[50] Burrows (n 31) 523.

[51] ibid 523. See also Grantham and Rickett (n 24) 105: 'at the doctrinal level, the treatment of matters as going to a cause of action or to a defence can be viewed largely as a matter of convention'. And note G Dannemann, 'Illegality as a Defence against Unjust Enrichment Claims' in D Johnston and R Zimmermann (eds), *Unjustified Enrichment: Key Issues in Comparative Perspective* (Cambridge, Cambridge University Press, 2002) 310, 311–12: common law and civil law systems often characterise liability rules in unjust enrichment differently, so that 'one system's ground of restitution, put in the negative, is the other's defence against such a claim'.

(2) Possible Rationales

We are unconvinced that a satisfactory argument has yet been identified to support the existence of the distinction between actions in unjust enrichment and defences. The aim of this section is therefore to discuss whether a compelling case for the distinction can be made. Five possible arguments are considered. These are tentative. We set them out here in the hope that they may point the way towards fully fledged rationalisations of the distinction between actions and defences.

(a) The Efficient Administration of Justice

The distinction between actions in unjust enrichment and defences governs the allocation of the onus of proof. As a general rule, facts that pertain to the elements of actions in unjust enrichment must be proved by the claimant, whereas facts that go to defences must be established by the defendant.[52] As a result, litigation is conducted more expeditiously and economically than would be the case were the distinction between actions and defences dissolved (unless the law were changed so that the onus of proof was allocated according to a different criterion). If all of the defences to liability in unjust enrichment were drawn within the net of actions in unjust enrichment, the number of facts that the claimant would be required to prove in order to establish liability would be greatly increased. Every fact in issue that is currently a matter of defence would have to be disproved by the claimant. To obtain restitution in proceedings in unjust enrichment, every claimant would have to demonstrate that the defendant did not change position, that no limitation bar had descended, that he should not fail on the ground that the transaction in question was tainted with illegality and so on. This would result in trials becoming significantly more protracted and expensive than they are at present. These costs would be incurred for minimal return since, in the majority of cases, it is unlikely that multiple rules that are presently cast as defences will be in contention. Accordingly, the distinction between actions in unjust enrichment and defences saves time and money insofar as it ensures that the court will not need to decide whether rules that currently fall into the defence category are enlivened unless they are raised by the defendant.

(b) Procedural Fairness

Second, the divide between actions in unjust enrichment and defences promotes procedural fairness. Again, because the onus of proof is assigned by reference to the distinction between actions in unjust enrichment and defences, the distinc-

[52] English authority that directly supports these propositions is surprisingly scarce. But see *Birmingham* (n 14) 399–400; *Bank of Credit and Commerce International (Overseas) Ltd v Akindele* [2001] Ch 437, 456; *Getronics Holdings Emea BV v Logistic & Transport Consulting Co* [2004] EWHC 808 (QB) [22]–[24]. An exceptional situation where the claimant bears the onus of excluding a defence is discussed in the text accompanying n 25.

tion means that both parties are responsible for proving certain matters. If the distinction between actions and defences did not exist, so that the law of unjust enrichment consisted only in the elements of actions, the claimant would be the only party placed under a burden (unless, of course, the law governing the assignment of the onus of proof were changed and the onus distributed according to a different criterion). This would be contrary to a fundamental tenet of procedural justice. It is a basic principle of law that litigants in the civil sphere must be treated as even-handedly in terms of procedure as is reasonably possible.[53]

This argument can be taken a step further. Certain facts may tend to be significantly easier for claimants to prove than for defendants to disprove and vice versa. This may be because particular facts are usually peculiarly within the knowledge of one party (for example, whether the defendant had notice of a mistake made by the claimant) or because requiring one party to establish a certain fact would involve calling on that party to prove a negative (which would happen if, for example, the claimant bore the onus of proof in respect of the change of position doctrine). The distinction between actions and defences can be recruited to ensure that litigants as a whole are treated fairly in terms of what they are called upon to prove. For example, if a particular fact is normally much easier for claimants to prove than the defendants, it might be procedurally fairer to allocate that issue to the actions category so that claimants will be called upon to establish it.

(c) More Refined Liability Rules

According to conventional wisdom, when all of the elements of an action in unjust enrichment are satisfied, defendants fall under an obligation to make restitution.[54] In other words, when an action is constituted, a duty to make restitution arises. In contrast, defences do not create duties; rather, they identify situations where a defendant has the option of not complying with the relevant duty. So, for example, whereas the fact that the defendant has been unjustly enriched at the claimant's expense places the defendant under a duty to make restitution, the defence of change of position (assuming for the moment that change of position is a defence and not a denial[55]) merely affords a defendant who has been unjustly enriched at the claimant's expense a privilege, to use Hohfeld's terminology,[56] to spend money where such expenditure is induced by the enrichment and it is spent

[53] The principle is discussed in A Zuckerman, *Zuckerman on Civil Procedure: Principles of Practice*, 2nd edn (London, Sweet & Maxwell, 2006) 104–10 and in relation to the onus of proof specifically at 755–56. At 755–56, Zuckerman writes: 'Precisely because both parties are entitled to equal protection from the risk of error it makes sense to hold that while one party runs a higher risk on one issue, the opponent should bear the risk on another issue.'

[54] This traditional learning is rejected by Stephen Smith in ch 10 of this volume. Smith would prefer to say that if an action in unjust enrichment is constituted, then the defendant is merely liable to be ordered by a court to make restitution. In his view, defendants who are unjustly enriched at the claimant's expense owe no duty to make restitution prior to judgment being given against them.

[55] The categorisation of the change of position rule is discussed in Part E, section (6).

[56] W N Hohfeld, 'Some Fundamental Legal Conceptions as Applied in Judicial Reasoning' (1913) 23 *Yale Law Journal* 16, especially at 30–44.

in good faith. In other words, the defence of change of position does not oblige the defendant to do anything. By separating actions in unjust enrichment and defences, the law of unjust enrichment is therefore able to indicate to defendants when they will fall under a duty to make restitution and when they enjoy a privilege to disregard that duty. It is arguable that such guidance could not be given (or could not be given as clearly) if defences were assimilated within the definitions of actions in unjust enrichment.

(d) Promoting Rationality in Judicial Reasoning

It is arguable that the distinction between actions in unjust enrichment and defences should be maintained because it promotes rationality in judges' reasoning processes.[57] Organising rules that determine the scope of liability in unjust enrichment into actions and defences may help judges to keep their thoughts straight in at least three distinct ways. First, it increases the visibility of connections between rules that fall within the same category and distinctions between rules that belong to different categories. This increased visibility guards against the risk that judges will overlook links between related rules or conflate discrete rules. Second, by arranging the process of determining liability in unjust enrichment into an action stage and a defence stage, judges may be more likely to systematically address all of the relevant liability rules rather than to lapse into an opaque determination of whether restitution should be permitted. This is because the rules are represented, to a degree, in a form resembling a checklist. Third, the distinction may help to prevent judges from dealing with rules in an illogical sequence. It is a principle that applies across the whole of the civil law[58] that judges should ascertain whether the claimant's action is complete before investigating the applicability of any defences.[59] The distinction between actions and defences can therefore be used to minimise the risk that judges will deal with certain rules in a nonsensical order. Rules that logically arise for consideration as anterior matters can be treated as part of an action, whereas rules that ought to be considered only after other rules have been addressed can be cast as defences.

(e) Subtle Relief

Another argument in favour of separating actions in unjust enrichment from defences runs as follows.[60] A successful denial normally leads to a verdict for the

[57] We believe that this rationale for recognising defences may be what Burrows alludes to when he writes that 'the scope of restitution is now more satisfactorily and openly controlled by defences' (see the text accompanying n 49).

[58] In relation to the law of torts, see *Perrett v Sydney Harbour Foreshore Authority* [2009] NSWSC 1026 [39]–[40].

[59] It is no accident that when judges enumerate the questions that need to be asked in determining whether a claimant is entitled to restitution, defences are mentioned last: eg, *Banque Financière* (n 7) 227.

[60] It has been inspired by the analysis of McLachlin J, in a different context, in *Hall v Hebert* [1993] 2 SCR 159, 184–85.

defendant, yet this might sometimes be inappropriate because it would not do justice to the merits of the claimant's action. Certain defences permit the court to respond more flexibly. For example, defences such as change of position and bona fide purchase (assuming that these rules are defences and not denials[61]) sometimes merely diminish the defendant's liability. Defences therefore on occasion give the court greater room for manoeuvre than denials. Hence, it is desirable to recognise defences because a system of law that permits the courts to respond in a nuanced way is preferable to a system that is constituted by blunter rules.

There are at least three weaknesses in this argument, all of which relate to the proposition that defences give the courts greater scope to resolve cases justly than denials. First, successful denials do not always eliminate liability. For example, a defendant might succeed in showing that he was only enriched by the receipt of $100 rather than $200, as alleged by a claimant. In this situation, liability will still arise, but it will be less extensive than asserted by the claimant. Second, very few defences merely reduce liability: most defences preclude liability from arising. Third, partial defences might not actually permit the courts much scope to dispense justice that is tailored to the facts of individual cases. Partial defences to liability in unjust enrichment do not operate, for example, in a manner equivalent to the apportionment provision in the law of torts,[62] which, when applicable, permits the courts to apportion damages in accordance with what is 'just and equitable' in view of the parties' shares in the responsibility for the claimant's damage. The apportionment provision is far more malleable than any of the partial defences in the law of unjust enrichment.

(f) Discussion

This part of the chapter was concerned with whether the law of unjust enrichment should recognise defences. This is an under-examined issue. Five arguments in favour of retaining defences were considered. These arguments were that defences promote the efficient administration of justice, advance procedural fairness, allow for more refined liability rules, promote rationality in judicial reasoning and enable the courts to afford more subtle relief. As the question of why defences exist has not previously been dealt with in any detail, the goal here has merely been to put some rationales for recognising defences on the table. The analysis, in other words, has been exploratory and the propositions advanced tentative. Some of the arguments may be less convincing than others and it may be that some of them should be rejected.

If the distinction between actions and defences is justifiable, the rationale or rationales that support it may bear upon how rules that govern liability should be classified. For example, if one is persuaded by the efficient administration of justice rationale, then one should conclude that rules which are infrequently in contention should be cast as defences to ensure that the court only needs to

[61] See Part E, sections (6) and (7), respectively.
[62] Law Reform (Contributory Negligence) Act 1945 (UK), s 1(1).

expend resources determining whether they are applicable if they are put in issue by the defendant. Some other rationales may not supply similar guidance on how individual rules should be presented. Consider, for instance, the procedural fairness rationale. This rationale, in addition to being concerned with how individual rules should be classified, is also interested in the treatment of the totality of rules that determine the scope of liability. It holds that the difficulty experienced by claimants in discharging the burden resting on them to establish that all of the elements of an action are present should be roughly commensurate to the difficulty of the task that defendants face in proving that defences apply. It should also be observed that if there are multiple sufficient rationales for the existence of defences, it is possible that different rationales might pull in different directions as to the way in which a given rule ought to be classified. In such a situation, a principle for resolving conflicts would need to be developed.

E. Classification

R3RUE identifies various arguments that defendants may be able to make to avoid or reduce their liability in unjust enrichment. In this part of the chapter we discuss whether some of these are denials or defences.[63] We look at the following arguments in turn: 'recipient not unjustly enriched' (§ 62), illegality (§ 32), incapacity (§ 33), 'equitable disqualification (unclean hands)' (§ 63), passing on (§ 64), change of position (§ 65), 'bona fide purchaser' (§ 66) and 'bona fide payee' (§ 67), limitation and laches (§ 70), disruption of public finances (§ 19(2)) and failure to make counter-restitution (§ 54(2)). We have chosen this running order for reasons of expository convenience. Most of these arguments appear in Chapter 8 of R3RUE,[64] but some are found elsewhere.

We assume that the law exists as it is described in R3RUE and we do not consider whether it accurately states the law of any particular American jurisdiction or of a majority of jurisdictions. Our only goal is to determine how the foregoing responses should be classified in view of their description in R3RUE. We stress that the analysis in this part of the chapter is descriptive rather than normative. We do not argue that any particular response should be available or unavailable or that the circumstances in which it should be accepted should be widened or narrowed. Nor do we contend that a given response should be re-defined so as to yield a different classification. This is not because we think that such normative analysis is unimportant. We have undertaken a descriptive project in this part of

[63] R3RUE does not address all of the responses open to defendants. For instance, the doctrine of set-off is not meaningfully treated. Because this chapter is primarily an analysis of R3RUE's handling of responses available to defendants, it ignores responses that are not discussed in R3RUE.

[64] Not all of the sections in Chapter 8 are intended to capture freestanding responses available to defendants. §§ 68 and 69 are respectively concerned with 'value' and 'notice'. These sections elaborate principles that are important to the application of certain responses discussed in other sections.

the chapter simply because we think it sensible to identify the present shape of the law before asking whether and, if so, how the law should be changed.

(1) Recipient Not Unjustly Enriched

§ 62 concerns cases in which all of the ingredients of an action in unjust enrichment would be established if the impugned transaction were 'viewed in isolation',[65] so that the law would prima facie give the claimant a remedy, but another source of rights entitles the defendant to be enriched at the claimant's expense. An example is given in § 62, Illustration 2, which concerns a claimant who owes separate contractual debts to two creditors and pays one while intending to pay the other. Even if the recipient takes the money with notice of the mistake, so that he is not a bona fide purchaser, he is not liable because he is entitled to receive the payment under his contract with the claimant.[66] This result is consistent with the 'limiting principle' described in § 2(2) that: 'A valid contract defines the obligations of the parties as to matters within its scope, displacing to that extent any inquiry into unjust enrichment.'[67]

In § 62, Comment a, the rule described in § 62 is said to be enlivened where:

> [T]he claimant alleges facts supporting a prima facie claim in unjust enrichment – typically a payment by mistake – but the recipient is able to show that the resulting enrichment is not unjust, in view of the larger transactional context within which the benefit has been conferred.

This could be interpreted as a statement that the defendant's argument is a denial, the element of the action being denied being the 'unjustness' of the defendant's enrichment, and this reading is reinforced by the title chosen for § 62: 'Recipient Not Unjustly Enriched'.[68] Against this, however, there is the Reporter's statement

[65] R3RUE (n 1) vol II, 482.

[66] Other examples given of the rule in § 62 concern natural obligations, ie, legally unenforceable obligations that are binding on the defendant's conscience (eg, § 62, Illustration 4: no recovery of money mistakenly paid to discharge an unenforceable gambling debt). It is controversial whether the law should give effect to such obligations, even to the extent of treating them as reasons for the retention of what would otherwise be an unjust enrichment. For discussion, see D Sheehan, 'Natural Obligations in English Law' [2004] *Lloyd's Maritime & Commercial Law Quarterly* 170; M McInnes, 'Natural Obligations and Unjust Enrichment' in E Bant and M Harding (eds), *Exploring Private Law* (Cambridge, Cambridge University Press, 2010) 175; A Rigoni, 'A Sin of Admission: Why Section 62 Should Have Been Omitted from the *Restatement (Third) of Restitution and Unjust Enrichment*' (2011) 68 *Washington and Lee Law Review* 1203. Examples of a stronger case, namely where the defendant's enrichment is mandated by a court order, are given at § 18, Comments e and g, and Illustrations 6 and 7.

[67] See too § 2, Comment c: 'Restitution is subordinate to contract as an organising principle of private relationships, and the terms of an enforceable agreement normally displace any claim of unjust enrichment within their reach.'

[68] Another way in which the rule might conceivably be interpreted would be to say that it operates as a denial that the defendant has been enriched. Douglas Laycock seemed to have this in mind when he wrote that § 62 concerns 'cases of apparent enrichment that turn out not to be': D Laycock, 'Restoring Restitution to the Canon' (2012) 110 *Michigan Law Review* 929, 940. *Cf Hills* (n 12) [73]. The argument would go that a defendant who has a contractual or other legal right to receive a money payment or other benefit from a claimant is no better off when this right is crystallised by the

that all of the responses discussed in Chapter 8 of R3RUE are 'presented as affirmative defenses'.[69] We are unsure what, precisely, the Reporter means by the phrase 'affirmative defence'. Perhaps he means it to refer to rules that we regard as defences. But he may intend for it to refer to rules in respect of which the defendant bears the onus of proof.[70] Scholars often preface the word 'defence' with the word 'affirmative' to indicate that they are referencing principles that the defendant is called upon to establish.[71] To decide whether § 62 describes a denial or a defence, we must ask what the Reporter means when he says that a defendant's enrichment is 'unjust', and how he thinks this 'unjustness' is affected by a contract or other source of rights entitling the defendant to receive the relevant benefit.

Consider the 'two creditors' example. One way to explain it might be to say that the payee's enrichment is 'unjust' only if the payor's mistake is an 'invalidating mistake' of the kind identified in § 5 *and* there is no basis for the payee's enrichment deriving from a contract. On this view, the absence of a contract between the parties is an element of the payor's action in unjust enrichment, and so the argument that the payee is contractually entitled to the money is a denial. Alternatively, if the making of an 'invalidating mistake' is sufficient in itself to render the payee's enrichment 'unjust', then the payee's appeal to his contractual rights is not a denial, because the 'unjustness' of the payee's enrichment deriving from the mistake cannot be 'nullified' by these rights. Instead, they provide a reason why restitution should not be awarded that is external to the definition of the action. On this view, § 62 describes a defence.[72]

Which version of 'unjust' is adopted in R3RUE? Adam Rigoni reads § 62 to mean that the rule operates as a defence.[73] Andrew Burrows concurs, but considers that 'the precise meaning of § 62 and the relationship of that defence to other parts of the Restatement – and even the relationship between that defence and the

claimant's performance of his obligation. However, this argument rests on the false premise that a legal right to be paid money, for example, is worth as much as having the money in hand.

[69] R3RUE (n 1) vol I, 481.

[70] See the text accompanying n 24.

[71] eg John Goldberg and Benjamin Zipursky write that to treat a rule as an 'affirmative defense ... is to say that it is the defendant's burden, rather than the plaintiff's, to raise [it] in court pleadings and to prove [it]': JCP Goldberg and BC Zipursky, *The Oxford Introductions to US Law: Torts* (Oxford, Oxford University Press, 2010) 110.

[72] For an apparent statement of English law to this effect, see G Virgo, 'Demolishing the Pyramid – The Presence of Basis and Risk-Taking in the Law of Unjust Enrichment' in A Robertson and Tang H W (eds), *The Goals of Private Law* (Oxford, Hart Publishing, 2009) 477, 488–504 and especially 489: 'once the elements of the unjust enrichment claim have been established by the claimant, restitution will follow save where a basis for the defendant's retention of the enrichment can be identified by the defendant'. This phrasing suggests that Virgo understands the presence of a legal ground for the defendant's enrichment to be a defence (as we use this term). Confusingly, however, he insists that the rule is a 'bar' and not a 'defence' (ibid 479, n 16 and text), and in other writing he seems to define 'bars' in the same way that we have defined denials: Virgo (n 42) 665: 'a bar relates to the establishment of the cause of action [whereas] a defence only arises once the defendant has established the cause of action'.

[73] Rigoni (n 66) 1204–05.

defence in § 67 – is not entirely clear.'[74] We agree that that the evidence supporting the 'defence' reading is strong, but inconclusive. As we have previously noted,[75] the Reporter has not overtly espoused an 'unjust factor' approach in preference to an 'absence of basis' approach, and although positive reasons for awarding restitution such as mistake and duress are identified in Chapter 2 of R3RUE, it is not explained exactly how these might be 'displaced' by the presence of a legal ground for the defendant's enrichment. Hence, while it may be conceptually possible for a legal system to roll the two approaches into one by requiring claimants to show both the presence of an unjust factor and the absence of any legal ground for the transfer,[76] it is unclear from the way in which actions in unjust enrichment are described in R3RUE that this is actually the approach that has been taken. We conclude that the proper classification of the rule in § 62, as it has been presented in R3RUE, is an open question.

(2) Illegality

§ 32 provides that restitution will be denied if the relevant transaction between the parties is unlawful. An exception to this rule is set out in § 32(2). Under § 32(2), restitution is permitted notwithstanding the illegal nature of the transaction to the extent necessary to prevent unjust enrichment if 'the allowance of restitution will not defeat or frustrate the policy of the underlying prohibition'. Insofar as § 32 provides that restitution is unavailable where the transaction is illegal, it is a defence. This is because pleading it is consistent with accepting that all of the elements of an action in unjust enrichment are present. It is clearly possible for a defendant to point to the fact that the transaction concerned was illegal while agreeing that he was unjustly enriched at the claimant's expense without contradicting himself.

(3) Incapacity

The starting position taken in R3RUE in relation to the incapacity of the defendant is that it is not an answer to liability. This rule is stated in § 33(1). However, § 33(3) provides that:

[74] See ch 7 in this volume, at p 182. Burrows has advanced the view elsewhere that this argument ought to be conceptualised as a denial: A Burrows, 'Restitution of Mistaken Enrichments' (2012) 92 *Boston University Law Review* 767, 774–79, especially 779; A Burrows, *A Restatement of the English Law of Unjust Enrichment* (Oxford, Oxford University Press, 2012) 36.

[75] See the text accompanying nn 9 and 10.

[76] Compare Jacques du Plessis' discussion in ch 4 of this volume, at p 102. Also, for the argument that English law should combine the two approaches to some extent, see Birks (n 44) 116–17, supported in TA Baloch, 'The Unjust Enrichment Pyramid' (2007) 123 *LQR* 636, but critiqued in A Burrows, 'Absence of Basis: The New Birksian Scheme' in Burrows and Rodger (n 10) 33. Burrows concludes that 'the best approach is . . . to apply the common law approach, while using the Birksian [absence of basis] scheme as a cross-check in difficult or novel cases': ibid 48.

> Notwithstanding the unjust enrichment of the recipient, restitution may be limited or denied if it would be inconsistent with the protection that the doctrine of incapacity is intended to afford in the circumstances of the case.

The Reporter understands § 33 to involve a balancing exercise. Comment c states that:

> [T]he contours of legal responsibility in . . . [cases in which § 33 is in issue] are determined, not by measuring 'capacity to contract' against some a priori standard, but by weighing at each point the value of the protection secured against the cost of securing it.

There is little in § 33(3) to suggest that, when it exceptionally prevents liability from arising, it does so other than by working as a defence. Relying on § 33(3) is consistent with accepting that the elements of an action in unjust enrichment have been established. Moreover, if § 33 involves a balancing exercise, as the Reporter asserts, it must be a defence since this balancing exercise does not appear among the elements of an action in unjust enrichment described in R3RUE.

(4) Equitable Disqualification (Unclean Hands)

§ 63 describes a doctrine referred to by R3RUE as 'equitable disqualification (unclean hands)'. This section is concerned with the claimant's inequitable conduct in relation to the transaction that is the source of the asserted liability. Although the Reporter tells us that §§ 32 and 63 are 'readily distinguishable',[77] it is unclear what the difference between them is, and it should be noted that the Reporter later writes that there is a 'significant overlap' between the rules[78] and seems to acknowledge that § 32 is a specific application of § 63.[79] This may explain why § 63 appears in § 32(3). If § 63 is merely a repetition of § 32, then it must be a defence too. Possibly supporting this interpretation is the fact that it is expressly stated on more than one occasion that § 63 is an 'affirmative defence'.[80]

Earlier in this chapter we discussed standing rules[81] and concluded that there is little indication that such rules exist in the law of unjust enrichment, at least in the modern world. It is worth noting that some sections of the commentary to § 63 are consistent with reading § 63 as a standing rule. In Comment a, it is said that:

> The possibility that a court may refuse relief . . . [by reference to the behaviour of the claimant] is classified within this Restatement, for convenience of organization, among the affirmative defences to a liability in restitution. But the principle involved is in fact one of judicial forbearance, and its concern is with the disqualification of the claimant rather than the rightful position of the recipient.[82]

[77] R3RUE (n 1) vol I, 513.
[78] ibid vol II, 489.
[79] ibid vol II, 493.
[80] ibid vol I, 513; and vol II, 488.
[81] Part C, section (1).
[82] R3RUE (n 1) vol II, 487–88.

This passage (and especially the words 'the disqualification of the claimant') suggests that § 63 describes a standing rule. The claimant is stripped of the right to maintain litigation, regardless of the merits of the underlying action. Of course, this is hardly conclusive evidence in favour of interpreting § 63 as a standing rule, and since there is no firm indication in R3RUE that standing rules exist, we conclude that the rule is intended to function as a defence.

(5) Passing On

§ 64(1) provides that a payee may escape liability in unjust enrichment if 'the economic burden of the payment has been passed on by the claimant to third persons' but 'restitution to the claimant would not facilitate recovery by the persons ultimately entitled to relief'. § 64(2) adds that:

> [T]he economic burden of a payment by the claimant to the recipient has been passed on by the claimant to a third person if and to the extent that such third person would be entitled to restitution of the payment from the claimant, if restitution were made by the recipient to the claimant.

In § 64, Comment a, these sub-sections are said to 'describe what is commonly known as the affirmative defence of "passing on".' However, the discussion in Comments a and b equivocates between two different explanations of the underlying reason for disallowing restitution in cases in which § 64 is enlivened. The first explanation is that where a benefit is passed along a chain of reversible transfers, such as a series of causally connected mistaken payments from a third party to the claimant, and from the claimant to a defendant, the best outcome would be to return the benefit received by the defendant to the third party. If that outcome is impossible to achieve, for example, because the third party can no longer be identified, then the benefit must either be left in the hands of the defendant or returned to the claimant, and since neither party deserves it, the preferable option is to let the gain lie where it falls (ie, in the defendant's hands). On this account, passing on is a defence because the claimant is denied restitution despite his being able to establish all of the elements of an action in unjust enrichment. He is denied restitution for the reason that ordering restitution would result in the claimant's unjust enrichment at the expense of the third party, so that restitution would produce the right result as between the claimant and the defendant, but the wrong result as between the claimant and the third party. It is true that denying restitution produces the wrong result as between the defendant and the third party, but there is no social interest in using scarce judicial resources to replace one wrong result with another by redirecting an enrichment gained at the third party's expense from the defendant to the claimant.

The second explanation of the rule in § 64 is more formalistic and (at least overtly) less policy-driven. This explanation depends on the rule stated in § 50(4) that: 'The liability in restitution of an innocent recipient of unrequested benefits may not exceed the cost to the claimant of conferring the benefits in question.' Where the claimant has passed on his loss to a third party, it is argued, he cannot recover because the cost to him of conferring the benefit on the defendant is zero. In other words, the defendant can escape liability in unjust enrichment by denying that the claimant has established one of the ingredients of the action, namely that the defendant's enrichment has been gained at the claimant's expense.

It seems that the first rather than the second of these interpretations was favoured by the Reporter, because it is otherwise difficult to explain why the principle is confined to the situations contemplated in § 64(2). This sub-section effectively defines the doctrine of passing on as a principle that is enlivened only where a third party has a better claim than the claimant to the benefit received by the defendant. Hence it deliberately prevents a defendant from arguing that he should escape liability in cases where the benefit he received was not gained at the claimant's expense because the claimant managed to pass on his loss to a third party who could not recover from the claimant if the defendant were ordered to repay the claimant. An example would be where a claimant pays money under duress to the defendant and then receives a gift from a friend to make good his loss on the shared understanding that he can keep the gift regardless of whether he recovers anything from the defendant.

(6) Change of Position

The doctrine of change of position is presented in § 65 as an 'affirmative defence'.[83] However, it is noted in § 65, Comment a that:

> [W]ith only a slight change of perspective, the same issues [with which the doctrine engages] appear to form part of the claimant's prima facie case in unjust enrichment: the need to establish that the recipient has in fact been unjustly enriched and (if so) by how much.

The Reporter continues:

> Broadly speaking, facts that our legal system would regard as giving rise to a defence of change of position are treated in civil-law systems as part of the problem of measuring the (surviving) enrichment for which the recipient is liable. The idea is crystallised in a section of the German Civil Code which provides, roughly translated, that 'to the extent that the recipient is no longer enriched, the duty of restitution or replacement of the benefit is excluded'.

The question whether the doctrine of change of position is a defence or a denial is therefore seen to turn on the resolution of an important debate concerning the requirement that a defendant must have been enriched, namely whether this

[83] ibid vol II, 176, 515 and 532.

requirement is tested at the time of receipt (the 'value received' model) or at the time when the action is brought (the 'value surviving' model). Suppose that C pays D $100 and D then spends $20 on a qualifying purchase in good faith. According to the 'value surviving' model, D's enrichment must be measured as $80 and so the remedy must be an order that D repay C $80. C is not entitled to more than $80 because one can never recover more than the amount of the defendant's surviving enrichment. According to the 'value received' model, in contrast, while D's enrichment is $100, the remedy remains an order that D repay $80, because although D was enriched by the larger amount, he can give a different reason for reducing C's remedy, namely that in the circumstances of the case, it would now be unfair to make him bear the loss of the $20 that he spent.

As noted in R3RUE, § 818 III of the BGB adopts the 'value surviving' model.[84] Conversely, R3RUE, at § 49, Comments b and c and Illustration 2, prefers the 'value received' model.[85] R3RUE's characterisation of change of position as a defence rather than a denial makes perfect sense on this model: the claimant can establish a cause of action in relation to the whole of the value received by the defendant, but once this value has been lost by the defendant's consumption or expenditure of the benefit in qualifying circumstances, the law ceases to be concerned with reversing the defendant's gain and concerns itself instead with the fair allocation of loss between the parties. This rationale for the defence is explained in § 65, Comment a and is reflected in § 50(3), which states that:

> The liability in restitution of an innocent recipient of unrequested benefits may not leave the recipient worse off (apart from the costs of litigation) than if the transaction giving rise to the liability had not occurred.

§ 50, Comment f observes that several other rules described in R3RUE are also intended to ensure that an innocent recipient is not left in a position inferior to that which he would have occupied had the impugned transaction never been made. For example, this consideration is also central to the limiting principle in § 2(4) that 'liability in restitution may not subject an innocent recipient to a forced exchange'[86] and the associated rules in § 49(3)(a) that a defendant's 'enrichment from the receipt of non-returnable benefits may be measured by the value of the benefit in advancing the purposes of the defendant' and § 50(2)(a) that 'unjust enrichment from unrequested benefits is measured by the standard that yields the smallest liability in restitution'. These rules embody a principle

[84] For an argument, which we do not find convincing, that 'value surviving' has become the de facto standard measure in all legal systems that recognise the change of position defence, see R Chambers, 'Two Kinds of Enrichment' in R Chambers, C Mitchell and J Penner (eds), *Philosophical Foundations of the Law of Unjust Enrichment* (Oxford, Oxford University Press, 2009) 242, 247–48.

[85] This dovetails with § 50(5), which provides that innocent parties are not liable for consequential gains (unlike wrongdoers against whom claims can lie for the disgorgement of profits that derive not from the law of unjust enrichment but from the law of wrongs).

[86] See also § 2, Comment e.

termed 'subjective devaluation' by some English courts and legal writers.[87] The idea underpinning this principle is that a defendant should not have to pay the market value of a benefit if this would unfairly deprive him of the right to choose not to take the benefit unless he can pay a lower price or have it for nothing. It appears from § 49, Comment d that the Reporter sees this as an argument that the claimant has failed to established market value as the appropriate measure of the defendant's enrichment, since he considers that 'value to the recipient' is 'the usual measure of enrichment in all cases where an innocent recipient has obtained unrequested, nonreturnable benefits'.[88]

(7) Bona Fide Purchaser and Bona Fide Payee

R3RUE deals with the doctrines of 'bona fide purchaser' and 'bona fide payee' in §§ 66 and 67, respectively. It is convenient to treat them together since the only difference between them, as described in R3RUE, is that the first responds to claims to recover real property and chattels, while the second responds to claims to recover money.[89] Both are expressly identified as defences.[90] The title-clearing function performed within property law by the bona fide purchase rule is said to be 'unrelated to unjust enrichment'[91] and it is not suggested that the purpose of these rules might be to avoid stultifying principles of property law by requiring those who receive good title by operation of these principles to pay over the value of the property.[92] Nor is it suggested that their purpose might be to prevent claims in unjust enrichment from subverting the contractual arrangements made between the defendant and the vendor from whom the defendant has received the claimant's property.[93] The function of both rules is rather said to be 'that they

[87] eg, *Cressman* (n 29) [28]; *Sempra* (n 46) [119]. The source of this terminology is P Birks, *An Introduction to the Law of Restitution* (Oxford, Clarendon Press, 1985) 109.

[88] Contrast *Sempra* (n 46) [48], [116]–[117] and [186], holding that objective market value will always be assigned to the use of money unless the defendant can show that it was worth less to him. On this view, subjective devaluation may be a defence.

[89] The *fons et origo* of § 67 is an article published by the Reporter: Kull (n 20). There he contends that the law of unjust enrichment admits a previously unrecognised answer to liability which he calls 'bona fide creditor' – which appears as 'bona fide payee' in R3RUE. At 924–25, Kull argues that this defence should be distinguished from the defence of bona fide purchaser. However, we are not convinced by his reasons for distinguishing the two, which seem to us to be the same defence, raised in response to claims generated by transfers of money and non-money benefits, respectively.

[90] R3RUE (n 1) vol II, 540. Young (n 26) 1336–37 writes that characterising these rules as denials rather than defences would be 'a turnabout of at least 160°, and maybe as much as 175°' from the position taken in the cases.

[91] R3RUE (n 1) vol II, 542

[92] For this view, see eg, Birks (n 44) 240-4; W Swadling, 'Ignorance and Unjust Enrichment: The Problem of Title' (2008) 28 *OJLS* 627, 656–57.

[93] For this view, see, eg, K Barker, 'After Change of Position: Good Faith Exchange in the Modern Law of Restitution' in P Birks (ed), *Laundering and Tracing* (Oxford, Clarendon Press, 1995) 191, 192; Burrows (n 31) 577–80. Had the 'bona fide purchaser' and 'bona fide payee' rules been presented in this way in R3RUE, an argument might have been made that they operate as denials of enrichment, given the Reporter's view that a defendant 'is not enriched' if he receives a benefit under a contract that requires him to make counter-performance: A Kull, 'Restitution as a Remedy for Breach of Contract'

facilitate commercial exchange by favouring the security of receipt', and for this reason it is claimed that there is 'a significant conceptual overlap' between them and the change of position defence.[94]

This prompts the observation that the two responses, like change of position, could be understood as denials if the law provided for restitution of value surviving in the defendant's hands rather than restitution of value received. The argument would then go that a bona fide purchaser or bona fide payee could deny that he was enriched once he had given value in exchange for the benefit received – and since the adequacy of the value provided would not be investigated, this would be an even stronger denial than change of position, which could only work *pro tanto*. As discussed in the previous section, however, value received rather than value surviving is treated by R3RUE as the standard measure of a defendant's enrichment, and bona fide purchase and bona fide payee, like change of position, are therefore more plausibly characterised as defences.

(8) Limitation of Actions and Laches

Limitation bars and the doctrine of laches are addressed in § 70, where they are treated as defences. There can be no argument against this classification. They are transparently rules that are external to the definitional elements of actions in unjust enrichment. The only point that is worth making for present purposes with regard to limitation bars and the doctrine of laches concerns the fact that R3RUE deals with them together. The reason given by R3RUE for doing so is that the period of delay that amounts to laches will generally be coloured by an analogous limitation period.[95] This reason is sufficient to justify this treatment. However, there is a much more fundamental basis for merging these bars to liability within a single rule in R3RUE: namely they are closely related in terms of their rationales. They both exist in recognition of the fact that it is unfair for defendants to be pursued in respect of long-forgotten events. They both acknowledge that certain types of evidence tend to deteriorate with the passing of time and that the accuracy of judicial decision-making is, consequently, generally diminished by delay. Finally, they are both premised on the idea that claimants who delay in bringing proceedings perhaps do not really need a remedy and that scarce court resources should be spent resolving other disputes.

(9) Disruption of Public Finances

The recovery of money paid as tax that is not due is treated in § 19 as a discrete topic, although actions to recover such payments are often grounded on mistake

(1993) 67 *South California Law Review* 1465, 1482, critiqued by Frederick Wilmot-Smith in ch 3 of this volume at p 74.

[94] R3RUE (n 1) vol II, 540.

[95] ibid vol II, 620. The English authorities are discussed in *Goff & Jones* (n 39) [33-38].

and sometimes on duress. The subject might therefore have been addressed in § 6, which provides that mistaken payments trigger restitution to the extent that they are not due, and § 14, which states that transfers induced by duress will trigger restitution. However, as explained in § 19, Comment a, the topic is treated separately because actions to recover money paid as tax that is not due are usually determined by 'principles thought to be specially applicable to tax cases'. These include the principle in § 19(2) that:

> If restitution . . . would disrupt orderly fiscal administration or result in severe public hardship, the court may on that account limit the relief to which the taxpayer would otherwise be entitled.

The structure of § 19 entails a deliberate departure from the way in which claims in this area are conceptualised by many American state courts.[96] As explained in § 19, Comment d, the strategy adopted in R3RUE is, first, to provide in § 19(1) that the payment of money as tax which is not due is a transaction that results in unjust enrichment. Then, in § 19(2), the disruption of public finances is presented as a 'countervailing equitable consideration'[97] or, in our terminology, as a defence. § 19(2) rests on the policy consideration that the public interest in fiscal stability outweighs the public interest in redressing unjust enrichment. Most jurisdictions do not overtly balance these considerations and instead conceal their policy calculations behind 'traditional formulas purporting to establish that an action to recover an illegal tax is not available as a matter of restitution law itself', the formula chiefly relied on being that payment of the illegal transaction is 'voluntarily' made.[98] In other words, most jurisdictions make 'non-voluntariness of the payment' an ingredient of an action in unjust enrichment to recover overpaid tax, and then, in an 'arbitrary and opaque fashion', they permit government defendants to deny that this has been established, for policy reasons that they do not clearly identify.[99] R3RUE does not argue against these policy assessments, but in the interests of transparency and descriptive accuracy, it eliminates 'non-voluntariness of payment' as an ingredient of the action and characterises the disruption of public finances as a defence.

One advantage flowing from this way of doing things is that it makes it easier to understand how a court might respond to an argument that restitution would seriously disrupt public finances not by disallowing recovery altogether, but by giving structured relief with a view to balancing the parties' interests in a more

[96] We note in passing that fiscal chaos has been rejected as a reason for denying liability in some other countries because it unfairly casts the burden of paying for the government's unlawful act onto an innocent taxpayer: eg, *Kingstreet Investments Ltd v New Brunswick (Department of Finance)* [2007] SCC 1, [2007] 1 SCR 3 [28] (Bastarache J). For discussion, see N Cleary, 'Property, Proportionality, and the Change of Position Defence' in S Elliott, B Häcker, and C Mitchell (eds), *Restitution of Overpaid Tax* (Oxford, Hart Publishing, 2013) 127, 136–39.

[97] R3RUE (n 1) vol II, 263.

[98] ibid vol II, 263.

[99] ibid vol II, 262. *Cf* Laycock (n 68) 934: 'when a court holds that . . . payments of erroneously assessed taxes were "voluntary", the word is being used in a Pickwickian or perhaps Orwellian sense to accomplish some purpose that might or might not make sense if openly stated and examined'.

nuanced way. In practice, a finding that a taxpayer has paid money that was not due 'voluntarily' leads inexorably to the conclusion that he is not entitled to restitution. Identifying the disruption of public finances as the true reason for a court's disinclination to allow immediate recovery might enable the court to proceed differently, in a way that is fairer to the taxpayer. An example of this mentioned in § 19, Comment f is 'allowing refunds in the form of credits against future assessments'.

(10) Counter-Restitution of Benefits Received by the Claimant

§ 54(2) provides that 'rescission requires a mutual restoration and accounting in which each party . . . restores property received from the other, to the extent such restoration is feasible'. § 54(3) limits rescission to 'cases in which counter-restitution by the claimant will restore the defendant to the status quo ante' unless 'the defendant is fairly compensated for any deficiencies in the restoration made by the claimant', the defendant is at fault, or the defendant agreed to bear the risk of uncompensated loss. Thus, a good faith defendant can resist an action for rescission if he can show that the claimant is unable to make specific or substitutive restitution of property received from him. However, given that a claimant will almost invariably be able to comply with this requirement by paying a money sum, the main question with regard to § 54 is not how one should classify the effect of a claimant's failure to make counter-restitution, but rather how one should classify the rule that counter-restitution must be made before rescission will be ordered.

§ 54(5) states that:

> [R]estitution or a tender of restitution by the claimant is not a prerequisite of rescission if affirmative relief to the claimant can be reduced by (or made subject to) the claimant's reciprocal obligation of restitution.

The point of this sub-section is to eliminate procedural requirements that have been imposed by many American state courts in the past, stipulating that a claimant must tender restitution to the defendant as a precondition for rescission. The justification for doing this offered by R3RUE is that the defendant can be protected by a judicial order to 'make restitution by one party conditional on counter-restitution by the other'.[100] However, there remains an interesting question as to how one should interpret such orders. There are two possibilities.[101] The first is to treat § 54 as a set-off rule and thus as a defence: the claimant and the defendant each has an action in unjust enrichment against the other for the full value of the benefit received, and the defendant is permitted to set off the amount

[100] R3RUE (n 1) § 54, Comment j.

[101] *cf* Grantham and Rickett (n 24) 95: 'The requirement of *restitutio in integrum* . . . can be regarded as either a condition of liability or a defence to a liability already established.'

of his action against the amount of the claimant's action.[102] The second way of understanding the rule described in § 54 is to see it as a netting off of the enrichments that each party has received, and thus as a denial by the defendant that he has been enriched by the full amount of the benefit he has received, because the measure of his enrichment is rather the amount the defendant has received minus the amount of the benefit received from him by the claimant.[103]

The difference between these two interpretations of § 54 would be well understood by German legal scholars working in this field. In accordance with the 'two claims theory' (*Zweikondiktionentheorie*) espoused by some writers, transactions under which a mutual exchange of benefits has taken place should be unwound by giving the parties independent claims against each other, each of which is potentially vulnerable to defences. In contrast, the 'difference theory' (*Saldotheorie*) espoused by other writers holds that there is only one enrichment and one party enriched: a claim will lie against the party who received the greater value on the basis that he has been enriched by the difference between what he received and what he gave, and the claimant is not considered to have been enriched at all.[104] On this theory, losses suffered by the claimant other than those which correspond to the benefits received by the defendant are ignored.[105] These theories reflect different conceptions of the reason for requiring claimants to make counter-restitution: the point of a rule that claim and counter-claim must be netted off is to reduce multiplicity of suits, while the point of a rule that enrichments transferred and received in a process of exchange must be netted off is to ensure that the mutual reciprocity of the parties' performances is duly reflected in the unwinding process that follows failure of the basis for the parties' exchange.

R3RUE describes the rule under consideration as a rule requiring 'mutual accounting',[106] 'mutual restoration of performance'[107] or 'mutual restitution' that often 'leads to offsets and a net liability on one side only'.[108] These descriptions do not make it clear whether the rule is thought to be a denial or a defence.

(11) Summary

R3RUE identifies numerous responses that the defendant can make in the hope of avoiding or reducing liability in unjust enrichment. In this part of the chapter we

[102] *cf Kerr v Baranow* [2011] SCC 10, [2011] 1 SCR 269 [109]–[116].

[103] *cf Kleinwort Benson Ltd v Sandwell BC* [1994] 4 All ER 890, as interpreted in *Goff & Jones* (n 39) [31-21].

[104] '*Saldo*' means 'balance' or, here, 'difference'.

[105] For discussion in English, see R Zimmermann and J du Plessis, 'Basic Features of the German Law of Unjustified Enrichment' [1994] *Restitution Law Review* 14, 41–42; P Hellwege, 'Unwinding Mutual Contracts: *Restitution in Integrum* v Change of Position' in Johnston and Zimmermann (n 51) 243, 258–60; BS Markesinis, W Lorenz, and G Dannemann, *The German Law of Obligations Volume I: The Law of Contracts and Restitution* (Oxford, Oxford University Press, 1997) 764–66; B Häcker, *Consequences of Impaired Consent Transfers* (Tübingen, Mohr Siebeck, 2009) 71–77.

[106] R3RUE (n 1) vol II, 282.

[107] ibid vol II, 284.

[108] ibid vol II, 285.

have considered a selection of these responses and asked whether they operate as denials or defences. This has not always been a straightforward task. This was partly because some responses are described in R3RUE rather imprecisely and without attention being paid to the separation between denials and defences. It was also because the classification of some responses depends on the way that actions in unjust enrichment are formulated, and R3RUE is also rather vague on this score in important respects. Consequently, we have had to look at several fundamental questions about the constitution of actions in unjust enrichment.

The results of our analysis are as follows:

(1) 'Recipient not unjustly enriched' could be a denial that the defendant's enrichment is unjust, but it could also be a defence.
(2) Illegality is a defence.
(3) A defendant's incapacity is generally irrelevant to liability. However, when, exceptionally, incapacity is admitted as an answer to liability, it is a defence.
(4) The plea of 'equitable disqualification (unclean hands)' is probably a defence.
(5) Passing on could be a denial that the defendant's enrichment was gained at the claimant's expense, but it is probably a defence.
(6) Change of position would be a denial of enrichment if the test for enrichment were 'value surviving' in the defendant's hands. However, the test for enrichment seems to be 'value received', and so the rule is probably a defence.
(7) Bona fide purchaser and bona fide payee are defences.
(8) Limitation of actions and laches are defences.
(9) Disruption of public finances is deliberately characterised as a defence in a departure from the practice of many American courts of making 'involuntary payment' an element of an action to recover money paid as tax that is not due.
(10) The requirement that a claimant make counter-restitution of benefits could be a denial that the defendant is enriched, but it could also be a defence.

F. Conclusion

Legal scholars have paid scant attention to the distinction between actions and defences in the law of unjust enrichment. Insufficient thought has been given to the question whether defences should exist in this area of the law, and scholars are often unconcerned with whether particular liability rules operate as denials or defences. If, as we believe, actions in unjust enrichment consist in identifiable and isolable elements, then more attention should be paid to the separation between actions and defences. To achieve conceptual clarity, it is essential to know whether particular liability rules operate as denials or defences.

A major part of this chapter sought to classify selected responses by defendants to actions in unjust enrichment, as these are described in R3RUE. Although

R3RUE is largely inattentive to this distinction, it was possible to ascertain, with a reasonable degree of confidence, how most of these responses function. However, this was not universally true. Some responses cannot be classified with any certainty because they are imprecisely described and because the elements of actions in unjust enrichment are insufficiently particularised.

This chapter did not address the normative question of how responses by defendants ought to operate. We have remained deliberately agnostic about this issue. This is not because we think it unimportant whether any given response is a denial or a defence; rather, we have said nothing about this primarily because we think that it is better to ask whether particular liability rules should function as denials or defences after it has been determined how they currently operate. Once this work has been completed, the question falls to be considered as to whether these rules operate in a justifiable way. Would it be better if some of the elements of actions in unjust enrichment were recast as defences? Should certain defences be recast as the elements of actions?[109] These are important questions to which answers are needed.

[109] As argued in Young (n 26) 1336, who contends that defences do not 'merit a large place in a Restatement about restitution'. His argument runs as follows. Unlike claims in contract which 'depend on the advertent activity of promise making', claims in unjust enrichment 'depend commonly on inadvertent activity by the claimants'. Hence 'a person making a claim in restitution might well be expected to circumvent obstacles that are not in the path of a contract claim'. Hence the liability rules in unjust enrichment should generally be characterised as 'elements in stating the claim' rather than as defences. This reasoning contains several non sequiturs.

7

Is There a Defence of Good Consideration?

ANDREW BURROWS

A. Introduction

The *Restatement Third: Restitution and Unjust Enrichment*[1] is a wonderful achievement and all of us interested in the subject owe a huge debt of gratitude to the Reporter, Professor Andrew Kull, his advisers and the American Law Institute. It is my fervent hope that R3RUE will stimulate both a renewal of interest in the subject in the US and increased comparative work on the Anglo-American law of unjust enrichment. It remains a deep puzzle as to how it can be that the dynamic interest in this subject in England has been matched by the equally dramatic decline in interest in the US. The effect of legal realism, the general decline in interest in doctrinal analysis, the widespread belief that an economic analysis of private law is the best way of understanding its workings and the concentration on public law rather than private law have all had a role to play in shaping developments in the US. There is also no doubt that individuals have changed the course of events. Would the English interest in the subject have been as intense without the driving passion of Peter Birks?

If Anglo-American comparison is to be used to maximum effect, it is important at the outset to appreciate that the approach taken to this area by English commentators and courts differs from the approach taken by R3RUE.[2] R3RUE is more contextual and less conceptual than that which would be adopted by restitution scholars in England. This is not intended as a criticism, but is rather designed to ensure that English and American scholars are fully aware that, in trying to learn from each other, we have rather different starting points. So, for example, in Chapter 1 on 'General Principles' there are only four black-letter propositions, none of which deals with what is meant by 'enrichment', 'at the expense of the claimant' or the approach to deciding 'injustice'; moreover, no

[1] American Law Institute, *Restatement Third: Restitution and Unjust Enrichment* (St Paul, MN, American Law Institute Publishers, 2011) (hereinafter 'R3RUE').

[2] For this point, see also A Burrows, 'Restitution of Mistaken Enrichments' (2012) 92 *Boston University Law Review* 767, 768–70.

fundamental distinction is drawn in these general principles between restitution for unjust enrichment and restitution for wrongs.[3] Admittedly, there is a sentence on the meaning of 'at the expense of' in the commentary on § 1[4] as well as some more extensive discussion of 'enrichment' in the commentary to § 1[5] and in the commentary to some of the other black-letter rules, such as § 9 on 'benefits other than money' conferred by mistake. The distinction between restitution for unjust enrichment and for wrongs is referred to very briefly in the commentary to § 1 (where it is said that 'nothing practical turns on this . . . except the identification of the applicable period of limitations').[6] There is barely any discussion[7] of the 'unjust factors' as opposed to the 'absence of basis' approach to injustice that has traditionally distinguished common law and civilian approaches to the subject and underpinned Birks' dramatic change of heart in *Unjust Enrichment*.[8] Moreover, there is no place for the four-step analysis that now guides English courts (enrichment, at the expense of, injustice and defences).[9] On the contrary, albeit that these particular four steps are not directly in mind, it is said that a 'checklist of factors' and 'formulas' are 'not helpful and . . . can lead to serious errors'.[10]

B. The Subject-matter of this Chapter

The subject-matter of this chapter raises a central question that has long troubled me. It may be expressed as follows: is there a defence of good consideration to a claim for restitution of an unjust enrichment? English and Australian commentators have found it difficult to give an answer to this apparently simple question. Hence, if we examine the leading textbooks, we find that, in contrast to the consistent treatment of, for example, change of position and bona fide purchase,[11]

[3] But note that 'wrongful gain' is the subject matter of the separate black-letter rule which is § 3.

[4] R3RUE (n 1) vol I, 3.

[5] ibid 7–8.

[6] ibid 10. There are other consequences of this division in England as regards, for example, the applicable defences (especially change of position) and private international law.

[7] What there is is at R3RUE (n 1) vol I, 6 and 13.

[8] P Birks, *Unjust Enrichment*, 2nd edn (Oxford, Oxford University Press, 2005).

[9] That these are the four questions to be answered was expressly approved by Lord Steyn in *Banque Financière de la Cité v Parc (Battersea Ltd)* [1999] 1 AC 221, 227; by the Court of Appeal in *Cressman v Coys of Kensington (Sales) Ltd* [2004] EWCA 47, [2004] 1 WLR 2775 [22] and *Chief Constable of the Greater Manchester Police v Wigan Athletic AFC Ltd* [2008] EWCA Civ 1449; by Lightman J in *Rowe v Vale of White Horse DC* [2003] EWHC 388 (Admin), [2003] 1 Lloyd's Rep 418 [11]; and by Henderson J in *Investment Trust Companies (in liq) v HMRC* [2012] EWHC 458 (Ch), [2012] STC 1150 [38]–[39]. See similarly, albeit not identically, Lord Hoffmann, in the *Banque Financière* case, at 234; and *Portman Building Society v Hamlyn Taylor Neck* [1998] 4 All ER 202, 206 (Millett LJ).

[10] R3RUE (n 1) vol I, 8 and 14.

[11] But note that, in contrast to the other works cited, G Virgo, *The Principles of the Law of Restitution*, 2nd edn (Oxford, Oxford University Press, 2006) treats bona fide purchase as a defence only to restitutionary claims vindicating proprietary rights and not to restitution for unjust enrichment.

there is a marked split of views as to whether or not good consideration is a defence. There is no mention of this as a defence anywhere in the work of Peter Birks, whether in the Old or New Testament.[12] For what it is worth, there is also no mention of this as a defence in any of the three editions of my textbook. In contrast, in Graham Virgo's *The Principles of the Law of Restitution*,[13] 'good consideration provided by the defendant' is treated as a defence to restitution of an unjust enrichment, albeit one that is specific to claims for restitution for mistake. In James Edelman and Elise Bant's book, 'good consideration' is treated as a general defence that conceals two different defences which they label 'receipt in satisfaction of a right' and 'set-off for failure of consideration.'[14] Keith Mason, John Carter and Greg Tolhurst treat 'consideration' as sometimes being a defence,[15] but by this they principally appear to have in mind the separate defence of contractual compromise (which is outside the scope of this chapter and is clearly a defence to restitution for unjust enrichment):[16] within their mistake chapter, they also refer to a defence which they label 'moneys due anyway'.[17] Perhaps most intriguingly of all, good consideration suddenly appeared as a general defence, with its own chapter separate from the chapter on bona fide purchase, in the sixth and seventh editions of *Goff & Jones*. In the new eighth edition by Charles Mitchell, Paul Mitchell and Stephen Watterson, it is retained but treated alongside bona fide purchase in a single chapter and the new authors express doubts as to whether it should be regarded as a separate defence. They point out that the work done by it may be regarded as covered by the defendant's entitlement to the benefit as a general justifying ground (which they deal with earlier in chapters two and three)[18] or by the defence of bona fide purchase or change of position.

The central argument in this chapter is that there is no defence, as such, of good consideration;[19] rather, the main issues thought to be raised by this defence relate to the much bigger question of the interplay between the 'unjust factors' and the fact that the enrichment was owed by the claimant to the defendant. This interplay is of fundamental importance in determining prima facie liability in the law

[12] Respectively, P Birks, *An Introduction to the Law of Restitution*, revised edn (Oxford, Clarendon Press, 1989) and *Unjust Enrichment* (n 8). For the references to the Old and New Testaments or 'Birks Mark 1' and 'Birks Mark 2', see Lord Rodger of Earlsferry and A Burrows, 'Peter Brian Herrenden Birks 1941–2004' in PJ Marshall (ed), *Proceedings of the British Academy, vol 150: Biographical Memoirs of Fellows, vol VI* (Oxford, Oxford University Press, 2008) 3.

[13] Virgo (n 11) 172–76. See also the 1st edn (Oxford, Oxford University Press, 1999) 169–73.

[14] J Edelman and E Bant, *Unjust Enrichment in Australia* (Melbourne, Oxford University Press, 2006) 344–48.

[15] K Mason, JW Carter and GJ Tolhurst, *Mason and Carter's Restitution Law in Australia*, 2nd edn (Chatswood, LexisNexis Butterworths, 2008) 875–88.

[16] So they write that 'in the contract context, the only situation in which it is meaningful to speak of the defendant having the onus of proving contractual consideration is where the defence is the compromise of a restitutionary claim': ibid 880.

[17] ibid 167–69.

[18] However, there is some ambiguity as to whether the authors regard the 'justifying grounds' in their chs 2 and 3 as defences or not. On the one hand, they do not appear in the part of the book dealing with defences. On the other hand, they are perceived as countering a prima facie right to restitution.

[19] In James Goudkamp and Charles Mitchell's terminology, 'good consideration' is a 'denial' and not a 'defence': see ch 6 of the present volume.

of unjust enrichment. Moreover, it is of central significance in understanding that the differences between the common law unjust factors scheme and the civilian absence of basis approach may not be as great as at first appears. Yet, traditionally, it is an interplay that has rarely been confronted and analysed head-on.

Having looked at these matters through the eyes of an English lawyer, with a focus especially on mistaken payments, I turn towards the end of the chapter to see how the matter is dealt with in, and whether any lessons can be learned from, R3RUE.

It is important to stress two points at the outset. First, this chapter does not examine the bona fide purchase defence and its relationship to a possible defence of 'good consideration'. For the purposes of this chapter, it will be assumed that the bona fide purchase defence in the law of unjust enrichment is concerned to 'track' the operation of that defence in relation to title conflicts in the law of property. It prevents the inconsistency that would arise if a recipient of property from a third party were to take good title to the property, applying the rules for title conflicts of the law of property, while at the same time being held liable for restitution in the law of unjust enrichment.

Second, reference is made throughout this chapter to the importance that should be attached to the fact that the enrichment was owed to the defendant. The principal focus is on the situation where the enrichment was owed *by the claimant* to the defendant, as exemplified by a 'two-creditor' example.[20] However, we shall also look at the situation where the enrichment was owed *by a third party* to the defendant, as exemplified by the leading case of *Lloyds Bank plc v Independent Insurance Co Ltd*.[21] That factual distinction appears to mark an important conceptual divide and yet this is not a division that has been sharply drawn in the past.

C. Robert Goff J's Second Qualification in *Barclays Bank v WJ Simms*

Let us assume that C entered into a contract with D mistakenly believing that the goods he was buying were made of top-quality material. There was no term, express or implied, to that effect and D made no representation to that effect. In fact, the goods were made of much cheaper material and were worth far less than C paid for them. It is clear that C has made a causative mistake whereby he would not have paid the agreed price had he known the truth. Applying the established approach to mistake in the law of unjust enrichment, first clearly established in the classic judgment of Robert Goff J, as he then was, in *Barclays Bank Ltd v WJ Simms, Son and Cooke (Southern) Ltd*,[22] C has made a mistake but for which he

[20] Below, p 174.
[21] *Lloyds Bank plc v Independent Insurance Co Ltd* [2000] QB 110.
[22] *Barclays Bank Ltd v WJ Simms, Son and Cooke (Southern) Ltd* [1980] QB 677.

would not have made the payment. Yet it is elementary that satisfying this standard test for restitution of a mistaken payment is insufficient to justify restitution where the payment has been made under a valid contract. C would not be entitled to restitution (even in return for counter-restitution of the goods). As Millett LJ said in obiter dicta in *Portman Building Society v Hamlyn Taylor Neck (a firm)*:

> It is fundamental that where money is paid under a legally effective transaction, neither misrepresentation nor mistake vitiates consent or gives rise by itself to an obligation to make restitution.[23]

Is this what Robert Goff J also had in mind with the second of his three qualifications (qualification 2(b)) to recovery for a causative mistake in *Barclays Bank v Simms*? The well-known scheme he set out was as follows:

> From this formidable line of authority certain simple principles can, in my judgment, be deduced: (1) If a person pays money to another under a mistake of fact which causes him to make the payment, he is prima facie entitled to recover it as money paid under a mistake of fact. (2) His claim may however fail if (a) the payer intends that the payee shall have the money at all events, whether the fact be true or false, or is deemed in law so to intend; or (b) the payment is made for good consideration, in particular if the money is paid to discharge, and does discharge, a debt owed to the payee (or a principal on whose behalf he is authorised to receive the payment) by the payer or by a third party by whom he is authorised to discharge the debt; or (c) the payee has changed his position in good faith, or is deemed in law to have done so.[24]

For the purposes of the theme of this chapter, four important points should be noted about this famous passage. First, Robert Goff J chose to express the qualification in 2(b) as being one where the payment was made for good consideration rather than being that the payment was made under a valid contract. Second, he chose to stress in particular that the qualification applies where the payment is made to discharge a debt, whether of the payer or, where authorised, of a third party. In addition, in what he termed the 'footnote' to the second qualification, he said that it was based on the decision in *Aiken v Short*,[25] which concerned a claimant bank, under a prior agreement with the debtor (Carter), paying off Carter's debt to the defendant under a mistaken belief that that debt was secured by a charge over land belonging to the bank, so that paying off the debt would make the land more valuable. One might have thought that, if Robert Goff J had in his mind the general proposition that a valid contract defeats restitution, it was rather odd for him to have chosen to focus on such a specialised example of a contract (discharging another's pre-existing debt) to illustrate the point. Third, again in his 'footnote', there is a rather oblique reference to the payee's good faith as having some possible relevance. Fourth, Robert Goff J saw each of his three qualifications as countering a 'prima facie' right to restitution and the third of them is what is now clearly recognised as the *defence* of change of position.

[23] *Portman Building Society v Hamlyn Taylor Neck (a firm)* [1998] 4 All ER 202, 208.
[24] *Barclays Bank* (n 22) 695.
[25] *Aiken v Short* (1856) 1 H & N 210, 156 ER 1180.

These points suggest that Robert Goff J had it in mind that he was setting up a defence of 'good consideration' with particular reference to the discharge of debts rather than recognising an initial starting point that restitution of an unjust enrichment cannot override a valid contract. Yet, if that was so, one would have expected there to have been an immediate reference in Robert Goff J's scheme to the fact that a unilateral mistake cannot justify restitution where money has been paid under a valid contract. But the only such reference was in what he termed a footnote to his first proposition. The rather unsatisfactory conclusion is that the best way of interpreting Robert Goff J's judgment is far from obvious and that the exact role of good consideration was left unclear.

These uncertainties resurfaced in *Lloyds Bank plc v Independent Insurance Co Ltd*.[26] W Ltd owed the defendant insurance company £162,388 (comprising premiums it had collected for the defendant). W Ltd requested its bank, the claimant, to pay that sum to the defendant's account. In the mistaken belief that three cheques for £172,132 in total payable to W Ltd had been cleared, the claimant bank made a credit transfer of £162,388 to the defendant's account. In fact, one of the three cheques, which was for £168,000, had not been cleared, so that W Ltd's account was substantially overdrawn. The claimant bank sought restitution from the defendant of £107,388 (which was the £162,388 paid minus £55,000 which was subsequently paid into W Ltd's account). The Court of Appeal refused restitution on the ground that the claimant bank's payment to the defendant, albeit made by a mistake of fact, had discharged a debt owed by W Ltd to the defendant. It was therefore paid for good consideration and, so it was reasoned, Robert Goff J's qualification 2(b) applied (as did *Aiken v Short*) to rule out restitution. In contrast to the facts of *Barclays Bank v Simms*, the claimant bank was acting with the actual authority of W Ltd in making the payment to the defendant and this payment did therefore operate to discharge W Ltd's debt to the defendant.

Although the decision in the *Lloyds Bank* case seems correct, the difficult question is how the decision should be best analysed: in particular, is it an illustration of Robert Goff J's 2(b) qualification and, if so, is that a *defence*?

One approach is to say that this is indeed an example of qualification 2(b) and that the defendant provided good consideration for the payment by the claimant bank by accepting that payment as a discharge of W Ltd's debt to the defendant. But instead of seeing this as a defence, one might say that the good consideration provided by the defendant was important because it showed that there was a valid contract between the defendant and the claimant bank. In other words, one might argue that there was a contract between the claimant bank (C) and the defendant (D) whereby, in return for the payment from C, D promised to discharge, and did discharge, the debt owed to it by W Ltd. In accordance with normal principle, it would be insufficient to render that contract void or voidable that C made a unilateral mistake not shared, known about or induced by D.

[26] *Lloyds Bank* (n 21). See also *Hills Industries Ltd v Australian Financial Services and Leasing Pty Ltd* [2012] NSWCA 380 which was decided in December 2012 and therefore came too late for coverage in this chapter.

Some support for the view that no defence was in play is provided by the judgment of Peter Gibson LJ.[27] Although he talked in the early part of his judgment about 'the defence of good consideration', he later indicated that qualification 2(b) was in line with Lord Hope's proposition, put forward in obiter dicta in *Kleinwort Benson Ltd v Lincoln CC*,[28] that a mistaken payor cannot have restitution – because there is no unjust enrichment – where the payee was entitled to receive the sum paid to him. Lord Hope said:

> *Subject to any defences that may arise from the circumstances*, a claim for restitution of money paid under a mistake raises three questions: (1) was there a mistake? (2) did the mistake cause the payment? and (3) did the payee have the right to receive the sum which was paid to him? . . . The third question arises because the payee cannot be said to have been unjustly enriched if he was entitled to receive the sum paid to him. The payer may have been mistaken as to the grounds on which the sum was due to the payee, but his mistake will not provide a ground for its recovery if the payee can show that he was entitled to it on some other ground.[29]

A difficulty with both the 'good consideration as a defence' and the 'valid contract' analyses is that they assume that the payment was made by the claimant bank to the defendant to discharge W Ltd's debt. This may be thought to be in line with the extensive discussion in the case as to whether the bank was acting with W Ltd's authority. But there is surely a difference between the claimant bank having W Ltd's authority to make the payment and the bank having authority to discharge W Ltd's debt. It would appear that the claimant bank had no knowledge of the underlying purpose of the payment and did not know that it was to discharge a debt. Indeed, it is significant that in *Barclays Bank v Simms*, Robert Goff J precisely spoke of the payment being made to discharge the debt. Therefore, it is submitted that, given C's lack of knowledge that a debt was being discharged, there may be some difficulty in saying that there was a valid contract to discharge the debt between C and D or in saying that D, by discharging the debt, provided good consideration to C for the payment by C.

It is perhaps for this reason that Waller LJ, who gave the leading judgment, appeared to take the view that qualification 2(b), and the decision in *Lloyds Bank*, should be regarded as an example of the change of position defence. The discharge of the debt meant that the defendant creditor would be worse off if the payment now had to be repaid. This would only not be so (that is, the defendant would not be worse off if he had to repay the mistaken payment) if the debt would be revived (without any other detriment to the defendant) by the repayment of the mistaken payment. However, it seems unlikely that a debt can be revived where the debtor has adopted the discharge. It may therefore be that change of position is a possible explanation of the *Lloyds Bank* case. However, as Peter Gibson LJ pointed out, this cannot be what Robert Goff J had in mind by his

[27] ibid 132.
[28] *Kleinwort Benson Ltd v Lincoln CC* [1999] 2 AC 349.
[29] ibid 407–08 (emphasis added).

qualification 2(b). This is not only because, as we have just seen, he required an intention to discharge the debt rather than just its discharge, but also because change of position was his separate qualification 2(c).

There is an even more fundamental problem regardless of whether one takes a 'good consideration as a defence' or a 'valid contract' or even a 'change of position' interpretation of *Lloyds Bank*. All these analyses are dependent on there being a debt owed by W Ltd to the payee. But what if the payee had been a donee to whom W Ltd was making a gift through the payment by the claimant bank? Surely one would still wish to deny restitution to the claimant bank. Yet, clearly, the mere receipt of the gift would not in itself constitute a change of position by the donee. And in a three-party situation – where the enrichment was owed by a third party (not by the claimant) to the defendant – it is hard to see why it should have any relevance to the claimant's right to restitution from the defendant whether the third party had a liability to the defendant or not. The consideration constituted by the discharge of the third party's liability appears to be of no crucial significance because there ought to be a denial of restitution even if there was no such consideration.

Birks made this precise point, in typically robust fashion, in his analysis of the *Lloyds Bank* case. He wrote:

> The bank tried and failed to recover from the creditor-payee. The reason given was that the bank got what it paid for. It obtained the discharge of the debt. That cannot be quite sufficient. It is inconceivable that the result would have been any different if the payee had been a donee receiving a birthday present by the wish of the customer.[30]

He went on to explain that, in his view, the wider and true reason for the denial of restitution in that case (and in *Aiken v Short*, which he viewed as having 'materially identical' facts)[31] was rather different. Although this does not tie in with qualification 2(b) or the Court of Appeal's reasoning, he argued that D's enrichment was *at the expense of* W Ltd (the customer) and not C (the bank).[32] In other words, C was paying D because it was requested to do so by W Ltd under a contract with W Ltd. The correct claimant (although the claim would not have succeeded) should have been W Ltd, not the bank. The claimant bank had no valid claim because this would have involved illegitimate 'leapfrogging' out of, and over, the valid contract between W Ltd and the bank.

Birks' reasoning is persuasive. However, even if, contrary to his view, one were to regard both the bank and W Ltd as direct providers of D's enrichment, one would still be in line with much of Birks' thinking if one reasoned that the bank

[30] Birks (n 8) 90.

[31] The bare facts of the case are set out at p 169. For Birks' analysis, it is crucial to note that the bank had agreed with Carter to pay off Carter's debt. There was therefore a contract between them. Birks' analysis would not be applicable if the bank had simply mistakenly paid off Carter's debt without any agreement between them. Note that in *Aiken v Short*, unlike *Lloyds Bank*, there was also a contract between the bank and the creditor under which the bank paid the creditor precisely in order to discharge Carter's debt.

[32] Birks (n 8) 90–91.

should not be entitled to restitution from D because this would undermine the contractual risks (especially the risk of the customer's insolvency) undertaken by the bank in the contract with its customer (W Ltd). This was the reason relied on by the Court of Appeal in denying restitution for building work carried out for a third party under a contract between the builders and another party in *Costello v Macdonald*.[33] The argument that, in any event, restitution should be denied because the benefit to the third party should be treated as coming indirectly, rather than directly, from the builders was also carefully referred to in the judgment of Etherton LJ, but he put that to one side in reaching his decision because it had played no part in the submissions to the court.

Therefore, the crucial point to emerge is that, whether one takes Birks' analysis of 'at the expense of' or the wider policy analysis focusing on the risk-taking involved in a contract, the denial of restitution in a situation where the enrichment was owed by a third party (rather than the claimant) to the defendant – as in *Lloyds Bank* – does not turn on the fact that the enrichment was owed by the third party and hence on the consideration constituted by the discharge of the third party's debt. Nor is it determinative whether the defendant has changed its position or not. The true explanation, which alone can properly explain the denial of restitution where the third party is making a gift to the defendant, rests on the contract between the claimant (the bank) and the third party (the bank's customer). Yet there was no hint at all of this reasoning in *Lloyds Bank*.

The conclusion to be reached is that the English law of unjust enrichment has adopted a rather muddled approach towards 'good consideration'. Its role has not been clearly identified, it is unclear whether or not it is viewed as a defence, and 'good consideration' is not the best explanation where the enrichment was owed by a third party (rather than the claimant) to the defendant.

D. The Interplay between 'Unjust Factors' and 'Enrichment Owed by the Claimant'

Assuming, therefore, that there has as yet been no clarity in the English cases or in the textbooks about the role of 'good consideration', the way is open to set out the best approach. It is submitted that, in order to move forward on this question, one should recognise that it is part of a wider and fundamental issue about the relationship between the 'unjust factors' scheme and the fact that the enrichment was owed to the defendant by the claimant. Until recently – and consistently with the uncertainty as to the role of 'good consideration' – this fundamental issue has not been directly addressed in accounts of the unjust factors scheme. There was no reference at all to this by Peter Birks in *An Introduction to the Law of Restitution*.

[33] *Costello v Macdonald* [2011] EWCA Civ 930, [2011] 3 WLR 1341.

Virgo did not mention this in his textbook and nor did I until the third edition of my book in 2010.[34] And while, with the exception of their first edition in 1966, each edition of *Goff and Jones*, from the second edition in 1978 to the seventh edition in 2007, included as a limit on the principle of unjust enrichment that 'the plaintiff conferred the benefit . . . in pursuance of a valid common law, equitable or statutory obligation which he owed to the defendant', the content of that limit was not tightly explained.

Although applicable to all unjust factors, it is helpful to focus on mistaken payments. So the question being asked is this: what is the position if a mistaken payor was under a valid contractual, statutory or other legal obligation to make that payment to the payee? The following hypothetical example illustrates the question. C owes £1,000 to each of X and D. C intends to pay off X, but by mistake of identity pays D £1,000 instead of X. Is C entitled to restitution from D by reason of mistake, even though C has a legal obligation to pay that sum to D?

Despite the dearth of analysis of this type of question, it would appear that the normal position, and the answer in the given example, is that C has no right to restitution from D. Hence, in setting out the requirements for restitution of a mistaken payment, Lord Hope in the passage from *Kleinwort Benson* set out above[35] said that, in addition to there being, first, a mistake which, second, caused the payment, there was the third requirement that the payee did not have the right to receive the payment: 'the payee cannot be said to have been unjustly enriched if he was entitled to receive the sum paid to him'. It is worth interjecting at this point that this third qualification was so far away from standard thinking at the time that most of us were very puzzled as to what Lord Hope meant by it and as to whether it was correct. So, for example, in the second edition of my book, I wrote that 'it is far from clear that Lord Hope's novel proposition is correct in so far as it goes beyond being an application of the "but for" causation test'.[36] However, it is now clear to me what Lord Hope meant and that he was correct and that, applying his qualification to the above example, C has no right to restitution from D. This is because the injustice by reason of the mistake is overridden by the fact that the money was owed anyway. It is also important that Lord Hope made clear that he saw this requirement as relating to prima facie liability rather than as a defence.

Lord Hope's qualification was subsequently relied on by Arden LJ in giving the judgment of the Court of Appeal in *Test Claimants in the FII Group Litigation v HMRC*.[37] In this case, the claimants argued that they were entitled to restitution

[34] See now A Burrows, *The Law of Restitution*, 3rd edn (Oxford, Oxford University Press, 2010) 88–91.

[35] See the text to n 29. See also the obiter dicta in the joint judgment of Mason CJ, Deane, Toohey, Gaudron and McHugh JJ in *David Securities Pty Ltd v Commonwealth Bank of Australia* (1992) 175 CLR 353, 376, that restitution for mistake of law 'would not, for example, extend to a case where the moneys were paid under a mistaken belief that they were legally due and owing under a particular clause of a particular contract when in fact they were legally due and owing to the recipient under another clause or contract'.

[36] A Burrows, *The Law of Restitution*, 2nd edn (London, Butterworths, 2002) 137.

[37] *Test Claimants in the FII Group Litigation v HMRC* [2010] EWCA Civ 103, [2010] STC 1251 [181].

not only of unlawful corporation tax paid plus interest but also for the value of the reliefs or allowances (eg, group relief and management expenses) that they had used up on unlawfully exacted tax and which they were therefore unable to use to offset lawfully exacted tax. They argued that the correct test to apply was simply one of 'but for' causation between the mistake and the relevant enrichment, and hence that the relevant enrichment was the lawful tax that, but for their mistake, they would not have paid. The Court of Appeal rejected that argument for two reasons. First, it said that the enrichment in paying more lawful tax than the claimants would have paid, but for the exaction of the initial unlawful tax, was too indirectly related to the mistake and was therefore too remote. The second explanation, which is the one we are concerned with here, was that, in contrast to the initial unlawful corporation tax paid, the secondary payment of tax was lawfully exacted and was due. There could be no restitution of tax that was legally owed. Very significantly, Arden LJ cited Lord Hope's statement in *Kleinwort Benson*. She then continued: 'The short answer to the claim is that the tax paid in . . . subsequent years was lawfully due and so cannot be the subject of recovery . . . as a payment under a mistake.'[38]

Lord Hope's qualification is also the best explanation of the recent New Zealand Court of Appeal decision in *Commissioner of Inland Revenue v Stiassny*,[39] albeit that the court accepted and applied a defence of good consideration. A company (CNIFP) paid goods and services tax to the Inland Revenue that was owed on a sale of its assets. The payment of the tax was made because the receivers controlling the company thought, mistakenly, that if the tax were not paid, it would be personally liable to pay it. This was a mistake of law but for which the tax would not have been paid. However, there was no doubt that the tax was owed by CNIFP to the Revenue. The claim for restitution on behalf of CNIFP, based on mistake, failed because, it was said, the Revenue had provided good consideration for the payment in discharging CNIFP's tax liability, and insofar as good faith by the Revenue was required, this was held to be satisfied. Yet it is precisely in line with the central theme of this chapter that the court drifted onto irrelevancies like good faith because of the incorrect view that what was in issue was a defence of good consideration. The decision should have been simple. There was no unjust enrichment because the Revenue was entitled to the tax paid by (or on behalf of) CNIFP. Indeed, this was the very point being made when the court said the following:

> [T]he giving of good consideration has been accepted as a proper ground upon which a court may determine that the defendant has not been unjustly enriched. This follows on the simple footing that, if the defendant is entitled to the money, then it cannot be said to be unjust, or against conscience, to require repayment.[40]

[38] ibid.

[39] *Commissioner of Inland Revenue v Stiassny* [2012] NZCA 93. I am most grateful to Charles Mitchell for drawing this case to my attention. The Court of Appeal's decision was upheld on 28 November 2012 by the New Zealand Supreme Court: [2012] NZSC 106.

[40] ibid [94]. The court comprised Glazebrook, Randerson and Harrison JJ, but the judgment of the court was delivered by Randerson J.

Significantly, as authority for this proposition, the court in a footnote referred to the passage in Lord Hope's speech in *Kleinwort Benson* set out in the text above.[41] Unfortunately, the court saw all this, with respect incorrectly, as an aspect of a 'good consideration' defence.

Commentators have not helped matters by only recently explicitly recognising the importance of the general restriction of the enrichment being owed by the claimant on the 'unjust factors' scheme. Yet it should not be thought that it is somehow a new problem. On the contrary, the relationship between a contractual or statutory obligation and unjust enrichment has long been an implicit issue for commentators, albeit one that has tended to be pushed off into the background rather than dealt with upfront. Bringing it out upfront (and no doubt this has been stimulated by the close comparison between the common law and civilian approaches to the subject triggered by the advocacy of an 'absence of basis' approach in Birks' *Unjust Enrichment*) makes clear that the difference between the common law unjust factors approach and the civilian 'absence of basis' approach is less marked than has sometimes been thought.[42]

An added difficulty, however, is that this restriction is not always applied. So, for example, two much-discussed cases on mistake, one in Australia and the other in England, go the other way and allow restitution for a mistaken payment even though the money was owed under a valid legal obligation. In the Australian case of *Roxborough v Rothmans of Pall Mall Australia Ltd*,[43] an identified part of the price of cigarettes being bought by a retailer, C, from a wholesaler, D, represented a tax that it was thought D would have to pay over to the state. The tax was subsequently held to be invalid so that that part of the price did not have to be paid over by D (and was not paid over or was refunded to D). Although the contract for the payment of the full price was valid, so that the full payment, including the tax, was contractually owed by C to D, C was held to be entitled to restitution of that part of the payment that represented the tax as paid by mistake. In *Deutsche Morgan Grenfell plc v IRC*,[44] C paid advance corporation tax under a statutory scheme that was ultra vires the

[41] See the text to n 29. They also referred to *David Securities Pty Ltd v Commonwealth Bank of Australia* (1992) 175 CLR 353.

[42] See, for similar reasoning, R Stevens, 'Is There a Law of Unjust Enrichment?' in S Degeling and J Edelman (eds), *Unjust Enrichment in Commercial Law* (Sydney, Lawbook Co, 2008) 11, especially 17; G Virgo, 'Demolishing the Pyramid – the Presence of Basis and Risk-Taking in the Law of Unjust Enrichment' in A Robertson and Tang Hang Wu (eds), *The Goals of Private Law* (Oxford, Hart Publishing, 2009) 477–508. But there is no need, as appears to be suggested by Goudkamp and Mitchell in their chapter in the present volume, at p 153, to see this approach as involving both unjust factors and the absence of legal basis. The idea of an enrichment owed to the claimant by the defendant is only one aspect of the absence of legal basis scheme and is being stressed both because that is the best interpretation of English law but also because there is an upfront problem of inconsistency in saying that C owed D the enrichment and yet that D must make restitution to C. In contrast, nothing is said here, for example, about the unjust factors scheme being qualified by the law on gifts.

[43] *Roxborough v Rothmans of Pall Mall Australia Ltd* (2001) 208 CLR 516. It should be noted that this case is also important for its rejection at common law in Australia of a defence of 'passing on'. This has also been rejected at common law in England: see *Kleinwort Benson Ltd v Birmingham CC* [1997] QB 380. In contrast, R3RUE (n 1) § 64 accepts such a defence.

[44] *Deutsche Morgan Grenfell plc v IRC* [2006] UKHL 49, [2007] 1 AC 558.

Revenue (D) because, contrary to EU law, the scheme did not give C an option to avoid paying the tax by making a group income election. The House of Lords held that C was entitled to restitution from D for mistake even though C had a statutory duty to pay the tax unless and until it validly exercised a group income election which, because that had not been provided, it had not done.

Are these two decisions correct? This has been hotly debated and in each of the two cases there was a powerful dissent (by Kirby J and Lord Scott, respectively) precisely on the ground that the money was legally owed and therefore could not be recovered in the law of unjust enrichment. It is submitted that the decisions are correct. They illustrate that the rule that one cannot have restitution for mistake where the mistaken payment was legally owed is not an absolute one, but permits limited exceptions. How, then, does one explain the exceptions?

At the root of the issue is whether the legal entitlement of D to the payment from C is outweighed by the injustice constituted by D receiving a payment that C mistakenly did not mean to make. In each of the two cases mentioned above, one might say that the legal entitlement was easily outweighed by the unjust factor. In the *Roxborough* case, this was because the tax element was a fixed separate element from the rest of the price and did not conflict with the valid contractual allocation of risk in the contract, given that the tax element was imposed outside the risks bargained for. Separated out in this way, one might even say that, once the tax was held not to be owing, that part of the price was not, in substance, owing, albeit that no particular clause could be struck down as void. Similarly, in the *Deutsche Morgan Grenfell* case, one can say that, as the exaction of advance corporation tax (ACT) was unlawful in relation to UK companies with non-resident parent companies because it did not allow them to make a group income election that they would have made had it been possible, it was (to adopt the words of Lords Hoffmann and Walker) 'over-analytical'[45] to say that the tax was due unless and until that group income election was made. As the operation of the group election scheme in relation to UK companies with non-resident parent companies was unlawful, no ACT was properly due and those who paid believing that it was due were entitled to restitution. The force of the unjust factor clearly outweighed the force of the tax being due.

It would therefore seem that a helpful way to understand at least some of the exceptions to the general rule that money legally owed cannot be recovered is where that legal obligation is easily outweighed by the unjust factor. It is helpful to contrast the facts of *Deutsche Morgan Grenfell* with a case where there is no doubt that the tax paid was lawfully due, but the claimant argued that it would not have paid so much tax had it exercised an election in a deed of variation, which it mistakenly failed to make.[46] In that situation, where the tax regime was lawful and the

[45] ibid [143].

[46] This hypothetical example (concerning inheritance tax) was suggested in argument in *Test Claimants in the FII Group Litigation v HMRC* [2008] EWHC 2893 (Ch), [2009] STC 254 [257]. Similarly, could it seriously be said that a tenant can reclaim rent paid to his landlord because he mistakenly failed to make an application for a rent review that would have reduced the rent?

claimant had simply mistakenly failed to operate it to its advantage, there should be no restitution. The obligation to pay the tax was not outweighed by the unjust factor and there is no question of describing the legal obligation to pay the tax as 'over-analytical'.

Although Lord Scott dissented in *Deutsche Morgan Grenfell*, it is of particular interest to the theme of this chapter to see that he analysed Robert Goff J's 2(b) qualification in *Barclays Bank v Simms* as an 'upfront' qualification of the unjust factor of mistake rather than seeing it as a defence. Having set out Robert Goff J's words in s 2(b), Lord Scott said the following:

> If a contract has been entered into that would not have been entered into but for a mistake, but the contract is then completed by a payment of the price for the goods or services that the payee has supplied, the payment cannot be recovered unless the contract can be set aside. The proposition seems such an obviously correct one that it may seem pointless to ask why it is that it is correct. But I think the question does need to be asked for the answer casts, in my opinion, valuable light on the nature of the restitutionary remedy for the recovery of money paid under a mistake . . . The reason, it seems to me, why the proposition is correct is that the mistake does not necessarily undermine the legal obligation which required the payment of the money or for the discharge of which the money was paid. If the mistake does enable the contract to be set aside, then, subject to a change of position defence, the money should be recoverable. If the contract was void from the outset (as in the 'swaps' cases) or had been avoided before the payment was made, the money should be recoverable. But if the legal obligation under which the money was paid cannot be, or has not been, invalidated, then, in my opinion, whether or not it can be shown that 'but for' the mistake in question the money would not have been paid, a restitutionary remedy for the recovery of the money would not be available.[47]

Finally, there is the question whether the qualification of an 'obligation owed' applies beyond a *legal* obligation owed by C to pay D. It is submitted that the better view is that the force of an unjust factor easily outweighs the force of a merely moral obligation so that there should be restitution. This would also avoid considerable uncertainty in deciding what constitutes a moral or natural obligation. Thus, say that C gratuitously promises D £1,000. This promise is not legally binding (in England). C no longer wishes to pay D but, mistakenly believing that he is legally bound to do so, C pays D the £1,000. Although there is no authority in English law on this, it would appear that C would be entitled to restitution of £1,000 from D as paid by a mistake of law. The natural or moral obligation that, one might say, C owed D is overridden by the mistake.

[47] *Deutsche Morgan Grenfell* (n 44) [84]–[85].

E. The *Restatement Third: Restitution and Unjust Enrichment*

Is any help on these matters to be derived from R3RUE? There is an initial difficulty in locating the relevant discussion. If one first turns to the topic of benefits conferred by mistake within Chapter 2 on 'transfers subject to avoidance', § 6 reads: 'Payment by mistake gives the payor a claim in restitution against the recipient to the extent payment was not due.' However, it is clear from the context that the fact that the payment is not due is being treated as a category of mistake, like mistake as to identity, and not as a restriction on when there can be a claim for mistake. Indeed, there appears to be no direct black-letter rule in Chapter 2 dealing with the interplay between mistake and the enrichment being owed, albeit that it is made clear at various points throughout the commentary that restitution cannot be given for mistake where there is a valid contract to make the payment or where a contract of compromise has been entered into to deal with the risk that the payment might not be due. If one then turns to Chapter 4 on 'restitution and contract', § 34 deals with 'mistake or supervening change of circumstances' in avoiding a contract. However, no attempt is made to clarify how this links back to, or is consistent with, the earlier sections on mistake in Chapter 2 on 'transfers subject to avoidance'.

It would therefore appear that one must largely turn to the defences to find a black-letter rule dealing with the interplay question. There appear to be two relevant defences: 'recipient not unjustly enriched' (§ 62) and 'bona fide payee' (§ 67). The first of these is wide-ranging and reads as follows:

> Even if the claimant has conferred a benefit that results in the unjust enrichment of the recipient when viewed in isolation, the recipient may defend by showing that some or all of the benefit conferred did not unjustly enrich the recipient when the challenged transaction is viewed in the context of the parties' further obligations to each other.

A two-creditor mistaken payment is given as one of the illustrations, as is a mistaken payment of a statute-barred debt.[48] There is also reference to there being no unjust enrichment by reason of this defence where the benefit has been conferred under an unenforceable agreement.

Four features of this approach are noteworthy. First, the interplay issue is here being resolved by a defence. As we have seen, while English law has flirted with 'good consideration' as a defence there is also support for the view that the benefit being owed should be treated as a prima facie liability question before one gets to defences.[49] Second, there was no equivalent defence set out in the *Restatement*

[48] R3RUE (n 1) vol II, 482–83. As authority, the Reporter's note, at 485, refers to hypothetical cases put by Lord Mansfield in *Moses v Macferlan* (1760) 2 Burr 1005, 97 ER 676.

[49] This division between matters relating to prima facie liability and defences corresponds to the division between denials and defences drawn by James Goudkamp and Charles Mitchell in ch 6 of the present volume.

First and so it would appear that this is a novel approach. Third, there is no detailed discussion of how this defence precisely works. It has been indicated above that, in English law, there may be exceptions to the general rule where the liability owed is 'technical' only. All that the commentary says in relation to how one applies § 62, and how wide a defence it is, is that whether the defence will operate turns on whether the transactional context makes the prima facie unjust enrichment not unjust:

> [The cases in mind] arise when the claimant alleges facts supporting a prima facie claim in unjust enrichment – typically a payment by mistake – but the recipient is able to show that the resulting enrichment is not unjust, in view of the larger transactional context within which the benefit has been conferred.

Plainly this is very open-ended. Fourth, it is not clear why § 62 talks about the parties' *further* obligations to each other. To do so seems misleading because one is normally concerned about obligations that were owed but which are no longer owed. So, for example, in the two-creditor situation, the question is about the existing obligation to the mistaken payee, which has been discharged, not about any 'further' obligation. The reference to 'further obligations' may therefore merely be loose drafting designed to cover any contractual statutory or other obligation under which the benefit was owed to the defendant.

In addition to the defence in § 62, there is the defence of 'bona fide payee' in § 67. By this defence, the payor has no right to restitution of a payment discharging a legal obligation owed to the payee provided that the payee had no notice of the mistake (or other ground for restitution) prior to the discharge of the obligation. In other words, there is a defence where the payee, in return for the payment, discharges a debt owed to the payee by the payor or another person provided that the payee does so 'without notice' of the facts underlying the restitution claim. It is explained in the commentary that this defence is to be seen as analogous to § 66, which sets out the 'bona fide purchaser for value without notice' defence, but that that is seen as applying to property other than money: 'although there is a close relationship between the rules of §§ 66 and 67, distinctive features of the law's treatment of money payments make it convenient to state the rules separately'.[50]

The first illustration referred to under § 67[51] is where, as in *Barclays Bank v Simms*, a bank mistakenly overlooks a valid countermand by its customer and

[50] This is problematic. There is no peculiarity about the operation of the bona fide purchase rules of title in relation to money. The situation is merely that the bona fide purchase exception to *nemo dat* applies very widely (ie, it is the rule) in relation to money as currency. So, if the bona fide purchase defence is merely tracking the title conflict rules in the law of property (as has been assumed in this chapter; see p 168), there is no good reason to set out the rules in relation to money separately from those for other types of property. So it is that the leading example of the bona fide purchase defence in the law of unjust enrichment, *Lipkin Gorman (a firm) v Karpnale Ltd* [1991] 2 AC 548, concerned money. It is therefore better to see §§ 66–67 as one defence (bona fide purchase for value without notice) which applies to all property including money: 'good consideration' should then be seen as a separate defence (essentially dealt with in § 62 and covering the payment of debts) that stands or falls on its own terms.

[51] R3RUE (n 1) vol II, 559.

therefore mistakenly pays the defendant. It is pointed out that there is a conflict in the US authorities between the majority of cases which apply the defence as set out in § 67[52] and the minority of cases which require instead that there has been a change of position by the payee (for example, by giving up a security that it had for the debt).[53]

Several points should be made about the defence in § 67. The first is that § 67 does not just apply to a payment discharging *another's* debt. Although the analogy drawn with § 66 and the bona fide purchaser for value defence would suggest that one is purely concerned with a three-party situation, the drafting includes the payor paying off its own debt to the payee. Second, there appears to be no explanation of the relationship between § 67 and § 62. Yet, on the face of it, § 62 swallows up at least part of § 67, although it may be that § 62 includes only two-party cases, whereas § 67 includes three-party cases. Perhaps the best analysis of what is envisaged is that § 67 sets out more specifically how § 62 operates in the context of the discharge of debts (or other payment obligations) owed by the claimant. Third, the title of the defence 'bona fide payee' may be considered to be misleading. It is not being suggested, for example, that there is a defence wherever a person receives a payment without notice that it is mistakenly paid. In other words, no doubt at all is being cast on the strict liability approach to mistaken payments. It would seem, therefore, that the title of the defence that was used in the tentative drafts of the Restatement – 'payment for value (bona fide creditor)' – was more accurate. Fourth, this defence is not new to R3RUE. It has its origins in § 14 of the *Restatement First* which, within the coverage of mistake, was headed 'discharge for value'. However, significantly, that defence was confined to three-party situations. Fifth, this defence seems very similar to qualification 2(b) in Robert Goff J's formulation in *Barclays Bank v Simms*. The difficulties that we have considered above in relation to 2(b), and which resurfaced in the *Lloyds Bank* case, can also be raised in relation to § 67. Given the views in the *Lloyds Bank* case, it is of particular interest that the question as to whether the defence in § 67 is better recast as merely an aspect of the change of position defence has produced a split of view in the leading US cases. But it is also of interest that Robert Goff J's qualification 2(b) did not require (albeit that there was an oblique reference to this being a possibility in what he termed a footnote) that the payee, who was giving consideration by accepting the mistaken payment in discharge of a debt, had no notice of the mistake. This is in line with the English rules on mistake in relation to contracts, where it is largely irrelevant whether one party had knowledge of the other's mistake. In contrast, § 67 requires that the payee has no notice of the mistake.

[52] As in *Banque Worms v BankAmerica Int'l*, 77 NY 2d 362, 570 NE 2d 189 (1991). The decision in this case is defended in A Kull, 'Defenses to Restitution: The Bona Fide Creditor' (2001) 81 *Boston University Law Review* 919.

[53] As in *Manufacturers Hanover Trust Co v Chemical Bank*, 160 App Div 2d 113, 559 NYS 2d 704 (1990); *Wilson v Newman*, 463 Mich 435 (2000).

A further difficulty[54] is that there is an earlier section of R3RUE, § 24, which deals with what one might call contracts for the benefits of third parties and lays down that, in certain situations, there can be a claim for restitution against the unjustly enriched third party.[55] It is not at all clear why this section could not be invoked to give the claimant, on the facts of a case like the *Lloyds Bank* case, a claim for restitution against the payee.

It would therefore appear that, in trying to unravel the muddle in English law on the issues raised in this chapter, limited assistance is derived from R3RUE. Certainly, it is of great interest that the entirely new § 62 appears to push the 'enrichment owed' enquiry into a defence. But the precise meaning of § 62 and the relationship of that defence to other parts of the Restatement – and even the relationship between that defence and the defence in § 67 – is not entirely clear.

F. The Way Forward?

The issues raised in this chapter involve recognising that there is a wide and fundamental issue about the relationship between the 'unjust factors' scheme and the fact that the enrichment was legally owed to the defendant by the claimant. It would be possible – and arguably more elegant – to hive off that fundamental interplay to be solved by one or more defences, and this approach may be said to derive support from § 62 (and § 67) of R3RUE. However, it is submitted that the better way forward, which reflects the strategy clearly favoured by Lord Hope and Lord Scott, is that the fact that the enrichment was legally owed by the claimant should be treated as an 'upfront' matter going to prima facie liability.[56] There are at least three reasons why this is the preferable approach.[57]

First, to hive off the obligation owed by the claimant as a defence gives the misleading impression that where, for example, a contract has been entered into by a unilateral ('but for') mistake of the claimant, it is sufficient for the claimant who seeks restitution of money paid under the contract to show that the mistake it made was a unilateral mistake in entering into the contract and paying the money. Second, although the defence of limitation is an anomalous exception to this,[58] in principle the legal burden of proving a defence should be on the defendant.[59] Yet

[54] I am most grateful to Birke Häcker for drawing this to my attention.

[55] The terminology in § 24 needs to be treated with care because the third person referred to is the other contracting party and the defendant is the third party. In other words, in a contract between A and B for the benefit of C, B is referred to as the 'third person' and C is referred to as the 'defendant'.

[56] ie, as a 'denial', not a 'defence' in the language used by James Goudkamp and Charles Mitchell in ch 6 of the present volume.

[57] Goudkamp and Mitchell in their chapter leave open this 'normative' question.

[58] The best-known authorities on this are tort cases: see *Clerk and Lindsell on Torts*, 20th edn (London, Sweet & Maxwell, 2010) para 32-03. See also ch 6 in the present volume at p 138.

[59] For the importance of the burden of proof in deciding whether one has a true defence, see ch 6 in the present volume at pp 138 and 146.

it is surely clear that the legal burden of proving the invalidity of an apparent legal obligation, under which the enrichment was owed by the claimant to the defendant, is most appropriately placed on the claimant. If we go back to the two-creditor example discussed above, D is merely receiving what D was, on the face of it, entitled to receive from C. Even though C is mistaken, it can immediately be seen that D is not *unjustly* enriched because he is entitled to the enrichment. Why should D be put to the burden of proving that the obligation was valid rather than putting the burden on C, who after all is bringing the claim, to prove that the prior obligation is not as it seems? Third, once one sets up 'enrichment legally owed' as a defence, there is immediate pressure to explain how it fits alongside the leading defence of change of position. This can then lead to the erroneous belief that, somehow, this is not a distinct defence from change of position. We have seen this tension in the *Lloyds Bank* case, but it is particularly clearly shown in the chapter on 'the defence of good consideration' in the sixth and seventh editions of *Goff & Jones*,[60] and in the discussion of this defence in the mistake chapter in Virgo's book.[61] These commentators suggest that 'good faith' should probably be an integral part of the defence (and, perhaps misled by these commentators, the New Zealand Court of Appeal thought the same in *Stiassny*)[62] and that it might be more acceptable in principle if the defence were to operate *pro tanto* to the extent of the value of the consideration provided. Neither of these modifications is at all appropriate. So, if one takes Lord Scott's contract of sale example referred to in the text above,[63] the question is whether the contract is valid and neither good faith nor *pro tanto* apportionment have any relevance to this question. This is plainly understood if one regards 'enrichment owed by the claimant' as relating to prima facie liability in unjust enrichment rather than being a defence.

G. Conclusions

The overall conclusions of this chapter are as follows.

First, it is unclear whether or not 'good consideration' is a defence to restitution for unjust enrichment in English law and uncertainty on this question pervades the analysis in the textbooks.

Second, cases like the *Lloyds Bank* case, where the enrichment was owed *by a third party* to the defendant, have correctly denied restitution. But 'good consideration' is not the best explanation for that denial. The best explanation of such cases – 'best' because it can also explain why restitution should be denied if the

[60] G Jones (ed), *Goff & Jones: The Law of Restitution*, 7th edn (London, Sweet & Maxwell, 2007) [41-002].

[61] Virgo (n 11) 172–76.

[62] *Stiassny* (n 39).

[63] In the text to n 47. Or my own hypothetical example set out at p 168.

customer was making a gift to the defendant – focuses on the contract between the bank and its customer.

Third, there is a fundamental interplay between unjust factors and enrichment owed by the claimant. This interplay normally results in the unjust factor being overridden by the enrichment being owed. However, it is important to see that there are exceptions to this outcome in situations where the force of the obligation owed is outweighed by the force of the unjust factor.

Finally, it is possible to deal with this interplay by treating enrichment owed as a defence, and this approach derives strong support from § 62 of R3RUE. However, the preferable approach, which reflects the strategy clearly favoured by Lord Hope and Lord Scott, is that the fact that the enrichment was owed by the claimant should be treated as an 'upfront' matter relating to prima facie liability, with the legal burden being on the claimant, and not as a defence. At a deeper level, this involves recognising that the unjust factors and the civilian 'absence of basis' approaches are closer than has traditionally been thought.

8

The Distinctiveness of Law and Equity and the Taxonomy of the Constructive Trust

KEITH MASON*

A. Introduction

Restitution offers many opportunities to observe the interaction of legal and equitable doctrines and remedies. Using the historical labels, we see that 'equitable' doctrines and remedies may partially trigger 'common law' restitutionary causes of action, for example, when a contract is avoided for misrepresentation, thereby making way for the unjust factor of failure of consideration. Each 'system' can also offer differing responses to a single situation, as represented by the debate in the House of Lords over whether a newly recognised right to compound interest in restitutionary claims for the time value of money is legal and *therefore* recoverable as of right in particular circumstances[1] or is equitable and *therefore* recoverable somewhat at the discretion of the court, as the minority held.[2]

Law and equity also intersect where substantive 'equitable' principles affect the scope of claims derived from the 'common law' action for money had and received,[3] and where 'equitable' proprietary remedies offer additional benefits to claimants who establish additional criteria. The taxonomies of these two intersections are the primary concerns of this chapter, particularly when they suggest what is happening with the law/equity duality.

Professor Andrew Kull has identified the First (1937) *Restatement's* 'most significant innovation [as] its unified treatment of law and equity, presenting

* Thanks to Simone Degeling and Derek Wong for their assistance and helpful comments.

1 *See Sempra Metals Ltd (formerly Metallgesellschaft Ltd) v Inland Revenue Commissioners* [2008] 1 AC 561 [26] (Lord Hope), [112] (Lord Nicholls), [153] (Lord Scott). Their Lordships did not entirely agree on the circumstances that would generate recovery in every case.

2 ibid [183]–[187] (Lord Walker), [240] (Lord Mance).

3 As will be seen, this topic is traditionally viewed through the prism of the responses to *Moses v Macferlan* (1760) 2 Burr 1005, 97 ER 676.

quasi-contract and constructive trust as alternative responses to the problem of unjust enrichment'.[4] The American Law Institute (ALI) planned in the 1930s to address the subject of constructive trusts as a topic within the *Restatement of Trusts* and to sponsor a separate *Restatement of Quasi-Contract*, before deciding that these topics would be better treated together.[5] The ALI then 'took the radical step that carried Lord Mansfield's propositions in *Moses v Macferlan* to their natural conclusions, giving us the modern law of unjust enrichment in unmistakeable form'.[6]

In the article from which these quotations are taken, Andrew Kull may have been smiling with his suggestion that the modern law of restitution has achieved an 'unmistakeable form'. Leaving aside the unjust enrichment sceptics and the equity exclusivists, Peter Birks in his later writings banished restitution for wrongs from his framework of unjust enrichment, and the editors of the latest edition of *Goff & Jones* have dropped restitution itself from the book's title, while contracting the topic on the lines of Birks Mark II.[7] Wearing his Reporter's hat, Andrew acknowledges the controversy among English and Commonwealth writers about the structure of restitution, while stating without apology that the *Restatement Third: Restitution and Unjust Enrichment* follows a larger taxonomy that is both defensible and familiar to American lawyers.[8] As a co-author of a textbook based on Birks Mark I, I am with the Reporter all the way.

The 1937 *Restatement*'s 'significant insight and . . . boldly innovative step [in describing] the corresponding features of law and equity as parallel responses to the same problem'[9] was taken up, with due acknowledgement, by Robert Goff and Gareth Jones when they launched their treatise in 1966.[10] Peter Birks added zest to the crusade, especially when he squarely confronted the equity separatists in a characteristic review of *Meagher, Gummow and Lehane's Equity: Doctrines and Remedies*.[11] Two of that work's co-authors, Justices Gummow and Heydon, would later return Birks' fire from the judicial ramparts.

[4] Andrew Kull, 'James Barr Ames and the Early Modern History of Unjust Enrichment' (2005) 25 *OJLS* 297.

[5] The story is summarised in ibid 299–302. The first Restatement was entitled *Restatement of the Law of Restitution: Quasi-Contracts and Constructive Trusts.*

[6] Kull (n 4) 300.

[7] Charles Mitchell, Paul Mitchell and Stephen Watterson (eds), *Goff & Jones: The Law of Unjust Enrichment*, 8th edn (London, Sweet & Maxwell, 2011). The Preface indicates the editors' intention to include discussion of gain-based remedies for wrongdoing in a second volume, to be published at a later date.

[8] American Law Institute, *Restatement Third: Restitution and Unjust Enrichment* (St Paul, MN, American Law Institute Publishers, 2011) (hereinafter 'R3RUE') 12.

[9] Kull (n 4) 299.

[10] The reviews of the first *Restatement* by Lord Wright ((1937) 51 *Harvard Law Review* 369) and Sir Percy Winfield ((1938) 54 *LQR* 529) drew particular attention to this aspect of the *Restatement.* Winfield said (532) that: 'It may be a dreadful shock to the pure common lawyer and to the pure equity lawyer to find themselves compelled to embrace each other, but it is high time that they should realize that there is but one principle in this branch of the system.'

[11] (2004) 120 *LQR* 344.

There is no jurisdiction relevantly more mature than the US, where the merger[12] of law and equity commenced with Texas in 1845 and the Field Code in New York in 1848, and rapidly spread to most other states. Procedurally distinctive systems of law and equity also merged in the federal system when the Supreme Court promulgated the Federal Rules of Civil Procedure in 1938. These reforms ended separate courts or separate procedures within a single court and they created a single form of action, the civil action.

Maitland forecast that:

> The day will come when lawyers will cease to inquire whether a given rule be a rule of equity or a rule of the common law: suffice that it is a well-established rule administered by the High Court of Justice.[13]

How far have our American cousins travelled down this route? And what lessons can outsiders draw from their journey as reflected in R3RUE? I examine these topics as an outsider who admits to being a committed fusionist. My perspective is as one of Peter Birks' earliest pupils, a member of the academic and judicial divisions of the 'restitution industry' and a New South Wales lawyer. Readers will therefore know that (after a good education) I practised, taught and wrote in a jurisdiction that saw the very late arrival of a full judicature system and where our ultimate appellate court has recently developed hostility to the expansion of unjust enrichment, particularly where it seeks to enter an exclusion zone marked 'Equity – Keep Out'.[14]

B. The Moral Underpinnings of Unjust Enrichment

'The law and morality are inextricably interwoven. To a large extent the law is simply formulated and declared morality.'[15] There is a growing literature about the underlying moral justifications for the award of restitution,[16] indeed for all legal rules.

Some of the earlier American references to the 'equitable' aspects of the action for money had and received occurred when judges were more comfortable than

[12] Writers in the US use 'merger' rather than 'fusion'. In America, as elsewhere, the blending and borrowing of doctrines commenced before the merging of the jurisdictions and continued subsequently: see Austin Abbott, 'The Co-operation of "Law" and "Equity"; and the Engrafting of Equitable Remedies upon Common-Law Proceedings' (1893) 7 *Harvard Law Review* 76.

[13] J Brunyate (ed), *Equity: A Course of Lectures by F W Maitland*, revised edn (Cambridge, Cambridge University Press, 1947) 20.

[14] In *Friend v Brooker* (2009) 239 CLR 129 [7]–[8] and *Bofinger v Kingsway Group Ltd* (2009) 239 CLR 269 [85]–[98], respectively, the High Court saw no role for unjust enrichment in the analysis or development of 'the equitable doctrine of contribution' or 'the equitable doctrine of subrogation'.

[15] *Smith New Court Securities Ltd v Citibank NA* [1997] AC 254, 280 (Lord Steyn).

[16] See, eg, Robert Chambers, Charles Mitchell and James Penner, *Philosophical Foundations of the Law of Unjust Enrichment* (Oxford, Oxford University Press, 2009) and the articles cited in *Goff & Jones* (n 7) [1-08] n 20.

they are now in enunciating the moral values underlying their reasoning and when the blending of religious and civilian thinking into matters of common law raised few eyebrows. For example, when in 1849 the Georgia Supreme Court decided to allow restitution of money paid under mistake of law, the reasoning of Judge Eugenius Aristides Nisbet showed 'the freedom with which an American judge at mid-century might invoke Lord Mansfield, natural justice, Christian teachings, and civilian principles, all *in pari materia*'.[17]

R3RUE's opening Comment about unjust enrichment mentions Lord Mansfield's reference to 'the ties of natural justice and equity' and continues:

> Explaining restitution as the embodiment of natural justice and equity gives the subject an undoubted versatility, an adaptability to new situations, and (in the eyes of many observers) a special moral attractiveness. Restitution in this view is the aspect of our legal system that makes the most direct appeal to standards of equitable and conscientious behavior as a source of enforceable obligations.[18]

Whatever the moral justifications for an award of restitution and whatever the normative influences on restitutionary claims and defences, it is now almost universally recognised that the 'unjust' element in unjust enrichment is a 'generalisation of all the factors which the law recognises as calling for restitution' and not 'an abstract moral principle to which the courts must refer when deciding cases'.[19] The latest edition of *Goff & Jones* suggests that the High Court of Australia has recently strayed from this orthodoxy,[20] but there has been a return to the mainstream in the plurality judgment in *Equuscorp Pty Ltd v Haxton*,[21] a decision that cites R3RUE on several occasions.[22]

C. 'Equity' in the Action for Money Had and Received in England and Australia

Lord Mansfield's famous summation in *Moses v Macferlan* included the following references to 'equity':

[17] Kull (n 4) 312.

[18] R3RUE (n 8) comment at 4.

[19] *Goff & Jones* (n 7) [1-07], quoting an unimpeachable source.

[20] ibid.

[21] *Equuscorp Pty Ltd v Haxton* [2012] HCA 7, (2012) 86 ALJR 296 [29]–[31] (French CJ, Crennan and Kiefel JJ). Their Honours re-asserted the Birksian taxonomical function of the unjust enrichment concept, quietly rebuffing earlier assertions that some form of proscribed 'top-down' reasoning was involved ([30]). The Court also maintained Australia's Mansfieldian approach that allows for a prima facie obligation to make restitution to be displaced 'by circumstances which the law recognises would make an order for restitution unjust' ([30]), including unconscionability of retention with unconscionability 'derived from the general equitable notions which found expression in the common law count for money had and received' ([32]).

[22] [2012] HCA 7, (2012) 86 ALJR 296 [38], [104].

> [T]he law implies a debt, and gives this action, founded in the equity of the plaintiff's case, as it were upon a contract . . .
>
> This kind of equitable action, to recover back money, which ought not in justice to be kept, is very beneficial, and therefore much encouraged. It lies only for money which, ex aequo et bono, the defendant ought to refund: it does not lie for [examples are given] because in all these cases, the defendant may retain it with a safe conscience, though by positive law he was barred from recovering. But it lies for [examples are given, including such 'equitable' ones as] oppression; or an undue advantage taken of the plaintiff's situation, contrary to laws made for the protection of person under those circumstances.
>
> In one word, the gist of the action is that the defendant, upon the circumstances of the case, is obliged by the ties of natural justice and equity to refund the money.[23]

Fourteen years later, in *Clark v Shee & Johnson*, Mansfield described the action as:

> [A] liberal action in the nature of a bill in equity; and if, under the circumstances of the case, it appears that the defendant cannot in conscience retain what is the subject matter of it, the plaintiff may well support this action.[24]

In each instance, Lord Mansfield well knew that he had been trying an 'action' before a jury on a count for money had and received. Nevertheless, he and those who followed him in the early nineteenth century[25] were happy, in ways that some successors were not, to also recognise the implications of the phrase 'to the use of the plaintiff' in the common money count and to engraft principles taken unashamedly from Chancery and Roman law.[26] Some of this blending would be derided as loose talk or confined to procedural matters by hard-nosed nineteenth and early twentieth-century jurists,[27] but this did not do justice to Mansfield's words or his vision. The restitutionary rulings of those stern positivists are now decidedly heterodox for other reasons as well.

Whatever its conceptual underpinning, quasi-contract around the turn of the twentieth century continued to recognise claims that were inexplicable on the basis of implied contract, and wise judges acknowledged this even through the dark winter.[28] Those who felt the need to voice a non-fictional principle used Mansfieldian phrases such as '(natural) justice and equity' and 'equity and good

[23] *Moses v Macferlan* (1760) 2 Burr 1005, 1008, 1012, 97 ER 676, 678, 680–81.

[24] *Clark v Shee & Johnson* (1774) 1 Cowp 197, 199–200, 98 ER 1041, 1042.

[25] See *Remon v Hayward* (1835) 2 Ad & E 666, 111 ER 256; *Roper v Holland* (1835) 3 Ad & El 99, 111 ER 351. See also Bullen and Leake, *Precedents of Pleading*, 3rd edn (London, Stevens, 1868) 44: the count 'is applicable wherever the defendant has received money which in justice and equity belongs to the plaintiff, under circumstances which render the receipt of it a receipt by the defendant to the use of the plaintiff'. In New South Wales, this work was the primary source of reference for the law of quasi-contract before the arrival of *Goff & Jones* in 1966 and it remained the pleading Bible for practititioners before the judicature reforms that commenced there in 1972.

[26] In Gummow J's words in *Roxborough v Rothmans of Pall Mall Australia Ltd* (2001) 208 CLR 516 [84] (footnotes omitted): 'Lord Mansfield sought to translate equitable principles, doctrines and procedures into the trial of actions at law; this reflected his appreciation of equitable doctrine for its flexibility and adaptability to modern needs, particularly in commercial law.'

[27] See *Miller v Atlee* (1849) 13 Jur 431; *Sinclair v Brougham* [1914] AC 398, 454–55 (Lord Sumner).

[28] See, eg, *Re Rhodes* (1890) 44 Ch D 94.

conscience' with reference to the action for money had and received (at least before they were jumped on from a great height in *Sinclair v Brougham*).[29]

Those who shunned such language were occasionally troubled by the idea that 'Equity' in the form of substantive Chancery law could intrude into a common law action.[30] But greater concern lay with an apparently overt role for morality in a well-established corner of the common law. The two concerns were not entirely unrelated, given that Chancery law maintained its link with matters of conscience even as its arteries appeared to be hardening and its womb showing reluctance to bring forth new issue.

When, in *Holt v Markham*,[31] Scrutton LJ described the history of money had and received as 'a history of well-meaning sloppiness of thought', he specifically endorsed Hamilton LJ's remarks in *Bayliss v Bishop of London*[32] to the effect that judges were no longer free in the twentieth century to administer that 'vague jurisprudence which is sometimes attractively styled "justice as between man and man"'. As this ethical bathwater was being hurled out, so too was the possibility of a change of position defence,[33] a personal action for restitution of money paid under an ultra vires contract[34] and the unjust enrichment concept itself.[35]

Implied contract would be rejected and the unjust enrichment concept ushered back[36] by the highest courts in Canada, Australia and England in 1954, 1987 and 1991, in the latter cases with due acknowledgement of the writings of Robert Goff, Gareth Jones and Peter Birks. These scholars in turn acknowledged their debt to the 1937 *Restatement* and to jurists like Lord Wright who had written warmly about it on and off the bench.

With the abandonment of the implied contract fiction and the acceptance of the unjust enrichment rationale for most[37] of the causes of action derived from the money had and received count, courts and scholars were free to invoke the concept for explaining existing situations and developing the law as well. There

[29] *Sinclair v Brougham* [1914] AC 398. See, eg, *Freeman v Jeffries* (1869) LR 4 Ex 189, 197–98; *White v Copeland* (1894) 15 LR (NSW) 281; *R v Brown* (1912) 14 CLR 17, 25.

[30] See *Miller v Atlee* (n 27); *Sinclair v Brougham* (n 27) 454–55 (Lord Sumner). This, in the language of *Meagher, Gummow and Lehane's, Equity: Doctrines and Remedies*, represents a 'fusion fallacy'. Successive editions of that book have included *Hedley Byrne v Heller* [1964] AC 464 as one of several instances. Surprisingly, *Moses v Macferlan* is not mentioned.

[31] *Holt v Markham* [1923] 1 KB 504, 513.

[32] *Bayliss v Bishop of London* [1913] 1 Ch 127, 139–40.

[33] *Bayliss* (n 32).

[34] *Sinclair v Brougham* (n 27).

[35] See *Morgan v Ashcroft* [1938] 1 KB 49, 62.

[36] In 1802, Sir William Evans published an *Essay on the Action for Money Had and Received*, based closely upon Lord Mansfield's synthesis. Evans observed that the maxim of the civil law – that it is naturally just that one man should not be enriched to the detriment of another – was particularly applied to the claims under consideration.

[37] Most, not all, because of the debate centring around cases where (to show my colours) the cause of action vindicates title unless one resorts to a strained notion of enrichment or treats 'ignorance' as an unjust factor. The leading cases include *Holiday v Sigil* (1826) 2 Car & P 176, 172 ER 81; *Banque Belge pour l'Etranger v Hambrouk* [1921] 1 KB 321; *Lipkin Gorman v Karpnale Ltd* [1991] 2 AC 548; *Trustee of the Property of FC Jones & Sons (a firm) v Jones* [1997] Ch 159. For a review supporting this conceptualisation, see *Armstrong DLW Gmbh v Winnington Networks Ltd* [2012] EWHC 10 (Ch), [2012] 3 WLR 835.

might be taxonomical debates about whether rescission and undue influence claims would be included in restitution textbooks. And Australian law would categorically reject unjust enrichment's intrusion into the fields covered by *Barnes v Addy*,[38] 'equitable subrogation'[39] and 'equitable contribution'.[40] However, for monetary claims relating to mistaken or pressured payments or claims regarding a total failure of consideration, most authorities would follow Goff, Jones and Birks in viewing the standard unjust enrichment claims as strict, albeit subject to defences. In Birks' words, the idea of considering whether receipt or retention was unconscionable was like having 'a fifth wheel on the coach'.[41] This approach left room for debate about whether 'equitable' notions required 'something more' for such things as proprietary restitution for mistaken payments, but in England and Australia, this debate requires separate examination of 'legal' and 'equitable' principles.

The High Court of Australia initially endorsed the English approach when it emphasised that proof of mistake generated a prima facie right of recovery without the need to prove independently that the recipient was unjustly enriched at the expense of the payer: the payer does not have to prove an additional factor of want of honest belief in entitlement to receive on the part of the claimant.[42] In *Farah Constructions Pty Ltd v Say-Dee Pty Ltd*,[43] the High Court would also reiterate that, for the standard categories, 'whether enrichment is unjust is not determined by reference to a subjective evaluation of what is unfair or unconscionable'. The Court was also prepared to see roles for unjust enrichment in traditional 'equitable' fields.[44]

Nevertheless, Gummow J in particular launched a two-pronged assault on what I shall call the Birksian position regarding the conceptual underpinning of restitution for unjust enrichment. First, he led resistance to exportation of the concept by contending that it is inherently unstable and lends itself to fallacious 'top-down' reasoning that has brought forth bastard issue in some areas.[45] (These

[38] *Barnes v Addy* (1874) LR 9 Ch App 244. See *Farah Constructions Pty Ltd v Say-Dee Pty Ltd* (2007) 230 CLR 89. For an excellent review of the current state of the Australian law on this and other topics associated with proprietary restitution for bribes, see *Grimaldi v Chameleon Mining NL (No 2)* [2012] FCAFC 6, (2012) 287 ALR 22 (Finn J's judicial swansong).

[39] *Bofinger* (n 14) [85]–[98].

[40] *Friend v Brooker* (n 14) [7]–[8].

[41] Peter Birks, 'Receipt' in Peter Birks and Arianna Pretto, *Breach of Trust* (Oxford, Hart Publishing, 2002) 226.

[42] *David Securities Pty Ltd v Commonwealth Bank of Australia* (1992) 175 CLR 353, 378.

[43] *Farah Constructions* (n 38) [150]. *cf* also the warning against loose and conclusory reasoning based on the concept of 'unconscionable conduct': *Tanwar Enterprises Pty Ltd v Cauchi* (2003) 217 CLR 315, 324.

[44] See *Dart Industries Inc v Decor Corp Pty Ltd* (1993) 179 CLR 101, 111, 123; *Burke v LFOT Pty Ltd* (2002) 209 CLR 282, 294, 298.

[45] See the High Court cases cited in *Goff & Jones* (n 17) 7, n 20, commencing with the attack on 'unjust enrichment theory' in Gummow J's judgment in *Roxborough* (n 26) [70]–[74]. According to the learned editors, these passages appear to have lost sight of Deane J's meaning in *Pavey & Matthews Pty Ltd v Paul* (1987) 162 CLR 221, 256–57 and to have 'mischaracterised unjust enrichment as an abstract principle of justice'. I respectfully agree: see the writings cited in the same footnote in *Goff & Jones*.

arguments contributed to some rulings suggesting a categorical estrangement between the unjust enrichment concept and matters equitable.) Fortunately, there are signs of a major corrective to this view in the plurality judgment of *Equuscorp Pty Ltd v Haxton* very recently,[46] not that recent key rulings are likely to be revisited any time soon.

But, on a second front, Gummow J has successfully promoted in Australia what I would respectfully term an appropriately fusionist approach to money had and received claims that deliberately reconnects with Lord Mansfield's vision in *Moses v Macferlan*. I therefore detect some space between the modern English and Australian law because of Australia's reluctance to see 'common law' restitutionary liability as invariably strict. The recent Australian cases show a greater willingness to allow Lord Mansfield's 'equitable' factors room to work broadly in the fields of defences to claims derived from the money had and received count. It may be up to the defendant to raise the matter, but a fixed canon of sharply defined defences such as change of position, estoppel and so on has been resisted.

In *Baltic Shipping Co v Dillon*, Deane and Dawson JJ indicated that the *indebitatus* count was framed in the traditional language of trust or use and continued:

> [I]n a modern context where common law and equity are fused with equity prevailing, the artificial constraints imposed by the old forms of action can, unless they reflect coherent principle, be disregarded where they impede the principled enunciation and development of the law. In particular, the notions of good conscience, which both the common law and equity recognised as the underlying rationale of the law of unjust enrichment, now dictate that, in applying the relevant doctrines of law and equity, regard be had to matters of substance rather than technical form.[47]

Very recently, in *Equuscorp*,[48] Gummow and Bell JJ referred to 'the degree of flexibility in fashioning the just measure of recovery on an action such as that for money had and received, given that, while it is a legal action not an equitable suit, it is settled in Australia that the action is a liberal action in the nature of a bill in equity'. One might, with respect, quibble about the acceptance in Australia of the statement concerning a 'bill in equity' which is, in any event, an extremely dated concept. But the substance of the point was repeated in the plurality judgment itself where restitution's coherence with legal, equitable and statutory principles was emphasised.[49] *Ford v Perpetual Trustees Victoria Ltd*[50] is a striking example of this Australian trend.

[46] *Equuscorp* (n 21) [29]–[31] (French CJ, Crennan and Kiefel JJ).

[47] *Baltic Shipping Co v Dillon* (1993) 176 CLR 344 at 376, quoted by Gummow J in *Roxborough* (n 26) [100]. See also *Roxborough* [16], where Gleeson CJ, Gaudron and Hayne JJ quoted Deane J with approval when he had referred to 'general equitable notions . . . find[ing] expression in the common law count' in *Muschinski v Dodds* (1985) 160 CLR 583, 619–20.

[48] *Equuscorp* (n 21) [114], citing *National Commercial Banking Corporation of Australia Ltd v Batty* (1986) 160 CLR 251, 268 (Gibbs CJ); *Roxborough* (n 26) [15]–[16], [62]–[63], [71], [83]–[100].

[49] See *Equuscorp* (n 21) [32]–[34].

[50] *Ford v Perpetual Trustees Victoria Ltd* (2009) 75 NSWLR 42, 257 ALR 658 (NSWCA), discussed by Elise Bant in (2009) 33 *Melbourne University Law Review* 368 (mentally disabled borrower who was being manipulated by his son received proceeds of a loan under contract ruled void for *non est factum* due to his mental disability. Bulk of proceeds handed over to son. Restitutionary claim by lender confined to money left in borrower's hands. As regards money handed over, the court found no injustice

As we shall see, such blending of legal and equitable considerations in the action for money had and received has always been commonplace in the US, without any need to arm-wrestle over the fusionist or strict liability issues.

D. Lord Mansfield's Insight and its Reception into American Law

The pre-War of American Independence dating of *Moses v Macferlan* meant that it could always be cited by American judges without embarrassment. And the early merging of the administration of law and equity in the US removed so-called jurisdictional inhibitions that, like the forms of action, continued to haunt from their graves in other nations.

Thus, we see the US Supreme Court repeatedly describing the action for money had and received in terms that would have pleased Lord Mansfield. In *Myers v Hurley Motor Co*, Sutherland J, with much reference to nineteenth-century American authority applying *Moses v Macferlan*, said of the action for money had and received:

> Such an action, though brought at law, is in its nature a substitute for a suit in equity; and it is to be determined by the application of equitable principles. In other words, the rights of the parties are to be determined as they would be upon a bill in equity. The defendant may rely upon any defense which shows that the plaintiff, in equity and good conscience is not entitled to recover in whole or in part.[51]

In 1934, in *United States v Jefferson Electric Manufacturing Co*,[52] the US Supreme Court approved the following passage from the judgment of the Massachusetts Supreme Judicial Court in *Claflin v Godfrey*:

> The action is assumpsit for money had and received by the defendant to the plaintiff's use, and for money paid by the plaintiff for the defendant's benefit. This is often called an equitable action and is less restricted and fettered by technical rules and formalities than any other form of action. It aims at the abstract justice of the case, and looks solely to the inquiry, whether the defendant holds money, which ex aequo et bono belongs to the plaintiff. It was encouraged and, to a great extent, brought into use by that great and just judge, Lord Mansfield, and from his day to the present, has been constantly resorted to in all cases coming within its broad principles. It approaches nearer to a bill in equity than any other common law action.[53]

in retention and no true benefit was received by borrower. Lender's failure to inquire taken into account ([130]). Ageny receipt cases found to be illustrative of wider principle given that unjust enrichment is concerned with substance and not form).

[51] *Myers v Hurley Motor Co* (1927) 273 US 18, 24. These and the following references are drawn from Gummow J's scholarly judgment in *Roxborough* (n 26) [85]–[86]. See also The Honourable Justice WMC Gummow, 'Moses v Macferlan 250 Years On' (2011) 68 *Washington and Lee Law Review* 881.

[52] *United States v Jefferson Electric Manufacturing Co* (1934) 291 US 386, 402–03.

[53] *Claflin v Godfrey* (1838) 38 Mass 1, 6.

When giving the judgment of the Supreme Court in *Atlantic Coast Line Railroad Co v Florida*, Cardozo J, with reference to *Moses v Macferlan*, described the action for money had and received as 'equitable in origin and function' and continued:

> The claimant to prevail must show that the money was received in such circumstances that the possessor will give offense to equity and good conscience if permitted to retain it.[54]

It is important to note that these blendings occurred at a time when American lawyers would have understood the references to a bill in equity and would have perceived more clearly than now that 'Equity' was a separate system of law derived from the Court of Chancery. However, American law also enjoyed a strong academic tradition that welcomed the merger of legal and equitable principles, both substantive and remedial, especially in the present field. As Professor Kull has demonstrated,[55] Professor Ames was teaching and writing as early as 1887 that unjust enrichment, not implied contract, formed the basis of quasi-contract. Ames also perceived that a similar principle underpinned 'constructive trusts and other equitable obligations created by operation of law (including implied or *quasi* contracts, which are really equitable remedies, upon which the common law assumes to give a remedy)'.[56]

R3RUE stands firmly in this tradition. It acknowledges that liabilities and remedies within the law of restitution for unjust enrichment may have originated in law, in equity or in a combination of the two.[57] R3RUE confidently (and slightly circularly) states that a claimant entitled to an equitable remedy need not demonstrate inadequacy of available remedies at law.[58] And the comment is at pains to demonstrate that 'following the modern unification of law and equity jurisdiction the question of origin would be of merely historical interest, were it not for two peculiarities of American law'.[59] The first concerns constitutional protection of trial by jury for suits 'at common law', an issue that for federal cases requires American courts to decide whether the case before them is one that would have been brought at law or in equity in 1791.[60] The second concerns a recent proliferation of federal statutes which provide, in one context or another, that the rights conferred by statute may be judicially enforced via 'equitable relief'.

[54] *Atlantic Coast Line Railroad Co v Florida* (1935) 295 US 301, 309.

[55] A Kull, 'James Barr Ames and the Early Modern History of Unjust Enrichment' (2005) 25 *OJLS* 297, 303–05.

[56] JB Ames, 'Purchaser for Value Without Notice' (1887) 1 *HLR* 1, 3.

[57] R3RUE (n 8) § 4(1).

[58] ibid § 4 (2), discussed further below.

[59] ibid 27.

[60] But see also *Grupa Mexicano de Desarrollo SA v Alliance Bond Fund Inc*, 527 US 308 (1999), where a narrowly divided Supreme Court rejected an equitable jurisdiction to grant a Mareva injunction (named for Mareva Compania Naviera SA v International Bulkcarriers SA [1975] 2 Lloyd's Rep 509). All justices approached the task as involving examination of equity's capacity to develop since American independence when, in 1776 or shortly afterwards (see generally BH McPherson CBE, *The Reception of English Law Abroad* (Brisbane, Supreme Court of Queensland Library, 2007), 285–88), the various colonies were taken to have received English law. The majority in *Grupa Mexicano* ruled that *Mareva* was more than a development of inherited Chancery jurisdiction, castigating the minority opinion as confusing equitable flexibility with 'omnipotence' (322 (Scalia J)).

Neither of these qualifications need concern these readers. Since, however, the 'equitable' label tends everywhere to carry a coded message about the flexible nature of all proprietary remedies,[61] I shall return to this point below.

E. R3RUE's Taxonomy of Remedies

In ways that would have been shocking to Birks in his monist phase,[62] R3RUE is perfectly relaxed in addressing rights and remedies separately, thereby recognising that litigants and courts exercise legitimate choices when addressing the consequences of establishing a substantive entitlement. In this, and in its coherent treatment of remedies, R3RUE reflects a long tradition of American law. Judging by textbooks, university courses and the structure of modern statutes, this message is now getting through to Anglo-Australian law as well.

R3RUE addresses remedies in Part III and Chapter 7. The Introductory Note[63] speaks of two principal kinds of remedies for unjust enrichment: monetary judgments (Topic 1) and 'what are traditionally known as the equitable remedies in restitution – notably constructive trust, equitable lien, and subrogation – permitting the claimant to obtain restitution via rights in specifically identifiable property in the hands of the defendant' (Topic 2).[64]

As to the internal taxonomy of monetary judgments, R3RUE discusses such topics as 'measures of enrichment',[65] 'disgorgement', 'accounting for profits'[66] and 'use value'[67] in a way that straddles the law/equity divide without reference to the duality, let alone embarrassment. (Anglo-Australian courts are showing halting signs of progress along similar lines, especially in relation to restitution for wrongs, although much ink continues to be spilt justifying the crossover of remedies, particularly the legitimacy of using 'common law' remedies for 'equitable' tasks such as profit-stripping and the award of compound interest.)[68] R3RUE's handling of the question of punitive or exemplary damages should also serve as an encouragement in other jurisdictions.[69]

[61] Leaving aside detinue, which is still a 'common law' tort in many jurisdictions outside England.

[62] See Peter Birks, 'Rights, Wrongs and Remedies' (2000) 20 *OJLS* 1.

[63] R3RUE (n 8) 173.

[64] ibid 174–75.

[65] ibid § 49.

[66] ibid § 51.

[67] ibid § 52.

[68] See, eg, *Gaba Formwork Contractors Pty Ltd v Turner Corp Ltd* (1991) 32 NSWLR 175; *Trustee of the Property of FC Jones & Sons* (n 37); *Sempra Metals Ltd* (n 1). *cf* also the endless debates over the legitimacy of *Attorney-General v Blake* [2001] 1 AC 268 and the extraordinary statement by the majority in *Hospitality Group Pty Ltd v Australian Rugby Union Ltd* (2001) 110 FCR 157 [162] that 'however described, it is not possible to slot an acount of profits into the general framework of remedies that are available in tort'. The High Court of Australia has yet to propose any taxonomical coherence in relation to non-statutory awards of interest.

[69] R3RUE (n 8) § 51, Comment k. 'Encouragement' in both senses of the word to this dissenter in *Harris v Digital Pulse Pty Ltd* (2003) 53 NSWLR 298.

As to the internal taxonomy of the proprietary remedies, R3RUE has sections dealing with rescission,[70] constructive trust, equitable lien, subrogation as a remedy, following property into its product and against transferees, tracing into or through a commingled fund, priority and profitable recovery restricted.[71]

(Anglo-Australian law remains bedevilled by the location of profit-stripping monetary remedies within a still muddled taxonomy of the constructive trust.[72] Their presence has reinforced arguments challenging the fictitious nature of the 'constructive trust', even if it is understood as shorthand for an 'equitable' obligation to account *as if* the defendant were a trustee, but not to the full extent of an express trustee. There is a related debate about whether the 'constructive trust' that may be invoked against the third party who benefits from abusing a relationship of confidence or when either arm of *Barnes v Addy*[73] is engaged is at bottom a personal liability, albeit one that can trigger proprietary and tracing responses in certain situations.[74] Australian law also sometimes uses the language of constructive trust when embarking on decisions about tracing and following or discussion that may result in a less intrusive proprietary remedy, such as an equitable charge or lien.)

R3RUE has none of this confusion, being precise in both its restricted usage of 'constructive trust' and under no delusions as to its limited affinity (in restitution) with other trusts, except in name and early history (see below).

F. R3RUE'S Taxonomy of the Constructive Trust

R3RUE's insights and lessons concerning the constructive trust in restitution can be addressed under three headings: (1) the constructive trust as a remedy that may respond to unjust enrichment or wrongdoing (and other events); (2) the flexibility of the remedial constructive trust; and (3) the situation in bankruptcy.

[70] No distinction is recognised between rescission 'at law' and 'in equity', even in the part recognising that there are 'equitable defenses to rescission': see R3RUE (n 8) 285, 286–87.

[71] ibid §§ 54–61.

[72] See generally Keith Mason, 'Deconstructing the Constructive Trust in Australia' (2010) 4 *Journal of Equity* 98, 108, discussing cases such as *Giumelli v Giumelli* (1999) 196 CLR 101, 112; W Swadling, 'The Fiction of the Constructive Trust' (2011) 64 *CLP* 399, 405–06, 408, 412. The Reporter of R3RUE points out that 'the constructive trust metaphor is not necessary to the analysis' leading to a monetary accounting (315) and that references to the constructive trust in such cases 'are an inheritance from the era of divided law and equity jurisdiction: in particular, from the equity tradition in which the constructive trust (as a way to describe the restitutionary liability of a defaulting fiduciary) long antedated the idea of unjust enrichment as a generalized basis of liability. Unless the claimant's remedy in restitution involves specific restitution . . . the idea of constructive trust is at best superfluous and at worst misleading; but such references are still encountered' (329).

[73] *Barnes v Addy* (n 38).

[74] On this point, see the discussion in *Grimaldi* (n 38) [253]–[254].

(1) The Constructive Trust as a Remedy that May Respond to Unjust Enrichment or Wrongdoing (and Other Events)

American law has long held to a remedial view of the constructive trust. According to Cardozo J:

> A constructive trust is the formula through which the conscience of equity finds expression. When property has been acquired in such circumstances that the holder of the legal title may not in good conscience retain the beneficial interest, equity converts him into a trustee.[75]

In Professor Langbein's words, the constructive trust 'was a transparent fiction, rooted in the chancellor's ability to overcome legal title by framing a decree to affect legal title'.[76]

(This perception of a remedial yet proprietary response to unjust enrichment or wrongdoing is quite independent of the issues about when the 'trust' actually arises or the circumstances in which a court may in its discretion withhold the full proprietary remedy. Concentration on the latter (exceptional) aspects of the 'remedial constructive trust' has contributed to English courts shunning the remedial constructive trust entirely.[77] All this, in the face of ancient understanding about the *in personam* origins of the express trust. As indicated below, some of this debate is also driven by contestable views about bankruptcy law. Across the jurisdictions, the debate has been infected by lack of commonality in the use of terms such as 'institutional' and 'remedial' that has seen misrepresentation of the truly responsive functioning of the trust when it is imposed to nullify wrongdoing or unjust enrichment.)[78]

On the timing of arrival issue, R3RUE firmly supports the proposition that (quoting Scott) there is 'no foundation whatever for the notion that a constructive trust does not arise until it is decreed by a court'. The Reporter explains[79] that it is wrong to suggest that Bogert held a different view: 'his point is merely that there may be no constructive trust if the claimant seeks another form of relief.' Several authorities are cited and the contrary decision in bankruptcy in *In re Omegas Group Inc* (discussed below) is castigated with the observation that 'a

[75] *Beatty v Guggenheim Exploration Co*, 122 NE 378, 380 (1919). In an article, 'Constructive Trusts' (1955) 71 *LQR* 39, 41, Austin Scott wrote that the idea of a constructive trust as a remedial and not a substantive institution was stated by Roscoe Pound in his article 'The Progress of the Law' (1920) 33 *Harvard Law Review* 420, 421. Professor Kull traces that matter back further to the teaching of Ames: see Kull (n 4) 307–09.

[76] JH Langbein, 'The Later History of Restitution' in WR Cornish et al (eds), *Restitution: Past, Present and Future: Essays in Honour of Gareth Jones* (Oxford, Hart Publishing, 1998) 58.

[77] It has also produced much fictional talk about the 'common intention' of domestic partners who fall out: see *Stack v Dowden* [2007] 2 AC 432; *Jones v Kernott* [2012] 1 AC 776. Contrast *Baumgartner v Baumgartner* (1987) 164 CLR 137.

[78] On this point, see Hayton and Mitchell, *Commentary and Cases on the Law of Trusts and Equitable Remedies*, 13th edn (London, Sweet & Maxwell, 2010) 623–24.

[79] R3RUE (n 8) 325–26.

court that regards constructive trust as a source of injustice will not be the most reliable exponent of the traditional equitable theory of the remedy'.[80]

America's long perception of the constructive trust as an available response to unjust enrichment and wrongdoing has had further taxonomical implications. Its role in the ALI's decision in the 1930s about the structure of the *Restatement* has already been noted. These attitudes have, in turn, exposed the dangers of the 'trust' fiction. Going by R3RUE, the re-alignment has also challenged the perceived utility of using the 'equitable' label as well. This has encouraged R3RUE to spell out the particular principles engaged when a particular remedy is claimed rather than using the weak portmanteau 'equitable'. Let me explain.

We have it on Professor Kull's authority[81] that 'it is nothing less than extraordinary, to a US lawyer, to hear anyone [in the twenty-first century] describe a constructive trust as a species of trust. To us this seems just as old-fashioned, and just as fundamentally misleading, as to describe a quasi-contractual obligation as a species of contract'. (Just how misleading the fiction of a constructive trust for English law is developed in William Swadling's excellent article 'The Fiction of the Constructive Trust'.[82] I too have endeavoured to show the damage that the conclusory label inflicts in Australia where courts have embraced discretionary, minimalist remedialism in the approach to proprietary remedies in restitution, including restitution for wrongs.[83] Each jurisdiction has some distance to travel on the fiction issue, even though they are poles apart in their approach to 'remedial constructive trusts'. So let us return to R3RUE.)

R3RUE treats Cardozo's insight into the constructive trust as an 'unimpeachable citation' for the definition of a constructive trust.[84] The concept's conclusory nature is taken for granted, with emphasis on the flexibility of the device. The comment informs us that:

> It is commonly repeated that a constructive trust is 'not a real trust' since it is 'only a remedy.' One might go further and explain that the term 'constructive trust,' used correctly to designate a remedy for unjust enrichment, is only a manner of speaking. Abandoning the metaphor, every judicial order recognizing that 'B holds X in constructive trust for A' may be seen to comprise, in effect, two remedial components. The first of these is a declaration that B's legal title to X is subject to A's superior equitable claim. The second is a mandatory injunction directing B to surrender X to A or to take equivalent steps.
>
> The flexibility of constructive trust is significantly enhanced because this implicit injunction – the order to surrender specific property to the claimant – can easily be (and is frequently) made conditional on further remedial steps necessary to complete justice in a particular case.[85]

[80] ibid 326.

[81] Andrew Kull, 'Deconstructing the Constructive Trust' (2004) 40 *Canadian Business Law Journal* 358, 359.

[82] William Swadling, 'The Fiction of the Constructive Trust' (2011) 64 *CLP* 399.

[83] Mason (n 72).

[84] R3RUE (n 8) 321.

[85] ibid 298.

Of further interest to this chapter as a whole is R3RUE's recognition that modern America's absence of a 'shared professional understanding of the word "equity" '[86] drives the *Restatement* to paraphrase Cardozo. I shall later discuss the extent to which the modern American law's relatively insouciant attitude to a distinctive 'Equity' is a problem or an opportunity. For the moment, I merely set out the propositions in § 55 that give us the constructive trust almost shorn of the 'trust' fiction:

(1) If a defendant is unjustly enriched by the acquisition of title to identifiable property at the expense of the claimant or in violation of the claimant's rights, the defendant may be declared a constructive trustee, for the benefit of the claimant, of the property in question and its traceable product.
(2) The obligation of a constructive trustee is to surrender the constructive trust property to the claimant, on such conditions as the court may direct.

(2) The Flexibility of the Remedial Constructive Trust

The final words of § 55(2) (quoted above) highlight that relief is not automatic and this point is underscored in the comment.[87] Elsewhere, the Reporter acknowledges that:

> Given their antecedents in equity jurisprudence, it is a commonplace to observe that the remedies permitting restitution from property are to be flexibly applied, in the interests of justice, and in the sound discretion of the court. This means (among other things) that a court may structure a remedy to meet particular circumstances: for example, by requiring reimbursement or an accounting as a condition to the recognition of a constructive trust (see § 55, Comment l), or by imposing conditions to the foreclosure of an equitable lien (see § 56, Comment c). It means, also, that a claimant who satisfies the usual requirements for the availability of restitution from property may nevertheless be denied such relief, if the outcome sought would be inequitable under the circumstances of the particular case.[88]

I would be surprised to find in R3RUE any endorsement of the notion of 'doing equity', expressed in those terms, but that is the spirit of these remarks about the flexibility of the remedy.

Modern Australian law, which has embraced the remedial constructive trust, also emphasises 'the cardinal principle of equity that the remedy must be fashioned to fit the nature of the case and the particular facts'.[89] These considerations trigger acknowledgement that the court must have regard to the interests of third parties,[90] a factor that may lead to an order deferring the date on which a security

[86] ibid 296.
[87] ibid 298, being the second paragraph of the comment quoted above.
[88] ibid 262.
[89] *Bofinger* (n 14) [1].
[90] *Bathurst City Council v PWC Properties Pty Ltd* (1998) 195 CLR 566 [42]; *John Alexander's Clubs Pty Ltd v White City Tennis Club Ltd* (2010) 241 CLR 1 [126]–[129].

or trust takes effect.[91] I venture to suggest that recognition of these aspects of the 'remedial constructive trust' would help undermine the fear, if not misrepresentation, surrounding the remedy in the English case law.

Australian law adopts a vigorously minimalist approach to proprietary restitution. With some exceptions,[92] a full-blown 'trust' will be withheld if a lesser remedy would ensure complete and practical justice.[93] Thus, a monetary order may suffice against a solvent defendant and a lien may be preferred to a full constructive trust.

R3RUE would appear to hold to a similar position, although it is not spelt out expressly.[94] The *Restatement* has a section on the equitable lien (§ 56). § 56(3) states that a claimant who would be entitled to ownership of particular property via constructive trust may elect to obtain an equitable lien on the property instead. This is explained on the basis that the greater includes the lesser,[95] so the converse may not always be true. However, an earlier comment suggests that the choice between lien and constructive trust is the claimant's.[96] More significantly, we have it on the authority of § 4(2) of R3RUE that:

> A claimant otherwise entitled to a remedy for unjust enrichment, including a remedy originating in equity, need not demonstrate the inadequacy of available remedies at law.

The Comment adds that: 'An argument to the contrary should appear antiquated today.'[97] That said, the proposition is qualified by an acknowledgement that a constructive trust may be refused if the defendant has more than sufficient funds to meet a monetary judgment.[98]

Could this possibly be an instance where R3RUE's fusionist taxonomy has failed to drive home a point of real substance? It is one thing to break the yoke that prevents the mixing of the egg's legal and equitable contents; it may be another thing to whisk the mixture quite so vigorously that all distinctions are obliterated, even those supportable on policy grounds. Perhaps the acknowledgement that a constructive trust will be withheld in America against a solvent defendant shows that the differences are marginal at best.

[91] See *Bathurst City Council* (n 90) [42], explaining the order in *Muschinski.*

[92] For example, if the principles of proprietary estoppel are also engaged. See also *Grimaldi* (n 38) [510].

[93] For general statements about minimalism, see *Bathurst City* (n 90) [42]; *Giumelli v Giumelli* (n 72) [10]; *Farah Constructions* (n 38) [200] ('Ordinarily relief by way of a constructive trust is imposed only if some other remedy is not suitable'); *John Alexander's Clubs* (n 90) [128].

[94] See § 56, Comment b.

[95] R3RUE (n 8) 333.

[96] ibid 314.

[97] ibid 28. This proposition is explained and demonstrated at length at in ibid 34–37, 40–41.

[98] ibid 36–37.

(3) The Situation in Bankruptcy

R3RUE recognises that the reasons why a claimant would seek property-based remedies are broad, the most important being that 'the various forms of specific relief – by recognizing the claimant's interest as owner or lienor of the property in question – often give an effective priority to the restitution claimant over the general creditors of the recipient'.[99]

Priority achieved in consequence of a court declaring the existence of a proprietary interest on equitable grounds is both 'effective' and as old as the hills. Judges have nearly always been conscious of this consequence and have either embraced the opportunity in a proper case or eschewed it in the full realisation that the claimant will have to join a queue full of unsecured creditors in a bankruptcy or corporate liquidation. Regrettably, there has been a lot of circular reasoning on both sides, as has been pointed out recently by the Master of the Rolls in *Sinclair Investments (UK) Ltd v Versailles Trade Finance Ltd*[100] and by the Full Federal Court of Australia in *Grimaldi v Chameleon Mining NL (No 2)*.[101]

But some things have been clear for a long time and are supported in statute and case law relating to insolvency, namely that (as a general proposition) trust property does not form part of the estate and secured debts take priority over unsecured claims. The modern English and Australian enactments are referred to in the Appendix to this chapter: none of them distinguishes between categories of 'trust' and all of them deserve, prima facie, to be interpreted on the basis that the constructive trust was conceived as a 'trust' when the provision was first enacted. More importantly, the statutory principles reflect the pre-statutory history of insolvency where one finds very early statements that the trustee in bankruptcy stands in the shoes of the bankrupt with any assignment of property on insolvency passing 'only such property as the bankrupt is conscientiously entitled to'.[102] These decisions do not turn upon arguments over the remedial or discretionary nature of constructive trusts because, like the reasoning in *Attorney-General for Hong Kong v Reid*,[103] they proceed on the basis that the trust relevantly arose upon receipt. As indicated, this is the position taken in R3RUE as well.

In R3RUE and elsewhere the learned Reporter bemoans the decision in *In re Omegas Group Inc*,[104] the bankruptcy case in which a defrauded purchaser failed to recover its payments as on a constructive trust. The Court of Appeals, Sixth

[99] ibid 261.

[100] *Sinclair Investments (UK) Ltd v Versailles Trade Finance Ltd* [2011] EWCA Civ 347, [2011] 3 WLR 1153 [78].

[101] *Grimaldi* (n 38) [573].

[102] Lord Kenyon CJ in *Harrison v Walker* (1792) Peake 150 at 151, 170 ER 111. See also *Scott v Surman* (1743) Willes 400, 125 ER 1235. Australian cases recognising that a constructive trust (when appropriately declared) will not be defeated merely because legal title passes on bankruptcy include *Parsons v McBain* (2001) 109 FCR 120, 126; *Crouch v Abell* [2005] NSWSC 1308.

[103] *Attorney-General for Hong Kong v Reid* [1994] 1 AC 324.

[104] *In re Omegas Group Inc*, 16 F 3d 1443. See also Kull's note on the case in [1995] RLR § 294. See also Swadling (n 72) 428.

Circuit ruled that the remedy of constructive trust was not available in bankruptcy to enable a defrauded party to obtain priority over other creditors. The Court held that the 'trust property' that is not part of the bankrupt's estate is limited to property held on express trust. One strand of the reasoning merits qualified approval, namely that constructive trusts were 'not really a trust', but a 'legal fiction, a common-law remedy in equity that may only exist by the grace of judicial action'. But any approval should be severely qualified for two reasons. First, the 'by grace' description misrepresents what is at play when a court decides that it is appropriate to grant 'equitable' proprietary relief.[105] Second, *Omegas Group* really turns on a more fundamental proposition, namely the demonstrably false idea that constructive trusts are 'anathema to the equities of bankruptcy'. Thus expressed, it applies to all species of constructive trust, but even if confined to the remedial ones now in question, the proposition is unsupportable.

As the Reporter points out, several contrary 'better judicial authorities' proceed on the basis that the constructive trust comes into existence when the insolvent receives property and is unjustly enriched by such receipt, with the result that there is no improper derogation of the rights of unsecured creditors in bankruptcy.[106] This point is further developed in a later comment on *Restitution in Bankruptcy*,[107] prefaced by the following observation:

> An unintended consequence of the merger of law and equity procedure has been that many American lawyers know little or nothing about the property rights that were traditionally recognised and protected in equity. Property interests of this kind, created by state law, are neither defined nor explained by the federal bankruptcy statutes; though a century of decisional law makes it clear that the bankruptcy statutes were written to accommodate them. Lawyers unacquainted with these equitable interests tend to look to the bankruptcy statutes for answers to questions the statutes have never addressed.

In my opinion, the English Court of Appeal fell into almost identical error in *Re Polly Peck International plc (in administration) (No 2)*,[108] as I explain in the Appendix below.

R3RUE recognises a distinction between what it calls 'two-party' and 'three-party' contests, the latter occurring where the defendant's assets are insufficient to satisfy the defendant's obligations and the defendant's general creditors. The effect of the defendant's insolvency makes the defendant's general creditors the real parties in interest in opposition to the restitution claim. Significantly, however, this does not mean that the claim is necessarily defeated by bankruptcy;

[105] As well as the law on the constructive trust as described in R3RUE, see also the emphasis on equitable relief by way of subrogation being granted 'on well settled principles and in defined circumstances' (*Boscawen v Bajwa* [1996] 1 WLR 328, 335 (Millett LJ) and according to 'principles . . . not operat[ing] at large and in an idiosyncratic fashion' (*Bofinger* (n 14) [94] (*per curiam*)).

[106] See R3RUE (n 8) 325–26.

[107] ibid 465. The Reporter cites *Collier on Bankruptcy* for the proposition that the trustee in bankruptcy 'stands in the shoes of the bankrupt subject to all the valid liens, claims and equities that existed against the bankrupt, and has no higher or better right except as given him [by statute]'.

[108] *Re Polly Peck International plc (in administration) (No 2)* [1998] 3 All ER 812.

rather, the claimant in a three-party contest must argue – in effect – that restitution is justified by the unjust enrichment of *the defendant's creditors* at the claimant's expense.[109] There has been a good deal of academic discussion about the circumstances in which a claimant in restitution may or may not have legitimate grounds for obtaining otherwise appropriate proprietary relief in insolvency.[110] Exploring this difficult area goes beyond the scope of this chapter. Suffice it to say that the problem needs to be grappled with rather than swept away by circular reasoning, as occurred in *Omegas Group* and *Polly Peck*. Surprisingly, *Polly Peck* does not even mention the statutory provision about trust property not being divisible amongst creditors.

This much can be said about the taxonomy of the constructive trust and insolvency. Given what I have termed the modern understanding of the conclusory, if not fictional, nature of the constructive trust concept, however narrowly it is viewed, it might be worthwhile if bankruptcy legislation clarified the matter (in England at least). I am not suggesting that a proper construction of present-day bankruptcy legislation would justify a distinction being drawn between various categories of 'trust' such as to justify the categorical jettisoning of the 'constructive trust' as the courts did in *Omegas Group* and *Polly Peck*. But why take the risk, especially if, as William Swadling has contended, contrary to my views on the topic, that (for England at least) significant policy issues remain to be decided before the result in *Polly Peck* is reversed, however unsatisfactory its reasoning?[111]

G. Conclusion

No-one discusses the law of negligence by describing the tort as a common law wrong. And no-one expounds the rules on subpoenas or discovery by suggesting that we are dealing with equitable remedies. Historical differences between tracing 'at law' and 'in equity' are also passing into history and this will eventually see the adjectival labels disappearing as well.

Why do lawyers in England and Australia (and to a lingering degree in America) hang on to the 'common law' label for claims derived from money had and received[112] and the 'equitable' label for the proprietary remedies under consideration? What signals, apart from our historical learning, are we seeking to convey?

One answer in the present context is that statute law draws the distinction, as when it provides a particular rule for the assignment of a 'debt and other legal

[109] See R3RUE (n 8) 299, 301–03. See also § 60 ('Priority').

[110] An early discussion is by David Paciocco, 'The Remedial Constructive Trust: A Principled Basis for Priority over Creditors' (1989) 68 *Canadian Bar Review* 315. See generally Andrew Burrows, *The Law of Restitution*, 3rd edn (Oxford, Oxford University Press, 2011) 173–81.

[111] See W Swadling, 'Policy Arguments for Proprietary Restitution' in S Degeling and J Edelman (eds), *Unjust Enrichment and Commercial Law* (Sydney, Thomson, 2008) 365–66.

[112] See, eg, *Equuscorp* (n 21) [114] (Gummow and Bell JJ), [159] (Heydon J).

things in action'.[113] Another answer is that the labels are generally harmless, especially since they convey truths of sorts to the legal historian. However, the American law on the scope of the 'action' in money had and received shows the potential danger of using the 'legal' label. The 'equitable' label can also be dangerous if it is suggested that all things equitable are flexible and discretionary. After all, there are parts of equity that are extremely hard-nosed just as some parts of the common law (the notion of abuse of process, for example) are very nuanced.

An Introductory Note in R3RUE sets the scene for its fusionist discussion of proprietary remedies.[114] The Reporter explains that:

> The remedies in question were most fully developed in equity, and they are often referred to as the 'equitable remedies' in restitution. It should be noted, however, that the remedies described in the present Chapter are not strictly divided by historical origins. This Restatement presents the full scope of the remedies available in a court where law and equity have been merged, taking the least account possible of the historical distinctions between the jurisdictions. Lingering effects of those distinctions or on the right to jury trial are outside the scope of this Restatement.[115]

Nevertheless, the Reporter is at pains to remind us that the proprietary remedies under discussion must be applied with flexibility and discretion, in both senses of the word (see above). The 'equitable' label continues to be used as shorthand extensively throughout R3RUE, notwithstanding that we are outside the 'two peculiarities of American law' said to be the only justifications for any principled distinction continuing to be drawn.[116]

Generalisations about the nature of 'equitable' remedies in restitution can also be detected in recent English[117] and Australian[118] decisions. These may be reinforced by statements affirming the distinctiveness of equity because there is still considerable support for the idea that equity retains enduring and unique ties with conscience and justice in the particular.[119] Some of these claims may be overbroad, to use an American legal idiom, but that does not make them dangerous, especially since the discretionary aspects need emphasis in the present context.

As far as I can gauge, American universities have not taught equity as a separate topic for over 100 years. Of course, there is the law of trusts, but (as we have seen) its only contribution to restitution was through the fictional constructive trust, an institution that had no future, in the ALI's eyes, from the 1930s onwards. Some parts of 'Equity' involved with restitution might be addressed in the remedial sub-

[113] In *Equuscorp* (n 21), the High Court split over whether a right to restitution of benefits derived from illegal contracts was assignable under statute.

[114] R3RUE (n 8) 261.

[115] There is a reference back to § 4, Comment a.

[116] See above, text to n 60.

[117] See the discussion above about 'equitable' restitution by way of compound interest in *Sempra Metals Ltd* (n 1).

[118] See especially the discussion in *Bofinger* (n 14) [92]–[94].

[119] See, eg, Lionel Smith, 'Fusion and Tradition' in S Degeling and J Edelman (eds), *Equity and Commercial Law* (Sydney, Thomson, 2005) 19; PA Keane, 'The 2009 W A Lee Lecture in Equity: The Conscience of Equity' (2010) 84 *Australian Law Journal* 92.

sets to treatises on contract, but, increasingly, they were all viewed as part of a more coherent law of remedies that was taught at law schools and attracted its own texts, treatises and chapters in legal encyclopaedias. Dan Dobbs' influential treatise entitled *Law of Remedies: Damages – Equity – Restitution* shows that, for a time at least, restitution joined equity in this taxonomical rearrangement.

I have detected only a trickle of modern journal articles focusing directly upon 'Equity' in American legal literature. The silence speaks louder than anything in showing how the Americans have gone past the historical duality of law and equity. The index to the *Oxford Companion to the Supreme Court of the United States* has no item for 'Equity' and its item for 'Equitable remedies' states: 'See INJUNCTIONS AND EQUITABLE REMEDIES.' If you consult the index of *The Cambridge History of Law in America*, 'Equity's' only mention is a reference to Delaware, which is atypical on many fronts, and then only in the context of corporations law.

In Professor Kull's words, 'doctrines of equity have long been slipping out of our professional grasp, and the consequences for American law are not always the changes one would make as the result of informed choice'.[120] Presumably Kull had cases like *Omegas Group* in mind. But if I am correct in my analysis, the English counterpart of *Re Polly Peck* shows that a capacity for making categorically wrong turnings is universal and that they cannot always be explained by a non-dualist mindset.

The American experience points to what other jurisdictions may expect in the future. We are told in R3RUE and elsewhere that, over the last century, 'the law of equity has become unfamiliar to most judges and lawyers' in the US.[121] This is not a problem if the parts needing to be taught and expounded are (as with R3RUE) addressed in places more appropriate than a stand-alone 'Equity' context. I am not suggesting that equity ignorance is invariably blissful, only that its necessary lessons deserve to be addressed in a broader context and without a taxonomy of separation and triumphalism.

I am on the side of Professor Laycock, who has written:

> The war between law and equity is over. Equity won. We should stop thinking of equity as separate and marginal, as consisting of extraordinary remedies, supplemental doctrines, and occasional exceptions, as special doctrines reserved for special occasions. Except where references to equity have been codified . . . we should consider it wholly irrelevant whether a remedy, procedure, or doctrine originated at law or in equity. We should invoke equity just as we invoke law, without explanation or apology and without a preliminary showing that this is a case for equity.[122]

Not everyone would agree, even in America. The debate about fusion/merger depends, in part, on one's attitude to the past as a guide for the present and the

[120] Kull (n 81).

[121] Ashley S Hohimer, 'Constructive Trusts in Bankruptcy: Is an Equitable Interest in Property More than just a "Claim"?' (2003) 19 *Bankruptcy Developments Journal* 499, 500.

[122] Douglas Laycock, 'The Triumph of Equity' (1993) 56 *SUM Law & Contemp Probs* 53.

future. Judges and scholars who are familiar with legal history and conservative in outlook will tend to keep ancient learning alive and treat it with greater reverence than others. Those who value coherence may be bolder spirits, even if their views can trigger unexpected eruptions.

In none of these observations do I intend to convey criticism or praise. But I do finish on a note of praise for R3RUE and its Reporter. A taxonomical *tour de force*!

Appendix: A Note on *Re Polly Peck International (No 2)*[123]

English law has so far been most reluctant to embrace the remedial and discretionary aspects of the constructive trust, especially in bankruptcy. The leading case is the 1998 Court of Appeal decision in *Re Polly Peck International plc (in administration) (No 2)*.[124] Some of the Court's reasoning is coloured by what I would respectfully describe as mischaracterisation of the concept as 'driven in a vehicle of discretion'[125] and 'an order of the court granting, by way of remedy, a proprietary right to someone who, beforehand, had no proprietary right'.[126] Neither summary does justice to the body of law described in R3RUE and the recent Australian cases.

After a generally hostile review of North American authorities that supported a broad-based remedial constructive trust, the Court of Appeal rejected the concept in categorical terms. Nourse LJ was shocked with the notion that a court could even contemplate permitting property rights to arise in the absence of statutory authority, regardless of insolvency. But he and his fellow judges were especially concerned with the perceived capacity of a remedial constructive trust to 'give a preference to another person who enjoys no preference under the statutory scheme'.[127]

I venture to think that a serendipitous force may have contributed to the flawed reasoning and outcome in *Re Polly Peck*. The Court of Appeal surveyed the Canadian cases, finding them wanting for reasons that included the Canadian reliance upon Lord Denning's new model trust. However, the Court made no reference to any Australian cases, despite the judgments in *Muschinski*[128] and *Baumgartner*[129] having been delivered respectively three years and five months previously. The oversight (for which counsel take the traditional blame) was

[123] This is substantially an extract from my article, 'Deconstructing Constructive Trusts in Australia' (2010) 4 *Journal of Equity* 98, 111–12.

[124] *Re Polly Peck* (n 108) (delivered on 7 May 1998).

[125] ibid 827 (Mummery LJ).

[126] ibid 830 (Nourse LJ).

[127] ibid 827 (Mummery LJ). See also at 831 per Nourse LJ ('a variation of the manner in which the administrators are directed to deal with PPI's assets by the Insolvency Act 1986').

[128] *Muschinski v Dodds* (n 47).

[129] *Baumgartner v Baumgartner* (n 77).

probably influenced by Millett LJ's omission to notice the divergent Australian position in a speech he gave to the Chancery Bar Association two years earlier that was published in the *Law Quarterly Review*.[130] Millett LJ, whose views in this field were and remain highly influential in England, had strongly criticised the North American jurisprudence for having overlooked the distinction between personal and proprietary rights which was, in his words, 'fundamental to the law of insolvency'. Millett LJ stated that Australian law remained hostile to the remedial constructive trust and he made no reference to the High Court decision in *Muschinski*.

In a further irony, the New Zealand Court of Appeal was to embrace the remedial constructive trust in the same year that *Re Polly Peck* was decided, although no blame can be assigned to anyone in London for being unaware of a decision delivered only 37 days before judgment in *Re Polly Peck*.[131]

However, I am more interested here in looking at the Court of Appeal's approach to the English insolvency legislation. As Mr Swadling has demonstrated, there is a categorical answer to the categorical and essentially circular reasoning in *Re Polly Peck*.[132] Bankruptcy law provides expressly that property held by a bankrupt on trust for another person does not become part of the bankrupt estate.[133] A similar outcome applies to corporate insolvency due to well-established case law.[134] The rights of secured creditors are also preserved on insolvency, by common law in England and by statute in Australia.[135] This leaves room for debate about the role of the judiciary in framing proprietary remedies in restitutionary and other contexts touching insolvency, but the judicial role is not foreclosed by statute, as the English Court averred.[136]

The reasoning in *Re Polly Peck* is all the more curious given equity's long history of recognising species of 'equitable property' in contexts that include administration in insolvency. One can understand judicial reluctance to expand property categories and to displace the apparent rights of unsecured creditors, but a blanket refusal to contemplate the recognition of any species of constructive trust once insolvency intervenes surely went too far. The reasoning illustrates the capacity of broad yet contestable taxonomic assumptions (such as the distinctiveness and primacy of property and the rigidity of modern equity) being capable of driving the inevitable choices in judicial reasoning.

[130] The speech was given to the Chancery Bar Association in June 1996 and it is reported in an article entitled 'Restitution and Constructive Trusts' (1998) 114 *LQR* 399.

[131] *Fortex Group Ltd (in rec & liq) v Macintosh* [1998] 3 NZLR 171 (delivered on 30 March 1998).

[132] Swadling (n 111) 365–66.

[133] Insolvency Act 1986, s 283(3)(a). As far as I can see, there is no reference to this provision in *Re Polly Peck*, although Mummery LJ did state (827) that Parliament had erected a 'No Entry' sign. In Australia, the Bankruptcy Act 1966 (Cth), s 116(2) excludes property held in trust from the property divisible among creditors.

[134] *Re Barclays Bank Ltd v Quistclose Investments Ltd* [1970] AC 567, 581.

[135] See *Re Wallis* [1902] 1 KB 719; *In re Caine's Mortgage Trusts* [1918] WN 370; Bankruptcy Act 1966 (Cth), s 58(5).

[136] The policy arguments for and against proprietary remedies in restitution are canvassed by Swadling (n 111). He concludes that judges should keep out of this field. In Australia they have not (see (2010) 4 *Journal of Equity* 98, 113–14), which is not the same as saying that the rules of cautious engagement are completely clear.

9

Proprietary Remedies for Unjust Enrichment: Demystifying the Constructive Trust and Analysing Intentions

LUSINA HO*

A. Introduction

One aspect of the American law of unjust enrichment that has slowly been gaining ground in other common law jurisdictions is the use of the remedial constructive trust to effect proprietary relief for unjust enrichment.[1] While such a trust offers real advantages to claimants,[2] it can have damning effects on third-party transferees and the defendant's creditors. The US (and now also Canadian[3] and Australian)[4] approach addresses these policy considerations by allowing the court to fashion the remedy to suit the circumstances of the particular case.[5] Yet even R3RUE acknowledges that, as such, the constructive trust is but a 'conventional shorthand' for the court's customary analysis in proprietary language.[6] R3RUE

* The author would like to thank Birke Häcker, Rebecca Lee and William Swadling for valuable comments on earlier drafts of the present chapter. All errors are mine.

[1] American Law Institute, *Restatement Third: Restitution and Unjust Enrichment* (St Paul, MN, American Law Institute Publishers, 2011) (hereinafter 'R3RUE') § 55.

[2] A claimant who is granted an equitable proprietary interest over the trust asset can take the assets out from the bankruptcy assets, reap the increase in the value of his lost assets, obtain monetary awards on compound interest, benefit from exemption from limitation period and bring personal claims against third-party assisters and recipients of the trust assets, to name but a few.

[3] See *Soulos v Korkontzilas* [1997] 2 SCR 217.

[4] See *Grimaldi v Chameleon Mining NL (No 2)* [2012] FCAFC 6; Keith Mason, 'Deconstructing Constructive Trust in Australia' (2010) 4 *Journal of Equity* 98; Elise Bant and Michael Bryan, 'Constructive Trusts and Equitable Proprietary Relief: Rethinking the Essentials' (2011) 5 *Journal of Equity* 171.

[5] R3RUE (n 1) Chapter 7, Topic 2, Introductory Note.

[6] ibid § 55, Comment d. For critical commentary of the US approach, see Lionel Smith, 'Legal Epistemology in Restatement (Third) of Restitution and Unjust Enrichment' (2012) 900 *Boston University Law Review* 899; Andrew Kull, 'The Metaphorical Constructive Trust' (2012) 18(10) *Trusts and Trustees* 945. For a critique of the English approach, see William Swadling, 'The Fiction of the Constructive Trust' (2011) 64 *CLP* 399.

explains the label as meaning that the defendant's legal title over property is subject to the beneficial interest of the claimant who has a right to claim restitution. However, both the shorthand and the explanation beg the question of why the claimant's personal right to restitution should outflank the rights of the defendant's judgment creditors.

In light of these observations, this chapter seeks to: first, examine the rationale, criteria and content of proprietary relief for unjust enrichment as found in R3RUE, with a view to showing the difficulties in extracting clear and stable guidelines from the elusive concept of the constructive trust espoused there; and second, postulate a criterion for awarding proprietary relief consistently and independently of the trust discourse.

B. Proprietary Relief under R3RUE

Topic 2 in Chapter 7 of R3RUE recognises the granting of 'rights in specific property' of the defendant as a remedy for unjust enrichment. In particular, ownership rights may be awarded through the constructive trust (§ 55) and security interests through the lien (§ 56).[7] The principle for imposing the constructive trust is stated in § 55(1) and explained in the Introductory Note to Topic 2. Where there is a right to personal restitution arising from unjust enrichment in the form of the acquisition of identifiable assets, and such assets are traceable in the hands of the defendant, the court *may* grant a constructive trust. Alternatively, a lien under § 56 may be granted in lieu at the claimant's election or the court's discretion in order to protect innocent recipients (§ 50) or limit profitable recovery (§ 61).[8] However, it is clear that the availability of the constructive trust does not depend on showing that the remedies at law are inadequate.[9]

Many important questions are left open in this simple and 'prosaic'[10] formula. It is thus necessary to survey R3RUE to tease out: (1) the range of purposes which the constructive trust serves; (2) how these purposes interact with other factors to mould the particular court order in each case; (3) the precise content of the order; and ultimately (4) the rationale for granting proprietary relief beyond *in personam* remedies.

[7] Topic 2 also enumerates other 'asset-based' remedies such as rescission (§ 54) and subrogation (§ 57), which have the effect of giving the claimant rights in specific assets but are not themselves such rights.

[8] R3RUE (n 1) § 56(3) and (4), Comment g.

[9] ibid § 4, Comment e.

[10] ibid § 55, Comment a.

(1) Purposes behind the Constructive Trust

Although R3RUE portrays the constructive trust as a remedy for unjust enrichment, the incidents of constructive trust mentioned in R3RUE are not limited to enrichment arising from impaired intent (such as mistake, misrepresentation, undue influence or incapacity) or qualified intent (such as failure of basis).[11] The constructive trust is also used to deter wrongdoing,[12] to award fractional ownership in real estate to unmarried cohabitants[13] and even to specifically enforce informal oral trusts and secret testamentary trusts. However, on proper analysis, the last two categories are instances of express trusts, with the problem being only a lack of admissible evidence to prove the allegation of a declaration.[14]

In treating all these instances as involving unjust enrichment justifying the discretionary award of the constructive trust, R3RUE has stretched the concept of unjust enrichment so widely that it fails to offer any meaningful guidelines on how the discretion will be exercised. Although R3RUE provides illustrations of situations where the constructive trust will be awarded, there are no intermediate guidelines as to whether and how considerations such as the purpose served by the proprietary award, the degree of fault of the defendant or the immediate recipient and the nature of interest protected will be weighed in the discretionary balancing exercise. For example, in some instances, such as the secret trust and the interception of an informal gift of real property by a conscious wrongdoer, R3RUE describes the award of the constructive trust as 'almost beyond controversy'[15] or 'virtually certain',[16] without explaining why this is so. It is difficult to surmise what features in these illustrations account for the certainty of the award – could it be the lack of third-party interest or the purpose behind the constructive trust (such as deterrence of conscious wrongdoing or protection of the expectation interest) or is it merely a haphazard choice of words?

(2) Constructive Trust or Equitable Lien

R3RUE permits the court to replace the constructive trust with a lien to protect innocent recipients and limit recovery of profits.[17] This may go some way towards

[11] These include impaired intent transfers such as mistake (ibid § 11, Comment d, Illustrations 19 and 23; § 12, Comment a, Illustrations 4 and 10), fraud and misrepresentation (§ 13, Illustrations 7, 11, 19, 22 and 25), undue influence (§ 15, Illustration 7), incapacity (§ 16, Illustration 9) and vindication of ownership rights (§ 40, Illustration 19; § 41, Comment e, Illustration 9; § 42, Comment e; § 43, Comment c; §§ 44, 47–48). For a comprehensive survey of the purposes served by the constructive trust, see Robert Chambers, 'Constructive Trusts in Canada' (1999) 37 *Alberta Law Review* 137.

[12] These include wrongdoing by parties in a fiduciary or confidential relation (R3RUE (n 1) § 43, Comment b; §§ 44–46).

[13] ibid § 28, Comment d.

[14] ibid § 55, Comment j.

[15] ibid § 55, Comment j.

[16] ibid § 55, Comment c, Illustration 3.

[17] ibid § 56(3) and (4).

mitigating the harsh effects of the constructive trust, although it does not provide a complete solution to policy conflicts. First, although the lien can cap proprietary recovery at the claimant's loss, it is still a form of proprietary relief and, as such, depletes assets from the insolvency pool at the expense of innocent creditors just like the constructive trust.

Second, it is unclear what theoretical grounds justify the factors restricting relief to the grant of a lien and why they are only sufficient to deny a constructive trust but not a lien. As a result, it is difficult to assess whether these criteria operate consistently. For example, §§ 50(3)–(5) and 60 provide that the liability of innocent recipients or creditors should not exceed the loss of the claimant, extend to consequential gains or make the recipients worse off than they were before the receipt.[18] Accordingly, when an innocent recipient receives misappropriated funds through the wrongdoer and invests it profitably in shares, there will only be a lien over the shares to secure the original amount received.[19] It appears from these rules that there must be deprivation of the claimant's pre-existing property to raise proprietary rights against innocent recipients. However, if such deprivation is necessary, it cannot consistently explain why the constructive trust is imposed over the original bribe received by an innocent recipient through a fiduciary who obtained it without depriving the claimant of his pre-existing property, or for that matter a lien to secure the original bribe if the innocent recipient profitably invested the bribe.

Third, the emphasis on the discretionary choice of remedy at the date of judgment also clouds doctrinal formulation as to the nature of the claimant's rights. Does the black-letter provision of § 55(1) mean that whenever assets are received in circumstances where personal restitution is available, the claimant also has an *in rem* right over those assets, which can be transposed to traceable products of the assets? Crucially, is this in the nature of an *in rem* right to ownership through a constructive trust, which can be abated to a security interest through a lien once the product reaches the hands of innocent recipients or the recipient becomes insolvent? Alternatively, does the claimant only have a non-specific *in rem* right at the date of the transaction, the nature of which is determined at the date of judgment? The latter analysis conflicts with R3RUE, which stresses that the claimant's proprietary interest is created by the parties' transaction and is merely recognised by the court's subsequent decree.[20] The former analysis raises theoretical issues as

[18] See also ibid § 41, Comment e, which suggests that the outcome depends on rules determining priority (§ 60) and defences (§§ 65–67). For example, the constructive trust will typically be awarded against the original asset misappropriated or wrongfully obtained, as well as its appreciated value or consequential gains, if they were held in the hands of the conscious wrongdoer, a knowing recipient or a fiduciary in breach (§ 41, Comment d, Illustration 5; Comment e, Illustration 13; § 55, Comment i). Additionally, the constructive trust may also be awarded over the original asset or its traceable product received by an innocent recipient (§ 40, Illustration 19), but conditional upon reimbursing him for unwitting contribution to the property (§ 41, Comment d, Illustration 7).

[19] ibid § 41, Comment e, Illustration 13; § 50(3) and (4); § 53(3). By the same token, the claimant's claim over profitable recovery is subordinated to the claims of the wrongdoer's creditors (§ 41, Comment d, Illustration 6; § 61(a)).

[20] ibid § 55, Comment e.

to why, if the claimant already has equitable ownership in the whole of the final traceable product (and not just in the original asset), his ownership can be overreached by recipients who are not bona fide purchasers. After all, if he has ownership rights, innocent recipients and unsecured creditors will be unjustly enriched at the expense of the claimant, which is precisely the justification offered by R3RUE for the imposition of the constructive trust.[21]

(3) Constructive Trust as Conventional Shorthand

R3RUE notes the traditionally unnoticed role played by equitable remedies (in particular the constructive trust) in restoring unjust enrichment.[22] It explicitly recognises the constructive trust as a restitutionary remedy and seeks to detach it from the metaphorical language of equity[23] by explaining the content of the order of the constructive trust as comprising a declaratory and an injunctive component as follows. The order declares that the defendant's title is subject to a superior (equitable) property right[24] and compels him to transfer the property to the claimant on such conditions as the court may direct.[25] Due to its effect in reassigning title, the constructive trust entails ownership over specific assets and through it priority against third parties and the recovery of appreciated value.[26] Once the content of the order of constructive trust is deciphered and demystified, it is but a conventional shorthand or even a manner of speaking.[27]

Nonetheless, R3RUE does not go the whole hog and abandon the label 'constructive trust'. Its attitude is ambivalent. On the one hand, it seeks to define the constructive trust 'without depending so directly on a shared professional understanding of the word "equity"'; on the other hand, it holds on to the trust metaphor as conveying the idea that the defendant's legal title must yield to the claimant's superior (and equitable) right of ownership.[28]

In continuing to use the label 'constructive trust', a terminological and classificatory issue arises as to its relation with the resulting trust and whether the latter should be siphoned off to the *Restatement Third: Trusts*.[29] The Reporter's Note of R3RUE affirms that 'unjust enrichment is clearly one of the central concerns of the doctrine of resulting trusts', but excludes it on the pragmatic ground that it

[21] ibid § 55, Comments b and d.

[22] ibid § 4, Comment b, citing the observations of early American scholars in the law of restitution.

[23] R3RUE, § 55, Comment a: 'The object of the present, more prosaic description is to define constructive trust without depending so directly on a shared professional understanding of the word "equity".'

[24] ibid § 55, Comment b.

[25] ibid § 55(2), Comment b; § 4, Comment d.

[26] Thus, the constructive trust is superfluous if the claimant only wishes to obtain restitutionary awards in money in two-party situations (ibid § 4, Comment e and Reporter's Note to Comment e).

[27] ibid § 55, Comment b.

[28] ibid § 55, Comments a and b.

[29] American Law Institute, *Restatement Third: Trusts* (St Paul, MN, American Law Institute Publishers, 2003).

has been 'firmly situated within the law of trusts'.[30] Yet the doctrine of resulting trust in the *Restatement of Trusts* is neither discretionary nor subject to the court's power to award a lien.[31] By not rationalising the resulting trust within R3RUE, the opportunity for developing a coherent framework of proprietary restitution may have been missed.

As a preliminary step towards rationalising the legal doctrines that effect proprietary restitution, it would be useful to spell out the content of the relevant court order independently of the edifice of the trust. For example, while the conditions for establishing the resulting or constructive trust may differ, the content of the order is the same, namely that the claimant A has an *in rem* right against property held by B, such that B must convey his title to A. In relation to the constructive trust, the court may lay down conditions for awarding such a right to A, but this does not affect the nature of the order itself. Where a lien is awarded, the order can be understood as saying that A has the right to apply to court to order the sale of specific property held by B in order to discharge B's obligation to make restitution to A.

Even if the contents of the orders are clear, it is not easy to identify intermediate principles to flesh out the broad formula in §§ 55(1) and 56 in light of the limited clues given by R3RUE about the rationale for proprietary restitution.

(4) The Rationale for Proprietary Relief

Commentators in the US and other common law jurisdictions have offered two main policy grounds for proprietary restitution: either that the claimant has not taken insolvency risks or has swollen the insolvent's assets.[32] The former ground, however, does not explain why tort victims, who have likewise not taken insolvency risks and who have in fact suffered losses, should rank behind restitution claimants. Nor should one assume that all mistaken and defrauded claimants fail to take insolvency risks. At the same time, any ranking of the individual merits of creditors and factual enquiry as to whether they did take insolvency risks in each individual case will unnecessarily augment the cost of litigation and (ironically) deplete the bankruptcy pool.[33]

[30] R3RUE (n 1) § 31, Comment g, Reporter's Note.

[31] *Restatement Third: Trusts* (n 29) §§ 7–9.

[32] C Mitchell, P Mitchell and S Watterson, *Goff & Jones: The Law of Unjust Enrichment*, 8th edn (London, Sweet & Maxwell, 2011) [37-16], [37-24]; Andrew Burrows, 'Proprietary Restitution: Unmasking Unjust Enrichment' (2001) 117 *LQR* 412; A Burrows, *The Law of Restitution*, 3rd edn (Oxford, Oxford University Press, 2010) 176–79; Emily L Sherwin, 'Constructive Trusts in Bankruptcy' [1989] *University of Illinois Law Review* 297, 298; David M Paciocco, 'The Remedial Constructive Trust: A Principled Basis for Priorities over Creditors' (1989) 68 *Canadian Bar Review* 315.

[33] R Calnan, *Proprietary Rights and Insolvency* (Oxford, Oxford University Press, 2010) [1.151]–[1.152]; Anthony Duggan, 'Proprietary Remedies in Insolvency: A Comparison of the Restatement (Third) of Restitution & Unjust Enrichment with English and Commonwealth Law' (2011) 68 *Washington and Lee Law Review* 1229, 1244.

The latter ground is adopted by R3RUE, which justifies proprietary relief in insolvency on the basis that since the enrichment will swell the defendant's assets, the defendant's creditors will be unjustly enriched at the claimant's expense should a proprietary award not be made.[34] With respect, this begs the question whether the relevant property is beneficially owned by the insolvent recipient.[35] The claim that the unjust enrichment without more swells the wealth of the recipient is ambiguous and may mean one of the following two legal propositions: (1) that the recipient owes an *in personam* duty to make restitution; or (2) that the recipient's enrichment is subject to the claimant's *in rem* power or right. While the first statement can be established by showing the existence of unjust enrichment as required by R3RUE, the latter cannot. Its validity depends on how property or trusts law responds to the unjust enrichment, after taking into account factors such as the specific cause of unjust enrichment, the intention of the transferor and the type of property involved, to name but a few.[36] Ultimately, even the policy argument based on swollen assets hinges on the finding of an *in rem* power or right consistent with well-established principles in the existing laws of property, trusts or insolvency, which have had long experience in addressing policy considerations.

In response to these criticisms, *Goff & Jones* maintains that, albeit insufficient independently, the two criteria of insolvency risk and swollen assets when combined together justify proprietary restitution. Surely the combination strengthens the argument, but whether it then becomes sufficient depends on whether these are the only relevant reasons for granting proprietary restitution. It is submitted that they are not. What of the negative impact of the creation of (hidden) proprietary rights on third-party transferees and those who deal with the initial recipient – in other words, the smoothness of commerce and the security of transactions? Such concerns cannot be addressed by asking whether the claimant has taken an insolvency risk. Resort to judicial discretion such as that in R3RUE is a possible way out, but does not provide stable guidelines for analysis.

C. Analysing Intentions

The previous sub-section argued that the swollen asset theory adopted by R3RUE can justify proprietary restitution only if at the time of the transaction giving rise

[34] R3RUE (n 1) § 55, Comments b and d.

[35] William Swadling, 'Policy Arguments for Proprietary Restitution' (2008) 28 *LS* 506, 527–28; Duggan (n 33) 1237.

[36] For example, the rules with regards to goods, chattel money and funds are different. Title to goods does not pass if the contract is void (*Load v Green* (1846) 15 M & W 216, but see William Swadling, 'Rescission, Property and the Common Law' (2005) 121 *LQR* 123), whereas title to chattel money does. Strictly speaking, fund transfers do not involve the passing of title, but rather novation of contracts (*R v Preddy* [1996] AC 815, discussed in R Goode and E McKendrick, *Goode on Commercial Law*, 4th edn (London, Penguin, 2010) 493).

to the defendant's enrichment and notwithstanding it, the claimant can still be said to have an *in rem* power or right in the relevant asset under existing property and trust principles. The ensuing task is to extract situations from all grounds of unjust enrichment and wrongful gains where this criterion is met, and distil intermediate principles for organising them. While this is a mammoth task, far beyond the scope of the present chapter, a modest attempt will be made in the confined scope of unjust enrichments based on impaired intent.[37] Needless to say, this chapter does not exclude proprietary restitution in other circumstances should a new policy justification be identified in future. It hopes, as a start, to justify proprietary restitution where it is least controversial. Specifically, it takes as a given the legal principles pertaining to the award of proprietary relief, whether immediately on transfer or subsequently on exercising a right of rescission,[38] and seems to provide a coherent explanation why trusts are raised in these instances.

In this connection, debate in English law concerning proprietary restitution through the resulting trust doctrine provides a useful perspective. Drawing from the traditional scope of this doctrine, it is submitted that the key to raising an *in rem* power or right in impaired intent cases lies in analysing the intention of the claimant in relation to his parting with his property. As has been seen, the relevance of the resulting trust doctrine to unjust enrichment is positively affirmed in R3RUE, which recognises unjust enrichment as one of the central concerns of the resulting trust.[39] Furthermore, *Restatement Third: Trusts* bases the resulting trust on the 'inference that the transferor of the property did not intend that the person taking or holding title is to have the beneficial interest'.[40]

In light of these observations, this chapter argues that the claimant who transfers his property upon impaired intent should have an *in rem* power or right over the unjustly enriched asset of the defendant if either there is no valid intention to transfer his property right from the start or, notwithstanding an initially valid but impaired manifestation of intention to transfer, he has subsequently communicated an *unimpaired* intention to the immediate recipient not to benefit him (that is, not to give him the property beneficially).[41] A few remarks about this proposed rationalisation are necessary.

[37] In this chapter, 'impaired intent' refers to impairment of the transferor's autonomous agency, eg, where the transfer is due to mistake (spontaneous and induced), duress and undue influence. It does not include cases of 'qualified intent', where the tranferor makes an autonomous transfer upon a basis or condition that later fails.

[38] For a contrary view that no proprietary award should be raised, see Swadling (n 36).

[39] R3RUE (n 1) § 31, Reporter's Note to Comment g.

[40] *Restatement Third: Trusts* (n 29) § 1, Comment e; § 7, Comments a and d.

[41] While this view appears similar to that of Birks and Chambers, it differs from their thesis in at least three significant ways: (1) the transferor must have a positive intention not to benefit, rather than merely a lack of an intention to benefit (see R Chambers, *Resulting Trusts* (Oxford, Oxford University Press, 1997) 19, 33, 93, 104, and 111). The narrower formulation advanced in the present chapter excludes transferors who are indifferent, for they lack an intention to benefit, but also do not have an intention not to benefit; (2) an objective but impaired intention at the time of the initial transfer will still vest the title with the recipient until when the claimant evinces an unimpaired and objective intention not to benefit him; (3) the present proposal does not compel the granting of an immediate interest at the time of the initial transfer.

First, despite the prominence of intention in existing debates about the award of proprietary relief in impaired intent cases, relatively little attention has been paid to analysing the concept of intention, such as whether the relevant intention should be the claimant's manifest intention (albeit that it is the result of impaired consent)[42] or his putative intention based on what he must have intended if his autonomous judgment has not been impaired, and at which point of time is his intention to be ascertained. Resolution of these issues can identify the relevant intention to decide when to raise proprietary rights. It is submitted that consistent with the existing law to determine contract formation and declarations of trust,[43] the intention of the claimant should be his manifest intention as objectively assessed in the eyes of a reasonable person. This makes good policy sense in protecting the reasonable expectations of the party dealing with the claimant, as well as those dealing with this immediate recipient on the faith of his good title. It is therefore appropriate to adopt the same approach in ascertaining the intention of the claimant in impaired intent enrichments.

Second, it follows from the relevance of the manifest rather than putative intention of the claimant that even if it is impaired by such factors as spontaneous mistake, misrepresentation, duress and undue influence, the recipient will nevertheless obtain title over the transferred asset, at least until the point when the claimant communicates his unimpaired intention to the recipient not to benefit him. This is because, despite the impairment, the claimant still manifests an intention at the time of the initial transfer to transfer the property outright. The only exceptions are in cases of theft and fundamental mistake, which will be discussed below.[44]

Third, notwithstanding the prima facie validity of the initial intention, its impairment means that the claimant has not made an autonomous judgment or a conclusively valid expression of his intention with respect to the transfer of title. Thus, drawing an analogy to the law of rescission, it is submitted that when he subsequently communicates his unimpaired intention to the recipient that he does not intend to transfer property to him beneficially, this subsequent intention should be given effect to by raising an *in rem* right from this point of time. The proposed test of intention will now be applied to existing categories of impaired intent enrichment.

[42] In impaired intent transfers, the transferor's objective and subjective intention is the same, namely to make an outright transfer.

[43] See, eg, *Smith v Hughes* (1871) LR 6 QB 597, 607, discussed in E Peel, *Treitel on the Law of Contract*, 13th edn (London, Sweet & Maxwell, 2011) [2-002]–[2-003]; *Twinsectra Ltd v Yardley* [2002] UKHL 12, [2002] 2 AC 164 [71] (Lord Millett) discussing when a *Quistclose* (resulting) trust arises under *Barclays Bank Ltd v Quistclose Investment Ltd* [1970] AC 567; and *Brynes v Kendle* [2011] HCA 26. The line of authority based on *Aluminium Industrie Vaassen BV v Romalpa Aluminium Ltd* [1976] 1 WLR 676 also recognises the seller's contractual stipulation to retain legal title over goods delivered to the buyer. As terms of the contract, the scope of such *Romalpa* clauses are ascertained in line with the objective theory of contract espoused in *Smith v Hughes*.

[44] See text to nn 70–86.

(1) Impaired Intent

(a) Payments under Voidable Contracts Not Involving Fundamental Mistakes Induced by Fraud

It is well established under English and American law that payments made upon voidable contracts (such as those induced by duress, undue influence and misrepresentation)[45] transfer a valid title to the recipient subject to the transferor's power to rescind the contract and re-vest (legal or equitable) title in him.[46] In this sense, the recipient obtains a valid but defeasible title, which terminates upon rescission.[47]

These rules pose problems for arguments that treat proprietary restitution as arising immediately upon receipt (the immediate interest model), be it on the ground that the impairment entails a lack of intention to benefit the recipient (such as Birks and Chambers)[48] or that no insolvency risk has been taken (such as Burrows and *Goff & Jones*).[49] To justify the postponement of the resulting trust until after rescission, Chambers concedes that the claimant's lack of intention is not sufficient to justify awarding proprietary restitution and can be subject to rescission and defences protecting honest buyers.[50] *Goff & Jones* also express a preference for the power model on pragmatic grounds. Under the power model, which is exemplified by rescission and rectification cases, the claimant has no proprietary interest in the relevant asset until he exercises his power once and for all to establish a proprietary right in it. They recognise that the power model can better take into account the rights of bona fide purchasers. Unfortunately, in allowing exogenous policy considerations to override prima facie proprietary awards, Chambers and *Goff & Jones* have compromised the elegance and simplicity of their theories. In contrast, the power model proposed by Häcker provides a natural and elegant fit to voidable transfers.[51] Nonetheless, insofar as it is justified negatively upon its ability to avoid conceptual difficulties of the immediate interest

[45] For examples in R3RUE, see the imposition of constructive trust for fraud and misrepresentation (§ 13, Illustrations 7, 11, 19 and 22) and undue influence (§ 15, Illustration 7).

[46] If the contract is voidable at common law, such as for duress, fraud or non-disclosure, the legal title will be re-vested. If the contract is voidable in equity, a new equitable title will arise, but since the claimant is the absolute *sui juris* owner in equity, he can compel the recipient-trustee to transfer legal title back to him. The result is practically the same. See R3RUE(n 1) § 54; for mistake in *inter vivos* gifts, see § 11, Comment d, Illustrations 19 and 23).

[47] There are uncertainties as to whether equitable rescission takes effect upon the claimant's action to rescind or only upon court order and whether, once rescinded, the equitable right arises retroactively from the date of the initial transfer or from the date of rescission: D O'Sullivan, S Elliott and R Zakrzewski, *The Law of Rescission* (Oxford, Oxford University Press, 2007) [16.22] ff.

[48] Peter Birks, 'Restitution and Resulting Trusts' in S Goldstein (ed), *Equity and Contemporary Legal Developments* (Jerusalem, Harry & Michael Sacher Il, 1992) 335; Chambers, *Resulting Trusts* (n 41).

[49] *Goff & Jones* (n 32) [37-26]–[37-28]; Burrows, *The Law of Restitution* (n 32).

[50] Robert Chambers, 'Resulting Trusts' in A Burrows and Lord Rodger (eds), *Mapping the Law: Essays in Memory of Peter Birks* (Oxford, Oxford University Press, 2006) 261.

[51] Birke Häcker, 'Proprietary Restitution after Impaired Consent Transfers: A Generalised Power Model' [2009] *CLJ* 324.

model and positively upon its practical advantages over the latter, the power model does not in itself explain – nor is it intended to explain – why in some cases an immediate interest may deservedly come into existence at the time of transfer.

The test of intention offered in this chapter provides a simple and coherent explanation of the postponement of proprietary restitution as follows. Notwithstanding the impairment, the transferor's initial intention to transfer outright still takes effect as such, albeit only insofar as the claimant has not yet communicated his unimpaired intention not to benefit the recipient.[52] The impairment at the time of the transaction means that there is as yet no conclusively valid expression of the claimant's intention in relation to the transfer of his property. This gives him a *power in rem* which he can exercise subsequently by evincing his intention to not benefit the recipient. Once he has exercised this power, usually by invoking the law of rescission if a voidable transaction is involved or by communicating his intention to the immediate recipient where no transaction is involved (as in payments made upon spontaneous mistakes), he will have a *right in rem* over the relevant property. Besides, its effect can be calibrated to avoid undue prejudice to third parties. Since the *right in rem* does not arise right from the start, it will not upset bona fide purchasers who have acquired rights in between. Nor will it be unfair to the immediate recipient, who no longer has a reasonable expectation of enjoying unrestricted ownership.

(b) Payments upon Spontaneous Mistakes

On the availability of proprietary restitution for spontaneous mistakes, where rescission is generally not possible, English law remains unsettled. In US law, a constructive trust arises at the point of receipt.[53] Existing theories in the English debate only consider the claimant's intention at the time of transfer and hence either treat a *resulting* trust as arising immediately because the transferor did not intend to benefit the recipient[54] or not arising at all because he intended to make an outright transfer.[55] The latter view was propounded in *Westdeutsche Landesbank Girozentrale v Islington LBC*,[56] but as Lord Browne-Wilkinson's rationalisation of *Chase Manhattan Bank NA v Israel-British Bank (London) Ltd*[57] shows, the court has to rely on the recipient's affected conscience when he subsequently knows

[52] See *Hodgson v Marks* [1971] Ch 892, 929: 'any such case assumes a transfer of the beneficial interest, but in circumstances which entitle the transferor to recall it' (Russell LJ).

[53] R3RUE, §§ 6 and 55. See discussion in Duggan (n 33) 1234–46.

[54] James Edelman, 'Australian Challenges for the Law of Unjust Enrichment', Speech to the University of Western Australia Seminar Summer School (24 February 2012), http://www.supremecourt.wa.gov.au/_files/Australian_Challenges_for_the_Law_of_Unjust_Enrichment_-_Edelman_J_27022011.pdf (last accessed July 2012) 14–16.

[55] Sir Peter Millett, 'Resulting and Constructive Trusts' (1998) 114 *LQR* 399, 413.

[56] *Westdeutsche Landesbank Girozentrale v Islington LBC* [1996] AC 669.

[57] *Chase Manhattan Bank NA v Israel-British Bank (London) Ltd* [1981] Ch 105. In this case, the claimant bank informed the recipient of its mistake two days after the payment and almost a whole month before the latter petitioned for winding up. Most recently, Ward LJ noted that Lord Browne-Wilkinson's rationalisation of *Chase Manhattan* formed no part of the ratio in *Westdeutsche*: *Maqsood v Mahmood* [2012] EWCA 251.

about his personal obligation to make restitution to raise a *constructive* trust. However, such reasoning allows knowledge to elevate personal rights to proprietary ones.

The analysis put forward in the present chapter offers a more coherent and elegant analysis. It recognises the temporary validity of the claimant's objective intention to make an outright transfer and hence pass legal title to the defendant. At the same time, the mistake justifies an immediate *power in rem* that the claimant can exercise subsequently to justify a *right in rem* over the relevant property. There is no need to invoke the affected conscience of the recipient or the constructive trust.[58]

Admittedly, there is opinion in favour of confining the claimant to personal restitution on the grounds that he is the author of his own misfortune[59] and has no right of rescission anyway.[60] Taking the second argument first, a spontaneous mistake may take three forms: (1) it may lead to a payment rather than the entry into a contract, as in *Chase Manhattan*; (2) it may be a unilateral mistake which induces a party to enter into a contract, as in *Cundy v Lindsay*;[61] and (3) it may be a common mistake which causes the entry into a contract, as in *Raffles v Wichelhaus*.[62] Rescission is not available in these three situations for different reasons, though none of them entails that proprietary restitution should also be denied simply because rescission is not available. Taking the last situation first, if the common mistake renders the contract void at common law and so title over *goods* purportedly transferred does not pass to the recipient, rescission is otiose. Yet insofar as the common law preserves the property of the claimant by not recognising any passing of title, it achieves substantially the same if not a better result as equity would have by raising a trust in the claimant's favour. Similarly, in relation to the second situation, if the unilateral mistake is operative and renders the contract void at common law, as in *Cundy v Lindsay*, rescission is also otiose because the claimant's property right has already been preserved. If the unilateral mistake is not operative and the contract remains valid, as is generally the case, rescission is irrelevant. Here, once the objective test of contract formation is satisfied, a party is held to his bargain irrespective of his mistake.[63] However, in the first situation pertaining to spontaneous mistakes which do nothing more than cause a payment, there is no concern about unraveling a contractual bargain. Besides, the unavailability of rescission in these cases is simply due to the fact that the mistake does not cause entry into a contract. It would be odd to rest the availability of proprietary relief on this fortuitous circumstance.

[58] For criticisms, see Millett (n 55) 410–13; William Swadling, 'Property' in Peter Birks and Francis Rose (eds), *Lessons of the Swaps Litigation* (Oxford, Mansfield Press, 2000) 242, 261–64.

[59] Peter Watts, 'Constructive Trust and Insolvency' (2010) 3 *Journal of Equity* 250.

[60] Calnan (n 33) [4.114]–[4.116].

[61] *Cundy v Lindsay* (1877–78) LR 3 App Cas 459.

[62] *Raffles v Wichelhaus* (1864) 2 Hurl & C 906.

[63] See Peel (n 43) [8-047]. If the recipient obtains any legal title to cash handed over under such a void contract and if proprietary restitution were granted, such restitution can be explained by the intention analysis proposed in the present chapter.

Let us now turn to the first argument – that the claimant was the author of his own misfortune. This may mean that proprietary restitution should be denied because the recipient was at fault in inducing the mistake and/or that the claimant was at fault in making the mistake. It is doubtful if either reason is relevant for denying restitution, whether personal or proprietary. It is now well established that the basis of personal restitution in cases of mistake, duress, undue influence and misrepresentation is the claimant's impaired intention, not any wrongful conduct on the part of the recipient in inducing the mistake or coercing the claimant to enter into the transaction. The recipient's degree of fault should also be irrelevant to proprietary restitution, which is based on the payor's intention not to vest the payee with beneficial interest. The payor has the same intention whether the mistake was self-induced or brought about by some act of the recipient.

In a similar vein, it is well established that the claimant's negligence in a mistaken payment does not affect his right to personal restitution.[64] Should his negligence nonetheless be relevant in denying proprietary restitution, especially against an innocent recipient? First, bona fide purchasers of the legal interest will always be protected from the raising of the trust, hence only volunteers and the recipients are adversely affected.[65] In an ideal world, justice might be best achieved by weighing the parties' relative fault and apportioning loss in each case,[66] but as the *Twelfth Report of the Law Reform Committee on Transfer of Title to Chattels* notes, the uncertainty and increased cost of litigation show that such an approach is impractical.[67]

(c) Fraudulent Misrepresentation

Fraud cases deserve separate treatment, not least because judges appear at times to show greater indulgence in favour of proprietary restitution. It has long been established that a contract entered into upon a fraudulent misrepresentation is valid until the innocent party rescinds it,[68] albeit that it would be void if the mistake induced by such misrepresentation was fundamental.[69] This doctrine is currently under pressure from the view of Lord Browne-Wilkinson in *Westdeutshe* that knowledge of a mistake justifies the raising of a trust. His Lordship justified the finding of the constructive trust in *Chase Manhattan* on the basis that innocent receipt of mistaken payment did not give rise to a constructive trust, but retention of it after the recipient had knowledge of the mistake would. Applying the logic of this reasoning to its end, does it entail that fraudulent recipients, who by definition know about the payors' mistake at the time of receipt, will always be subject to a (constructive) trust right from the start? *Re Farepak Foods and Gifts Ltd* seems to suggest so.[70] In this case, a company that operated a Christmas

[64] *Kelly v Solari* (1841) 9 M & W 54.
[65] Bad faith purchasers will also be affected, but they are also as at fault as the claimant.
[66] See the suggestion of Devlin LJ in *Ingram v Little* [1961] 1 QB 31.
[67] Cm 2958, 1966.
[68] *Alati v Kruger* [1995] HCA 64, (1995) 94 CLR 216; *Shalson v Russo* [2003] EWHC 1637.
[69] *Cundy v Lindsay* (n 61).
[70] *Re Farepak Foods and Gifts Ltd* [2006] EWHC 3272.

savings scheme allowed customers to keep paying in even though it had resolved to cease trading, and went into administration three days later. The disgruntled customers sought to establish proprietary interest in the monies paid during this period. Mann J found it strongly arguable that a constructive trust could be raised on the facts and possible to rationalise such a trust on the basis of Lord Browne-Wilkinson's dictum. His Lordship warned, though, that the time pressure under which the case was heard and decided was 'not a promising basis for making new law'.[71]

While it falls outside the scope of the present chapter to resolve these emerging controversies, the proposed approach based on the claimant's intention can provide a better reconciliation with existing law than that offered by Lord Browne-Wilkinson in *Westdeutsche* and reluctantly followed by Mann J in *Farepak*. Just as in other cases involving impaired consent, the victim of a fraudulent misrepresentation still has a manifest intention to enter into the contract and transfer property outright. If the mistake is not fundamental, such as one in relation to the turnover of a medical practice,[72] it does not negate his intention. After all, even if he had known about the fraudulent misrepresentation, the victim might still have entered into the contract.[73]

Accordingly, even if the fraudulent misrepresentor knows about the claimant's mistake, it is still fair to allow him and especially bona fide purchasers through him to rely on the claimant's previously expressed intention. It is only when the victim discovers the fraud and evinces a clear intention to rescind the contract that a trust should be raised to award a beneficial title in his favour. As Rimer J explained in *Shalson v Russo*:

> A typical case of a voidable contract induced by deceit is one in which C overpays for a house as the result of a fraudulent misrepresentation by D as to its physical condition. In such a case, when C pays over the purchase price he intends D to become the legal and beneficial owner of it, as D does; and D has a like intention in relation to the house when he assures it to C on completion. The contract remains voidable despite completion; but until it is avoided those respective beneficial entitlements to price and house remain the same.[74]

The proposed analysis can also explain why fundamental mistakes arising from fraud can render a contract void. This is because the objective theory of contract formation does not apply if the other contracting party knows that in spite of the appearance of the intention, the contracting party does not so intend.[75] Where the fraudulently induced mistake is fundamental, such as when the victim is mistaken about the identity of the other contracting party or the very subject matter of the contract, he would clearly not have intended to enter into the contract had he

[71] ibid [36].

[72] See, for example, the facts of *With v O'Flanagan* [1936] Ch 575.

[73] It is not necessary for a victim of fraudulent misrepresentation to show that he would not have entered into the contract had the representation been made.

[74] *Shalson v Russo* (n 68) [108].

[75] Peel (n 43) [2-003].

known the truth. The fraudulent misrepresentor also knows this. In such a case, the victim should not be bound by his objective intention. *Cundy v Lindsay* is a good case in point.[76] Here, the sellers only intended to deal with the real Blenkarn. The imposter who induced their fundamental mistake about his identity knew that they had no intention to contract with him, let alone transfer title to him outright. He could not rely on the appearance of their objective intention to do so. There was, accordingly, no intention to sell to the imposter; the purported contract was void and no title passed.

The same analysis can be applied beyond fraud to explain why an immediate trust can arise in cases such as *Neste Oy v Lloyds Bank plc*[77] and *Re Farepak Food and Gifts Ltd.*[78] At first blush, they appear to be anomalous decisions in which contractual payments made without the payors realising that the recipients had ceased trading were subject to immediate trusts, without any need on the part of the payors to rescind the contracts. On closer examination, however, the trusts arose because the recipients had actual knowledge of a sufficiently fundamental mistake of the payors. Both Bingham J in *Neste Oy* and Mann J in *Farepak* remarked on the seriousness of the payors' mistake in not realising that the payments were made 'at a time when there was bound to be a total failure of consideration'.[79] It can fairly be said that if they had known the truth, the payors would not have made the transfer at all. Furthermore, since the recipients who had ceased trading knew about the mistake, they could not rely on the objective appearance of the payors' intention to transfer outright. Admittedly, the judges in these two cases did not adopt this explanation for imposing trusts, but appealed instead to the recipient's knowledge of the mistake as affecting its conscience and therefore raising a constructive trust. As such, the reasoning is open to the same criticisms leveled against *Westdeutsche* in elevating personal rights to proprietary ones.[80]

For the sake of completeness, it may be noted that the present analysis in theory justifies raising an immediate *right in rem* in relation to all transactions affected by vitiating factors if the claimant would not have made the transfer had there been no impairment and the recipient knows about it. In particular, duress, undue influence involving wrongful conduct and fraudulent misrepresentation will become likely candidates for immediate proprietary relief. While that may be a possible direction for the future, the factual enquiry in each individual case in ascertaining what the claimant would have intended and whether the recipient knew about the impairment is time-consuming and may not be cost-effective. After all, the costs and delay associated with the resolution of these issues will ultimately be borne by the claimants themselves. The need for a straightforward and efficient insolvency regime at least militates against drawing fine distinctions

[76] *Cundy v Lindsay* (n 61).
[77] *Neste Oy v Lloyds Bank plc* [1983] 2 Lloyd's Rep 658.
[78] *Re Farepak* (n 70).
[79] *Neste Oy* (n 77) 666; ibid [37].
[80] See n 58.

within, say, undue influence cases and hence treating them equally for the purposes of determining proprietary relief.[81]

(d) Theft

In both English and US law, the treatment of theft by common law principles is fairly clear. The victim's legal title over the original stolen asset is treated as undestroyed by theft, thus justifying his right to bring an action for conversion[82] against the thief and, save when *nemo dat* applies, transferees from the thief, as well as their trustees in bankruptcy. Profits obtained from the use of the stolen asset can be recovered by bringing claims in restitution for wrongs. The victim's immediate right of possession can also be enforced against the thief's trustee in bankruptcy. As far as the original stolen asset is concerned, the common law response is adequate and renders otiose the raising of a trust over the original stolen asset. Yet the irrelevance of the trust is not because the law refuses to recognise any proprietary relief; quite the contrary, it is because common law has already done so by creating an *immediate, in rem* right to possession on the part of the victim.

In relation to proceeds of sale of the stolen asset, the victim's right to possession also allows him to claim the proceeds in tort as an alternative to his claim for compensatory damages.[83] There are limits to this legal property right, however; when the thief passes the money into currency, the victim's right will be lost. At this juncture, the law may either leave the victim without remedy or it may enhance the protection offered to him through creating an equitable proprietary right in the proceeds, which will ring-fence them from insolvency risks. Here, there is a great divergence of approach amongst common law jurisdictions. In English law, there is only tentative conjecture by way of much-criticised dictum in *Westdeutsche* that a constructive trust may be awarded in this context.[84] In contrast, R3RUE is unequivocal that a constructive trust will arise over the *proceeds* of the original asset.[85] Australian authorities go further to award an immediate trust over the *original* asset.[86] The bone of contention lies in the justifications for imposing a trust over the proceeds, if not also the original asset. At least three grounds

[81] See AH Oosterhoff et al, *Oosterhoff on Trusts: Text, Commentary and Materials*, 7th edn (Toronto, Carswell, 2009) 792–93; Calnan (n 33); Duggan (n 33).

[82] See Torts (Interference with Goods) Act 1977, s 3(2). The claim in conversion allows the victim to recover the original asset *in specie* (albeit subject to judicial discretion), in addition to consequential damages.

[83] *Lamine v Dorrell* (1701) Ld Raym 1216; 92 ER 303.

[84] *Westdeutsche* (n 56) 716.

[85] R3RUE (n 1) § 41, Illustration 1; *cf Newton v Porter*, 69 NY 133 (1877), discussed by Dickson J in *Rathwell v Rathwell* (1978) 83 DLR (3d) 289, 305.

[86] *Black v FS Freedman & Co Ltd* [1910] HCA 58; (1910) 12 CLR 105, 110, followed in *Robb Evans v European Bank Ltd* [2003] NSWSC 204; *White City Tennis Club Ltd v John Alexander's Clubs Pty Ltd* [2009] NSWCA 114; *Port of Brisbane Corp v ANZ Securities Ltd* [2003] 2 Qd R 661. See also the debate between Susan Barkehall-Thomas, 'Thieves, Owners, and the Problem of Title: Part 1 – Chattels' (2001) 5 *Journal of Equity* 228, 'Thieves, Owners and the Problem of Title: Part 2 – Money' (2012) 6 *Journal of Equity* 1 and John Tarrant, 'Thieves as Trustees: In Defence of the Theft Principle' (2009) 3 *Journal of Equity* 170.

have been offered: deterrence,[87] the claimant's lack of knowledge about the transfer[88] and his lack of intention to benefit the thief.[89]

Given the range of issues involved, discussion of the relative merits of these approaches, and in particular the growing trend in favour of the creation of the trust, will have to remain for another occasion. Nonetheless, the intention analysis proposed in the present chapter can help explain the emerging trend, on the basis that a victim of theft cannot be said to have any valid intention in relation to the transfer, let alone to benefit the thief. If equity were to raise a trust, it is but following the approach of the common law in creating a new *in rem* right to enhance protection of the victim's pre-existing ownership.[90] Here, unlike impaired intent cases, the claimant had no initial intention to benefit the recipient, who as a thief is well aware of this. The path is cleared to create the *in rem* right immediately at the time of theft.

(2) Qualified Intent

Although the main purpose of the proposed approach is to rationalise the availability of proprietary restitution in impaired intent cases, it also explains the general non-availability of proprietary restitution in qualified intent cases such as failure of consideration.[91] In these cases, the claimant manifests an intention at the time of the transaction to transfer outright, only that the basis of his transfer fails. Qualified intent transfers are, however, distinguishable from impaired intent transfers in that there was no impairment of the transferor's initial intention to transfer outright. Such an unimpaired intention is therefore fully valid in passing unencumbered title to the recipient, and hence there is no justification to take into account the claimant's subsequent intention when the basis of payment fails.[92]

[87] *Westdeustche* (n 56) 716.

[88] Edelman (n 54) 13. This echoes Birks' view of ignorance as the unjust factor, which was expressly rejected by the Australian High Court in *Farah Constructions Pty Ltd v Say-Dee Pty Ltd* [2007] HCA 22, (2007) 230 CLR 89 [156]. It is submitted that lack of intent per se is insufficient. Imagine a thief steals a bicycle from its owner. When the owner discovers the theft and sees the thief leave the bicycle outside a bookshop before going in for a browse, he seizes possession of the bike without the thief knowing it. The thief is unaware of the transfer of his possessory title, but the owner, who has superior title over the bicycle, is unlikely to be liable for conversion, let alone bound by any trust of the bicycle or any property rights over it. He is merely exercising the self-help remedy of recaption.

[89] Robert Chambers, 'Trusts and Theft' in E Bant and M Harding (eds), *Exploring Private Law* (Cambridge, Cambridge University Press, 2010) ch 10, arguing that a purchase money resulting trust is raised before the purchase price was provided by the victim.

[90] The author is grateful to Birke Häcker for discussion on this point.

[91] There is a dearth of illustrations in R3RUE on the imposition of the constructive trust over assets unjustly received on these grounds, even though the remedy is potentially available for all grounds of unjust enrichment.

[92] In resulting trust cases, the court never takes into account subsequent conduct (such as the parties' payment of mortgage instalments) in determining what initial intention to presume.

D. Conclusion

The present chapter has drawn from the English debate in the context of the resulting trust to postulate a nuanced test of intention that can justify proprietary relief for unjust enrichment in a simple and coherent manner that is consistent with existing legal doctrines and the policy considerations. It is hoped that this will also provide a useful starting point for developing intermediate principles for the exercise of judicial discretion in jurisdictions such as the US that adopt the remedial constructive trust.

Although the organising idea of a nuanced concept of intention is derived from the context of the resulting trust, it can be utilised to rationalise impaired intent cases, which are situated within the broad notion of constructive trust in R3RUE. After all, once stripped of their metaphorical labels, the resulting and constructive trusts involve orders of the same content. As such, for present purposes, the debate about the relative suitability of the two concepts based on their historical scopes can be put aside for the time being.

If the present proposal is accepted, the granting of proprietary restitution for impaired intent transfers will rest on a simple and coherent framework, which asks what the intention of the claimant was, both at the time of the initial transfer and subsequently at any time before a competing proprietary claim arises. This test provides an inherent conceptual basis for accommodating immediate *rights in rem* arising at the time of transfer,[93] the *power in rem* which re-vests title upon a subsequent exercise of such power,[94] as well as the general denial of proprietary restitution in transfers of qualified intent. The only type of proprietary restitution it does not encompass is policy-motivated restitution, where even the granting of personal restitution is determined by policy rather than the claimant's intent.[95]

[93] Chambers (n 40) ch 5.

[94] Häcker (n 51).

[95] For example, an ultra vires tax payment is recoverable whether the payor objectively intends to make an outright transfer or not, for it is based on the policy of ensuring government compliance with the law: P Birks, *Unjust Enrichment*, 2nd edn (Oxford, Oxford University Press, 2005) 106; R3RUE (n 1) § 17, Illustrations 13 and 19.

10

The Restatement of Liabilities in Restitution

STEPHEN SMITH*

The American Law Institute's Restatements share with civilian codes the aim of stating the law in a series of short propositions. And while they are not strictly binding on courts, the operative parts of Restatements (the 'sections') are similar to codal articles in that they are quoted in judgments, analysed in law review articles and legal treatises, and generally play a foundational role in American lawyers' and judges' understanding of their law. This well-recognised role helps to explain why drafting Restatements is a lengthy process: the Reporters know it is important that they get the law right.

Against this background, a striking feature of *Restatement Third: Restitution and Unjust Enrichment*[1] is the way it describes the legal relationships that are its basic subject matter. Throughout its sections, comments and notes, R3RUE describes individuals who have been unjustly enriched[2] not as being under obligations (or duties)[3] to reverse their enrichments, but as incurring liabilities – and only liabilities – to make restitution.[4] More specifically, R3RUE describes such individuals as liable to be ordered[5] by a court to make restitution.[6] These descriptions are striking because the literature on unjust enrichment law assumes that someone who has been unjustly enriched has an obligation, and not merely a liability, to make restitution. In Peter Birks' words: 'A person who receives a

* I would like to thank Nicola Langille and Zain Naqi for research assistance.

[1] American Law Institute, *Restatement Third: Restitution and Unjust Enrichment* (St Paul, MN, American Law Institute Publishers, 2011) (hereinafter 'R3RUE').

[2] I adopt this terminology (and the parallel description of R3RUE's subject matter as 'unjust enrichment law') for convenience. As will become evident, I query whether these terms are in fact appropriate labels.

[3] I use the terms 'obligation' and 'duty' interchangeably.

[4] See n 27 below.

[5] I adopt the current English practice of describing court awards that require a defendant to make restitution and/or that authorise involuntary restitution (ie, seizure of assets) as 'orders'. In the US, awards that require monetary restitution are described as 'judgments'. The differences between orders (as this term is understood in contemporary English law) and judgments are unimportant for this chapter's argument.

[6] R3RUE does not say explicitly that recipients' liabilities are 'liabilities to court orders', but it is clear that this is how it understands liabilities to make restitution, since it treats such liabilities as equivalent to recipients being subject to a 'claim in restitution' by the impoverished party: see n 27 below.

mistaken payment of a non-existent debt is unjustly enriched, and from that unjust enrichment he comes under an obligation to make restitution.'[7] Other common law writers are rarely as explicit, but the broader idea – central to Birks' work – that the rules Birks was writing about in his scholarship on unjust enrichment and restitution fall (for the most part)[8] within 'the law of obligations' is accepted without comment.[9] Indeed, the idea that these rules impose obligations is one of the very few things that Birks believed about unjust enrichment law that not only escaped self-criticism[10] but also – as far as I am aware – challenges from others.[11] Civilian writers make the same assumption about their law.[12]

R3RUE's apparent rejection of an 'obligation model' of unjust enrichment in favour of a 'liability model' raises three questions: first, does R3RUE actually mean what it appears to mean?; second, does the liability model accurately describe the positive law?; and third, and finally, why does it matter (if it matters at all) if unjust enrichment law is concerned only with liabilities and not with obligations? I will say relatively little about the first and second questions – just enough to show that R3RUE plausibly means what it appears to mean and, further, that the liability model is a prima facie plausible description of the positive law in common law jurisdictions.[13] My main interest is the third question. Specifically, I seek to explore the implications of the liability model for resolving a theoretical or 'justificatory' puzzle that arises on the obligation model. According to the obligation model, if you accidentally wire money into my bank account, the

[7] Peter Birks, *Unjust Enrichment*, 2nd edn (Oxford, Oxford University Press, 2005) 31. In his position as editor of *English Private Law* (Oxford, Oxford University Press, 2000), Birks classified unjust enrichment law as a part of the law of obligations.

[8] I describe Birks as believing that unjust enrichment law was 'for the most part' within the law of obligations because he held that some unjust enrichments may, in addition to giving rise to obligations, generate proprietary rights (Birks, *Unjust Enrichment* (n 7) 38).

[9] Insofar as scholars have discussed the assumption that unjust enrichment law deals in obligation-creating rules, they have focused on the question of whether, as Birks believed, unjust enrichments sometimes also generate property rights: see, eg, Graham Virgo, *The Principles of the Law of Restitution*, 2nd edn (Oxford, Oxford University Press, 2006) 11–18. Some scholars also argue that obligations to do things like return mistaken payments are imposed to protect property rights (see n 25 below) rather than, as Birks supposed, in order to reverse a substantively unjust enrichment. However, these scholars have not challenged Birks' view that the rules they are trying to explain impose obligations.

[10] In his later work, Birks rejected many positions that he had advanced earlier: 'Almost everything of mine now needs calling back for burning' (Birks, *Unjust Enrichment* (n 7) xii).

[11] I provide no citations because my point is not that scholars have openly defended or even consciously adopted Birks' assumption. Indeed, many writers (and even Birks on occasion) employ non-obligational terminology when describing unjust enrichment law (see n 45 below). My point is that (in contrast with almost everything else he wrote) Birks' assumption that the law imposes obligations to do things like return mistaken payments has not been challenged. The assumption's validity is a non-issue in the unjust enrichment literature.

[12] See, eg, David Johnston and Reinhard Zimmerman, 'Unjust Enrichment: Surveying the Landscape' in David Johnston and Reinhard Zimmerman (eds), *Unjustified Enrichment* (Cambridge, Cambridge University Press, 2002) 3, 8. The traditional civilian view is explicitly adopted in Christian von Bar et al (eds), *Principles, Definitions and Model Rules of European Private Law: Draft Common Frame of Reference* (Munich, Sellier, 2009), Art VII.-1:101 of which states: 'A person who obtains an unjustified enrichment which is attributable to another's disadvantage is obliged to reverse the enrichment.'

[13] The positive law of unjust enrichment is not identical across common law jurisdictions, but the differences are unimportant in respect of the rules discussed in this chapter.

law imposes a legal obligation on me to pay you an equivalent sum of money. Why? What is the justification for imposing that obligation – a positive obligation to benefit you – in a situation where I have not undertaken to do something, or committed a wrong, or indeed done anything at all? To be clear, the puzzle is not the final result: few people would think I should be allowed to keep the money. The puzzle lies in explaining how that result is meant to be achieved. Why am I obliged to fix a problem that I had no hand in creating?

R3RUE was not written to resolve theoretical puzzles. Nonetheless, I would like to explore the possibility that its language points towards a resolution of the justificatory puzzle. The possibility arises because justifying liabilities to make restitution is different from justifying duties to make restitution. Certain objections to attempts to explain unjust enrichment law can be avoided when those explanations are interpreted not as explanations of obligations, but of liabilities. Specifically, I will argue that the main objection to what I will call 'property-based' explanations of unjust enrichment law can be overcome insofar as these explanations are interpreted as explaining legal liabilities, not legal duties.

This chapter is divided into five parts. Part A describes the justificatory puzzle in more detail. Part B defends the claim that R3RUE adopts a liability model of unjust enrichment, while Part C defends the claim that the liability model is a prima facie plausible description of the positive law. Part D then explains why it matters, from the perspective of the justificatory puzzle, whether unjust enrichment is a law of obligations or liabilities. Finally, Part E explains why property-based explanations of unjust enrichment, if interpreted as explanations of liabilities to make restitution, both avoid the justificatory puzzle and provide a prima facie plausible explanation of the law.

The discussion throughout focuses exclusively on the part of unjust enrichment law dealing with what are usually termed 'defective transfers'. A defective transfer is a transfer of property or other legal rights that, due to a mistake, ignorance, compulsion or other similar flaw, is unintended or at least undesired, but is nevertheless effective to pass legal title to the recipient. A standard example is the mistaken payment of a non-existent debt. On any account of unjust enrichment law, the rules governing such transfers are of central concern. These rules are, however, only part of the law discussed in R3RUE and in the standard texts on unjust enrichment. It follows that if the rules discussed in R3RUE constitute a single legal subject, the limited reach of this chapter's arguments might count against them. It is, of course, possible (though I do not make the argument here) that the distinction between obligation rules and liability rules sheds light on other parts of unjust enrichment law. But in any event, the just-mentioned assumption need not be made. R3RUE itself explicitly leaves open the possibility that the law it discusses is part of more than one legal subject.[14]

[14] The Reporter's Note to § 1 of R3RUE states that materials covered in R3RUE 'may not self-evidently constitute a single subject' (12).

A. The Justificatory Puzzle

The obligation model supposes that the law imposes obligations on recipients of defective transfers to return the transferred thing or its value in money.[15] Thus, the model assumes that the recipient of a mistaken payment – for example, the recipient of a misdirected bank transfer – is under an obligation, from the moment of receipt, to return the sum transferred to the transferor.[16] This assumption raises a puzzle since, as already mentioned, recipients of mistaken transfers frequently, indeed typically, play no part in the transfer. We normally assume, exceptional cases aside, that individuals should only be placed under legal obligations to do things for others where they have agreed to the obligation[17] or where they have done something – for example, harming someone or bringing someone into the world – that makes them responsible for that person's circumstances.[18] Few defective transfer cases fit this model. In many cases, recipients are not only entirely innocent but also play no role at all in the transactions that enrich them.

Positive obligations are not unknown in the law. For instance, citizens in common law jurisdictions normally have obligations to pay taxes. In many parts of Canada, citizens have obligations to clear snow from the sidewalks in front of their houses. Other countries impose obligations to do military service. But in each of these examples, the obligations are owed to the state. Most civil law jurisdictions (though few common law jurisdictions) recognise duties to rescue,[19] but such duties are exceptional and are typically heavily qualified. They do not extend,

[15] Some writers, including Birks, believed that in the normal case, the recipient's duty is limited to handing over the value of the transferred thing: Birks, *Unjust Enrichment* (n 7) 163. I adopt the broader description for convenience and because, even if there is no duty to return the transferred thing, the duty to hand over the value of the thing is extinguished (save for possible interest) if the thing is handed over.

[16] Although Birks believed that the obligation to make restitution arose at the time of receipt (see Birks, *Unjust Enrichment* (n 7) 169), it is possible to imagine the obligation arising later (see Part C below). The timing of the obligation is unimportant for understanding the justificatory puzzle because, on any view, the obligation is imposed on individuals who may have played no part at all in the transaction that enriched them.

[17] For the purposes of this chapter, agreeing to the obligation includes agreeing to assume a role or position that normally carries with it obligations to others.

[18] The philosophical foundations of this assumption – and the difficulty of reconciling it with obligations to make restitution – are explained by Dennis Klimchuk, 'The Normative Foundations of Unjust Enrichment' in Robert Chambers, Charles Mitchell and James Penner (eds), *Philosophical Foundations of the Law of Unjust Enrichment* (Oxford, Oxford University Press, 2009) 81. Klimchuk devotes particular attention to Ernest Weinrib's argument that the solution to the justificatory puzzle is that recipients are deemed to have 'accepted' the benefits as given non-gratuitously ('Put at its broadest, the obligation-creating condition on the defendant's side is that the defendant accepted the benefit as non-gratuitously given . . . If the defendant can be regarded as having accepted a benefit as non-gratuitously given, then in fairness the benefit cannot be retained gratis': Ernest Weinrib, 'The Normative Structure of Unjust Enrichment' in Charles Rickett and Ross Grantham (eds), *Structure and Justification in Private Law* (Oxford, Hart Publishing, 2008) 1, 37)). Klimchuk argues (convincingly, in my view) that the hypothetical concept of acceptance that Weinrib's argument employs cannot do any justificatory work.

[19] See, eg, *Charter of Human Rights and Freedoms*, RSQ c C-12, s 2 (Quebec).

for example, to duties to save property.[20] All civil law (and some common law) jurisdictions recognise duties to act in good faith, including positive duties to disclose information, but none of these duties involves transferring or otherwise expending significant resources, and all arise in the context of ongoing relationships.[21] It has never been suggested that there might be good faith duties to, for example, alert someone who has left goods on a bus or dropped their wallet on the street. These observations are not meant to deny that assisting others is admirable and praiseworthy; rather, the point is that we do not generally think it is the law's role to compel us to be admirable and praiseworthy.[22]

Does it matter that the obligation to reverse a defective transfer is only an obligation to return the property or its value, and that even this obligation is reduced (according to the conventional view) in cases where recipients change their position prior to becoming aware of the defect?[23] The change of position defence ensures that innocent recipients are not left worse off after fulfilling their putative obligation than they were prior to the transfer. Birks often remarked that these limitations on the scope of recovery were crucial because of the very slight facts giving rise to the recipient's duty.[24] However, this observation does not explain why the law imposes an obligation at all: if it is my money, why do I have to do anything?

One possible explanation for imposing obligations on recipients of defective transfers is that they are not entitled to what was transferred.[25] The recipient of a misdirected bank transfer was never intended to have the money, and so, it might be thought, has no valid claim to hold on to it. According to this explanation, the mistaken recipient's situation is not materially different from that of a recipient of stolen property. In each case, the property should be returned because it should not have been conveyed to the recipient in the first place.

[20] This limitation is implicit in the wording of s 2 of the Quebec *Charter* (ibid): 'Every human being whose life is in peril has a right to assistance . . .'

[21] See, eg, the range of examples that are thought to raise possible good faith issues in Reinhard Zimmerman and Simon Whittaker, *Good Faith in European Contract Law* (Cambridge, Cambridge University Press, 2000).

[22] The law governing 'necessity' cases (eg, where someone is lost in a snowstorm and breaks into a cabin to save her life) are sometimes thought to be an exception to this rule on the basis that courts find that the defendant has done no wrong, but is nonetheless required to pay damages. However, these cases are not an exception, because there are no duties to pay damages; there are only liabilities: see Stephen A Smith, 'Why Courts Make Orders (And What This Tells Us About Damages)' (2011) 64 *CLP* 51, 71–76. And even if there were a duty to pay damages, defendants in necessity cases differ significantly from defendants in defective transfer cases in that they are responsible, in a straightforward sense, for the losses suffered by those whose property they have taken or damaged.

[23] Andrew Burrows, *Remedies for Torts and Breach of Contract*, 3rd edn (Oxford, Oxford University Press, 2004) 524–26.

[24] Birks, *Unjust Enrichment* (n 7) 208.

[25] Versions of this argument are defended in Samuel Stoljar, *The Law of Quasi-Contract*, 2nd edn (Sydney, Law Book Company of Australia, 1989) 5–9; Peter Watts, 'Restitution – A Property Principle and a Services Principle' [1995] *Restitution Law Review* 49, 49–70; Joachim Dietrich, *Restitution: A New Perspective* (Sydney, Federation Press, 1998) 208–13; Peter Jaffey, *The Nature and Scope of Restitution* (Oxford, Hart Publishing, 2000) 275–79; Charlie Webb, 'Property, Unjust Enrichment, and Defective Transfers' in Chambers, Mitchell and Penner (n 18) 335; Ben McFarlane, 'Unjust Enrichment, Rights, and Value' in Donal Nolan and Andrew Robertson (eds), *Rights and Private Law* (Oxford, Hart Publishing, 2012) 581.

In Part E, I argue that property-based explanations of unjust enrichment law come very near to the truth, but, as described above, they are vulnerable to two objections. First, regardless of recipients' entitlements, it remains the case that they are passive participants in the relevant transactions. An absence of entitlement might explain why recipients should, for example, permit transferors to recover their property, but it does not explain positive obligations to return property. The second objection is that property-based explanations are inconsistent with the clear rule that in the defective transfers that (according to the obligation model) give rise to obligations, title passes to the recipient. Certain defects can, it is true, preclude title from passing (for example, a mistake about identity), but in such cases it is assumed that no obligation arises because there is no unjust enrichment to reverse. It is only where title passes that (according to the obligation model) such an obligation is needed and arises. Unlike recipients of stolen property, then, recipients of defective transfers are, according to the law, the true owners of the transferred property. The objection to property-based theories, it follows, is that they must suppose that the law attributes ownership of the property to the recipients and, at the same time, imposes an obligation to give up the property or its value. If the attribution of ownership was an obvious sham, this contradiction might be ignored. But the attribution is no mere facade: the change of position defence, the ability of bona fide third party purchasers to obtain good title and the transferor's status as an unsecured creditor all depend on the law's view that the recipient acquires legal title at the time of the transfer.

B. R3RUE

For anyone interested in the justificatory puzzle and, more broadly, in the validity of the obligation model, R3RUE's language is striking. As already mentioned, R3RUE describes unjust enrichments not as giving rise to 'obligations', but to 'liabilities'. § 1 of R3RUE states: 'A person who is unjustly enriched at the expense of another is *subject to liability* in restitution.'[26] Volume II, which includes the sections describing the circumstances giving rise to unjust enrichments, is entitled 'Liability in Restitution'. And with a single exception, the operative sections in Volume II describe unjust enrichments as giving rise to a 'liability in restitution' on the part of the recipient or (what is treated as the same thing) to the transferor acquiring 'a claim in restitution'.[27] In short, rather than expressing the obligation

[26] Emphasis added.

[27] In vol I of R3RUE, the phrase 'liability [or "liable"] in restitution' is used to describe the legal consequence of an unjust enrichment in § 1, 2, 5, 13, 14, 15, 16 and 17, while the phrase 'claim in restitution' is employed in § 6, 7, 8, 9, 10, 11, 12, 18 and 19. The single counter-example is sub-§ 2(4), which appears to treat liabilities and obligations as equivalent: 'Liability in restitution may not force an innocent recipient to a forced exchange: in other words, an obligation to pay for a benefit that the recipient should have been free to refuse' (14). There are also five references to obligations to reverse unjust enrichments within the notes and comments to vol I, the clearest of which states: 'the name

model's view that a defective transfer gives rise to an obligation to make restitution, R3RUE says that such transfers give rise to the recipient incurring a liability in restitution.

Liabilities are not obligations. To say that individuals have legal obligations to do X means that, from the law's perspective, they must do X. In contrast, to say that someone has incurred a legal liability to Y means that the liable person may have Y done to or imposed upon her if another person (or institution, etc) exercises a legal power. As Hohfeld explained, the correlative of an obligation is a right, while the correlative of a liability is a power.[28] This difference in meaning explains why we do not say that contracting parties are liable to perform their contracts: what we say (and R3RUE adopts this usage)[29] is that contracting parties have obligations to perform their contracts.[30] The difference also explains why we do not say that committing a traffic offence gives rise to an obligation to pay the requisite fine: we say instead that offenders are liable to be fined. Liability terminology is used in the traffic offence case because 'being fined' is something that happens only insofar as government officials exercise their power to prosecute and pass judgment on the defendant. In contrast, while contractual obligations can be waived by the right holder, their obligational force exists independently of the right holder (or anyone else's) exercise of a legal power.

As I explain in a moment, legal liabilities arise in different forms. The natural and straightforward interpretation of R3RUE's references to 'liabilities in restitution', however, is that they refer to liabilities to be made the subject of a court order requiring that one make restitution (voluntarily or not). As noted already, in cases where R3RUE does not specifically say that unjust enrichments give rise to 'liabilities' in restitution, what it says instead is that they give 'the [transferor] a claim in restitution'.[31] The word 'claim' clearly refers to a legal action. In short, in R3RUE, liability in restitution means liability to a court-issued remedy.

"restitution" . . . remains the word most commonly employed throughout the common law world to refer to this set of legal obligations and their associated remedies' (7; other references are 6, 9 and 16). These are the only references to obligations to make restitution (or something similar). By way of contrast, vol I contains 185 references to 'liability in restitution'/'liability in unjust enrichment'/'liable in restitution'/'liability for restitution'/'liability for unjust enrichment' and 408 references to a 'claim in restitution'/'claim in unjust enrichment'.

[28] Wesley Hohfeld, 'Fundamental Legal Conceptions' (1913) 23 *Yale LJ* 29, 44–54.

[29] See, eg, § 7 (referring to the 'mistaken performance of another's obligation') and § 8 (referring to the 'mistaken discharge of an obligation or lien').

[30] It is, of course, common to say that contracting parties who fail to perform their obligations are liable to pay damages and, in some cases, liable to be ordered to perform their contracts. In the case of damages, we use this language precisely because there is no legal obligation to pay damages – there is merely a liability to be ordered by a court to pay damages (Smith (n 22) 71–76; Nathan B Oman, 'Why There Is No Duty to Pay Damages: Powers, Duties, and Private Law' (2011) 39(1) *Florida State University Law Review* 137). In the case of a liability to be ordered to perform, the language is again appropriate because such orders are not automatic consequences of contractual obligations, but are made only where the defendant has failed or threatened to fail to perform the obligation and the co-contracting party exercises her power to bring a legal action.

[31] See § 7. Further support for this interpretation is found in R3RUE's discussion of remedies. This discussion, which occupies a separate and subsequent chapter in R3RUE, focuses on rules that determine 'how to measure the defendant's enrichment' and those that govern the availability of equitable

Of course, R3RUE's position that recipients of impaired transfers are liable to be subject to court orders does not preclude the possibility that R3RUE also recognises that recipients were, are, or may in future be under obligations to make restitution. Liabilities are often closely connected to obligations, but none of the possible ways in which liabilities can be related to obligations fits with the kinds of liabilities described in R3RUE. The first possibility – which supposes that an obligation to make restitution arises before the liability arises – is, in principle, perfectly plausible. Legal liabilities frequently arise when, and because, an obligation was breached. For instance, if D breaches a legal obligation not to assault C, D becomes liable to be punished by the state; similarly, if D breaches a legal obligation to convey Blackacre to C, D normally becomes liable to be ordered by a court to convey Blackacre. It is possible, then, that R3RUE's references to liabilities are intended merely to highlight that individuals who fail to comply with their obligations to make restitution are liable to be forced to do this by a court. There is a long tradition in the common law of describing the law in terms of the availability of judicial remedies rather than the obligations whose breach gives rise to those remedies. And it might be thought unsurprising that R3RUE – a document intended primarily for practising lawyers and judges – would follow this tradition. As Holmes famously opined, what most clients care about is not their legal obligations, but the likelihood of being subjected to sanctions.[32]

However, this suggestion faces two major obstacles. First, consistent with the conventional English view, R3RUE holds that liability in restitution arises at the moment of the defective transfer, ie, the moment of enrichment.[33] It is not logically possible, therefore, that the liability contemplated by R3RUE arises because of a breach or even a threatened breach of an obligation to make restitution. Second, if it were the case that liability in restitution arose from the breach of an obligation to make restitution, then in a document as carefully written as R3RUE, one would expect that this assumption would be made explicit somewhere. When discussing contractual obligations, R3RUE describes them as just that – contrac-

remedies (constructive trust, liens, etc) (vol II, 173). From the perspective of the obligation model, R3RUE's discussion of remedies seems odd because it appears to assume that the rules for quantifying enrichments, etc, only come up for consideration when courts are contemplating making an award. This way of classifying the rules governing the measurement of enrichment is perfectly straightforward, however, from the perspective of the liability model. As the example of liability to criminal punishments shows, a liability can be a liability to an as-yet-unspecified consequence. There is therefore nothing odd about assuming – as R3RUE appears to do – that a recipient has incurred a liability in restitution at the moment of receipt, notwithstanding that the content of the liability is not certain until a court issues an award.

[32] Oliver W Holmes, 'The Path of the Law' (1897) 10 *Harvard Law Review* 457, 459.

[33] In England, this rule is normally explained by saying that the 'cause of action' is complete at the moment of enrichment: see Birks, *Unjust Enrichment* (n 7) 169, citing *Baker v Courage & Co* [1910] 1 KB 56, 65. R3RUE adopts the same position (see vol II, 627). The phrase 'cause of action' is, of course, another way of describing a liability (not an obligation), since a cause of action is the set of facts that the claimant must establish to obtain the desired court award. In cases where the recipient is unaware of the circumstances giving rise to the unjust enrichment, R3RUE sometimes refers to a 'prima facie' liability to allow for the possibility of a defence of change of position (see, eg, vol II, 169). In cases where the recipient has knowledge of the defective transfer, the liability is unqualified.

tual obligations.[34] Yet none of the references to liabilities in restitution mentions or even hints that those liabilities arise because the defendant breached an obligation to make restitution.

It may be worth adding that it is not a logical or legal truth that liabilities to court orders presuppose an obligation to do the thing that the order requires. Criminal wrongdoers who are liable to be fined do not have legal obligations to pay those fines prior to an order. The same is true of a civil wrongdoer who is liable to an order to pay punitive damages; the wrongdoer is under no obligation to pay punitive damages on commission of the civil wrong (and, indeed, could not be as the quantum is unknown prior to judgment). Indeed, civil wrongdoers have no obligations to pay damages of any kind prior to judgment; rather, they are (as we usually say when we are careful with our language) merely 'liable' to pay damages.[35] In these examples, the wrongdoer has, of course, breached an obligation, but in none of them is the obligation to do the thing that the court award requires.[36] In contrast, the obligation model supposes that court awards to make restitution replicate existing obligations to make restitution.

A second possible way to reconcile R3RUE's focus on liabilities with the obligation model is to suppose that the obligation to make restitution and the liability to be forced by a court to make restitution arise simultaneously. According to this suggestion, recipients are subject to obligations to make restitution immediately upon receiving a benefit and, at the same moment, the transferor also acquires the power to obtain a court order requiring restitution. As was true of the previous suggestion, this suggestion has no textual support. If obligations to make restitution arise on enrichment, why does R3RUE not indicate this? A further objection is that the suggestion supposes that the law would permit claimants to bring actions to enforce obligations without requiring proof that the defendant had failed or even threatened to fail to perform the obligation. The suggestion therefore contemplates that defendants may be judicially forced to perform an obligation without having been given a chance to perform the obligation voluntarily. Aside from its substantive unattractiveness, the suggestion is therefore inconsistent with the well-established practice of not granting injunctions or specific performance except on proof that a breach has been committed or, exceptionally, on proof that a breach is imminent.[37]

The third and final possibility is that the liability described in R3RUE is a liability to fall under a future legal obligation. Many liabilities are related to obligations in this way. For example, an offeror is liable to incur a contractual obligation if the offeree exercises her power to accept the offer. It seems clear, however, that

[34] See § 7 (referring to the 'mistaken performance of another's obligation') and § 8 (referring to the 'mistaken discharge of an obligation or lien').

[35] See Smith (n 22) 71–76. The rule is the same in the US: Oman (n 30) 137.

[36] Although I cannot defend the proposition here, it also appears that there are cases, aside from those involving unjust enrichments, in which individuals are liable to be ordered to pay damages notwithstanding that they have not committed a legal wrong. Necessity cases are an example.

[37] Burrows (n 23) 544–45; Dan B Dobbs, *Law of Remedies: Damages, Equity, Restitution*, 2nd edn (St Paul, MN, West Publishing Company, 1993) 164.

R3RUE does not understand liabilities to make restitution in this way. If the liability to make restitution were a liability to fall under an obligation, we would again expect R3RUE to explain how – and when – the liability is turned into an obligation. More to the point, we would expect the liability to be described as a liability to fall under an obligation. As already noted, R3RUE regards a recipient's liability to make restitution as equivalent to a transferor having a 'claim in restitution'. Admittedly, once a transferor successfully pursues her claim to restitution, the recipient will be required to make restitution. Yet it is not obvious that orders to make restitution create true obligations to make restitution,[38] and even if they do create obligations, these are not the kinds of obligations that the obligation model supposes arise from unjust enrichments. The obligation model supposes that court awards confirm, not create obligations to make restitution.

Nor is it plausible to suppose that the recipient's liability is a liability to fall under an obligation if and when the transferor (as opposed to the court) makes a request or demand for restitution. Aside from its lack of textual support and inconsistency with the clear rule that the cause of action in restitution is complete on transfer,[39] this suggestion is vulnerable to two substantive objections.[40] Each arises from the fact that a request for restitution (or even the initiation of a lawsuit seeking restitution) clearly cannot be sufficient, on its own, to create an obligation. Suppose D learns that an unexpected payment of $1,000 was made into her bank account and suppose that shortly afterwards, C requests restitution of $1,000 from D. In these circumstances, it is not even prima facie plausible to suppose that D is under an obligation to make restitution to C unless two further things are true. First, it must be the case that it was C who transferred the money and that the transfer was impaired. This requirement is problematic because in many cases D will not know that C made the transfer or why the transfer was made. Of course, the law could require that C inform D of these facts.[41] But how is D to know if C is telling the truth? Suppose C asserts that the transfer was made on the basis of a mistaken understanding of the law, or a mistaken belief in a debt owed

[38] As I explain in Part D, 'legal obligations' are meant to reflect reasons – moral reasons – that already apply to the subject. As the example of punitive orders shows, court orders do not carry this meaning (even if it is the case that many orders replicate legal obligations). Of course, the law believes that citizens should obey court orders, but this is different from believing that citizens have, apart from the order, moral reasons to do what the order requires.

[39] If the cause of action is complete on transfer, it follows that all of the facts that a claimant must provide to obtain a judicial order to make restitution can be proven at that point. Thus, it cannot be part of the cause of action in restitution that the claimant must make a demand or otherwise inform the defendant that an impaired transfer occurred.

[40] The basic idea underlying these objections (namely that it is not reasonable to expect the parties to an alleged obligation to make restitution to know of the existence or content of the obligation) could also be directed at the previous suggestions. However, I discuss the objection now because the obvious reply when attempting to rebut the objection is to suggest that the obligation arises only when the transferor makes a request for restitution.

[41] Although the law does not impose any such requirement, it might be supposed that the statement of claim that claimants provide defendants at the commencement of a legal action offers just this information – and therefore that it is not possible to obtain an order to make restitution without having earlier informed the defendant of the factual basis for the order.

to the recipient, or because of coercion by a third party. D might reasonably wonder whether C was in fact making a gift, or took the risk that the debt was not owed, or was not actually coerced by a third party. Indeed, in some cases it will not even be clear that C was the transferor – perhaps a third party transferred the money or perhaps C was a mere conduit. Must C therefore produce evidence that she was the transferor, that the transfer was made under mistake, etc? And who assesses the evidence? Must D and C have a mini-trial?

It is, of course, not unusual that the facts giving rise to legal obligations may be uncertain. The parties to an alleged contract may be unclear as to the content or even existence of the contract. But the uncertainty that arises with respect to alleged restitutionary obligations is different because the relevant information is in the hands of the obligation's beneficiary. For D in my example to know she is under an obligation, she must believe what C tells her, and what C tells her must be the truth. The consequence is that if D wants to comply with her alleged legal obligations, she has no choice but to accept any reasonably plausible request for restitution from C. Yet the apparent plausibility of C's request does not ensure its validity, as C may be lying or mistaken.[42]

The second thing that must be the case in order for D to fall under an obligation to make restitution of the $1,000 is that D cannot have changed her position in reliance on the transfer prior to becoming aware (by whatever means) that the transfer was impaired. If D has innocently changed her position in reliance on the transfer, her putative obligation will be less than it would be otherwise, and indeed she may be under no obligation at all. The possibility that D has changed her position is a problem for the obligation model because the facts that prove a change of position will in this case be in D's hands. Thus, just as D cannot be sure of the facts that (if the matter went to trial) C must prove, C cannot be sure of the facts that (if the matter went to trial) D might offer by way of defence. Again, D might inform C of her change of position (though there is clearly no requirement to do this), but even if this happens, C will be left with no option but to accept on faith any seemingly plausible explanation. Being uncertain that one is the beneficiary of an obligation is admittedly less serious than being uncertain that one has an obligation, but it is serious nonetheless. The law's obligation-supporting rules are meant to guide not just those who are bound by obligations but also those who benefit from obligations. In short, even if it were supposed that an obligation to make restitution arises only when the transferor requests restitution (or initiates a lawsuit), it would still be the case that neither the creditors nor debtors of such obligations could reasonably be expected to know that the obligation exists. In other words, it is not reasonable to expect recipients and transferors to accept on faith each other's explanations – yet this is exactly what the obligation model requires.

[42] Given the complexity of many unjust enrichment cases, there is a real possibility that a request for restitution, though bona fide, may be based on a mistaken view of the law or the facts.

Finally, it might be asked whether it is possible that R3RUE simply understands the word 'liability' to mean the same thing as 'obligation'. Legal writers and judges occasionally use these terms as if they were interchangeable.[43] It seems unlikely, however, that R3RUE understands them in this way. Aside from the rare exceptions mentioned earlier, R3RUE consistently refers to liabilities to make restitution (or claims in restitution).[44] This usage cannot be explained on the basis of distaste for the language of obligations. R3RUE frequently refers to 'obligations' when discussing contract law and other legal fields outside of unjust enrichment law. Further, whatever the plausibility of supposing that 'liability' might mean 'obligation', it is not plausible to suppose that 'claim in restitution' means 'obligation to make restitution'. The availability of a claim in restitution can only refer to the claimant's ability to bring a legal action leading to a judgment or order to make restitution.

C. The Law

Restatements are meant to describe the law, but it cannot be assumed that their descriptions are accurate. Notwithstanding R3RUE's language, it is possible that American law (and the common law generally) recognises obligations to make restitution. No doubt, many supporters of the obligation model – assuming they accept my argument thus far – will take this view. To be sure, even if R3RUE gets the law wrong – indeed, especially when it gets the law wrong – it will influence both the law's future content and scholars' understanding of that content. R3RUE's language matters, even if it is inaccurate. For anyone trying to understand the current law, however, the first question that R3RUE's adoption of the liability model raises is whether it is accurate.

We have already seen two reasons for querying the obligation model. The first is that the model raises the justificatory puzzle. If the obligation model is correct, then it must be supposed that, in contrast to the law's usual approach, in cases involving defective transfers, the law imposes positive obligations on citizens who have neither agreed to such obligations nor indeed done anything at all. The second reason is that if the model is correct, then it must be supposed that the law imposes obligations with which citizens cannot reasonably be expected to comply. This second objection arises most clearly on the conventional understanding of the obligation model, which assumes that the obligation to make restitution arises at the moment of enrichment. Recipients are often unaware at the moment of receipt that a transfer has been made. Admittedly, it is not strictly impossible to comply with a duty to make restitution on receipt: it is not physically impossible for me to pay mistaken transferors whatever sums they have paid to me immediately after the payments. But the only way that I could come even reasonably close

[43] See, eg, Hohfeld (n 28) 63.
[44] See n 27 above.

to being certain of complying with such a duty is to check my bank account constantly and to immediately investigate all unexpected payments. The law clearly cannot want me to undertake such actions. Further, this objection cannot be avoided by assuming that obligations to make restitution arise only when a demand for restitution is made or when the recipient is otherwise told that she is the beneficiary of an impaired transfer. As we saw in Part B, making a demand cannot be sufficient to give rise to an obligation to make restitution because the demand may be unfounded. The consequence (given that the relevant facts can only be known by the transferor) is that recipients who wish to comply with their alleged obligations to make restitution have no choice but to accede to plausible demands, even if they are in fact unfounded. Again, the law cannot possibly want citizens to undertake such actions. Further, transferors would be placed in a parallel situation, because they can never know whether the recipient has changed position and so can never know – except if they take on faith what the recipient tells them – whether they are owed an obligation to make restitution.

The question that I want to address now is whether, aside from these conceptual concerns, there are any specific features of the positive law that support or contradict the obligation model. This question has received little attention from legal scholars; indeed, the question seems to have almost never been raised.[45] As already mentioned, R3RUE does not defend or explain its terminology. It is clear that Peter Birks believed in the obligation model,[46] but he did not think it necessary to explicitly defend this belief. Consistent with his Romanist approach to private law,[47] Birks appeared to assume that, insofar as an individual is liable to be required by a court to make restitution, that individual is necessarily under a legal obligation – from the moment of enrichment – to do what the prospective order would require.[48] For Birks, the proof that an obligation to make restitution arises

[45] Although the obligation model has not (as far as I am aware) ever been challenged, legal scholars working in unjust enrichment law rarely refer to obligations to make restitution. Like the Reporters for R3RUE, scholars typically describe the law in terms of liabilities or claims in restitution: see, eg, Virgo (n 9); Webb (n 25) 354; McFarlane (n 25). Peter Birks himself often described unjust enrichments as giving rise to liabilities. The introductory chapter to *Unjust Enrichment* is replete with references to liabilities: 'The previous paragraphs have shown that a striking feature of the liability to make restitution of mistaken payments is that the liability is strict' (Birks, *Unjust Enrichment* (n 7) 8). The introductory chapter to Andrew Burrows' *The Law of Restitution*, 3rd edn (Oxford, Oxford University Press, 2011) is notable for not referring to liabilities to make restitution, though Burrows also never refers to obligations to make restitution. Instead, he refers to a 'right to restitution', which presumably means a right correlative to an obligation, though it could also mean a right to a court award. The only discussion of which I am aware that consistently and without ambiguity describes unjust enrichment law in terms of obligations to make restitution is Klimchuk (n 18) 81.

[46] See n 8.

[47] On the Romanist framework and its clear endorsement of the assumption that court awards confirm existing obligations, see Helge Dedek, 'The Relationship between Rights and Remedies in Private Law: A Comparison between the Common and the Civil Law Tradition' in Robert J Sharpe and Kent Roach (eds), *Taking Remedies Seriously* (Montreal, Canadian Institute for the Administration of Justice, 2010) 63.

[48] This assumption underlies the entirety of Birks' essay 'Rights, Wrongs, and Remedies' (2000) 20 *OJLS* 1. Punitive damages – to mention just one example – show that at least some court awards do not replicate existing duties.

at the moment of enrichment is that the cause of action was complete at that moment.[49] This only follows, however, if one assumes that a liability to make restitution presumes an obligation to make restitution. Rafael Zakrzewski, the only writer who appears to have directly questioned the status of obligations to make restitution, accepts without qualification that such obligations exist.[50] However, Zakrzewski offers no supporting evidence aside from Birks' 'complete cause of action' argument and a single judicial reference to an obligation to return a payment.[51]

If the assumption that court awards necessarily give effect to existing obligations is relaxed, it is no simple matter to determine if the positive law recognises or assumes the existence of obligations to make restitution. Judicial language is not consistent (though it is rare for judges to refer explicitly to legal obligations to make restitution).[52] In any event, the tangled history of unjust enrichment law makes it dangerous to place much weight on judicial language or, more broadly, on the historical classification of claims for restitution. For example, it would be unwise to put much stock in the once-prevalent classification of restitutionary claims arising from defective transfers as contractual or quasi-contractual.[53] A full examination of the positive law, either American or English, is outside this chapter's scope. Instead, I limit myself to noting two reasons supporting the liability model. These reasons are insufficient, standing alone, to justify rejecting the obligation model, but together with the conceptual objections mentioned above, they are sufficient to justify asking (in Parts D and E) whether adopting the liability model might help resolve the justificatory puzzle described earlier.

The first reason for querying the existence of obligations to make restitution is that damages are not available for failing to make restitution.[54] The common law's normal response to a legal wrong is to hold the wrongdoer liable to pay damages. And if there is an obligation to make restitution, then failing to make restitution must be a legal wrong. If I breach a contractual obligation or an obligation recognised by tort law, I become liable to a judgment to pay damages. Even if the breach causes no loss, nominal damages are available. Indeed, awarding nominal dam-

[49] Birks, *Unjust Enrichment* (n 7) 169, citing *Baker v Courage* (n 33) 65. R3RUE adopts the same position: R3RUE (n 1) vol II, 627.

[50] Rafael Zakrzewski, *Remedies Reclassified* (Oxford, Oxford University Press, 2005) 112–14. The related question whether, in 'unjust enrichment' cases that are resolved by declaring a constructive trust, courts merely affirm existing property rights or, instead, create new property rights is discussed in William Swadling, 'The Fiction of the Constructive Trust' (2011) 64 *CLP* 399.

[51] The reference is to Hamilton J's statement in *Baker v Courage* (n 33) 65 that notice of a mistake was not necessary 'to raise an obligation in Mr Baker to pay the overpayment back'. The fact that Hamilton J assumed that the obligation can arise without knowledge of the enrichment suggests, as I explain below, an odd understanding of a legal obligation.

[52] Counter-examples include Hamilton J's statement in *Baker v Courage* (n 33) 65 and Lord Steyn's comment in *Banque Financière de la Cite v Parc (Battersea) Ltd* [1999] AC 221, 227 that 'unjust enrichment ranks next to contract and tort as part of the law of obligations [as] an independent source of rights and obligations'.

[53] See the discussion in R3RUE (n 1) vol II, 623.

[54] I took a different position in Stephen A Smith, 'Unjust Enrichment: Nearer to Tort than Contract' in Chambers, Mitchell and Penner (n 18) 187–89.

ages is how the common law makes it clear that a wrong has been committed, and thus that an obligation exists to not do what the defendant has done. Nothing similar is available in the case of alleged obligations to make restitution. No matter how tardy the payment and regardless of the consequences, damages (nominal or otherwise) are unavailable for failing to make restitution.[55] Pre-judgment interest is now available on restitutionary awards,[56] but the sums awarded on this basis often differ from the losses that could have been avoided by an earlier payment. Consistent with this interpretation, both R3RUE and the English courts have affirmed that interest is awarded because it represents part of the value of the enrichment.[57]

It is sometimes suggested, or at least implied, that damages are not available for breaching an obligation to make restitution because the facts that give rise to the obligation are – to adopt Birks' language – so slight.[58] It is the thinness of these facts, Birks stressed, that makes the defence of change of position central to the law of unjust enrichment. It would be intolerable if the law required an innocent recipient to give up more than that which she had received.[59] This observation is undoubtedly correct, but it does not explain why damages are unavailable. The weakness of the causative facts explains why the content of the recipient's obligation is limited, but does not account for the absence of liability for breaching the obligation. If the obligation exists, then failing to comply with it is, by definition, a legal wrong.

As mentioned earlier, the conventional understanding of the obligation model supposes that the obligation to make restitution arises at the moment of enrichment. It follows that, if damages were available for failing to make timely restitution, defendants could be liable for losses arising from failing to comply with an obligation of which they were completely unaware. This would be difficult to justify. The idea that the law might recognise unknowable positive legal obligations raises its own problems.[60] However, for the moment, it is sufficient to note that the difficulty of justifying damages for breaching such an obligation does not explain why the law does not award damages for losses arising after the recipient becomes aware of the relevant facts. It would be a simple matter to hold that liability for damages arises from the moment of knowledge.

[55] Damages are also not available for failing to pay damages on commission of a tort or a breach of contract: *President of India v Lips Maritime Corporation* [1988] AC 395, 475. This rule is consistent with the liability model because, as a matter of positive law, there is no obligation to pay damages prior to a court award: see n 30 above.

[56] See R3RUE (n 1) vol II, § 53(4); *Sempra Metals Ltd v Inland Revenue* [2007] UKHL 34, [2008] 1 AC 561; Supreme Court Act 1981, s 35A (UK).

[57] 'Liability for the use-value of money may be imposed by an award of prejudgment interest . . . whenever the failure to award interest would contribute to the unjust enrichment of the defendant': R3RUE (n 10 vol II, § 53(4); *Westdeutsche Landesbank Girozentrale v Islington LBC* [1996] UKHL 12, [1996] 2 AC 669, 696, 736; *Sempra Metals Ltd* (n 56) [34]–[50], [116], [132], [178]–[179]. See also Birks, *Unjust Enrichment* (n 7) 53; Burrows, *Restitution* (n 45) 55–56.

[58] Birks, *Unjust Enrichment* (n 7) 18.

[59] ibid 208.

[60] See Part E below.

A final possible explanation for the unavailability of damages for failing to comply with alleged obligations to make restitution is that these obligations do not carry a fixed date for performance. It has never been suggested, by courts or scholars, that the alleged obligation to make restitution must be performed within a given time period. Thus, one possible explanation for why damages are unavailable is that, without a deadline for performance, it is not possible to breach the obligation. Again, however, if obligations to make restitution were thought to be similar to other positive obligations (for example, to pay for goods delivered pursuant to a contract of sale), it would be relatively simple to stipulate that the obligation must be performed in a timely manner. The fact that no time for performance has been stipulated is not so much an explanation for the no-damages rule as a reason for querying the existence of an obligation in the first place. An obligation that cannot be breached is hardly an obligation.

The second reason for questioning the accuracy of the obligation model is that it appears inconsistent with the rules allowing claimants, in certain situations, to make an election at trial between personal and proprietary restitution.[61] The possibility of election means that the content of the alleged obligation may not be known until a judgment is made against the defendant. At that point, it is too late for the defendant to comply with the obligation. Defendants are, of course, normally (though not always) given time to comply voluntarily with a court award,[62] but satisfying an award voluntarily is not the same as complying with an obligation. The award typically extinguishes the obligation. Thus, the possibility of choosing between remedies again raises the objection that the obligation model assumes the existence of obligations that are not capable of being fulfilled. It is no response to say that the obligation in such cases is simply a 'conditional obligation' similar to, for example, a contractual obligation to deliver goods on request. In unjust enrichment cases, the election need not be made until judgment, at which point it is too late for the defendant to fulfil the putative obligation. In addition, if one regards the content of the defendant's obligation, prior to judgment, as an inchoate or unspecified obligation, then the proper award (including in cases where the claimant has elected personal restitution) is a declaration rather than a monetary judgment. A declaration is the appropriate way to specify previously unspecified obligations.[63]

[61] See especially R3RUE (n 1) vol II, Topic 2, 'Restitution via Rights in Identifiable Property' (269, 271, 278, 286–87, 295, 412 and 414). See also Birks, *Unjust Enrichment* (n 7) 163.

[62] Adrian Zuckerman, *Zuckerman on Civil Procedure*, 2nd edn (London, Sweet & Maxwell, 2006) 790.

[63] I defend this proposition in more detail in Stephen A Smith, 'Duties, Liabilities and Damages' (2012) 125 *Harvard Law Review* 1727, 1746–48.

D. Why the Obligation–Liability Distinction Matters

The above comments are too brief to establish conclusively that the liability model accurately describes the positive law. However, they do provide sufficient grounds to justify asking the third question raised by R3RUE's apparent adoption of this model: why does it matter if the law recognises only liabilities, and not obligations, to make restitution?

The distinction matters in various ways, but I would like to focus on one in particular that has implications for the justificatory puzzle. The distinction matters for the puzzle because the kinds of reasons that might potentially justify legal obligations are different from those that might potentially justify legal liabilities. As HLA Hart explained, we describe legal obligations as *obligations* because they announce, from the law's perspective, what citizens ought to do.[64] The rules that set out legal obligations are normative propositions. It is part of their meaning that they are meant to reflect reasons – moral reasons – that apply to those subject to them.[65] When courts or legislatures declare that 'there is an obligation to do X', they are declaring that citizens are morally obliged to do X. Courts and legislatures can, of course, be mistaken: they may declare a legal obligation to do something that is not in fact morally justified. It is, however, part of the meaning of obligation-imposing rules that the actions they stipulate are morally obligatory.

This feature of obligation-imposing rules helps to explain why the obligation model of unjust enrichment raises a justificatory puzzle. The puzzle is not merely that obligations to make restitution are difficult to justify – many perfectly intelligible legal obligations are difficult to justify. The puzzle is that the acts required by obligations to make restitution appear to be the wrong kind of acts to even plausibly be the subject of a moral obligation. More specifically, such acts seem incapable of being moral obligations – at least from the law's perspective – given the legal system's other commitments. As explained earlier, an obligation to reverse a transfer in which title to the relevant property has passed to the recipient is an obligation to give back something (or its value) that the law has told the recipient she owns. Thus, an explanation of the law that includes the existence of such an obligation does not merely suppose that the law is imperfect or mistaken: it supposes that the law is conceptually confused. In short, the explanation fails as an explanation.

[64] HLA Hart, *The Concept of Law* (Oxford, Clarendon Press, 1961) 82–91. This aspect of Hart's work has been developed most fully by Joseph Raz: see *The Authority of Law* (Oxford, Oxford University Press, 1979) 3-232; *Ethics in the Public Domain* (Oxford, Oxford University Press, 1994) 210–37.

[65] This proposition is true even where, without the legal obligation, there would be no moral obligation to do what the legal obligation requires. Thus, a rule that solves a coordination problem – for example, which side of the road to drive on – fits this explanation because everyone has moral reasons to do whatever is reasonably necessary to ensure the safe and efficient flow of traffic: see generally Raz, *Ethics* (n 64).

Liabilities are different from obligations, in particular, the kind of liabilities contemplated by R3RUE (that is, liabilities to court orders). To justify such liabilities, one must not defend rules that impose obligations, but rather must defend rules that authorise courts to make orders. The distinction is important because, unlike in the case of a legal obligation, it is not part of the meaning of an order that the order reflects reasons, moral or otherwise, that apply to the subject. This is evident not just from the language in which orders are framed ('It is ordered that . . .'),[66] but from the characteristic situations in which the law relies exclusively on orders to achieve a desired result. The clearest example is punishment. The law does not impose obligations on wrongdoers to punish themselves. There is a bylaw in Montreal that authorises a fine of $300 to be imposed on anyone who allows their dog to run unleashed in city parks.[67] The bylaw does not, however, impose an obligation on citizens who allow their dogs to run free to send the city a cheque for $300; it merely provides that citizens are liable to be fined $300. The explanation for why there is no such obligation is not just the practical difficulty of ensuring that the obligation is known or of specifying its content in advance. An obligation to pay a fine is a contradiction in terms because legal obligations are meant to give effect to moral reasons that apply to the subject, and we do not have moral obligations to punish ourselves. The point is not that punishment is unjustified, it is that whatever justification exists is not based on reasons for action that apply to the wrongdoer. This is why an attempt to impose a legal obligation to pay a fine would fail: the putative fine would be interpreted as imposing a tax.[68] Employing orders to punish wrongdoers is, however, perfectly intelligible because, in both law and ordinary life, orders carry a different meaning from rules. Orders are essentially commands.

The example of punitive orders is not meant to deny the point that legal orders may stipulate actions that the law regards as morally obligatory. Such 'replicative' orders are common. Orders requiring defendants to pay contractual debts or to refrain from trespassing stipulate actions that the law views as moral obligations. In such cases, however, the actions are, as one would expect, also required by a legal rule that imposes an obligation to perform the actions. Indeed, the order is made in such cases precisely because the defendant failed to comply (or threatened to fail to comply) with that obligation.[69] However, as the example of punitive

[66] The point made above applies even more strongly to jurisdictions like the US in which monetary awards are framed as 'judgments' that 'the defendant shall have and recover' the relevant sum: see Dobbs (n 37). This language is directed as much at bailiffs as at the claimant.

[67] City of Montreal, bylaw RCG 10-016, *By-law Concerning Parks Under the Authority of the Urban Agglomeration Council of Montréal* (26 August 2010), ss 7, 14.

[68] It would be interpreted as a tax because moral duties to pay taxes are intelligible.

[69] The common feature of orders that replicate obligations and orders that, like punitive orders, are non-replicative is that neither attempts to motivate compliance through a plea to moral reasons for action. Although replicative orders may require actions that, from the law's perspective, are morally obligatory, an order – unlike an obligation – is not presented as a moral obligation. This is entirely appropriate given that the basic justification for making replicative orders is that the defendant has shown herself unwilling to comply with her legal, and hence (from the law's perspective) moral, obligations. I discuss these issues in more detail in Smith (n 22) 54–64.

orders shows, orders need not replicate existing legal obligations. And when, as in the case of punitive orders, an order is not a replication of a prior obligation, the implication is that the law employs the order – and only the order – because it wants something done that is not properly the subject of a legal obligation.[70] If the desired action were properly the subject matter of a duty-imposing rule, we would expect the law to declare a rule. Imposing legal duties through rules is an obvious and practical way for the law to guide the behaviour of large groups of people. Many citizens accept that they have a moral obligation to obey the law and act on this belief.[71] It follows that when, as in the case of punitive orders, the law declines to use a rule, we should assume that the law is trying to do something that it thinks rules are not supposed to do.

E. Property-Based Theories Re-interpreted

The reference to punitive orders as an example of non-replicative orders is not intended to suggest that restitutionary orders are punitive; rather, the point of the comparison is to suggest that the kinds of reasons one should look for to justify non-replicative court orders will be similar, at least in structure, to the kinds of reasons that might be used to justify punitive awards. More specifically, the suggestion is that one should not seek to justify restitutionary orders (and thus restitutionary liabilities) on the basis of moral reasons that might apply to the orders' subjects. Instead, one must look for reasons that (like reasons that might justify punishment) apply specifically to *courts*, that is to say, reasons for which courts (not citizens) ought to do things. In theory, such reasons might take various forms, but rather than canvassing the possibilities, I would like to explore one reason that is already well known in the unjust enrichment literature: the law's interest in protecting property rights. My suggestion is that this reason gains new traction when interpreted as a justification specifically for liabilities – not obligations – to make restitution.

[70] We might think that another reason for employing orders in cases where there is no legal obligation to do the thing required by the order is to fix an uncertain moral obligation. Thus, we might suppose that there are situations where an obligation's content is too variable to be specified by way of a legal rule and where, therefore, courts employ orders to specify the obligation. Yet, even assuming that it makes sense to speak of uncertain *legal* obligations, this suggestion must be rejected because the obvious and appropriate way for a court to specify an uncertain legal obligation is to make a declaration. A declaration is the individualised counterpart to a legal rule: both rules and declarations announce what *ought* to happen. Ordering defendants to comply with obligations (or, as where a judgment is issued, authorising legal officials to seize their property) without first giving them the opportunity to comply voluntarily makes a nonsense of the very idea of an obligation. It implies – without any proof to the contrary – that defendants are unwilling to comply with their legal obligations. As the law governing requests for injunctions to prevent future wrongs shows, common law courts hesitate to order defendants to comply with legal obligations in advance of clear proof that the defendants are unwilling to do so voluntarily. See generally Smith (n 63) 1744–49.

[71] I discuss the evidence in Stephen A Smith, 'The Normativity of Private Law' (2011) 31 *OJLS* 215.

I noted earlier that a common, if controversial, justification for reversing defective transfers is to protect transferors' property rights in the transferred goods.[72] Writers who adopt property-based explanations of this kind suppose that the basic justification for reversing defective transfers is to support property-owners' interests in controlling their property. In the words of one proponent, 'these claims [to reverse defective transfers] arise as a means of protecting and effectuating the claimant's interest in exclusively determining the disposition of his assets'.[73] According to property-based explanations, the part of unjust enrichment law that deals with defective transfers is in substance an appendage to property law; the rules governing defective transfers are ancillary property law rules.

I also noted that the standard objection to property-based explanations is that they appear to conflict with property law itself. The only cases where transferors of defectively transferred property must turn to the law of unjust enrichment for relief are where property law holds that title has passed to the recipient. The objection, then, is that property-based explanations must suppose that the law of unjust enrichment requires, for property-based reasons, the undoing of transfers that the law of property declares to be perfectly valid.

This objection appears reasonable insofar as one assumes that the law undoes defective transfers by imposing obligations on recipients to return the property or its value. An obligation to hand over something that you own (or its equivalent value) in circumstances where you made no promise, nor are responsible for the way in which the property came to be yours, seems odd. We teach our children that they should return things to their owners, but, except perhaps when we are trying to teach charitableness, we do not teach children that they should hand over their own things. As mentioned earlier, the point is not that a moral obligation to return defectively transferred property is implausible; many people believe that such an obligation exists. However, the reason they believe this is almost certainly that they believe that the transferor owns, or at least should own, the property. Yet the law cannot suppose that such an obligation exists because the law says that the defective transfer (or at least the kind of defective transfer that is our present concern) passes title to the property. The law is, in effect, estopped from declaring obligations to undo legally valid transfers.

However, property-based explanations can avoid this objection if they are presented as explanations of liabilities, not obligations, to make restitution. Stripped to their essentials, property-based explanations suppose that the rules governing defective transfers are intended to fix a problem that the law, in particular the law of property, has itself created or at least authorised. In Ben McFarlane's words: 'On the model proposed here, the liability principle [which requires that defective

[72] See n 25 above. The Introduction to R3RUE comes very close to adopting a property-based explanation of its subject matter: 'Unjust enrichment is enrichment that lacks an adequate legal basis; it results from a transaction that the law treats as ineffective to work a conclusive alteration in ownership rights' (5).

[73] Webb (n 25) 335. Webb's reference to 'claims' is an example of describing unjust enrichment law in terms of liabilities.

transfers be reversed] is justified at one remove. The function of the principle . . . is to mitigate the effects on C [the claimant] of other legal rules.'[74] One might ask, of course, why it is not possible simply to revise the rules governing the passing of title to mitigate the effects of the current rules. The short answer – a full answer would require another chapter – is that the proposed revision is not easily achieved: if it were, it would have happened by now. A second possible response is for the law to ask citizens to fix the problem, which it could do by creating obligations to undo defective transfers. The main objections to this solution have already been discussed. It only remains to be added that imposing obligations is a prima facie inappropriate way for the law to 'mitigate the effects' of its own rules. Why place the burden on citizens? The third possibility, and the one which appears to have been adopted, is for the law, or more strictly the courts, to fix the problem themselves. Interpreted as liability rules, the rules governing defective transfers provide a means by which citizens who have been disadvantaged by the rules governing the passing of title can approach the courts for relief. It is as if the law says to citizens: 'Here are the rules governing property transfers. They work well most of the time, but in rare cases they lead to undesirable results. When that happens, come to us and we will fix the problem.'

Re-interpreting property-based theories as theories of liabilities leaves untouched the substance of their arguments as to why the law responds to defective transfers. The re-interpretation accepts that the law responds in order to protect citizens' interests in controlling their property. The sole modification to property-based theories is to introduce the idea that the law's response takes the form of imposing a liability rather than an obligation. This modification is crucial, however, because it allows property-based theories to overcome the objection that they suppose the law requires citizens to fix a problem that the law created. Of course, the liability model accepts that the law involves citizens in fixing defective transfers, but citizens' involvement is limited (in the case of transferors) to asking the courts for relief and (in the case of recipients) to submitting to the court's decision. Strictly speaking, the recipient does not need to do anything – not even go to court. If you transfer money into my bank account while I am on vacation, I can stay on vacation: the courts will render judgment and seize the necessary assets without my participation.[75] Of course, I might prefer that my assets not be seized, but if the substantive arguments underlying property-based theories are correct, I have no complaint. In an ideal legal system, I would not have obtained good title in the first place. This fact is not sufficient reason to put me under an obligation to return the property (or a substitute for it), but it is a good reason to allow courts to authorise legal officials to bring about this result.

[74] McFarlane (n 25) 607. McFarlane's explanation is more properly described as a 'legal rights-based' explanation rather than a property-based explanation because it applies – correctly in my view – to transfers of legal rights generally, not just to transfers of property rights.

[75] If I return the transferred money prior to litigation, the court should (and would) refuse to make an award because the problem that the award is meant to cure has already been resolved. The fact that the method the law provides to fix a problem involves going to court does not mean that the problem cannot be resolved in other ways.

Understood as explanations of liabilities to make restitution, property-based theories of unjust enrichment law (or at least a part of that law) thus avoid the objection that they are inconsistent with the rules governing the passing of title. Other objections to property-based theories are no doubt possible, but rather than pursue these objections, I would like to conclude by mentioning four ways in which the theory presented here connects with widely shared views about the nature of unjust enrichment law. The first connection is to the idea that unjust enrichment is a subsidiary or complementary body of law. For instance, Robert Stevens has recently described unjust enrichment law as playing a 'second order vacuum filling role'.[76] This description sounds strange if it is assumed that the subject matter is a body of law that imposes obligations on individuals. Few individuals would be pleased to hear that the reason they have an obligation to pay a sum of money to another citizen is to help fill a vacuum in the law. On the liability model, however, there is nothing odd about unjust enrichment playing a second-order role. Liability to punishment and liability to damages in private law are also second-order. Neither exists as a freestanding body of law; each depends for its existence on a body of law that sets out substantive legal obligations.

The second, related connection is to the widespread recognition of the complexity of unjust enrichment law.[77] This complexity is an embarrassment if one supposes that unjust enrichment law is obligation-imposing. Citizens should be able to understand their legal obligations without going to lawyers. Yet even lawyers rarely possess more than a rudimentary understanding of unjust enrichment law. The liability model gives us no reason to applaud this complexity, but if the model is correct, then the complexity ceases to be an embarrassment. In the liability model, the rules governing relief for defective transfers are primarily intended to guide judges, not citizens. Citizens should, of course, be able to determine with reasonable certainty if they are likely to succeed if they go to court, but at this point we enter the world of litigation, where it is generally understood that legal advice is necessary. Not coincidentally, the rules governing the assessment of damages – the other major body of private law governing liabilities – exhibit a similar complexity. Like unjust enrichment law, the law of damages is 'lawyers' law'.

The third connection is to the widely voiced (though often criticised) idea that unjust enrichment law has a special connection to 'equity'.[78] Relatively little of the law governing defective transfers originated in the courts of equity, and little of the law governing the kinds of relief available for defective transfers is subject to the courts' discretion in the way that, for example, the availability of injunctions and specific relief is subject to discretion. From the perspective defended in this

[76] Robert Stevens, 'Is There a Law of Unjust Enrichment?' in Simone Degeling and James Edelman (eds), *Unjust Enrichment in Commercial Law* (Sydney, Lawbook Co, 2008) 11, 23. The subsidiary nature of unjust enrichment law is a recurrent theme in writings on unjust enrichment: see, eg, Lionel Smith, 'Property, Subsidiarity, and Unjust Enrichment' in Johnston and Zimmerman (n 12) 596.

[77] See, eg, Smith (n 76) 623.

[78] See Burrows (n 45) 25–26; Virgo (n 9) 45–46; Smith (n 76) 610–12.

chapter, however, unjust enrichment law is equitable in the sense that it is meant to provide relief for, broadly speaking, *legal* injustices. The rules governing defective transfers, like the rules first developed in the courts of equity, provide a means by which citizens who are aggrieved by the operation of other rules can approach a court and obtain relief. From the perspective of the liability model, unjust enrichment law is equitable in the core sense that it provides a corrective to other laws.

The final connection is to the name (or at least one of the names) conventionally given to R3RUE's subject matter: unjust enrichment. To describe a situation as 'unjust' may simply indicate that it is thought to be undesirable; however, in its traditional and accepted core meaning, the term refers to situations that are thought to raise fairness concerns and, in particular, fairness concerns that are attributed to, or considered the responsibility of, an authority – paradigmatically the state.[79] Matters of interpersonal morality – lying, stealing, breaking promises and so on – are not usually thought to raises issues of justice. We say that stealing is wrong, not that it is unjust. It is only when the state or another authority becomes involved that stealing raises justice concerns. Thus, if a judge trying an alleged thief is biased, if the substantive rules that led to a thief's conviction are unfair or if a thief's sentence is disproportionate to the crime, issues of justice arise. Similarly, one might think it unfair that some people are born stronger or more intelligent than others, but such advantages only become a matter of justice when one assesses how the state (and other authorities) respond to them.

The idea that defective transfers give rise to 'unjust' enrichments fits neatly with this understanding of justice – or at least it fits neatly if one adopts a property-based (or similar) explanation of why such transfers give rise to problems. On the property-based account, the problems are a consequence of the rules governing the passing of title. The recipient is enriched because the law of property declares that she obtains good title. The enrichment is unfair because the transferor did not intend to enrich the recipient. And the unfairness is a matter of justice because property law holds that the transfer is valid notwithstanding the absence of intent.

This explanation (or any similar explanation) as to why unjust enrichments are unjust fits awkwardly with the obligation model. If the problem raised by defective transfers is one of justice (in the sense just described), then it would be unusual, indeed inappropriate, for the state to attempt to solve it by imposing obligations on citizens. If the problem is indeed one of justice, then it is one that, if not strictly created by the state, is the state's responsibility. The state is, of course, involved when law makers introduce obligation-imposing rules. But in the case of alleged obligations to make restitution, the involvement takes the form of placing responsibility for a problem on citizens whose only connection to it is that the law says they own the relevant property. In the liability model, by con-

[79] 'Justice is the first virtue of social institutions': John Rawls, *A Theory of Justice* (Cambridge, MA, Harvard University Press, 1971) 3.

trast, responsibility for fixing the law's problems remains with the law, in particular, the courts. Aggrieved transferors must initiate a legal action to obtain relief, but the relief is brought about by courts making awards. Those awards require that defendants hand over money or other property, but the responsibility for ensuring that this happens remains, in the end, with the state. No blame is attached to the recipient because no obligation on her part is presumed. In short, the model of unjust enrichment defended in this chapter supposes that unjust enrichments are indeed 'unjust' and, as a result, are properly cured not by imposing obligations on citizens, but by providing means by which citizens can obtain relief from courts.

11

Restitution for Wrongs

NICHOLAS MCBRIDE*

A. Introduction

In this chapter I will set out the key provisions in the *Restatement Third: Restitution and Unjust Enrichment*[1] as to when gain-based damages (and analogous remedies) may be awarded against a wrongdoer. I will go on to argue that the justifications that R3RUE offers for awarding such damages against a wrongdoer are flawed. I will then conclude by sketching out an account of what a soundly based law on restitution for wrongs would look like.

B. Summary of R3RUE's Provisions

(1) What Sort of Wrongs?

§ 3 of R3RUE boldly proclaims that: 'A person is not permitted to profit by his own wrong.' This would tend to suggest that there is no limit on what kinds of wrongs may be the subject of an award of gain-based damages under R3RUE.[2] However, six provisions in the main body of R3RUE that deal with restitution for wrongs are carefully targeted at certain discrete types of wrong:

* One sub-section of this chapter (C(2)(b)) has profited a great deal from conversations I have had with Jason Varuhas about the nature and function of damages awards. All remaining errors are, of course, my own responsibility.

[1] American Law Institute, *Restatement Third: Restitution and Unjust Enrichment* (St Paul, MN, American Law Institute Publishers, 2011) (hereinafter 'R3RUE').

[2] See also § 39, Comment a: 'If a profitable interference has . . . occurred, the law of restitution allows a claim to disgorgement of profits, as an alternative to damages, in cases of intentional interference with legal entitlements *of any kind*' (emphasis added).

- § 39 deals with breach of contract.
- § 40 deals with trespass to property, conversion and 'comparable wrongs', where a wrong will be 'comparable' to trespass or conversion if it involves a 'comparable interference with other protected interests in tangible property'.[3]
- § 41 deals with the misappropriaton of financial assets.
- § 42 deals with the 'misappropriation or infringement of another's legally protected rights in any idea, expression, information, image or designation'.
- § 43 deals with a breach of fiduciary duty or the breach of 'an equivalent duty imposed by a relationship of trust and confidence'.
- § 45 deals with the case where someone who has killed someone else, or who has participated in killing someone else 'by an act that is felonious, intentional, and without legal excuse or justification', has benefited, or stands to benefit, from the killing; the 'slayer rule' laid out in § 45 prevents him from doing so.

For the purpose of knowing what kinds of wrongs are covered by R3RUE's provisions on restitution for wrongs, § 44 is the most important. It is a catch-all provision entitled 'Interference with Other Protected Interests'. Its key provision is §44(1), which provides that:

> A person who obtains a benefit by conscious interference with a claimant's legally protected interests (or in consequence of such interference by another) is liable in restitution as necessary to prevent unjust enrichment, unless competing legal objectives make such liability inappropriate.

§ 44(2) goes on to explain that:

> [I]nterference with legally protected interests includes conduct that is tortious, or that violates another's legal duty or prohibition (other than a duty imposed by contract) if the conduct constitutes an actionable wrong to the claimant.

This seems very general, but the accompanying Comments and Illustrations to § 44 make it clear that § 44 is intended to apply centrally to: (1) a tortious interference with a species of property not covered elsewhere by R3RUE;[4] (2) the case

[3] Some of § 40's Illustrations give us an idea what this means: Illustration 7 involves the violation of the term of a lease; Illustration 8 involves an interference with an easement (which would amount to private nuisance in English law); Illustration 9 involves a shipowner lawfully mooring his ship to a dock during a violent storm; Illustration 15 involves making unauthorised use of the facilities of an Internet service provider to send spam email to its customers; and Illustration 16 involves the unauthorised use of a crane that the owner of the crane (who is the claimant in the Illustration) has leased for six months to someone else, with the result that the owner has no claim in conversion against the user of the crane.

[4] See § 44, Comment a; and § 44, Illustration 1 (offering Polish-language television programming to cable subscribers without authority from the broadcaster with worldwide exclusive rights to that programming) and Illustration 3 (an owner of adjacent tracts, Blackacre (with a house on it and mortgaged to Bank A) and Whiteacre (unimproved and mortgaged to Bank B), moves a house from Blackacre to Whiteacre to make it more attractive to potential purchaser of Whiteacre. The house cannot be moved back and in foreclosure proceedings, bank B gets $75,000 more than it would have had no house been on Whiteacre. 'By the rule of this section, Bank A is entitled to restitution of $75,000 from Bank B').

where a defendant commits an economic tort in relation to the claimant;[5] (3) the case where a defendant tortiously violates the claimant's privacy;[6] (4) the case where a defendant commits a breach of a statutory duty imposed on the defendant for the benefit of the claimant.[7]

What does this leave over? Assault, battery, false imprisonment, defamation and negligence. It is possible to think of scenarios where a defendant could make a gain from consciously[8] committing any of these wrongs, but it is unclear what R3RUE would make of those situations. The ambit of § 44 is limited by § 44(3), which provides that:

> Restitution by the rule of this section will be limited or denied:
>
> (a) if the court would refuse to enjoin the interference, assuming timely application and an absence of procedural or administrative obstacles;
> (b) to the extent it would result in an inappropriate windfall to the claimant, or would otherwise be inequitable in a particular case;
> (c) if the benefit derived from the interference cannot be adequately measured; or
> (d) if allowance of the claim would conflict with liabilities or penalties for the interference provided by other law.

It may be that one or more of these provisions would apply to knock out a claim for restitution for wrongs under § 44 where the wrong committed was one of these 'leftover' wrongs – but the failure to mention any[9] of these wrongs in relation to § 44 creates uncertainty over whether they are even meant to be covered by that section.

[5] See § 44, Comment b: 'It applies generally to interference with contract or with prospective economic advantage, to the extent that such interference is tortious under applicable law.'

[6] See § 44, Comment b: 'Profitable interference with other protected interests, such as the claimant's right to privacy, gives rise to a claim under § 44 if the benefit to the defendant is susceptible to measurement.' The example supplied is Illustration 10, where a local pharmacy sells customers' prescription information to a national chain. Illustrations 2 ('theft' of the claimant's identity enables a conman to buy a house with help of mortgage from Bank A and on which he later raises loan from Bank B; the claimant is entitled to what is left over from the sale of the house after the conman absconds with Bank B's loan money and Bank A and Bank B recover the value of their loans from sale) and 8 (recordings of an actor reading the Bible are marketed on basis that they are endorsed by actor) could also fit here.

[7] See § 44, Comment c; and § 44, Illustration 11 (bids invited for municipal construction work are set aside for 'small businesses' only; the winning bidder misrepresents that he is a small business; the runner up can sue the winner for the net profits he makes on his contract).

[8] I hope that we have by now left behind the fallacy that the tort of negligence cannot be committed deliberately: see NJ McBride and R Bagshaw, *Tort Law*, 4th edn (Harlow, Pearson Education, 2012) 93–94.

[9] § 44, Illustration 11 (a doctor extracts blood cells from patient for testing; he recognizes that cells are unusually valuable for research and sells samples to researchers for $25,000; there is no conversion of the patient's body parts but the patient can still sue under the 'local law governing disclosure by physicians and informed consent' for $25,000) could be read as being a negligence case (if we think that the doctor here has breached his duty to treat his patient with a reasonable degree of care and skill), but is presented in R3RUE as being an invasion of privacy case.

(2) What Sort of Damages?

Restitution for wrongs may be effected by a variety of means, including the imposition of constructive trusts over gains that a wrongdoer has, or stands to make, from his wrong. R3RUE's provisions on restitution for wrongs contain plenty of examples of cases where constructive trusts are used to prevent a wrongdoer benefiting from his wrong, particularly in relation to breaches of fiduciary duty, and under the 'slayer rule'. But my interest in this chapter is in cases where we effect restitution for wrongs through awards of damages – which I will refer to as 'gain-based damages', following James Edelman.[10]

R3RUE follows Edelman in taking the view that there are *two* forms of gain-based damages. There are, first of all, damages that are designed to make the wrongdoer disgorge whatever tangible, in-hand gains he has made from doing what he did. These are straightforwardly known as 'disgorgement damages'.

The second set of gain-based damages seems to be designed to make the wrongdoer pay a reasonable sum for the privilege he has enjoyed from committing his wrong. These damages have no agreed-upon name.[11] Some scholars argue that they need no distinct name: they are simply a limited form of disgorgement damages. This is hard to accept. For example, suppose that A goes for a ride on B's horse without B's permission. The ride goes disastrously badly: it is so bumpy that A throws up at one point; he then falls off the horse and injures himself; finally, he is soaked in a flash storm as he rides the horse back to its stable and consequently develops pneumonia. A will be liable to pay B a reasonable sum for the use he has made of B's horse. This is so even though the outcome of A's ride has been so disastrous that we cannot say that the ride has resulted in A obtaining any kind of tangible gain.[12] However, A still has to pay for the mere fact that he has gone for a ride on B's horse.

If the damages payable in a case like A's cannot be characterised as 'disgorgement damages', then we need a name for them. Edelman likes 'restitutionary damages'.[13] I think we should avoid this name as it reflects a particular (and, as we will see, incorrect) view as to the basis of awards of damages in cases like A's. My own preference is for 'licence fee damages',[14] as damages awarded in cases like A's are usually awarded by reference to what it would have cost someone like A to obtain a licence to do what he did.

[10] J Edelman, *Gain-Based Damages* (Oxford, Hart Publishing, 2002) *passim.*

[11] 'User damages', 'reasonable fee damages', 'negotiating damages', 'restitutionary damages', 'licence fee damages' and '*Wrotham Park* damages' have all been suggested in the past.

[12] It might be argued that A can be *deemed* to have made a gain as a result of going for a ride on B's horse that he is not allowed to 'subjectively devalue' because he is a bad man. But how is that any better, or any less artificial, than saying that A is liable to pay B a reasonable sum for the use of the horse because he is *deemed* to have made a contract with B to pay him such a sum?

[13] Edelman (n 10) ch 3.

[14] McBride and Bagshaw (n 8) 807, following P Jaffey, 'Licence Fee Damages' (2011) 19 *Restitution Law Review* 95.

As we will see very shortly, R3RUE tends to reserve disgorgement damages for 'conscious' wrongdoers. Defendants who innocently commit a wrong tend *not* to be held liable under R3RUE for more than 'the value of what they have acquired – usually measured by the cost of a license – but not for consequential gains'.[15] This seems to refer to licence fee damages, but the reference to a wrongdoer being held liable under this measure for the 'value of what they have acquired' is liable to create confusion, as disgorgement damages also focus on the value of what has been acquired by the wrongdoer and make him give up that value.

(3) Fault Requirements

R3RUE tends to take the position that disgorgement damages may only be awarded against conscious wrongdoers, while innocent wrongdoers may still be liable to pay the victims of their wrongs licence fee damages. Let's get a more detailed view of these fault requirements by taking each measure of damages in turn.

(a) Disgorgement Damages

As we will see in the next part of this chapter, R3RUE is based on the view that disgorgement damages should be primarily aimed at discouraging people from committing wrongs by making it clear to those who are thinking about committing a wrong that they will not be allowed to profit from it. As a result of this, disgorgement damages are primarily to be awarded against those who *consciously* commit a wrong. As § 3, Comment a observes:

> Liability to disgorge profits is ordinarily limited to cases of what the Restatement calls 'conscious wrongdoing', because the disincentives that are the object of a disgorgement remedy are not required in dealing either with innocent recipients or with inadvertent tortfeasors (such as innocent trespassers and converters).

Despite this, R3RUE allows that disgorgement damages may be awarded against a wrongdoer who has inadvertently breached a duty owed to another.

§ 39, Comment g provides that someone who inadvertently breaches a contract term may be held liable to give up the money he has saved by committing that breach if the term that was breached was relevant to the calculation of the contract price. For example, in § 39, Illustration 13, a house builder who is contractually required to use Vermont granite in constructing the foundations of the house inadvertently uses New Hampshire granite instead, saving himself $15,000 in the process. He is required to give up that money saving, as the specification of the type of granite to be used in the foundations may well have inflated the contract

[15] § 40, Comment b. See also § 51(2): 'The value for restitution purposes of benefits obtained by the misconduct of the defendant, culpable or otherwise, is not less than their market value. Market value may be identified, where appropriate, with the reasonable cost of a license'; and § 51, Comment a: 'the unjust enrichment of tortfeasors without fault – such as innocent converters or trespassers, or unwitting infringers – is . . . measured by the rule of § 51(2)'.

price. In effect, the law on restitution for wrongs is being used here as a disguised form of recovery for failure of consideration.

§ 43 makes it clear that remedies aimed at making a fiduciary disgorge the gains that he has made as a result of a breach of fiduciary duty will be available even if the breach was inadvertent.[16]

R3RUE does not allow disgorgement damages (or analogous remedies) to be awarded against someone who inadvertently commits a proprietary tort.[17] In taking this stand, R3RUE is stricter than English law, which does allow someone whose property has been converted by selling it to someone else to sue for the proceeds of the conversion, even if the defendant who converted the property acted innocently.[18] However, consider the following example, from § 51, Illustration 20:

> Tenant plants millet in June; his lease expires in August; Landlord harvests the crop in September at a cost of $10,000 and sells it for $50,000. Tenant sues Landlord in restitution, alleging conversion of the millet crop. The court decides the controversy – a close question under local property law – in favor of Tenant. Because Landlord is not regarded as a conscious wrongdoer, his harvesting expenses of $10,000 are properly deducted in determining his liability for net profits of $40,000. (If Tenant's crop had been harvested and sold by a thief, the thief would be liable for $50,000 in proceeds without deduction.)

Here it looks like Landlord *is* being held liable to pay disgorgement damages even though he acted innocently in selling Tenant's crop. The fact that he can reduce his liability by $10,000 – the value of his harvesting expenses – does not turn his liability into a liability to pay Tenant licence fee damages. An elegant explanation of why Landlord can reduce his liability to Tenant by $10,000 when the thief cannot is that Landlord is entitled to a defence of change of position to Tenant's claim against him for disgorgement damages, while the thief is not. The relevant provisions of R3RUE (§ 65) are silent on the issue of whether an innocent wrongdoer can take advantage of a defence of change of position,[19] but § 51, Illustration 20 might support the idea that he can,[20] while undermining R3RUE's

[16] § 43, Comments d and h.

[17] See, for example, § 40, Illustration 14: Distiller converts corn worth $50 and makes it into whiskey worth $500. If Distiller is a thief, the owner of the corn can sue for the whiskey. If not, he is limited to a lien over the whiskey for $50. See also § 41, Illustration 13: Wrongdoer misappropriates $10,000 from Owner, gives the money to Donee, and Donee uses the money to purchase 100 shares of XYZ Corp. When the facts come to light, Donee's XYZ shares are worth $25,000. If Donee had notice of the source of the funds, Owner is entitled to ownership of the appreciated stock (via a constructive trust). If Donee had no notice of the misappropriation, Owner's remedy in restitution will be limited to an equitable lien on the stock, securing a claim to $10,000 plus interest. (It is noticeable that no authority is cited in support of this illustration.) See also § 58, Comment i.

[18] *Oughton v Seppings* (1830) 1 B & Ad 241, 109 ER 776.

[19] For discussion of the position in English law on this issue, see E Bant, *The Change of Position Defence* (Oxford, Hart Publishing, 2009) 166–72; and PA Walker, 'Change of Position and Restitution for Wrongs: "Ne'er the Twain Shall Meet"?' (2009) 33 *Melbourne University Law Review* 235.

[20] Against this, compare § 51, Illustration 4, where A innocently burns coal that has been stolen from C, and sold to him by B for $5 per ton. A could have got an equivalent supply of coal from D for $5.50 per ton, so using C's coal saves him $5.50 per ton. Despite this, A is held liable for $6 per ton, which is the market value of C's coal at the time he burns it. Illustration 5 says that a different result

position that so far as proprietary torts are concerned, disgorgement is only available against someone who *consciously* violates another's proprietary rights.

(b) Licence Fee Damages

There is no fault requirement for the award of such damages. They will be available against an innocent wrongdoer and as an alternative remedy to disgorgement damages against a conscious wrongdoer.[21] As such, they fix a '*minimum* liability in restitution . . . most often pertinent in cases involving conscious wrongdoers, but [also applying] to any case in which enrichment results from misconduct, with or without culpability, on the part of the defendant'.[22]

There are three cases where licence fee damages will *not* be available against a wrongdoer. First of all, where the wrong consists in the breach of a fiduciary duty, the remedy will be disgorgement of the benefit that the fiduciary has obtained that has put him in breach of his fiduciary duty.

Second, the 'slayer rule' operates simply to prevent someone who has committed an unlawful homicide benefiting from that homicide: it does not impose on him a liability to pay a reasonable sum for killing the victim of his homicide.

Third, § 39 provides that gain-based damages will only be available in a breach of contract case where 'a deliberate breach of contract results in profit to the defaulting promisor' and in such a case 'the promisee [will have] a claim to restitution of the profit realized by the promisor as a result of the breach'. So the only measure of damages that will be available in a breach of contract case is disgorgement damages.[23] It follows that had *Experience Hendrix LLC v PPX Enterprises Ltd*[24] been decided under R3RUE, Jimi Hendrix's estate would have been entitled to sue the defendants in that case for the profits they had made as a result of marketing recordings made by Hendrix, in breach of their contract with Hendrix's estate. The actual remedy that the estate was awarded – 'reasonable payment for [the defendants'] use of masters in breach of the settlement agreement'[25] – would not be available under R3RUE.[26]

would be reached if B sells coal to C and mistakenly delivers it to A. A burns the coal, saving himself $5.50 per ton which he would otherwise have had to pay to D for coal. His liability is limited to $5.50 per ton. But surely A is an innocent converter of the coal in Illustration 2 just as much as he is in Illustration 1? As such, his liability should be the same in both cases.

[21] For a situation where disgorgement and licence fee damages are available as alternatives, see § 42, Illustration 3. Manufacturer wrongfully exploits the results of research carried out by Professors to obtain a patent, which Manufacturer exploits. R3RUE says that on Professors' suit, they will be able to obtain a money judgment against Manufacturer, measured 'as the court finds appropriate, by the amount Manufacturer would have paid to acquire the rights [to exploit Professors' research], or by the profits it has derived from exploitation of the patent'.

[22] § 51, Comment d (emphasis added).

[23] § 39 is the only provision in R3RUE that deals with the availability of gain-based damages in breach of contract cases. § 44 (the catch-all provision) is carefully framed *not* to apply to cases involving breach of 'a duty imposed by contract': § 44(2).

[24] *Experience Hendrix LLC v PPX Enterprises Ltd* [2003] EWCA Civ 323, [2003] 1 All ER (Comm) 830.

[25] ibid [42].

[26] Compare § 39, Illustration 11: Developer agrees to build no more than 100 houses on land sold to him by Landowner. He builds 120, with a profit of $200,000. Landowner would have agreed to permit

(4) The Relevance of Other Remedies

We can split the discussion of this issue into two groups: (a) cases where the *presence* of another remedy will knock out the possibility of bringing a claim for gain-based damages; and (b) cases where the *absence* of another remedy will knock out the possibility of bringing a claim for gain-based damages.

(a) Presence of Another Remedy

The general rule under R3RUE is that the fact that the claimant has another remedy against a defendant will not prevent him suing the defendant for gain-based damages.[27]

§ 39 creates the sole – and very important – exception to this general rule. § 39 provides that disgorgement damages will *only* be available against someone who commits a deliberate breach of contract if 'the available damage remedy affords inadequate protection to the promisee's contractual entitlement'.[28]

So, for example, § 39, Illustration 15 presents a case where Farmer contractually agrees to sell his entire crop of wheat to A at $5 a bushel, but takes advantage of a sudden rise in wheat prices to sell his crop to B at $10 a bushel. By the time A discovers the breach, prices have settled back to $6 a bushel. R3RUE says that A will not be entitled to sue Farmer for disgorgement damages here, as a remedy of $1 a bushel in compensatory damages will fully protect his contractual entitlement to wheat at $5 a bushel.

In contrast, in Illustration 7, the Firefighters' Association skimps on the level of fire services that it has contractually agreed to provide City, saving $100,000 over the lifetime of its contract with City without in any way prejudicing its ability to put out the fires that break out in the city during the lifetime of the contract. Under R3RUE, City is entitled to disgorgement damages of $100,000 as a normal, compensatory remedy for breach of contract would not give City anything, it having suffered no loss as a result of the Association's breach.[29]

additional construction of 20 houses for $20,000. R3RUE says that Landowner should be entitled to sue Developer for $200,000 and not $20,000. The accompanying Reporter's Note e states that the remedy in the equivalent English case of *Wrotham Park Estate Co v Parkside Homes Ltd* [1974] 1 WLR 798 (Ch) was 'incorrectly' limited to 'such a sum of money as might reasonably have been demanded by the plaintiffs . . . as a quid pro quo for relaxing the covenant'.

[27] See § 3, Comment c: '"inadequacy of a remedy at law" is not a requirement of a claim in restitution to disgorgement of wrongful gain'.

[28] For criticism of this limit on awards of disgorgement damages for a deliberate breach of contract, see CL Roberts, 'The Restitution Revival and the Ghosts of Equity' (2011) 68 *Washington and Lee Law Review* 1027.

[29] Having said that, it strikes me that in a number of the illustrations where – according to R3RUE – disgorgement would be allowed against a contract breaker, an action for normal, compensatory damages for losses arising out of the breach of contract would provide a meaningful remedy. See § 39, Illustrations 1 (contract for sale of Blackacre for $100,000; Blackacre sold to third party for $110,000), 2 (contract for sale of Blackacre (including timber and gravel) for $100,000; vendor removes timber and gravel and sells for a net gain of $10,000), 5 (Mining Company undertakes to restore Landowner's land to its former state after it has been stripmined; it would cost $25,000 to restore the land) and 6

(b) Absence of Another Remedy

The fact that the victim of a wrong will not be able to obtain another remedy against the wrongdoer may, for R3RUE, be a reason for refusing to allow the victim to sue for gain-based damages. § 44(3) specifies that restitution under the catch-all provision set out in § 44(1) will be 'limited or denied . . . if the court would refuse to enjoin' the wrongful conduct that is the basis of the claimant's claim 'assuming timely application and an absence of procedural or administrative obstacles'.

As an example of this rule in action, § 44, Illustration 15, provides us with a case where a Meatpacking Plant's failure to treat its wastewater adequately results in Neighbor's land being polluted. Neighbor sues for an injunction, but this is denied as the effect of the pollution on his land is relatively trivial and the inconvenience to the Plant of putting in place a new wastewater treatment facility would be large. Alternatively, Neighbor seeks to make the Plant disgorge the money it has saved by not treating its wastewater adequately. This should be denied, R3RUE says, as allowing Neighbor to sue for the 'saved cost of abatement would be inequitable [given that] the court has refused, on equitable grounds, to order abatement itself'. The prejudice that the court has tried to save Plant from by not ordering it to install a new wastewater treatment facility would be inflicted on Plant in another way if it had to hand over to Neighbor the money it has saved by not installing that facility. Therefore, Neighbor will be entitled to sue Plant for licence fee damages instead.

(5) The Position of Third Parties

One of the most difficult aspects of R3RUE's provisions on restitution for wrongs is that, in many cases, a defendant can be liable under these provisions even if he himself is not a wrongdoer: it will be enough if he has, in fact, obtained a benefit as a result of a wrong committed by *someone else.*

So, § 40 provides that: 'A person who obtains a benefit by an act of trespass or conversion, by comparable interference with other protected interests in tangible property, *or in consequence of such an act by another*, is liable in restitution to the victim of the wrong.'[30]

§ 41 provides that: 'A person who obtains a benefit by misappropriating financial assets, *or in consequence of their misappropriation by another*, is liable in restitution to the victim of the wrong.'[31]

§ 42 provides that: 'A person who obtains a benefit by misappropriation or infringement of another's legally protected rights in any idea, expression, information, image or designation is liable in restitution to the holder of such rights.'

(breach of a non-compete agreement, resulting in Seller who has sold his business to Buyer for $500,000 making profits of $50,000).

[30] Emphasis added.

[31] Emphasis added.

The fact that the words 'misappropriation' and 'infringement' are used here, instead of the words 'misappropriating' and 'infringing' may indicate that the rule of liability under § 42 is meant to apply even in cases when a third party benefits from someone else's misappropriation or infringement of the claimant's intellectual property.

§ 43 provides that: 'A person who obtains a benefit . . . (c) *in consequence of another's breach* of [a fiduciary duty or an equivalent duty imposed by a relationship of trust and confidence] is liable in restitution to the person to whom the duty is owed'.[32]

§ 44 provides that: 'A person who obtains a benefit by conscious interference with a claimant's legally protected interests (*or in consequence of such interference by another*) is liable in restitution as necessary to prevent unjust enrichment, unless competing legal objectives make such liability in appropriate.'[33]

It is hard to avoid the impression that these provisions on third party liability have been drafted with one eye on the proprietary effects that committing a wrong in relation to someone else can have. For example, in § 41, Illustration 1, Thief steals $10,000 from Owner and uses $4,000 of it to purchase a car. Facing prosecution for theft, Thief retains Lawyer to defend him and transfers title to the car as Lawyer's fee. R3RUE provides that if Lawyer has notice of Owner's claim, and so is not a bona fide purchaser, Owner has a claim against Lawyer to restitution of the car (typically via a constructive trust). There is no problem with this: orthodox tracing rules would indicate that Owner has a claim over the car which will be good against anyone except a bona fide purchaser.

If the provisions in §§ 40–44 that deal with the liability of third parties who benefit from another's wrong were inserted to take account of the proprietary effects that wronging someone else can have, this might explain why the *only* person who can be held liable under § 39 is the contract breaker. A third party who objectively benefits from a breach of contract will not be held liable under § 39. So, for example, suppose that in § 39, Illustration 7,[34] the Firefighters' Association took the $100,000 it saved from skimping on its contract with City and donated the money to the families of members of the Firefighters' Association who had died in the line of action. No claim in restitution will be available against the families under § 39, as there is simply no basis for arguing that the $100,000 they received belongs to the City. That money always belonged to the Firefighters' Association and City had no proprietary interest in it.

However, the difficulty is that §§ 40–44, as drafted, give rise to the suggestion that claims *can* be brought under those sections against third parties in situations where there is no possibility of arguing that the third parties have received property that belongs to the claimant. The fact that the third party has benefited from some wrong done to the claimant is enough for liability to arise under §§ 40–44.

[32] Emphasis added.
[33] Emphasis added.
[34] See text to n 29.

For example, § 40, Illustration 8 provides us with a case where B, the owner of Whiteacre, has a right as against A, the owner of Blackacre, that no building be constructed on Blackacre that would obstruct the view of Whiteacre from the highway. A leases Blackacre to C and gives C permission to construct a building that would have the effect of blocking the view of Whiteacre from the highway. After the building is completed, R3RUE says that B will be allowed to sue A for the extra rental income that was obtained as a result of giving C permission to construct the building.

But what about C? § 40, as drafted, raises the possibility that B could sue C for whatever benefits he has obtained from constructing the building on Blackacre. It might be objected that the wrong that has been done to B here involves obstructing the view of Whiteacre from the highway, and C is not actually benefiting from the fact that people's view of Whiteacre from the highway is being obstructed. But what if he is? What if B's interest in people being able to see Whiteacre from the highway lies in the fact that he has a hotel on Whiteacre that people driving along the highway will see and decide to use for the night? And what if the building C has constructed on Blackacre was another hotel – which passers-by use because they cannot now see B's hotel from the highway? It is hard to understand why C should be accountable to B in this scenario for the extra profits he makes from running his hotel that are attributable to the fact that drivers on the highway cannot now see B's hotel from the highway, but that is the potential effect of § 40.

Again, in § 44, Illustration 11, a doctor extracts blood cells from a patient for testing. He recognises that the cells are unusually valuable for research and sells samples to researchers for $25,000. As the cells do not count as property that the patient has an immediate right to possess, the doctor does not convert the cells in selling them to the researchers. However, he does commit a wrong to the patient under local laws requiring a doctor to tell his patient what he is doing to the patient and to obtain the patient's informed consent to what he is doing. The doctor's infringement of those local laws warrants the patient being allowed to sue the doctor under § 44 to make him disgorge the gain he has made from that infringement – that is, $25,000.

But what about the researchers? What if work on the cells results in a researcher obtaining a patent, the exploitation of which makes him a multi-millionaire? As the cells that the researcher was using never belonged to the patient, orthodox tracing rules would not warrant our finding that the patient has any kind of interest in the patent obtained as a result of the work done on those cells. But § 44, as drafted, opens the door to the patient making some sort of claim for gain-based damages against our multi-millionaire researcher on the basis that he has obtained a benefit as a consequence of the patient's doctor infringing the patient's legally protected interests. In order to make such a claim, the patient would simply have to show that had he been asked, he would not have consented to his cells being used for research purposes. If he can show this, then a causal chain between the researcher's millions and the doctor's wrong would be established that would seem to entitle the patient to make a claim for gain-based damages against the researcher.

The examples in the previous two paragraphs are of cases where the way in which the provisions in R3RUE on restitution for wrongs have been drafted creates the potential that these provisions will misfire and hold a third party liable in situations where no liability was (probably) intended. However, one situation where R3RUE makes it clear that a third party beneficiary of a wrong *should* be held liable for the benefit he has received, even though that benefit cannot be said to take the form of property that belongs to someone else, is provided by § 45, Illustration 18.

In this scenario, T's current will leaves his $3 million estate to A and B. T proposes to make a new will leaving $500,000 to C. To prevent T from doing this, A murders T. A is barred from inheriting under the 'slayer rule', and so T's entire estate goes to B. The commentary on the Illustration goes on to note that a 'further effect of A's crime is . . . the unjust enrichment of B at the expense of C. Not being a slayer, B is not liable [under § 45]; but B still holds $500,000 in constructive trust for C'. This trust arises under § 46, which provides that:

> If assets that would otherwise have passed by donative transfer to the claimant are diverted to another recipient by duress, fraud, undue influence, or other intentional misconduct, the recipient is liable to the claimant for unjust enrichment. The misconduct that invalidates the transfer to the recipient may be the act of the recipient or of a third person.

I doubt very much whether it would be correct to apply § 46 to hold B liable in Illustration 18. T was only *proposing* to make a new will leaving $500,000 to C. As a result of this, it is hard to say – as § 46 requires to be shown – that had A not murdered T, the $500,000 received by B *would* have gone to C instead. As Lionel Smith has observed, 'intending something does not make it a certainty . . . intentions are often frustrated'.[35] Who knows what would have happened had A not murdered T? Maybe T would have changed his mind and left the old will in place. Maybe he would have made a new will and then later replaced it with a further will, under which C would have received nothing. It seems very difficult to justify stripping B of some of the money to which he is legally entitled on the basis of thoughts that T had in his head at the time he was murdered.

C. Discussion

The above is sufficient to set out the essential provisions of R3RUE on restitution for wrongs. In the second part of this chapter, I will discuss whether these provisions are justifiable. Let's begin by examining R3RUE's provisions on disgorgement damages.

[35] L Smith, 'Three-Party Restitution: A Critique of Birks' Theory of Interceptive Subtraction' (1991) 11 *OJLS* 481, 511.

(1) Disgorgement Damages

(a) R3RUE's Arguments for Awarding Disgorgement Damages

The principal argument that R3RUE makes in favour of awards of disgorgement damages being made is what we can call the *Dangerous Incentives* argument. The argument is best set out in § 3, Comment c:

> Restitution requires full disgorgement of profit by a conscious wrongdoer . . . because any lesser liability would provide an inadequate incentive to lawful behaviour. If A anticipates (accurately) that unauthorised interference with B's entitlement may yield profits exceeding any damages B could prove, A has a dangerous incentive to take without asking – since the nonconsensual transaction promises to be more profitable than the foregone negotiation with B. The objective of that part of the law of restitution summarized by the rule of § 3 is to frustrate any such calculation.

The *Dangerous Incentives* argument explains why R3RUE is not in favour of awards of licence fee damages being made against someone who has committed an opportunistic breach of contract:

> The purpose of the disgorgement remedy for breach of contract is to eliminate the possibility that an intentional and opportunistic breach will be more profitable to the performing party than negotiation with the party to whom performance is owed. For this reason 'profit realized . . . as a result of the breach' includes the gains that motivated the promisor's decision to breach the contract. If the defendant's liability in restitution were limited to the amount that might have been paid to obtain the necessary contractual modification in a voluntary transaction, there would be inadequate incentive to bargain over the entitlement in question.[36]

R3RUE backs this point up with § 39, Illustration 11, in which Developer agrees to build no more than 100 houses on land sold to him by Landowner. In fact, Developer builds 120, making a profit of $200,000 on the extra houses. Landowner would have agreed to permit the additional construction of 20 houses for $20,000. R3RUE would hold Developer liable to surrender the full $200,000 profit that he has made from constructing the extra houses, remarking that:

> If Developer's liability in restitution were limited to the $20,000 that would have been paid in a voluntary transaction, a party disposed to breach in these circumstances would have inadequate incentive to bargain over a release from the covenant.

For the same reason, R3RUE insists that in a case where a defendant has wrongfully disposed of the claimant's property, the claimant should have the option of suing the defendant for disgorgement damages and not be limited to suing the defendant for a reasonable sum for what the defendant did with the claimant's property:

[36] § 39, Comment e.

> Enrichment resulting from intentional trespass is not properly measured by ordinary rental value. A conscious wrongdoer will not be left on a parity with a person who – pursuing the same objectives – respects the legally protected rights of the property owner. If liability in restitution were limited to the price that would have been paid in a voluntary exchange, the calculating wrongdoer would have no incentive to bargain.[37]
>
> Because a liability limited to the use value of the claimant's property would prove inadequate incentive to bargain over the rights at issue, restitution authorizes the disgorgement of profits in all cases of conscious wrongdoing.[38]

Unfortunately for the *Dangerous Incentives* argument, *exactly the same objection* that R3RUE makes to confining a claimant to suing a defendant for licence fee damages can *also* be made against confining the claimant to suing the defendant for disgorgement damages, at least in cases where the claimant would never have agreed to allow the defendant to do what he did.

Take the example considered by Mance LJ in the *Experience Hendrix* case, where Farmer puts on a pop concert on his land, in breach of a restrictive covenant that exists for the benefit of Posh's neighbouring country estate.[39] Posh is out of the country at the time of the concert and suffers no harm as a result of the concert being put on. R3RUE rightly points out that confining Posh to suing Farmer for a reasonable sum for being allowed to hold the concert on his land does not give Farmer enough of an incentive to negotiate with Posh. Farmer will think: 'Why should I bother negotiating with Posh to get his permission to relax the covenant? If I get caught, the worst that can happen is that I will end up paying Posh exactly what I would have paid him anyway if I had negotiated with him.'

R3RUE argues that we will only give Farmer an adequate incentive to come to the negotiating table if we threaten him that if he does not, we will allow Posh to sue Farmer for the profits he makes by putting on the concert. This is true *if Posh is willing to negotiate.* But if Farmer knows that Posh will take an 'over my dead body' approach to any proposal that a concert be held on Farmer's land, allowing Posh to sue Farmer for disgorgement damages will *not* be sufficient to discourage Farmer from holding a concert on his land. Farmer will think: 'There's no point in negotiating with Posh and alerting him to my plans. I might as well go ahead. The worst that can happen if I get caught is that I'll have to hand over my profits to Posh. But if that happens, I'll be no worse off than I am now. On the other hand, I might not get caught, and even if Posh does find out what I did, he might not want to sue given how expensive and risky litigation can be. So overall, I don't really have any reason not to go ahead and hold the concert while Posh is away.'

The law could try to give Farmer a reason not to go ahead with his plans by threatening that if he does, he will be liable for *all* of the money he takes at the gate, with no discount or allowance being made for the expenses he incurs in putting on the concert. Making Farmer liable for what we might call *gross disgorgement damages* will threaten to turn holding the concert without Posh's permission

[37] § 40, Comment b.
[38] § 42, Comment g.
[39] *Experience Hendrix* (n 24) [35].

into a losing option for him, and might give him pause for thought about whether he should go ahead with his plans to hold the concert. R3RUE does contemplate that gross disgorgement damages might be awarded against a conscious wrongdoer,[40] but is uneasy about awarding such damages and goes out of its way to deny that gross disgorgement damages can be awarded generally against a conscious wrongdoer.[41] The reason for this is plain enough. Gross disgorgement damages are not really targeted at making Farmer disgorge the gain he makes from holding his concert; their real aim is to discourage Farmer from holding his concert by threatening him with a 'punitive sanction'[42] for violating Posh's rights. But if we regard it as legitimate to protect Posh's rights by threatening Farmer with such a sanction, then why not straightforwardly threaten him with an award of *exemplary* damages?

R3RUE acknowledges that in order to ensure that someone who is thinking about committing a wrong is properly deterred from doing so, the courts may *supplement* an award of disgorgement damages with an award of exemplary damages.[43] But in a case where the claimant would never have agreed to allow the defendant to do what he did, it is not clear why – if deterrence is our goal – we should have to go through the rigmarole of first awarding damages to the claimant that have no deterrence value *at all* before we award the claimant damages that *are* explicitly designed to discourage someone who is thinking of violating someone's rights by threatening him with the prospect that if he does so, he will be left worse off as a result.[44] It is the equivalent of going to the doctor with a

[40] See § 40, Illustration 1: A and B hold mining leases on adjoining tracts; A removes coal from B's tract; if the removal was deliberate, A is liable for money he makes from selling B's coal, with no credit for the costs of extraction and transportation.

[41] See § 42, Comment i and Illustration 22; § 43, Comment h.

[42] See § 42, Illustration 22. D produces and sells a distinctive line of goods that infringes P's trademark. D supplies evidence of increased general and administrative expenses attributable to its sales of the infringing goods. P's argument that a deduction for 'overhead' ought not to be allowed in a case of deliberate infringement is 'wrong in principle. The disallowance of any proven item of expense – assuming its relevance to the calculation of net profits – would transform an "accounting for profits" into a punitive sanction, increasing the award of profits by a fine of arbitrary amount'.

[43] See § 51, Comment k: 'Precisely because disgorgement, in theory at least, imposes no net loss on the defendant, there are situations in which a court may conclude that the threat of liability to disgorge profits will not adequately deter the misconduct revealed by the case before it. A court that reaches this conclusion will sometimes supplement the defendant's liability in restitution with an award of exemplary damages. See Illustration 26.' Illustration 26 is a case where Agent invests Client's funds in a real estate transaction that 'is structured in such a way that Agent will take any profits while Client will bear any losses'. After the facts come to light, Agent is held liable for the profits he has made on the transaction, but the 'court concludes . . . that a potential liability to disgorge profits in those cases where such a fraud might be detected is insufficient, by itself, to deter the misconduct in which Agent has engaged' and awards exemplary damages on top. The accompanying Reporter's Note k remarks that Illustration 26 is based on *Ward v Taggart*, 51 Cal 2d 736, 336 P 2d 534 (1959), in which the court said: 'Courts award exemplary damages to discourage oppression, fraud, or malice by punishing the wrongdoer . . . Such damages are appropriate in cases like the present one, where restitution would have little or no deterrent effect, for wrongdoers would run no risk of liability to their victims beyond that of returning what they wrongfully obtained.'

[44] It should be noted that certain restitution scholars' attempts to claim that awards of exemplary damages under the second head in *Rookes v Barnard* [1964] AC 1129 are really gain-based in nature threaten to emasculate completely any deterrent effect that such awards might have. This is because if

headache and being told to hop on one leg for a minute and then take some paracetamol. If we genuinely want to cure our headache, we should forget about hopping on one leg and go straight to the paracetamol.

So the *Dangerous Incentives* argument only works to support the award of disgorgement damages in a case where a defendant wrongs a claimant by doing something that the claimant would have allowed the defendant to do (in return for some consideration) had he been asked in the first place. In a case where that condition – the *hypothetical consent condition* – is not satisfied, the *Dangerous Incentives* argument indicates that awarding disgorgement damages against the defendant will not be enough and that we should instead make an award of exemplary damages against him. If this is right, then it blows a considerable hole in R3RUE's provisions on when disgorgement damages may be awarded against a defendant, as virtually all of these provisions are based on the *Dangerous Incentives* argument[45] and it is hard to imagine that the *hypothetical consent condition* will be fulfilled in all, or even most, of the cases covered by those provisions.

If this hole is to be filled, it can only be done by going beyond the *Dangerous Incentives* argument and considering other arguments for allowing a claimant to sue a defendant for disgorgement damages.

(b) Alternative Arguments for Awarding Disgorgement Damages

There is one really bad argument that is often made in favour of awards of disgorgement damages against wrongdoers generally. The argument is that: 'People should not be allowed to profit from their wrongs.' This is a terrible argument because it is really an assertion masquerading as an argument.

Suppose that A has committed a wrong in relation to B and made £100,000 as a result. Arguing that A should be made to give up the £100,000 because 'People should not be allowed to profit from their wrongs' gives rise to the following unprofitable exchange. 'But why shouldn't A be allowed to keep the £100,000?' 'Because A is a wrongdoer.' 'But why does that mean that A should have to give up the £100,000?' 'Because people should not be allowed to profit from their wrongs.' 'But why shouldn't people like A be allowed to profit from their wrongs?' 'Because they shouldn't.'

We need an argument as to *why* people should not be allowed to profit from their wrongs, not an assertion that it is simply the case that people should not be

such awards are genuinely gain-based, they should be limited to the gain made by the wrongdoer, with the result that they cannot deter a putative wrongdoer from going ahead with his plans. It is sad to note that in *Borders v Commissioner of Police of the Metropolis* [2005] EWCA Civ 197, [2005] Po LR 1 and *AT v Dulghieru* [2009] EWHC 225 (QB), the courts accepted the restitutionary analysis of awards of exemplary damages under the second head in *Rookes v Barnard*; a rare example of an argument about classification within private law turning out to have positively anti-social effects.

[45] The exception is disgorgement awards under § 43 (for breach of fiduciary duty) which – being available even against innocent wrongdoers – are not based on the *Dangerous Incentives* argument but on the prophylactic aim of preventing the fiduciary getting into a position where he may end up breaching his duty to his principal. See § 43, Comments d and h. This basis for making a fiduciary disgorge a gain that he has made is discussed further below: text to nn 56–60.

allowed to profit from their wrongs. I have never heard anyone make a good argument as to why wrongdoers *generally* should not be allowed to profit from their wrongs. However, it seems to me that a number of good arguments can be made as to why *particular* wrongdoers should not be allowed to profit from their wrongs. Let's have a look at these arguments.

(i) Institutional Arguments

In his article 'Restitution for Wrongs', Ian Jackman argued that:

> [T]he rationale for the right to restitution for wrongs is the protection of a variety of private legal facilities, or facilitative institutions, namely private property, relationships of trust and confidence, and . . . contracts. Such facilities require protection against those who seek to take the benefits of an institution without submitting to the burdens thereof, and in this way the right to restitution for a wrong is triggered not by harm to a person as such, but by harm to an institution.[46]

The idea that restitution for wrongs can work to prevent harm being done to an institution is unpromising insofar as it is applied to the 'institutions' (if such they are) of private property, or relationships of trust and confidence and contracts: (1) it is not clear how someone's committing (say) a breach of contract can damage the 'institution' of contracting; and (2) even if it does, it is not clear how restitution for wrongs can discourage this sort of damage occurring, given that awards of disgorgement damages have very little deterrent effect.

However, I do think that Jackman's idea has a lot going for it if it is applied to other institutions. For example, I think that (with one qualification) the 'slayer rule' can be justified on institutional grounds. The *Dangerous Incentives* argument cannot work to justify the 'slayer rule'. This is not only because making some disgorge a gain that they have made from their wrong cannot deter them from committing that wrong, as they might hope to get away with their wrongful conduct and retain the gain, it is also because – as R3RUE makes clear – the 'slayer rule' 'requires no showing that the crime was committed for economic motives'.[47] As such, the rule will operate even in cases where the prospect of obtaining some benefit from killing V did not provide D with a 'dangerous incentive' to kill V. But an institutional explanation does provide a good explanation of the 'slayer rule'.

The 'slayer rule' can be justified as attempting to ensure that people are punished equally for committing the same crimes. If A and B have each committed the same kind of homicide offence, and A has made a gain as a result of committing his homicide while B has not, giving A and B the same punishment for their crimes will not result in them being punished equally. The gain A has made will serve to mitigate his punishment and lessen its felt severity. The only way to ensure that A and B suffer equally for their crimes is to strip A of the gain he has made from committing his crime.

[46] Ian Jackman, 'Restitution for Wrongs' (1989) 48 *CLJ* 302, 302.

[47] § 45, Comment a. The same is true in English law: *Dunbar v Plant* [1998] Ch 412 (CA).

Seen in this way, the 'slayer rule' upholds the integrity of the institution of criminal punishment – as would a wider rule requiring those who have been convicted of a criminal offence to disgorge any gains they have made from committing their crime.[48] However, it must be admitted that the 'slayer rule', as set out in R3RUE, applies much more widely than this institutional justification of the rule would allow. This is because R3RUE insists that: 'Application of the slayer rule does not require that the slayer be convicted of a crime.'[49] My institutional justification of the 'slayer rule' suggests that the rule should *only* apply in cases where D has been criminally convicted and punished for killing V. It is only in this event that there is a need to strip D of any gain that he has made as a result of killing V, so that he will feel the full severity of the punishment for his crime.

(ii) Tracing Arguments

Let's consider the situation where D receives £5,000 that has been stolen from C and uses the money to buy shares that are now worth £10,000. A number of arguments have been made in favour of the view that C can sue D for the value of the shares, with the effect that D is made to disgorge the gain he has obtained as a result of dealing with C's money:

(a) Ross Grantham and Charles Rickett argue that C has a right to sue D for the value of the shares because the shares belong to C, and they belong to him because they represent the proceeds of money that belonged to C.[50] On this view, ownership of property not only gives you rights over that property, but also rights over the proceeds of that property, in the same way that ownership of an apple tree gives you rights over the apples that come from the apple tree.
(b) Peter Birks argued that C has a right to sue D for the value of the shares because he can claim that that value has come into D's hands from C, and it has done so without C's consent.[51] C can argue that the value of the shares in

[48] A rule which is given effect in English law by the Proceeds of Crime Act 2002. For a particularly clear account of the provisions of this complex Act, see A Eissa and R Barber, *Confiscation Law Handbook* (Haywards Heath, Bloomsbury Professional, 2011).

[49] § 45, Comment a. *Re Dellow's Will Trusts* [1964] 1 WLR 451 (Ch) is to the same effect. In that case, a husband and wife were found dead from coal gas poisoning. Ungoed-Thomas J found that the wife had killed the husband and prevented her estate from inheriting under the husband's will. See also pt V of the Proceeds of Crime Act 2002, which allows civil actions to make people disgorge the proceeds of their 'criminal' lifestyle even if they have not actually been convicted of any crime.

[50] R Grantham and C Rickett, 'Tracing and Property Rights: The Categorical Truth' (2000) 63 *MLR* 905; and 'Disgorgement for Unjust Enrichment?' (2003) 62 *CLJ* 159, 171–73.

[51] P Birks, 'Unjust Enrichment and Wrongful Enrichment' (2001) 79 *Texas Law Review* 1767, 1782 and 1785; '"At the Expense of the Claimant": Direct and Indirect Enrichment in English Law' in D Johnston and R Zimmermann (eds), *Unjustified Enrichment: Key Issues in Comparative Perspective* (Cambridge, Cambridge University Press, 2002) 509–10; and *Unjust Enrichment*, 2nd edn (Oxford, Oxford University Press, 2005) 82-86. For criticisms of Birks' analysis, see JE Penner, 'Value, Property and Unjust Enrichment: Trusts of Traceable Proceeds' in R Chambers, C Mitchell and JE Penner (eds), *Philosophical Foundations of the Law of Unjust Enrichment* (Oxford, Oxford University Press, 2009), and P Millett, '*Jones v Jones*: Property or Unjust Enrichment?' in A Burrows and Lord Rodger of Earlsferry (eds), *Mapping the Law: Essays in Honour of Peter Birks* (Oxford, Oxford University Press, 2006).

D's hands has come from him because the 'earning opportunity' inherent in his original £5,000 belonged to him, and so anything that has been acquired as a result of taking advantage of that opportunity has come from C. On this view, C's right to sue D for the value of the shares arises to prevent D being unjustly enriched at C's expense.

(c) Arthur Ripstein argues that C has a right to sue D for the value of the shares because the wrong that D has committed against C in dealing with his money is that D used that money for his own purposes, not C's.[52] In order to rectify this wrong, the law must make it as though that money was used for C's purposes. The only way to do this is to treat D as though he was dealing with C's money on C's behalf, and not his – with the result that the shares obtained by dealing with that money are treated as though they are C's, not D's. On this view, C's right to sue D for the value of the shares arises to rectify the wrong that D committed by using C's money to buy those shares in the first place.

It is possible to get so hung up on the differences between these views that one overlooks what they agree on: that C has a right to sue D for the value of the shares *irrespective* of whether D acted innocently or was at fault in dealing with C's money. All the above arguments agree that it is the *bare* fact that it was C's money that was used to buy the shares that gives C a right to sue D for the value of those shares.

Of course, R3RUE takes a different view, arguing that C can only sue D for the value of the shares in a case where the *Dangerous Incentives* argument applies. This, in turn, means that C can only sue D for the value of the shares (as opposed to the value of his original £5,000 that went into the shares) if D consciously did something wrong in dealing with C's money.[53] But for R3RUE's position to be correct, it would have to be shown that *all* of the arguments set out in (a)–(c) above are incorrect. This seems very unlikely. It is much more likely to be true that we can explain why C is entitled to sue D for the value of the shares that he bought with C's money without having to rely on the *Dangerous Incentives* argument.

(iii) The argument from the existence of anti-enrichment wrongs

In his *Introduction to the Law of Restitution*, Peter Birks suggested that disgorgement would be an appropriate response to someone committing an 'anti-enrichment' wrong.[54] He later gave up on the idea that it was possible to classify wrongs as either being 'anti-enrichment' or 'anti-harm' in nature.[55] I think the idea that there can be such a thing as an 'anti-enrichment' wrong is a useful one. Birks' problem was that he tried to make the idea do too much work, and when it proved unserviceable for all the work he wanted to make it do, he abandoned it. It is time to bring it back.

[52] A Ripstein, 'As If It Had Never Happened' (2007) 48 *William & Mary Law Review* 1957, 1991–95.
[53] See n 17.
[54] P Birks, *An Introduction to the Law of Restitution*, revised edn (Oxford, Oxford University Press, 1989) 328–30.
[55] P Birks, *Civil Wrongs: A New World* (London, Butterworths, 1991) 97.

D will commit an 'anti-enrichment' wrong in relation to C if he breaches a duty owed to C not to make a gain of some kind. All such duties seem to be *parasitic* in nature: they arise because D owes C some other kind of duty. These parasitic duties not to make a gain seem to be of two primary kinds.

First, D may owe C a duty not to make a gain of some kind because he is under a primary duty to make that gain for C. This will be the case, for example, where D is employed by C to search out lucrative investment opportunities for C. If D comes across such an opportunity in the course of his employment and takes advantage of it for his own benefit, he will commit an anti-enrichment wrong. D is held liable to give up to C the gain he has made as a way of enforcing the primary duty he owed C to make that gain for C, not himself.

Second, and more commonly, D will sometimes owe C a duty not to make a gain of some kind because the law fears that if D is allowed to make that gain, he *might* be led to breach some other primary duty that he owes C. In such a case, D is said to be a fiduciary for C. Therefore, if D is a fiduciary for C, he will commit an anti-enrichment wrong in relation to C if he makes a gain, the making or retention of which *might* result in D breaching a primary duty that he owes C. D is held liable to give up to C the gain he has made as a way of ensuring that D properly performs the primary duty that he owes C.

Where D is a fiduciary for C, different academics have different views as to: (i) *what* the primary duty is that the law attempts to ensure is properly performed by requiring D not to make a gain for himself; and (ii) *how* D's making a gain for himself might result in D's failing to perform properly the primary duty he owes C.

Lionel Smith argues that: (i) the primary duty D owes C is a (fiduciary) duty to act in *what he perceives* to be C's best interests; and (ii) the law requires D not to make a gain for himself in order to ensure that D *does* act in what he *actually* perceives to be C's best interests and not what he has fooled himself into thinking is in C's best interests because acting in that way is also in D's interests.[56]

Matthew Conaglen argues that: (i) the primary duty D owes C is a (non-fiduciary) duty to act *prudently* in looking after C's affairs; and (ii) the law requires D not to make a gain for himself in order to ensure that D is not *tempted* by the prospect of making that gain into doing something which is not in C's interests.[57]

For myself, I think Conaglen is right on (i), but Smith is closer to the truth on (ii). As Irit Samet has convincingly argued,[58] the reason why the law requires D not to make a gain for himself is to help him make good decisions about how best to administer C's affairs. The law recognises that human beings have a fantastic capacity for rationalisation – for identifying what is in their self-interest with what is the right thing to do. So if D were allowed to make a gain for himself as a result

[56] L Smith, 'The Motive, Not the Deed' in J Getzler (ed), *Rationalizing Property, Equity and Trusts: Essays in Honour of Edward Burn* (London, Butterworths, 2003).

[57] M Conaglen, *Fiduciary Loyalty* (Oxford, Hart Publishing, 2010).

[58] I Samet, 'Guarding the Fiduciary's Conscience: A Justification of a Stringent Profit-Stripping Rule' (2008) 28 *OJLS* 763.

of the decisions he made about (say) how best to invest C's money, he might end up making some very poor decisions about how to invest C's money which he had fooled himself into thinking were great decisions because he actually stood to make a personal gain for making those decisions. It is in order to ensure that D makes investment decisions on C's behalf with a clear head that the law requires D not to make a gain for himself from the decisions he makes.[59]

(2) Licence Fee Damages

(a) R3RUE's Arguments for Awarding Licence Fee Damages

R3RUE nowhere explicitly explains why licence fee damages should ever be awarded against a wrongdoer. However, one can get a sense of why awards of such damages are endorsed by R3RUE from the following passages:

> [E]ven an innocent and inadvertent interference with the claimant's property leads to a liability in restitution for the value of what has been taken, typically measured by the cost of a license.[60]
>
> The minimum liability in restitution for benefits obtained by misconduct is the value of anything wrongfully taken from the claimant, whether or not the taking causes measurable harm to the claimant . . . In the context of intellectual property, what is 'taken' is often an unauthorized use; the value of the use may often be determined – depending on the nature of the property – by a reasonable royalty or by the market price of a license.[61]
>
> Persons such as innocent converters, unconscious trespassers, and unwitting infringers are liable in restitution for the market value of the rights they have 'taken,' if this measure of enrichment exceeds any value actually realized by the defendant.[62]

Passages such as these suggest that R3RUE agrees with James Edelman that awards of licence fee damages are 'restitutionary' in the sense that they give 'back value transferred from a [claimant] to a defendant as a result of a defendant's wrong'.[63] However, this analysis of licence fee damages is very difficult to defend.

The principal difficulty afflicting the 'restitutionary' analysis of licence fee damages is this. In many cases where licence fee damages are routinely awarded, it is hard to see how there has been any *transfer* of value *from the claimant* to the defendant.[64] For example, in the case where A has gone for a ride on B's horse

[59] Conaglen (n 57) recognises (at 72) that the rules against making a gain for oneself as a fiduciary are based on fears about human nature, but goes wrong in identifying the relevant fear as being the fear that people can easily be corrupted by their self-interest into doing the wrong thing. As Irit Samet (n 58) observes, the real fear about human nature that underlies the law on fiduciaries is not that people can be tempted into doing the wrong thing, but that they can fool themselves into thinking that doing the wrong thing is actually the right thing to do.

[60] § 3, Comment e.

[61] § 42, Comment f.

[62] § 51, Comment c.

[63] Edelman (n 10) 66.

[64] See further C Rotherham, 'The Conceptual Structure of Restitution for Wrongs' (2007) 66 *CLJ* 172, 176–83.

without B's permission, one can certainly see that A could be said to have obtained *something* here – the freedom to ride on B's horse. But was that freedom obtained *from B*, so that we can say that that freedom was *transferred from* B *to* A? The more natural analysis is that the freedom A enjoys when he takes a ride on B's horse without B's permission is something that he has *manufactured for himself out of nothing*. As such, it has not been obtained *from anyone*. Edelman acknowledges the objection, but seeks to get round it by arguing that as the horse belongs to B, the freedom to ride on the horse also belongs to B – so when A takes the horse for a ride, the freedom to ride on the horse that he thereby obtains has been taken *from* B.[65]

The restitutionary analysis of awards of licence fee damages against someone who wrongfully appropriates an asset belonging to someone else is preserved at the cost of having to argue that the asset owner not only owns the asset but also the freedom to exploit the use value 'inhering' in that asset. But then what about the case where licence fee damages are awarded against someone who exploits his *own* asset but commits a breach of contract in so doing? For example, let's consider again the case where Farmer commits a breach of a contract that he has with Posh by putting on a pop concert on his (Farmer's) land.[66] Assume that Farmer is held liable to pay Posh a reasonable sum for what he has done. It is hard to see how Farmer can be said to have obtained anything *from Posh* in this situation, the transfer of which can be said to have been reversed through making Farmer pay Posh licence fee damages. Edelman argues that an award of licence fee damages in this kind of case is designed to reverse a wrongful transfer of 'contractual *rights*'.[67] But this is unsustainable. No contract lawyer would say that in a breach of contract case, the claimant's right to performance was transferred to the defendant as a result of the defendant's breach of contract. The claimant's right has been violated; it has not been transferred.

If a restitutionary analysis of licence fee damages as awarded against a contract breaker cannot be supported, there seems little reason why we should analyse awards of such damages against other wrongdoers as being restitutionary in nature. There must be better arguments available to us as to why such damages are awarded.

(b) An Alternative Argument for Awarding Licence Fee Damages[68]

A much better argument in favour of awarding licence fee damages takes as its starting point the observation that not all rights are the same. Some rights are

[65] Edelman (n 10) 67–68, quoting Birks, 'Unjust Enrichment and Wrongful Enrichment' (n 51) 1785.

[66] Discussed above, text to n 24.

[67] Edelman (n 10) 172 (emphasis in original). For an argument that *all* awards of gain-based damages against a contract breaker can be explained on this basis, see A Botterell, 'Contractual Performance, Corrective Justice, and Disgorgement for Breach of Contract' (2010) 16 *Legal Theory* 135.

[68] This section of my chapter owes much to discussions I have had with Jason Varuhas about an as-yet-unpublished paper of his on the nature of vindicatory damages.

designed to secure, or help secure, for us a certain level of material welfare. Other rights are designed to secure, or help secure, for us a certain level of liberty. So, for example, rights arising under the law of negligence can be seen, for the most part, as being welfare-oriented – as designed to help protect us from suffering material damage to our bodies, our minds, our property or our bank balances. In contrast, rights arising under the law of trespass can be seen as being liberty-oriented – as designed to help ensure that we are free to move about and can decide for ourselves who is allowed to touch us and who is not.

The two kinds of rights reflect and protect two different kinds of interests that we have: (i) the interest we have in things going well for us; and (ii) the interest we have in being allowed to determine for ourselves how things go for us. The difference between these two interests is well captured by Tim Mulgan, in discussing John Stuart Mill's work:

> Imagine you are approached by two committees: the *finance committee* offers to manage your money, and the *life committee* offers to run your whole life. Both committees are very experienced . . . Many . . . people would [accept] the first offer and [decline] the second. But why? Isn't life more important than money? . . . Mill's explanation was that a worthwhile life is something you must live *for yourself.* Individuality is essential to a flourishing life.[69]

Our interest in being allowed to determine for ourselves how things go for us is distinct from, and cannot be reduced to, our interest in having things go well for us.

The fact that not all rights are the same means that the law cannot and should not always respond in the same way to the violation of a right. When a welfare-oriented right is violated, it is appropriate to award the claimant compensation for any harm to his material welfare that he has suffered as a result of his right being violated. But when a liberty-oriented right is violated, it would be inappropriate to confine the claimant to suing the defendant for welfare-oriented compensation. As the right that was violated in the claimant's case was geared towards protecting his liberty, he may well not have suffered any material harm to his welfare as a result of that right being violated. However, the claimant will still have lost something – a liberty – that the law thinks he was entitled to have. Therefore, while the claimant may not have suffered any *material* loss as a result of his right being violated, he has still suffered a *normative* loss[70] – a loss not in the real world, but on the plane of the law.

What I want to suggest is that awards of licence fee damages are made in order to help rectify the violation of a liberty-oriented right. They do this by compensating a claimant for the normative loss that he has suffered as a result of one of his liberty-oriented rights being violated. The amount of licence fee damages that the claimant receives reflects the value of the freedom of which he has been deprived as a result of the defendant's wrong.

[69] T Mulgan, *Ethics for a Broken World: Imagining Philosophy After Catastrophe* (Durham, Acumen, 2011) 116 (emphasis in original).

[70] A phrase I owe to Jason Varuhas, though it does also occur in Ernest Weinrib's work.

For example, where A goes for a ride on B's horse without B's permission, he deprives B of a freedom that the law sought to grant him – the freedom to decide for himself who gets to ride on the horse and who doesn't. By allowing B to sue A for licence fee damages, the law seeks to compensate B for the loss of this freedom by giving him an amount of money that reflects the value of being able to say whether or not A could go for a ride on his horse. Similarly, if Farmer breaches a contract that he has with Posh by holding a pop concert on his (Farmer's) land, he deprives Posh of a freedom that the law sought to secure for Posh: the freedom to decide for himself whether or not pop concerts would be held on Farmer's land. If the law allows Posh to sue Farmer for licence fee damages, it does so in order to compensate Posh for the loss of this freedom.

Viewed in this way, licence fee damages are actually compensatory, not gain-based. They focus not on what the defendant has gained by committing his wrong (the freedom to do what he did), but on what the claimant lost when the defendant committed his wrong (the freedom to decide whether or not the defendant would be allowed to do what he did). But licence fee damages are *not* compensatory in the same way that damages in a negligence case are compensatory. They are *not* designed to compensate the claimant for any *material* loss that he has suffered as a result of the defendant's wrong, such as the loss of an opportunity to make some money out of the defendant by charging him for permission to do what he did.[71] What they are designed to do is to compensate the claimant for the intangible, immaterial loss that he has suffered in being deprived of a liberty that the law sought to secure for him.

(c) A Limit on the Availability of Licence Fee Damages

If this argument is correct, then it suggests that there should be an important limit on the availability of licence fee damages (other than that they can only be awarded in cases where a liberty-oriented right has been violated). Where the freedom of which the claimant has been deprived by the defendant's wrong is *beyond value*, the law cannot rectify what the defendant has done by awarding the claimant licence fee damages. In such a case, the claimant cannot be compensated for the loss of the freedom that has been taken from him, and the law should not try to do so. The law needs to respond to the defendant's wrong in some other way; for example, by awarding the claimant *vindicatory* damages that acknowledge that the claimant has been the victim of a wrong that cannot be rectified through an award of some other form of damages.[72]

For example, in a case where A rapes B, it would be inappropriate for the law to allow B to sue A for licence fee damages. The freedom of which A has deprived B by raping her – the freedom to refuse to have sex with A – and which the law sought to secure for B by giving her a liberty-oriented right against A, that he not

[71] RJ Sharpe and SM Waddams, 'Damages for Lost Opportunity to Bargain' (1982) 2 *OJLS* 290; F Giglio, 'Pseudo-Restitutionary Damages' (2009) 22 *Canadian Journal of Law & Jurisprudence* 49.

[72] For further discussion of vindicatory damages, see McBride and Bagshaw (n 8), ch 32.

touch her without her consent, is beyond value. B cannot be compensated for the loss of this freedom and the law should not attempt to try and do so. In contrast, where A commits a battery in relation to B by injecting her without her knowledge with an experimental drug to see what happens, and B suffers no ill effects from the injection but in fact benefits considerably from it, an award of licence fee damages against A might well be appropriate. Just as in the rape case, A has committed the tort of battery, but this time the freedom of which he has deprived B is a different one: the freedom to decide for oneself how one should be treated medically. This is a freedom that is not beyond value and the loss of this kind of freedom is something for which the law can realistically aim to compensate someone.

These examples suggest that awards of licence fee damages should be limited to cases where, in the language of R3RUE, 'the advantage acquired by the defendant is one that should properly have been the subject of negotiation and payment'.[73] Where a liberty that the law seeks to secure for a claimant is beyond value, the law will tend not to allow him to surrender that liberty in return for money, as doing so will be inconsistent with that liberty's status as being beyond value.[74] As such, the freedom to refuse to have sex with someone else is not something that the law allows anyone to turn into an object of trade: if that freedom is to be surrendered, it must be for nothing, and not for money. However, there is nothing objectionable in accepting money in return for being turned into a medical guinea pig, as the freedom to decide for oneself how one will be treated medically is not beyond value.

So in a case where a claimant's liberty-oriented right has been violated, a useful test for determining whether licence fee damages may be appropriately awarded to the claimant is to ask: is this a case where the law would regard it as legitimate for the claimant to have accepted money from the defendant in return for allowing the defendant to do what he did? For example, in the case where A commits a battery by beating B up, the law would not regard it as legitimate for B to have accepted money from A in return for allowing A to beat her up. This indicates that the freedom that A has deprived B of by beating B up is regarded as beyond value by the law, and B cannot therefore be compensated for the loss of this freedom through an award of licence fee damages.

D. A Redraft of R3RUE

The arguments in the second part of this chapter indicate that R3RUE's provisions on restitution for wrongs are in need of a redraft. The provisions on disgorgement that are based on the *Dangerous Incentives* argument need to be revised

[73] § 40, Comment b.

[74] See M Sandel, *What Money Can't Buy: The Moral Limits of Markets* (London, Allen Lane, 2012) for a very clear discussion of how allowing people to put a financial value on a particular good can end up degrading and corrupting that good.

to reflect the severe limitations of this argument. And the conditions for the award of licence fee damages need to be stated far more clearly to reflect the reasons for awarding such damages. In this section, I will set out a Redraft of R3RUE, and then illustrate some of the differences between the Redraft and R3RUE.

(1) The Redraft

§ 1 Definitions

(1) A person who breaches a legal duty imposed on him for the benefit of another is a wrongdoer, and that other is the victim of his wrong.
(2) Restitution for wrongs may be effected by:
    (a) an order requiring a wrongdoer to disgorge to the victim of his wrong a tangible gain he has obtained as a result of committing that wrong;
    (b) an order requiring a wrongdoer to pay a reasonable sum for what he has done.

§ 2 Disgorgement

(1) A wrongdoer (W) may be required to disgorge to the victim of his wrong (V) a tangible gain that W has obtained as a result of committing that wrong in *any* of the following circumstances:
    (a) W consciously failed to seek permission to act as he did from V when:
        (i) such permission would have been granted (either for free, or for some consideration) had it been sought, and
        (ii) making an order requiring W to pay V compensatory damages would not provide an adequate sanction for W's behaviour.
    (b) The gain represents the proceeds of property belonging to V.
    (c) W was under a duty to V not to make that gain.
    (d) The gain represents the proceeds of a crime committed by W for which W has been convicted and punished.
(2) In cases (a) and (d), W will be required to pay V a sum equal to the value of the gain that he is required to disgorge to V. In case (b), the gain that W is required to disgorge to V will be held on constructive trust for V. In case (c), the gain that W is required to disgorge to V will be held on constructive trust for V if W was under a duty to make that gain for V; if not, W will be required to pay V a sum equal to the value of that gain.
(3) If W committed his wrong in good faith, and has dissipated the tangible gain that he obtained as a result of that wrong in good faith, he will not be held liable to V under this rule.

§ 3 Punishment

(1) In the case where a wrongdoer (W) consciously failed to seek permission to act as he did from the victim of his wrong (V) because he knew such permission would not have been granted had it been sought, a punitive sum in damages may be awarded against W.
(2) Such a sum will always exceed the value of any tangible gain that W obtained as a result of committing his wrong, whether that gain has been retained or dissipated.

(3) A punitive award will not be made against W under (1), above, if W's conduct has been the subject of criminal proceedings, or if the combined effect of any other damages awards that can be made against W for what he has done is sufficient to punish W adequately for his conduct.

§ 4 Reasonable sum

(1) A wrongdoer (W) will be required to pay the victim of his wrong (V) a reasonable sum for what he has done if, in acting as he did:

(a) W violated a right of V's that was designed to help ensure that V enjoyed a specific liberty; and

(b) by violating that right, W obtained an advantage for which the law would normally require him to negotiate and pay.

(2) The reasonable sum will normally be assessed according to the going market rate for the advantage that W has obtained.

(3) The reasonable sum will be reduced below the going market rate if W committed his wrong in good faith, or was given no alternative but to commit that wrong, and requiring W to pay the going market rate would be inequitable.

(2) Illustrations

Illustration 1.[75] Landowner conducts tours of a cave on his land which features interesting rock formations. As Landowner is aware, the last third of the cave stretches underneath Neighbour's land, and Landowner regularly trespasses on Neighbour's land by taking the tours all the way to the back of the cave.

Under R3RUE, Neighbour would be entitled to require Landowner to disgorge the profits made by him by trespassing on Neighbour's land.[76] Under the Redraft, disgorgement is justified under § 2(1)(a). Landowner could have negotiated with Neighbour for access to Neighbour's land but chose not to do so, and now must pay the price of his failure in being made to give up far more than he would have had to had he negotiated. Merely requiring Landowner to pay Neighbour compensatory damages will not provide an adequate sanction for Landowner's trespass, as the trespass has caused no tangible harm to Neighbour's land and merely making Landowner compensate Neighbour for the loss of the opportunity to bargain that his trespass has triggered will give Landowner no incentive to respect Neighbour's rights.

If Landowner failed to negotiate because he knew Neighbour would refuse permission to access the part of the cave running under Neighbour's land, disgorgement will not be an adequate sanction for Landowner's wilful disregard of Neighbour's rights and a higher sum in exemplary damages should be awarded against Landowner instead under § 3.

Illustration 2. Promoter allows Band to practise for as long as they like in a basement owned by Promoter. In return, Band undertakes to pay Promoter five

[75] Based on *Edwards v Lee's Administrators*, 96 SW 2d 1028 (1936).

[76] § 40.

per cent of their earnings from their forthcoming tour. Band's practice sessions – which go on through the night – prove very disturbing to Neighbour, who lives in the property next to Promoter's basement. Band's tour is extremely successful and they end up paying Promoter £6,000.

Discussion of this scenario is complicated by the fact that there are not one but two wrongdoers here (Promoter and Band), and a variety of remedies that may be sought against them – either disgorgement of the gains they have made as a result of the Band's practice sessions or a reasonable sum for the privilege of being allowed to make so much noise on Promoter's land. The tables below sum up the different views taken by R3RUE and the Redraft, respectively, as to what remedies will be available in this situation.

	Disgorgement	Reasonable sum
Promoter	✓	✓
Band	✗	✓

1. *Position under R3RUE*

	Disgorgement	Reasonable sum
Promoter	✗	✗
Band	✗	✗

2. *Position under Redraft*

Looking at disgorgement first: this remedy would seem to be available against Promoter under R3RUE,[77] but not against Band, as Band did not deliberately wrong Neighbour in practising for as long as they did.[78] The Redraft agrees that there is no case for allowing Neighbour to sue Band for disgorgement. As Band did not consciously wrong Neighbour in acting as they did, § 2(1)(a) will not apply and no other basis for disgorgement will be available. Promoter is in a different category: he did deliberately wrong Neighbour in acting as he did, but whether disgorgement can be sued for under the Redraft depends on whether allowing Neighbour to sue Promoter for compensation for the interference with his use and enjoyment of land will provide an adequate sanction for Promoter's behaviour. If it does (and it seems likely to be the case that it will), § 2(1)(a) will not apply and no other basis for disgorgement will be available.

The main point of disagreement between R3RUE and the Redraft is over whether Neighbour can sue either Promoter or Band for a reasonable sum for their being allowed to disturb his peace and quiet. Under R3RUE, such a remedy will certainly be available against Promoter on the basis that if disgorgement is available, why should Neighbour not be allowed to sue for a reasonable sum in the alternative? And a reasonable sum might well be available as against Band as well, as such an award can be made under R3RUE without having to prove fault on the part of the defendant.[79]

[77] § 40, especially Illustration 8.
[78] § 40, Comment b.
[79] § 40, Comment b; § 51, Comment c.

Under the Redraft, things are much more difficult. Whether or not Neighbour can sue either Promoter or Band for a reasonable sum will depend on whether their actions violated a welfare-oriented right or a liberty-oriented right of Neighbour's. If the first, then Neighbour will be confined to suing for compensation for any material damage to his welfare suffered as a result of Band's practice sessions. If the second, then Neighbour should be entitled to sue for a reasonable sum to reflect the loss of the freedom to determine how he would use his own property that the law sought to secure for Neighbour and that he was deprived of by Band's practice sessions.

Although it is difficult to tell, it seems that the right that others not interfere unreasonably with one's quiet enjoyment of one's land is welfare-oriented rather than liberty-oriented. The right is designed to secure a material good for claimants: that they not be unreasonably *disturbed* in using their land. It is not designed to help ensure that claimants are left relatively *free* to determine for themselves how to use their land. Two factors militate in favour of this analysis. First, private nuisance is not a tort that is actionable per se: a claimant has to show that he has suffered some material harm before he can sue for private nuisance.[80] Second, the level of damages available to a claimant in a private nuisance is calibrated according to how much material harm he has suffered as a result of that nuisance occurring. Therefore, a claimant who has not been disturbed at all by noxious smells coming from the defendant's land will not be able to recover as much as a claimant who has been.[81]

If, as these features of the law seem to indicate, the rights arising under the law on private nuisance are welfare-oriented rather than liberty-oriented, there seems to be no basis for allowing Neighbour to sue either Promoter or Band for a reasonable sum for putting up with being disturbed by Band's practice sessions. Neighbour should be confined to suing for compensatory damages for the actual material harm that he has suffered as a result of those sessions.

Illustration 3.[82] Pimp forces Girl to work for him as a prostitute by locking her in a room where she is visited by clients and beating her up when she shows any sign of being unwilling to have sex with the clients.

It is not clear whether Girl would be allowed under R3RUE to require Pimp to disgorge the profits he has made by forcing her to work for him as a prostitute. It would be surprising if recovery were not allowed under § 44 (the catch-all provision), given that disgorgement damages are recoverable for much less serious torts under this section.

Under the Redraft, the outcome of the case would depend on whether Pimp had been criminally convicted and punished for his treatment of Girl. If so, disgorgement would be available under § 2(1)(d) so as to ensure that Pimp suffers to the full extent of the law his due punishment for the way he has behaved. (This

[80] *Nicholls v Ely Beet Sugar Factory Ltd (No 2)* [1936] 1 Ch 343 (CA) (though it is different in the case of a private nuisance involving an interference with a right to light).

[81] *Dobson v Thames Water Utilities Ltd* [2009] 3 All ER 319 (CA).

[82] Based on *Dulghieru* (n 44).

assumes, of course, that Pimp's gains from his treatment of Girl have not been seized by the government under some statutory provision.) If Pimp has not been criminally convicted and punished, disgorgement will not be available: it is a completely inadequate sanction for what Pimp has done.[83] Instead, exemplary damages should be awarded under § 3 and will be calibrated not according to how much money Pimp made from Girl, but according to Pimp's overall means, so as to ensure that the damages he pays will make him 'smart'. There can be no question of allowing Girl to sue Pimp for a reasonable sum for what he did to her under § 4: while what he did violated various liberty-oriented rights of Girl's, the freedom of which she was thereby deprived was beyond value and the loss of that freedom cannot be rectified through an award of damages.

Illustration 4.[84] Patient is terminally ill and is in continual pain. She asks Husband to help her commit suicide, and he does so. The authorities decline to prosecute Husband on the grounds that such a prosecution would not be in the public interest. Patient and Husband jointly owned a house, and Husband stands to inherit all of Patient's property under her will. Patient and Husband had three children, two of whom are strongly opposed to what Husband did.

It is not clear what the position would be under R3RUE. § 45, Comment a says that 'The exact contours of the slayer rule in a given jurisdiction . . . is not a principal concern of this Restatement', while Comment b says that 'Particular jurisdictions may impose a slayer rule that differs slightly in scope' and that 'the rules set forth in § 45 . . . apply to a person who is defined as a "slayer" . . . by the rules of the jurisdiction'. As such, R3RUE seems to be open-minded on whether the slayer rule would apply in a case of assisted suicide.[85] If someone who assisted another to commit suicide were regarded as a 'slayer' in Husband's jurisdiction, then under R3RUE, the 'slayer rule' would operate to prevent Husband benefiting from Patient's death, so that Patient's half-share of the house, and her goods, would be held on constructive trust for Patient and Husband's children.

Under the Redraft, it seems likely that the opposite result would obtain and that Husband would become sole owner of the house that he owned jointly with Patient and would inherit all her belongings under her will. As Husband has not been criminally convicted and punished, § 2(1)(d) does not apply. However, it

[83] Tsachi Keren-Paz argues in favour of disgorgement here on the basis that the profits made by Pimp represent the proceeds of Pimp's disposing of Girl's property (viz her body): T Keren-Paz, '*AT v Dulghieru* – Compensation for the Victims of Trafficking, But Where Is the Restitution?' (2010) 18 *Torts Law Journal* 1. The objection to this is that bodies cannot be counted as property as they are not separable from us: JE Penner, *The Idea of Property in Law* (Oxford, Oxford University Press, 1997) 121–22. Keren-Paz counters by arguing that it would be 'poetic justice' if those who treat other people's bodies as property were held liable on that basis: 'Poetic Justice: Why Sex-Slaves Should Be Allowed to Sue Ignorant Clients in Conversion' (2010) 29 *Law & Philosophy* 307. Maybe so, but it is not clear why the law should follow pimps and their customers into barbarism by reifying the bodies of those they exploit.

[84] Based on *R (on the application of Purdy) v Director of Public Prosecutions* [2009] UKHL 45, [2010] 1 AC 345.

[85] The English equivalent of the 'slayer rule' *does* apply in cases where the defendant has assisted someone to commit suicide: *Dunbar* (n 47).

might be argued that § 2(1)(c) does apply. The argument would be that someone who is deciding whether or not to assist another to commit suicide becomes a fiduciary for that other, so as to ensure that he makes his decision whether or not to assist in the suicide with a completely clear head, free of any influences that might encourage him to think that assisting someone to commit suicide is the right thing to do when it is actually the wrong thing to do. If this argument works, we could say that Husband has a duty to Patient not to make a gain from her death. However, the argument suffers from severe difficulties. If Patient wants Husband to help her kill herself, it is hard to see how Husband could owe *Patient* (as opposed to society as a whole) a duty not to help her kill herself. And if he did not owe Patient such a duty, there is no primary duty that Husband owes Patient that could form the basis of a duty owed to Patient not to make a gain from helping her to kill herself.

Illustration 5.[86] Factory undertakes to supply Manufacturer with steel for £700 per ton. Before Factory is due to deliver the steel to Manufacturer, war breaks out, with the result that the price of steel rises to £1,000 per ton. Factory immediately sells its entire supply of steel to Government for £1,000 per ton. By the time Manufacturer's consignment is due to be delivered, the war has finished and the price of steel has settled back to £750 per ton.

R3RUE would deny a disgorgement remedy here, as Manufacturer has an adequate remedy for Factory's breach of contract in that it can sue Factory for £50 per ton by way of compensatory damages – the difference between what it would have had to pay Factory for its steel and what it is going to have to pay to replace that steel on the open market.[87] In contrast, the Redraft would allow Manufacturer to sue Factory for disgorgement damages assessed at £300 per ton of steel that Factory undertook to sell to Manufacturer. § 2(1)(a) applies: Factory could have negotiated with Manufacturer to make an arrangement, but chose not to do so and must now pay the price of its failure. Compensatory damages would represent an inadequate sanction for what Factory has done as the prospect of being held liable for £50 per ton in compensatory damages would not deter Factory from committing a breach that would yield it £300 per ton profit.

Illustration 6.[88] Petrol Giant has an exclusive deal to supply Petrol Station with as much petrol as it needs. Under the terms of the deal, Giant's name is to be displayed prominently at the station, and Station is not allowed to sell Giant's petrol at more than the price charged by local competitors so as to fulfil a 'Price Guarantee' that Giant has widely advertised itself as undertaking to observe. Station regularly sells Giant's petrol at five per cent more than customers at competing local petrol stations are charged for their petrol.

Under R3RUE, Giant may well be able to sue Station to make it disgorge the profits it has made from breaching the contract it has with Giant. Station's breach

[86] Based on *Adras v Harlow & Jones GmbH* (1988) 42(1) PD 221 (Sup Ct of Israel) (English translation: (1995) 3 *Restitution Law Review* 235).

[87] See § 39, Illustration 15 (text to n 28).

[88] Based on *Esso Petroleum Co Ltd v Niad Ltd* [2001] All ER (D) 324 (Ch).

is deliberate, and a normal remedy for breach of contract might not prove adequate to protect Giant's interests, as it would prove difficult for Giant to establish that it has suffered any loss (either in the form of lost business or reputational damage) as a result of Station's behaviour.

The Redraft agrees that disgorgement damages should be available here, but for the simple reason that if Station undertook not to sell Giant's petrol for more than a certain price, then it had a duty to Giant not to sell the petrol at a higher price. It therefore had a contractual duty, owed to Giant, not to make the gain that it did. Therefore, § 2(1)(c) applies and a disgorgement remedy follows automatically.

Illustration 7.[89] Owner's house is insured with Greedy. The house burns down through no fault of Owner. Despite being aware that it is liable to indemnify Owner against the loss of his house under the terms of his insurance contract with Greedy, Greedy disputes Owner's claim, raising objections to his claim that it well knows are completely unjustified.

Under R3RUE, disgorgement damages would not be allowed here. If we focus on Greedy's breach of contract in failing to pay up, Owner has a perfectly adequate remedy for that breach: an action for debt. If we focus on Greedy's breach of contract in failing to deal with Owner's claim in good faith, it is not clear that Greedy will have actually made any gain from this breach once it has been required to pay up.

Under the Redraft, disgorgement damages will again not be available. In a case where the defendant's breach of contract involves a failure to pay money, disgorgement is a particularly useless remedy as it merely requires the defendant to do what he was supposed to do in the first place. As a result, limiting the claimant to a claim for disgorgement damages actually incentivises the sort of game-playing that Greedy has engaged in here. Instead, the only adequate remedy for Greedy's behaviour here will be exemplary damages. (We assume that Greedy has not already incurred some kind of regulatory sanction for its behaviour here.)

Illustration 8.[90] The *Daily Hound* infiltrates one of its photographers into the wedding reception of Mr and Mrs Brangelina. The Brangelinas have entered into a contract with *The Moon*, a rival newspaper, under which they undertook to allow *The Moon*'s photographers exclusive access to the reception. The *Daily Hound* publishes the photos that its photographer secretly took at the reception and enjoys a 50 per cent rise in sales on that day as a result. It has been established that in acting as it did, the Hound committed two torts – wrongful disclosure of private information vis-a-vis the Brangelinas and the tort of intentionally causing another harm using unlawful means vis-a-vis *The Moon*.

It seems likely that both the Brangelinas and *The Moon* would be able to sue to make the *Daily Hound* disgorge the gains it has made from its torts under § 44 of R3RUE. § 44 contemplates awards of such damages being made in invasion of privacy cases and in economic tort cases, and this case involves both. All of the

[89] Based on *Whiten v Pilot Insurance Co* [2002] 1 SCR 595.
[90] Based on *Douglas v Hello! Ltd (No 3)* [2007] UKHL 21, [2008] 1 AC 1.

conditions for a remedy under § 44 seem to be made out; in particular, had either of the claimants discovered beforehand the *Daily Hound*'s plans to publish secretly taken photos of the reception, they would have been able to get an injunction to stop the *Daily Hound* from going ahead with its plans.

In contrast, the Redraft would not allow a disgorgement remedy here. § 2(1)(a) does not apply as consent to publication of the photos in the *Daily Hound* would never have been forthcoming from either the Brangelinas or *The Moon*; in any case, a normal order for compensatory damages would probably provide an adequate sanction for the *Daily Hound*'s behaviour. The Brangelinas might try to invoke § 2(1)(b) by arguing that the *Daily Hound*'s gains from invading their privacy amount to 'proceeds of property' belonging to them, on the basis that private information about them amounts to property that belongs to them. Whether such an argument deserves to succeed is a matter for another paper, but in my view it does not. Property can be given to you or taken away from you.[91] *Private* information lacks the first quality: it isn't given to you; you just have it. Private *information* lacks the second quality: information, once obtained, cannot be taken away. Put together, information that is private does not have the characteristics required for it to amount to property.[92]

Illustration 9.[93] Girlfriend moves into Boyfriend's house. On her birthday, Boy lies to Girl and tells her that he has arranged with the Land Registry for her to be registered as legally owning the house they live in, jointly with him. As Boy anticipated, this news causes Girl to start spending time making improvements to the house that she never would have contemplated making had she not thought she had a stake in it. The market value of these improvements at the time they were undertaken – as measured by how much it would have cost to get a professional to make these improvements – was £5,000. After a while, Boy and Girl split up and Boy sells the house for £350,000, £50,000 of which is attributable to the work Girl did on the house. Girl has now discovered that Boy never gave her a half-share interest in the house.

It seems very likely that Girl would be able to invoke § 44 of R3RUE to require Boy to disgorge the gain he has made as a result of his fraudulent misrepresentation to her.[94] However, the gain he has made will probably be measured by the £5,000 Boy saved by not getting a professional in to make the improvements that Girl made, not by the £50,000 that Boy has now pocketed as a result of Girl's work.[95]

[91] A point summed up by James Penner's 'separability thesis' that 'Only those "things" in the world which are contingently associated with any particular owner may be objects of property': Penner (n 83) 111.

[92] *Oxford v Moss* (1979) 68 Cr App R 183 (QB).

[93] Based on *Eves v Eves* [1975] 1 WLR 1338 (CA).

[94] See § 44, Illustration 13 (by fraudulent misrepresentation, Developer gets permission from City for the demolition of a historic landmark as part of Developer's building project; had Developer not lied to City, he would have been required to move the landmark to an adjacent lot at a cost of $500,000; Developer is liable to City for the $500,000 he has saved as a result of his fraud).

[95] ibid.

The Redraft would get to the same result, although by different means. Girl would only be able to sue Boy for disgorgement if he had been criminally convicted and punished for his fraud, so as to ensure that he felt the full impact of his punishment. A Lockean argument that Girl's work belongs to her with the result that the £50,000 gained by Boy represents the 'proceeds of property' belonging to Girl is not likely to get off the ground. Girl would, however, be able to sue Boy for a reasonable sum for the work done by her under § 4 of the Redraft. Boy's lie violated a liberty-oriented right that Girl had against Boy that was designed to allow her to decide for herself what she would do for Boy and on what terms. As a result of this, Boy now has to pay a reasonable sum to compensate her for depriving her of that freedom. Such a sum will equal what he would have had to pay to get someone to do the work that his lie induced Girl to do for him for free. As such, Girl will be entitled to sue Boy for £5,000 under § 4 of the Redraft.

12

Comparisons with Book VII of the *Draft Common Frame of Reference*

GERHARD DANNEMANN

This chapter compares the unjust(ified) enrichment regimes contained in the American Law Institute's *Restatement Third: Restitution and Unjust Enrichment*[1] and in Book VII of the *Draft Common Frame of Reference*.[2] Part A presents some general observations concerning the different pedigrees, methodologies, time-frames, working patterns and drafting styles which were used for R3RUE and Book VII DCFR. Part B examines classification issues, namely a comparison of the approaches taken by R3RUE and Book VII DCFR. Part C looks at how these two sets of rules deal with a few well-known difficult cases or sets of factual situations. Finally, Part D presents some conclusions. The chapter is limited to grounds of restitution and excludes defences against unjust enrichment claims as well as questions relating to the measure of recovery.[3]

A. General Observations

Both R3RUE and Book VII DCFR form part of a larger project which seeks to formulate legal rules in the style of a codification. Nevertheless, there are many substantial differences in the way in which these rules have been drafted.

[1] American Law Institute, *Restatement Third: Restitution and Unjust Enrichment* (St Paul, MN, American Law Institute Publishers, 2011) (hereinafter 'R3RUE').

[2] *Principles, Definitions and Model Rules of European Private Law. Draft Common Frame of Reference (DCFR), Outline Edition* (Munich, Sellier, 2009).

[3] For the DCFR's relationship with gain-based measures of restitutionary recovery, see Erik Monsen, 'DCFR and Restitution for Wrongs' (2010) 4 *European Review of Private Law* 813.

(1) Timeframe

When R3RUE was launched at Boston University in September 2011, the reporter, Andrew Kull, summed up the 74 years which had passed between the first and the inappropriately named third edition of the American Law Institute's restatement of restitution (or unjust enrichment) rules, and the many more events which occasionally helped, but mostly hindered the progress towards R3RUE.[4] The drafting history of Book VII DCFR is, by comparison, brutally short. The Study Group for a European Civil Code apparently commenced its work on what it then called 'unjustified enrichments' in 2001[5] and adopted a full set of rules on unjustified enrichment in 2005.[6] With some revisions, the provisions on unjustified enrichment were eventually adopted as part of the DCFR by the so-called Compilation and Redaction Team, which was composed of members of both the Study Group and the Acquis Group,[7] appearing first in an Interim Outline Edition of 2008[8] and then in the final Outline Edition of 2009.[9] While the wording of the DCFR provisions underwent a vetting and voting procedure which may roughly compare to the adoption of restatement rules by the American Law Institute, no similar mechanism existed for the DCFR commentaries, which were largely left to the two drafters. Two (very similar) sets of commentaries appeared in 2009 and 2010, respectively, in the form of the Full Edition of the DCFR[10] and in the Study Group's series of 'Principles of European Law'.[11] The entire project was thus completed in less than a decade.

(2) Methodology

While R3RUE seeks to restate the existing case law in the US, the situation is more complicated with the DCFR. Some parts are also a restatement, namely of existing EU contract law, but this is not the case for the rules on unjustified enrichment, which have been derived from a comparative survey of European domestic laws.

[4] Unfortunately, this presentation was not published in the special edition of the Boston University Law Review that contains the conference papers: (2012) 92(3) *Boston University Law Review* 763–1079.

[5] The first mention of 'unjustified enrichments' which can be traced from the Study Group's website appears in the context of a meeting in December 2001: http://www.sgecc.net/pages/en/meetings/6.coordinating_group.htm.

[6] http://www.sgecc.net/pages/en/texts/index.draft_articles.htm.

[7] European Research Group on Existing EC Private Law (Acquis Group), http://www.acquis-group.org.

[8] *Principles, Definitions and Model Rules of European Private Law. Draft Common Frame of Reference (DCFR), Interim Outline Edition* (Munich, Sellier, 2008).

[9] *Principles, Definitions and Model Rules of European Private Law. Draft Common Frame of Reference (DCFR), Outline Edition* (Munich, Sellier, 2009).

[10] Christian von Bar and Eric Clive (eds), *Principles, Definitions and Model Rules of European Private Law. Draft Common Frame of Reference*, vol 4 (Munich, Sellier, 2009).

[11] Christian von Bar and Stephen Swann (eds), *Principles of European Law, Volume 6: Unjustified Enrichment* (Munich, Sellier, 2010).

Having said this, the Study Group's comparative methodology oscillates between three positions, which are reflected in the Group's statement of aims.[12] First, a comparative survey may reveal a common core of rules across Europe, which only appear to be different because of historical peculiarities. Second, however, the Study Group will use this survey for a discussion of merits, revealing the best amongst the available rules, however that is to be ascertained. Third, the Study Group may rise above the many domestic laws by formulating new, perhaps more general rules, with the domestic laws predominantly used as reference points for the results which are produced in given situations. In the present author's view, Book VII DCFR falls into the last category.

(3) Pedigree

R3RUE could build on the first edition, whereas the DCFR rules on unjustified enrichment had no predecessor. Comparative scholarship in unjust enrichment law came later, or at least remained on the sidelines for longer than comparative research on contract law. Thus, the DCFR provisions on contract law can claim roots in comparative studies by Ernst Rabel (1936)[13] and Schlesinger (1968),[14] leading to contract law unification or harmonization projects such as the 1964 Hague Uniform Sales Law, the 1980 Convention on the International Sale of Goods, the Lando Group's *Principles of European Contract Law*[15] and the UNIDROIT *Principles of International Commercial Contracts.*[16] The DCFR provisions on unjustified enrichment also show some ancestry in comparative research, including studies by Harold Gutteridge and René David (1935),[17] Wolfgang Friedmann (1938)[18] and John Dawson (1951),[19] but the actual drafting of rules based on a comparative survey had to start from scratch.

(4) Drafters

With Andrew Kull, the American Law Institute eventually appointed as Reporter for R3RUE one of the most experienced American scholars in unjust enrichment law. The Study Group for a European Civil Code initially appointed three reporters

[12] http://www.sgecc.net/pages/en/introduction/100.aims.htm.

[13] Ernst Rabel, *Das Recht des Warenkaufs*, vols I (de Gruyter, 1936) and II (de Gruyter, 1957).

[14] Rudolf Schlesinger (ed), *Formation of Contracts: A Study of the Common Core of Legal Systems* (Dobbs Ferry, NY, Oceana, 1968).

[15] Ole Lando and Hugh Beale (eds), *Principles of European Contract Law, Parts I and II Revised* (Dordrecht, Kluwer, 2002).

[16] International Institute for the Unification of Private Law (UNIDROIT), *Principles of International Commercial Contracts* (UNIDROIT, 1994).

[17] Harold Gutteridge and René David, 'The Doctrine of Unjustified Enrichment' (1935) 5 *CLJ* 204.

[18] Wolfgang Friedmann, 'The Principle of Unjust Enrichment in English Law' (1938) 16 *Canadian Bar Review* 243–67, 365–86.

[19] John P Dawson, *Unjust Enrichment: A Comparative Analysis* (Boston, Little Brown, 1951, quoted from the 1999 reprint).

for its unjustified enrichment provisions, namely the well-known Dutch and German scholars Arthur Hartkamp and Christian von Bar, and a young English colleague, Stephen Swann. Arthur Hartkamp soon dropped out of the picture. Stephen Swann was at the beginning of his academic career and Christian von Bar, while very well known for his work on comparative contract and tort law, and on conflict of laws, was not then known for his interest in issues relating to restitution. This fresh start may (or may not) explain some of the fresh perspectives taken by Book VII DCFR and of the short time taken for its completion when compared to R3RUE.

(5) Drafting Style

Given the many differences outlined above and the known peculiarities of common law style in legislative drafting,[20] it is surprising that the stylistic differences in terms of sentence structure, length of provisions and choice of words, and to a lesser degree terminology, are limited. This is partly to do with the fact that the American Law Institute's restatements were never written like English or US statutes, but were more concerned with clarity than with exhaustiveness, and never demonstrated the obsession for detail which is characteristic of Westminster-style drafting.

Terminology apart, the opening provisions of R3RUE and Book VII DCFR look remarkably similar:

> R3RUE, § 1. Restitution and unjust enrichment.
>
> A person who is unjustly enriched at the expense of another is subject to liability in restitution.
>
> Art VII-1:101 DCFR: Basic rule
>
> (1) A person who obtains an unjustified enrichment which is attributable to another's disadvantage is obliged to that other to reverse the enrichment.

But while R3RUE and DCFR Book VII appear stylistically so similar that the unsuspecting reader might hardly notice were the odd provision swapped, the common law's preference for detailed regulation shines through in the number of provisions – 70 in total for R3RUE, compared with 23 provisions in Book VII DCFR. This can be compared to the 11 provisions (§§ 812–22) which the German Civil Code designates to unjustified enrichment. As they are shorter, their 750 words in total amount to some 40 per cent of the words used for the DCFR provisions and are perhaps one-eighth of the length of R3RUE. This difference in size corresponds mostly to a difference in density of regulation. To a lesser degree, this can be explained by the more general approach taken to unjustified enrichment by both the DCFR and German law.

[20] See Sir William Dale, *Legislative Drafting: A New Approach. A Comparative Study of Methods in France, Germany, Sweden, and the United Kingdom* (London, Butterworths, 1977).

B. Scope and Taxonomy

The scope and taxonomy of Book VII DCFR are closely interlinked. The first provision, Art VII-1:101, which we have seen above, looks like a close relative of § 1 R3RUE. However, whereas the latter merely formulates a principle of unjust enrichment (and the relationship to restitution as a remedy), the former provides a basis for a restitutionary claim. Article VII-1:101 gives a right to restitution, though this is qualified by notions such as 'enrichment', 'unjustified', 'disadvantage' and 'attribution', which are then defined in subsequent provisions. This is why paragraph 2 of the first provision makes clear that this is not a stand-alone rule.

(1) Unitary Notion in DCFR

The comments nevertheless leave no doubt that the DCFR embraces a unitary notion of unjustified enrichment.[21] It includes restitution of transfers and wrongs-based restitution. It makes no differentiation between transfers of money, of other assets, or cases of improvement of somebody else's property. One and the same rule covers participatory and non-participatory enrichment. The present author knows of no continental legal system with such a strictly unitary notion of unjustified enrichment.

(2) Differences in Scope

On the other hand, the DCFR's approach excludes from its scope two entire areas which are not excluded from the R3RUE, or indeed common law notions of unjust enrichment. First, the DCFR's rules on unjustified enrichment are limited to rights *in personam*. No proprietary consequences whatsoever flow from an unjust enrichment. Both tracing and trusts are missing. The DCFR has a separate Book X on Trusts, but this does not attach any proprietary consequences to trusts which aim to prevent unjustified enrichment.[22] Second, restitutionary consequences of termination of a contract, or of withdrawal from a contract, are outside the scope of Book VII and are instead covered by Book III rules.[23] The same applies to restitution after excused non-performance of a contract, non-fulfilment of a condition and variation or termination by agreement. Moreover, the DCFR contains a separate chapter (Book V) entitled 'Benevolent Intervention in Another's Affairs', thus excluding most cases of *negotiorum gestio* from the ambit of the DCFR's rules on unjustified enrichment. So, the scope of Book VII DCFR is considerably narrower than that of R3RUE.

[21] Art VII-1:101 DCFR, Comment A.
[22] Art X-1:101 DCFR, Comment E, Illustration 2.
[23] Arts III-3:510–14 DCFR.

(3) Unjustified: Absence of Legal Ground or Unjust Factors?

While, on first overall impression, Book VII DCFR may have a Continental feel to Continental readers, it does not (or at least not explicitly) use the notion of 'absence of legal ground' (*sans cause*, *ohne Rechtsgrund*) as a controlling element. True, a Continental lawyer could read an 'absence of legal ground' notion into the very use of the term 'unjustified', but one look at the definition of 'unjustified' in Art VII-2:101 reveals that matters are a little more complicated. Jan Smits and Vanessa Mak even argue that this provision, in listing four categories in which an enrichment is unjustified, looks more familiar to the common lawyer in resembling an unjust factor approach;[24] common lawyers may agree or disagree. In the present author's view, this is a provision which can easily give a false impression of similarity to both the Continental and the common lawyer.

Paragraph (1) reads as follows:

> An enrichment is unjustified unless:
>
> (a) the enriched person is entitled as against the disadvantaged person to the enrichment by virtue of a contract or other juridical act, a court order or a rule of law, or
> (b) the disadvantaged person consented freely and without error to the disadvantage.

This provision cannot really be seen as an unjust factor. Sub-paragraph (a) resembles unjustified enrichment based on 'absence of legal ground', and Comment A confirms this view. On closer inspection, however, sub-paragraph (a) reverses the notion by stating that an enrichment is not unjustified if the recipient was entitled to it 'by virtue of a contract or other juridical act, a court order or a rule of law'. So, sub-paragraph (a) really operates as a 'justifying factor', complemented by an alternative second 'justifying factor' in sub-paragraph (b), namely unvitiated consent of the disadvantaged party.[25] This 'justifying factor' looks like the mirror image of two unjust factors in the common law, namely mistake and compulsion.

Paragraphs (2)–(4) could easily be understood as unjust factors in a common law sense. Paragraph (2) makes an enrichment unjustified if conferred under contract, etc, which is 'void or avoided or otherwise rendered ineffective', mirroring R3RUE's Chapter 2, 'Transfers Subject to Avoidance', including unjust factors such as mistake and compulsion. However, this reading as unjust factor ignores the fact that paragraph (2), by linking to 'the contract or other juridical act . . . referred to in paragraph (1)(a)', is really only an explanatory rule to the latter provision. It states no more and no less that a contract, etc, once it becomes void, avoided, etc, no longer provides an entitlement.

[24] Jan Smits and Vanessa Mak, 'DCFR, Book VII: Unjustified Enrichment' in Luisa Antoniolli and Francesca Fiorentini (eds), *A Factual Assessment of the Draft Common Frame of Reference* (Munich, Sellier, 2010) 249, 254.

[25] Note that C Mitchell, P Mitchell and S Watterson (edd), *Goff & Jones: The Law of Unjust Enrichment*, 8th edn (London, Sweet & Maxwell, 2011), while maintaining an unjust factor approach in Part 5 (Grounds for Restitution), also contains a Part 2 on 'Justifying Grounds', including notably statutes and contracts.

Paragraph (3) is about policy-based restitution, but, like paragraph (1), formulated the other way round: an enrichment is justified if keeping the enrichment corresponds to a legal policy. Policy-based restitution figures as a separate unjust factor in some textbooks on English law,[26] whereas § 34 R3RUE sees this, much like the German Civil Code in § 817, as a question of illegality. Again, though, paragraph (3) is not a stand-alone unjust factor, but an explanatory rule to what amounts to an entitlement under paragraph (1).

Paragraph (4) covers failure of purpose, similar to the English unjust factor 'failure of consideration', and what in the R3RUE (though it does not use this expression)[27] is mostly covered by Chapter 4, Topic 1, 'Restitution to a performing party with no claim on the contract'. As the wording of paragraph (4) ('. . . is also unjustified . . .') indicates, this provision operates independently of entitlements in paragraph (1). It is thus the DCFR's closest equivalent to an unjust factor. For German lawyers, this forms part of performance-based unjustified enrichment and is primarily an explanatory rule on the general clause.

It is worth mentioning that Roman lawyers will feel at home with Art VII-2:101 DCFR. Paragraph (1) could be seen as a rendition of the *condictio indebiti*. Paragraph (2) cannot easily be associated with one single *condictio*, but includes the *condictio ob causam finitam*. Paragraph (3) resembles the *condictio ob turpem vel iniustam causam*, while paragraph (4) resembles the *condictio causa data causa non secuta*.[28]

At any rate, this mixture of two justifying factors, two explanatory rules and one unjust factor in Art VII-2:101 DCFR can easily make it a false friend to common and civil lawyers alike. Or, as Smits and Mak put it: 'This provision makes very hard reading for anyone without a solid knowledge of the restitution law of several European jurisdictions.'[29]

Most of R3RUE's taxonomy, by contrast, appears almost self-explanatory, in particular its division into 'Transfers Subject to Avoidance' (Chapter 2), 'Unrequested Intervention' (Chapter 3, covered by the DCFR provisions on benevolent intervention in another's affairs in Chapter 5), and 'Restitution for Wrongs' (Chapter 5). It can nevertheless be argued that the headings of Chapter 4 (Restitution and Contract)[30] and Chapter 6 (Benefits Conferred by a Third Person) will not be instantly recognizable to somebody familiar with the unjust factor approach. In his contribution to this volume, Jacques du Plessis makes the case that for some cases of duress under § 14, R3RUE operates on what is at best a 'weak' unjust factor, which makes simultaneous use of an absence of basis approach.[31] The present author

[26] Peter Birks, *An Introduction to the Law of Restitution* (Oxford, Oxford University Press, 1989 (reprint)), ch IX, followed by Gerard McMeel, *The Modern Law of Restitution* (London, Blackstone, 2000) 205.

[27] See also the contribution by Frederick Wilmot-Smith in ch 3 of this volume.

[28] On the system of Roman *condictiones*, see Reinhard Zimmermann, *The Law of Obligations: Roman Foundations of the Civilian Tradition* (Oxford, Oxford University Press, 1996) 841–51.

[29] Smits and Mak (n 24) 259.

[30] See the contribution by Frederick Wilmot-Smith in ch 3 of this volume.

[31] Jacques du Plessis, ch 4 of this volume.

would argue that the predominant unjust factor, mistake, is similarly weak when compared to its counterpart in contract law and makes the same simultaneous use of an absence of basis approach; support for this view can be found in the contribution which James Goudkamp and Charles Mitchell have made to this volume.[32] Goudkamp and Mitchell generally see R3RUE as an exercise in fence-sitting between an unjust factor and absence of basis approach.[33]

Andrew Burrows concludes his contribution to this volume as follows: 'At a deeper level, this involves recognising that the unjust factors and the civilian "absence of basis" approaches are closer than has traditionally been thought.'[34] A comparison between DCFR and R3RUE lends support to this view.

For reasons of space, the present chapter will not discuss the DCFR's two next and probably uncontroversial requirements for a claim in unjustified enrichment, namely the enrichment of the defendant and the disenrichment of the claimant, or 'disadvantage' as it is called in DCFR terminology.[35]

(4) Attribution

An apparently novel requirement in the DCFR deserves more attention, namely what the DCFR calls 'attribution', defined in Art VII-4:101. Similar to what R3RUE and English law call 'at the expense of' (and German law likewise calls '*auf dessen Kosten*'), attribution provides the necessary link between enrichment and disadvantage. Its first function is that of a condition: without attribution, no claim will lie in unjustified enrichment. Its second function is (or rather should be) to identify the right claimant and defendant in a multipartite situation.[36] This is a task which German law, within transfer of assets, leaves to the notion of performance: once you know who performed this transfer of assets and towards whom, you have identified the right claimant and the right defendant to an unjustified enrichment claim.

The DCFR provisions give a much more limited role to the notion of performance in Art VII-2:102, which regulates whether an enrichment is unjustified if performance is made to a third party. Article VII-4:101, the rule on attribution, nevertheless first lists the standard situation of a transfer, namely that the disadvantaged person has transferred his own asset to the enriched person. Unfortunately, the reader is not told how the recipient of the asset should be identified. Should property law be decisive, ie, the question of who becomes the new owner of the assets? Or should this, at least in the case of failed contracts, be decided by contract law, with the defendant being the intended beneficiary under the contract?[37]

[32] James Goudkamp and Charles Mitchell, ch 6 of this volume (discussing § 62 R3RUE).
[33] ibid 135.
[34] Andrew Burrows, ch 7 of this volume.
[35] Arts VII-3:101 and 102 DCFR.
[36] See the contribution by Birke Häcker in ch 2 to this volume.
[37] The contractual perspective is decisive where Art VII-2:102 applies: see below, section C(3) (leapfrogging claims).

Alternatively, should this, as under the German notion of performance, be decided from the perspective of the person who was performing?[38]

The second instance of attribution demonstrates a similar vagueness. The defendant's enrichment is attributable to the claimant's disadvantage if 'a service is rendered to or work is done for the [defendant] by [the claimant]'. Which perspective will decide this 'for' – that of the recipient, of the service provider or of contract law? Presumably, if the service increases the assets of the recipient (for example, by repairing the defendant's car, as in *Greenwood v Bennett*),[39] attribution occurs under option (d), namely where 'an asset of the enriched person is improved by that other'. Is 'asset of' the same as 'asset belonging to' in a property law sense? Or, in the case of a hire-purchase or car rental, would the person who has rented or purchased the car be the enriched person? We will return to these issues below when comparing how R3RUE and the DCFR cope with some well-known problem situations in unjust enrichment law.

By comparison, attribution grounds (c) and (e) appear fairly straightforward. Attribution occurs under ground (c) through the use of another person's assets, 'especially . . . the disadvantaged person's rights or legally protected interest'. This is at the core of wrongs-based restitution, where it is usually not too difficult to find the right claimant and the right defendant.[40]

Ground (e), at first sight, appears all but self-explanatory: attribution occurs if 'the enriched person is discharged from a liability by that other'. It will usually be easy to find the right claimant and the right defendant under this rule. Common lawyers may marvel at the wide recovery which this potentially opens to officious intermeddlers paying somebody else's debt, a question about which R3RUE is, however, fairly relaxed.[41]

Nevertheless, the DCFR fails to clarify the relationship between attribution grounds (a) and (e). Assuming that grounds (a) and (e) both apply in a given case, but point to different defendants, which of the attribution rules should take precedence? Or should the claimant be free to choose? The commentary to Art VII-4:101 offers no help. We only learn that in 'triangular or chain arrangements of transactions . . . the complexity of the case is inescapable'.[42]

It should be mentioned that the list in Art VII-4:101 is not exhaustive ('. . . in particular where'). New instances of attribution can be found. This preserves flexibility, but at the cost of certainty.

[38] See Gerhard Dannemann, *The German Law of Unjustified Enrichment and Restitution* (Oxford, Oxford University Press, 2009) 52.

[39] *Greenwood v Bennett* [1973] 1 QB 195 (CA).

[40] For wrongs-based restitution under the DCFR, see Monsen (n 3).

[41] See eg, § 22 Comment b(3): 'such cases are mostly hypothetical'. See also Gerhard Dannemann, 'Is Unjust Enrichment Law an Officious Intermeddler?' (2012) 92 *Boston University Law Review* 991, 992, 1002.

[42] Art VII-4:101 DCFR, Comment A.

C. Application to Some Problem Cases

We will now examine how R3RUE and Book VII DCFR handle some well-known problem cases or situations. The selection may look arbitrary, but it consists of five textbook or real cases which have exposed problems or flaws in the classification of unjust enrichment claims, sometimes leading to results which are overly generous or overly parsimonious, sometimes requiring major twisting and bending of rules if such results are to be avoided, and sometimes leading courts to adopt a different approach to unjust enrichment claims in order to avoid both unjust results and twisting of rules.

The first two are textbook examples given by Peter Birks. The first is the famous window cleaner, which caused problems to the unjust factor approach then favoured by Birks. The second is the 'rising heat' scenario, which caused even greater trouble to the absence of basis approach which Birks propagated later. The third concerns leapfrog claims, which, in the case of *Boudier*, wreaked major havoc on French law and which accelerated a shift towards performance-based liability in German law. The fourth concerns cases of (non-)marital property disputes, which made the Supreme Court of Canada shift to its present juristic reason approach, while the fifth concerns payments under protest as the one major area in which the English unjust factor approach appears to be unable to reach satisfactory results.[43]

(1) Window Cleaner

The first example is taken from Peter Birks' *An Introduction to the Law of Restitution.*[44] It immediately caused trouble for the unjust factor approach presented in that book. The prospective claimant is a window cleaner who, without having been asked to do so, cleans the windows of the defendant's house in the hope of getting paid. The defendant watches this and decides to hang back unseen, hoping to get clean windows without having to pay for them. The window cleaner's hopes are fulfilled, and those of the house occupant thwarted, because of a controversial unjust factor of 'free acceptance'.

Article VII-2:101(4) DCFR reads as if it should cover the window cleaner. The cleaner did his job with an expectation which was not realised (namely that he be paid). The occupant 'knew or could reasonably be expected to know of the . . .

[43] An obvious sixth or alternative example would have been cases of deemed mistakes, in which recovery of a payment made without legal ground is allowed even in the absence of any convincing unjust factor. In *Deutsche Morgan Grenfell plc v Her Majesty's Commissioners of Inland Revenue* [2006] UKHL 49, [2007] 1 AC 558, Lord Hoffmann at [23] stated that the claimant in *Kleinwort Benson Ltd v Lincoln City Council* [1999] 2 AC 349 (HL) had arguably been 'deemed to have made a mistake'. See Dannemann (n 38) 211.

[44] Birks (n 26) 265.

expectation'. Moreover, 'the enriched person accepted or could reasonably be assumed to have accepted that the enrichment must be reversed in such circumstances'. This is the reason why Birks made the occupant hide: because he knew that watching visibly without sign of protest could be understood in this way.

And yet the DCFR commentary informs us that the occupant is right.[45] The illustration in question concerns car rather than house windows. The car owner (E) watches the cleaner (D) and fails to interfere. We are again informed of a result: 'E cannot be regarded as having accepted that D must be paid for his service.' The reader is also told that 'D intends to take the risk that he will not be paid.' This result may be right as a matter of legal policy, but did D really intend to take the risk of not getting paid even if E was watching over the scene with a benevolent smile? At any rate, the DCFR addresses the issue with its rule in Art VII-2:101(4).

The window cleaner will, by contrast, find R3RUE's rules disappointing. § 2(3) provides that restitution for the conferral of unrequested benefits will be allowed only if the intervention was justified. None of the rules on self-interested intervention (§§ 26–30) allow recovery. In particular, the residual rule in § 30 will not apply because the car owner or house occupant has not been saved any expense and because the benefit cannot be returned in kind. § 9 will not apply because the window cleaner was not labouring under any mistake.

(2) Rising Heat

The second example is taken from Peter Birks' *Unjust Enrichment*.[46] It caused great difficulty to his then proposal that English law should switch to an absence of basis approach. Because heat rises, anyone who heats an apartment in winter cannot help part of this heat dissipating upstairs, where it will heat the room occupied by his neighbour. The loss and gain of heat are enrichments and disenrichments (or disadvantages, in DCFR parlance). Birks finds a legal basis for this enrichment in a 'grudging gift' which the occupier of the lower flat makes to the occupier of the upper one.

This case is unproblematic for R3RUE, or for English law, provided the occupier of the bottom flat is aware of this effect. There is no mistake, no compulsion, no failure of consideration. The case is also unproblematic for German law. There is no performance, no wrong and no other obvious basis for a restitutionary claim.[47]

The DCFR rules find it considerably more difficult to defeat such a claim. The enrichment is unjustified under Art VII-2:101(1) because there is no legal basis which would entitle the upper flat occupant to this enrichment and because the lower flat occupant did not consent freely. There are also two possible grounds of

[45] Art VII-2:101 DCFR, Illustration 44.
[46] Peter Birks, *Unjust Enrichment*, 2nd edn (Oxford, Oxford University Press, 2005) 158–59.
[47] See Dannemann (n 38) 196–98.

attribution under Art VII-4:101 DCFR. This could either be a 'service rendered . . . for the enriched person' or a case where 'an asset of the enriched person is improved'. A more narrow construction of either 'service' or 'for' could exclude attribution on the first ground. However, in relation to attribution as an improvement, it is more difficult to argue why, when it is bitterly cold outside, the defendant's flat is not improved by the heat which rises from below. The DCFR commentaries do not discuss the 'rising heat' example. However, Illustration 36 to Art VII-2:101 DCFR uses the following, somewhat related situation:

> D, a landowning company, establishes an irrigation system for the benefit of its land. That system also happens to improve the irrigation of adjacent land belonging to E. E's enrichment (in so far as D has done work which benefited both D and E) is not unjustified under this Article because D undertook the work voluntarily and thus consented to doing the work. D's ignorance of the fact he was coincidentally benefiting E does not amount to an error.

In this example, D could freely choose whether to install an irrigation system and, if so, which system. If 'consent' is the reason why D should not recover, then it should follow that recovery should be allowed in the rising heat example, because no such choices are available to the claimant in that situation. The only choice given to the occupier of the lower flat is whether to heat more or less.

The present author has argued elsewhere that the unjust factor approach (and thus also R3RUE) is troubled by the 'rising heat' example if the claimant is unaware that the upstairs neighbour benefits from the rising heat.[48] Recovery should be allowed under mistake if the claimant additionally shows that he would otherwise have used the heat more sparingly. There appears to be no discussion of this example in the R3RUE comments and notes.[49] And the DCFR, having partially integrated mistake, will also have to do better than just stating that 'D's ignorance . . . does not amount to an error'.[50] Why not?

(3) Leapfrogging Claims

We move from English textbook cases to a leading French case and a leading German case.[51] Although different in many respects, both have in common that the claimant delivers goods (manure in the French case, electrical appliances in the German case) to a third party who is also in a contractual relationship with the defendant. The goods are mixed or connected with the defendant's real property.

[48] ibid 197.

[49] In discussion with the present author at the conference, Andrew Kull argued that it would be appropriate for the lower floor occupant to recover under § 9 R3RUE if the neighbour living on the floor above had saved expenses, so this appears to be an intended result.

[50] Art VII-2:101 DCFR, Illustration 36.

[51] Cass civ 15 June 1892, S. 1893.I.281, D. 1892.I.596 (*Boudier*); for an English translation, see Jack Beatson and Eltjo Schrage (eds), *Cases, Materials and Texts on Unjustified Enrichment* (Oxford, Hart Publishing, 2003) 39f; BGH 31.10.1963, BGHZ 40, 272; for an English translation, see Dannemann (n 38) 227.

The third party becomes insolvent. The disappointed claimant, leapfrogging over its insolvent contract partner, seeks recovery from the defendant as the owner of the improved property. The French Cour de cassation allowed this claim in the *Boudier* case, causing endless difficulties until French law eventually managed to hedge *Boudier* into insignificance.[52] The other case marked the shift of German courts in the direction of a performance-based approach towards unjust enrichment.[53]

On a literal application of the DCFR rules, the defendant is enriched and the claimant is disadvantaged. The defendant may be entitled to keep the enrichment under the contract with the third party, but not necessarily 'against the disadvantaged person' (ie, the claimant), as is required by Art VII-2:101(1) DCFR, making the enrichment unjustified. Attribution also appears to be unproblematic, this being a case of improvement of assets (Art VII-4:101(d)). Nevertheless, the DCFR Commentary tells us explicitly for the German case, the delivery of electrical appliances, that recovery is excluded (Art VII-1:101, Illustration 3), in line with the outcome of the German judgment. We simply learn that 'the enrichment of [the defendant] is nonetheless justified in relation to [the claimant]', but the reader is left to guess why this should be the case.

The explanation is actually found in the following provision, Art VII-2:102 ('Performance of obligation to third person'), which reads as follows:

> Where the enriched person obtains the enrichment as a result of the disadvantaged person performing an obligation of a supposed obligation owed by the disadvantaged person to a third person, the enrichment is justified if:
>
> (a) the disadvantaged person performed freely; or
> (b) the enrichment was merely the incidental result of performance of the obligation.

This provision would prevent the suppliers in both *Boudier* and the German case from jumping the insolvency queue by swapping their insolvent contract partner with a solvent defendant who never had a chance to negotiate that particular insolvency risk.

The same problem is covered by § 25 R3RUE, entitled 'Uncompensated Performance under Contract with Third Person':

> (1) If the claimant renders to a third person a contractual performance for which the claimant does not receive the promised compensation, and the effect of the claimant's uncompensated performance is to confer a benefit on the defendant, the claimant is entitled to restitution from the defendant as necessary to prevent unjust enrichment.[54]

[52] For a comparative discussion, see Peter Schlechtriem, *Restitution und Bereicherungsausgleich*, Vol II (Tübingen, Mohr, 2001) nos 18ff; Konrad Zweigert and Hein Kötz, *An Introduction to Comparative Law*, 3rd edn (Tony Weir tr, Oxford, Oxford University Press, 1998) 586.

[53] Dannemann (n 38) 23, 52.

[54] For leapfrogging claims under R3RUE, see also Birke Häcker in ch 2 of this volume (Primary Defendants, Contractual Performance).

What amounts to 'as necessary to prevent unjust enrichment' is discussed for a multitude of different situations. Liability is excluded if the owner has paid the insolvent main contractor or is still liable towards this party (§ 25, Comment b, Illustration 1). § 25 will nevertheless allow recovery in some situations, but only if the subcontractor's performance has left the owner with an enrichment beyond that owed by the main contractor under its contract with the owner.

(4) (Non-)Marital Property

When couples split up, the application of property law rules (or of marital property rules) can sometimes result in a windfall to one and a corresponding loss or hardship to the other party. Many unjust enrichment regimes have been tempted to provide a corrective for such (non-)marital property disputes. In *Pettkus v Becker*, the Supreme Court of Canada allowed recovery, using this case to shift to its 'juristic reason' approach.[55] The subsequent experience is mixed. One negative example is another Canadian case, *Rawluk v Rawluk*.[56] Under the Ontario Family Law Act 1986, property was to be divided equally on divorce, its value being determined at the earliest date within a list of five dates fixed in the statute. The value increased dramatically after that date. The Supreme Court used a constructive trust to outflank the legislation, effectively replacing the statutory valuation date with the value at the time of the division of the assets. Could this be done with Book VII DCFR or R3RUE?

For the DCFR rules, two issues arise. A *Rawluk v Rawluk* type of redistribution of marital property would be impossible under Art VI-2:101(1) DCFR, because any provision on marital property qualifies as a 'rule of law' which justifies an enrichment. However, the enrichment could nevertheless be unjustified under paragraph (4), the abovementioned failure of basis provision. The case will again hang on the question whether the enriched party 'accepted or could reasonably be assumed to have accepted that the enrichment must be reversed'. The DCFR commentaries provide no illustration for a divorce case. There is one illustration for a non-marital property dispute, concerning the joint renovation of property held in the name of the defendant alone. The reader is told in Illustration 1 that the disappointed partner 'may have a claim' and referred to Illustration 46, which continues to discuss the same case.[57] There, the reader is told that it all depends: 'The greater D's expense, the less realistic is the notion that D assumed the risk that he would [*sic*] short-changed in the event the relationship failed.'

It all depends a little less in R3RUE. There appears to be no provision which allows courts to correct the legislature's view on marital property. One specific provision, § 28, deals with non-marital property disputes. Recovery is allowed 'as necessary to prevent unjust enrichment'. It should also be noted that § 28 con-

[55] *Pettkus v Becker* [1980] 2 SCR 824.
[56] *Rawluk v Rawluk* [1990] 1 SCR 70.
[57] Art VII-2:101 DCFR, Illustrations 1 and 46.

tains its own subsidiarity clause: it 'may be displaced, modified, or supplemented by local domestic relations law'.

It appears that R3RUE does not interfere with marital property rules, but does give a claim to the disenriched party after the break-up of a non-marital (or unregistered) relationship where this is not provided for by applicable state law. By contrast, because Art VII-2:101 DCFR contains no subsidiarity rules for its four instances of 'unjustified', paragraph (4) could at least theoretically be used in a *Rawluk v Rawluk*-type fashion. It all depends on what the enriched partner 'accepted or could reasonably be assumed to have accepted'. Indeed, this is close to a similar case decided by the German Bundesgerichtshof.[58]

(5) Payment under Protest

Numerous English cases are slight variations on the following situation. The defendant makes an unjustified demand for payment and threatens grave consequences in case of non-payment. The claimant pays under protest and, after the danger is averted, requests repayment. As long as the defendant was bona fide in making the unjustified demand, the claim will fail under English law.[59]

By contrast, recovery appears straightforward under Book VII DCFR. This is a simple case of a payment made without legal ground under Art VII-2:101(1). The defendant was not entitled to this money, nor did the claimant consent 'freely and without error to the disadvantage'.

Interestingly, recovery is also possible under R3RUE's rules on duress. Illustration 15 of § 14 (there are further examples in Illustrations 14 and 16), modelled on *Still v Equitable Life Insurance*,[60] reads as follows:

> Insurer demands in good faith that Policyholder pay a scheduled premium, announcing that it will cancel the policy if payment is not received. Policyholder correctly interprets the policy to provide that further premiums are waived. To avoid the risk of a lapse in coverage, however, Policyholder pays the premium demanded, then sues in restitution to recover the payment. Under the circumstances, Insurer's threat to cancel amount to duress. Policyholder's payment was involuntary, and Policyholder may recover the amount of the disputed premium.

In applying duress as an unjust factor, *Still v Equitable Life Insurance* and R3RUE avoid a conceptual error of the common law which still affects English law. In English law, all agree that mistake as an unjust factor ('mistake light' in the parlance of Jacques du Plessis)[61] must be construed more widely than mistake as a

[58] BGH 9.7.2008, NJW 2008, 3277; for an English translation, see Dannemann (n 38) 290.

[59] *CTN Cash and Carry Ltd v Gallaher Ltd* [1994] 4 All ER 714 (CA); *Maskell v Horner* [1915] 3 KB 106 (CA); *Twyford v Manchester Corporation* [1946] Ch 236; for an ingenious recovery under mistake of law, see *Nurdin & Peacock v DB Ramsden & Co Ltd* [1999] 1 All ER 941. See also Dannemann (n 38) 200–02.

[60] *Still v Equitable Life Insurance*, 54 SW 2d 947. I am grateful to Jacques du Plessis for having pointed out to me that I misread this case in Dannemann (n 38) 200.

[61] Du Plessis, ch 4 of this volume 91 (referring to 'duress light').

ground of avoidance in contract law. Everyone also agrees that failure of consideration as an unjust factor must be construed more widely than contractual rules on frustration or termination of contract. But nobody seems to be willing to say the same about duress or undue influence as unjust factors.[62] Common wisdom and case law have it that they are to be construed as narrowly as the rules under which a contract is avoidable or can be set aside, producing absurd results in the above-mentioned cases. R3RUE shows that this conceptual error is not a necessary element of the common law. It has opted for 'duress light', ie, threat without wrongful coercion, for cases of overpayment.

Moreover, § 35 R3RUE, entitled 'Performance of a Disputed Obligation' contains a separate rule on payment under protest which covers situations where the demand for excess payment was made within a contractual relationship, as was the case, for example, in *CTN Cash & Carry* and in *Still v Equitable Life* (but not, for example, in *Twyford v Manchester Corp*).[63] Recovery is allowed if, under the circumstances, it was 'reasonable to accede to the demand rather than to insist on an immediate test of the disputed obligation'.[64]

D. Conclusions

R3RUE seems to get the right result in most cases. The window cleaner is paid voluntarily or not at all. No restitution is required for rising heat in the standard situation. Most cases of leapfrogging over an insolvent contract partner are excluded, admittedly at the loss of some certainty. Unjust enrichment can be used for sorting non-marital property disputes, but not where the legislature has provided otherwise. And when somebody is presented with an unjustified demand which is coupled with a threat, paying first and recovering later is still an option. At the same time, R3RUE does not have to bend or twist its rules in order to achieve the desired outcomes.[65]

The only real problem for R3RUE appears to be the rising heat example, where the owner of the bottom flat is unaware of this effect: mistake-based recovery should in principle be allowed if the claimant can show that he would otherwise have reduced the heat. That, however, appears to be the intended result.[66]

Book VII DCFR can handle the window cleaner under its 'failure of basis' rule, but at the expense of some discrepancy between the wording of Art VII-2:101(4) DCFR and the explanation given in Illustration 44. In the rising heat example,

[62] See Dannemann (n 38) 200–02.

[63] *CTN Cash and Carry* (n 59); *Still v Equitable Life Insurance* (n 60); *Twyford* (n 59).

[64] Illustration 2 to this provision is identical to Illustration 15 in § 14; § 35, Illustration 3 is similar to § 14, Illustration 16.

[65] But see Birke Häcker, ch 2 of this volume (under 'collateral-source rule') for an incident of R3RUE rule twisting.

[66] See n 49.

the enrichment is clearly unjustified. Some rule twisting would be necessary to defeat attribution as an improvement of the upper floor occupant's assets. As concerns leapfrog claims, these are largely excluded under Art VII-4:102. For the DCFR, the only other fully convincing test case result is the last, namely where a party is pressured into making what it knows to be an unjustified payment. Here, recovery under the DCFR rules is even more straightforward than under R3RUE's rules on duress.

If 'rising heat' and leapfrogging claims are discounted as ties, the overall score for the test cases is thus two to one in favour of R3RUE.

The DCFR's unitary notion of unjustified enrichment and its unitary construction through four elements – enrichment, disadvantage, unjustified and attribution – is certainly more elegant than R3RUE's restatement of an unjust factor approach. However, the contrast between how German law and the DCFR handle the 'rising heat' example shows the dangers of an absence of legal basis approach which is not hedged about by a restricting taxonomy, as is the case for performance-based unjustified enrichment under German law.

The test cases have exposed some weaknesses of the DCFR's construction of unjustified enrichment claims. They stem from the unresolved relationships between two justifying factors, two explanatory rules and one unjust factor in Art VII-2:101, and between five grounds of attribution in Art VII-4:101. Article VII-2:202 should exclude leapfrogging, at least for standard situations involving three parties, but will not, for example, preclude a claimant from jumping over a valid contract with the defendant by claiming restitution for failure of purpose under Art VII-2:101(4). Likewise, the five attribution rules in Art VII-4:101 can potentially point to different defendants for the recovery of the same disenrichment or to different claimants for the return of the same enrichment. Both flaws can be overcome: some more thought would have to go into the precise relationship between entitlement as a justifying factor and failure of purpose as an unjust factor, and also into the precise relationship between the five grounds of attribution, which could take the form of a subsidiarity rule.

We have also seen that the perceived weakness of the DCFR sometimes relates less to the quality of its rules and more to the way in which the commentary announces results for its illustrations without providing reasons. The same cannot be said about the commentaries and notes to R3RUE. We have seen above that the drafting environment and timeframes allocated were quite different for Book VII DCFR and R3RUE. This will also go some way towards explaining the different standards and density of the commentaries and notes.

INDEX

www.ingramcontent.com/pod-product-compliance
Ingram Content Group UK Ltd.
Pitfield, Milton Keynes, MK11 3LW, UK
UKHW020238290926
15470UKWH00002B/602

9 781849 464086